HEARTS OF FIRE

ALSO BY

KEMP BATTLE
Great American Folklore

HEARTS OF FIRE

Great Women of American Lore and Legend

KEMP BATTLE

Doubleday Direct, Inc. Garden City, New York

Permissions appear on page 431.

Published by Harmony Books, a division of Crown Publishers, Inc., 201 East 50th Street, New York,
New York 10022. Member of the Crown Publishing Group.

By arrangement with GuildAmerica® Books, an imprint and a registered trademark of Doubleday Direct, Inc.,
Dept. GB, 401 Franklin Avenue, Garden City, New York 11530

Random House, Inc., New York, Toronto, London, Sydney, Auckland

http://www.randomhouse.com/

Harmony and colophon are trademarks of Crown Publishers, Inc.

Printed in the United States of America

Design by Lynne Amft

Library of Congress Cataloging-in-Publication Data is available upon request.

ISBN 0-517-70397-1

10 9 8 7 6 5 4 3 2 1

First Edition

TO CAROLYN SLAUGHTER
AND OUR CHILDREN:
ALLY, TOM, EMILY AND JOE

C O N T E N T S

Ceremonies of Childbirth (Hopi) ~ "Here's to the Mothers . . ."   ~   Birth on
the Trail (1853)   ~   Onnie Lee Logan: "This is the way I did it."   ~   The
Cows Mooed and the Horses Neighed   ~   Weighing the Baby (1848)   ~
"He just ain't going to do it."   ~   Diana and Her Baby   ~   Elizabeth Cady
Stanton's Lesson in Self-Reliance   ~   "For that crippled baby I have kept an
affection that is ineffaceable."   ~   Wartime Birth (1966)   ~   Birth and
Infancy Superstitions

Aunt Jane's Quilting (Kentucky, 1908)   ~   Why Not Save Mother?   ~
Health Tips in Colonial America   ~   Share and Share Alike (1825)   ~
Lydia Maria Child's Household Hints (1832)   ~   Advice to the Victorian
Woman   ~   Aunt Weed's Rat Letter   ~   When Her Courage Failed Her   ~
There's Many an Empty Cradle (1858)   ~   Counting Your Blessings (1859)
~   "I am scareing the hogs out of my kitchen . . ." (1852)   ~   American
Cooking, Frontier Style   ~   Isabella Bird: "Epicures at home would have
envied us."   ~   All in a Day's Work   ~   Dust Bowl Observations   ~
Culpepper's Pride   ~   Billie Holiday Gets Her Start   ~   Cowgirls Carry On
~   Some Things My Ma Used to Say (at one time or another . . .)   ~   My
Mother, Myself

herself . . ." ∼ Carry Nation Gets Her Start ∼ The Wit of Abigail Scott Duniway ∼ Mother Jones ∼ Emma Goldman Goes to the Mines ∼ Helen Keller Remembers ∼ "I want to ride!" ∼ Rosa L. Parks ∼ Where Did You Go, Virginia Dare?

A C K N O W L E D G M E N T S

So much gratitude, so little space. To the women in the following pages—for the forthrightness of their words and the inspiration of their lives—belongs the greatest thanks of all. Among the many institutions from whom I received assistance and information: the Academy of Natural Sciences of Philadelphia; the Boston Atheneum; the British Museum; Childbirth Graphics, Inc. of Rochester, N.Y.; the Firestone Library at Princeton University (and in particular the Miriam Holden Collection housed there); the historical societies of Connecticut, Massachusetts, Minnesota, Illinois, Iowa, New York, North Carolina, Oregon, and Virginia; the magnificent Library of Congress; the National Museum of Women in the Arts in Washington, D.C.; the National Women's Hall of Fame in Seneca, N.Y.; the National Women's History Project in Windsor, CA.; the New York Public Library; the Princeton Public Library; Radcliffe's Schlesinger Library in Cambridge, MA.; the Smithsonian Museum of American History in Washington, D.C.; and the Widener and Houghton Libraries at Harvard University. The radical women's presses of the mid 19th century (*The Lily, The Una, The Woman's Advocate* and *The Sibyl* among them) were fascinating sources, filled with material. To the many able historians, scholars, and folklorists who have taken up the cause of women's lore in more recent years I am profoundly grateful. A particular note of thanks to Marion Tinling for her majestic *Women Remembered: A Guide to the Landmarks of Women's History,* which I carried all across the country with enthusiasm. Also a special thanks for the writings of Joanna Stratton, Laurel Thatcher Ulrich, Julia Spruill, Cathy Luchetti, Susan Griffin, Ann Russo, Cheris Kramarae, Zora Neale Hurston (again), and Margaret Forster, among others, for helping me to see what had been in front of me all along.

I have had the privilege of working with two accomplished, sensitive, and skillful editors—Barbara Greenman at GuildAmerica Books, who trusted my passion for good stories and believed in this project before anyone else, and

Shaye Areheart at Harmony Books, who proved to be as fine an editor as she has been a friend. I thank both of these wonderful women for their unfailing support and encouragement, as well as Dina Siciliano at Harmony, whose patience is exceeded only by her good judgment and humor. I am lucky for my association with these three women, and this book is much the better for their efforts. Thanks too to Phyllis Berk for her careful work on the manuscript.

Immense gratitude is due Stephanie Beddows, my talented colleague and resourceful research assistant, for the wisdom and insight she brought to this book. She trudged with me every step of the way and provided invaluable criticism and contributions from the first to the last. Thanks to Tom Cromer for his insight and research on notable women of crime.

Among the many individuals who deserve special acknowledgment for their friendship and goodwill: Elliot Illava (as always); Sam and Liz Hynes; Roy and Aisling Foster; Ned and Margaret Handy; Henry and Mary Reath; Nathan Schwartz-Salant; Ellie Wyeth Fox; Katherine Hughes; Robert Del Tufo; Bob Fagles; Chase Twitchell; Russell Banks; Mr. Miller; Frank Gill; Bob Peck; Alan Poole; Charlie Gerras; Amelia Silver; David Baxendale; Allen Wood; Anne and Craig, David, and John Battle; The GPL; Ryan Phelan; Matthew Murray; Jim Alexander; Kermit Hummel; Alex Hoyt; Lorraine Shanley; Donna Hayes; Brian Hickey; Ian Davis; Francis Baldwin Schaefer; Lee Quackenbush; Jamie Bolane; Harriet Hartigan; Kitty Ernst; Hyman and Reine Battle; Jim and Peggy Calvert; Deborah Hartzog; the steadfast support of Hope Van Winkle; and the tenacious, unwavering friendship of Logan Fox.

And finally, of course, to Carolyn Slaughter, whose own fiery heart led the way.

I N T R O D U C T I O N

If historians tell us who we were, storytellers reveal to us who we are. In the stories we tell about ourselves, in the facts we include and the details we omit, everything is revealed. So it is with Americans who love nothing better than stories about themselves and the celebration of virtues that underpin their notion of national identity: humor, tenacity, defiance and, best of all, a measure of outright audacity. The American landscape was not wrought out of humility as much as grit; we live with the absolute conviction that nothing less than sheer cussedness was necessary to lay the foundations and dig the graves. It is particularly odd, then, to note that the most consistent omission from the stories Americans treasure most is the American woman.

Where are the heroines of American lore and legend, and why do we have to look so hard to find them? Male folk heroes abound; the national ledger is teeming with tales of cowboys, sailors, soldiers, farmers, and fighters, men of passion, faith, and intellect; there is no end to the adventure narratives, hunting and fishing yarns, preacher stories, tall tales and ballads of great showdowns and broken-hearted boys. The books and anthologies that feature American heroes fill the shelves of our libraries. Why, then, when we look up "Heroines" in the library catalog are we lucky if we find a scattering of citations—most of which carry a still further classification, such as "Heroines in Fiction"?

The call for popular folk heroines all too often brings forth the usual volunteers: as schoolchildren we learned of Betsy Ross and her flag, Sacajawea, the intrepid Shoshone who, with her baby strapped to her back, led Lewis and Clark west, or Abigail Adams, the feisty observer, diligent wife and relentless letter writer. We were told about Annie Oakley and Calamity Jane (because they could shoot), and women of courage like Helen Keller, Amelia Earhart or Barbara Frietchie (who probably never existed at all). And yet, before the recent (and welcome) avalanche of books about the experience of American women, the extent to which popular folk collections actually ignored the nation's most vivid, powerful women is simply astounding. Why were we not taught about the faith and will of Anne Hutchinson, whose religious convictions challenged Boston's Puritan elders, or Mary Dyer, who died for her Quakerism? Should we not have known more about Harriet Ann Jacobs, whose account of slavery will endure as long as any people are oppressed, or Margaret Sanger, who fought to educate women about their own rights and potential? What about the inspiring defiance of rights activists like Mother Jones, Sojourner Truth, Emma Goldman, or Elizabeth Cady Stanton? Why do we have to look so hard to learn about the surprising adventures of Sara Edmonds, Poker Alice Tubbs, or Mary Read? Civil War nurses like Clara Barton or Mother Bickerdyke are as inspiring as their modern counterparts who served in Vietnam. Why have Lucy Stone, Susan Anthony, or the Grimké sisters often seemed more the property of academic historians when a wider world has so much to learn about their astonishing lives and words? The attention paid these women and countless others, whose lives embody the virtues Americans value most, seems minimal when compared with the demonstrations made over their male counterparts.

That isn't to say that there aren't a number of American heroines who have seemed bigger than life and who can't take a blustering bow alongside their folkloric brothers. Some are apocryphal frontier women like Sally Hooter and Big Lou (though their tales seem more like Davy Crockett in drag); others were real enough, but still seem outrageous to us now. Consider Victoria Woodhull, best known, perhaps, for her presidential candidacy in 1872 on a platform of free love ("I have an inalienable right to love whom I may and to change that love every day if I please"); less well known is that Woodhull was the first female member of the New York Stock Exchange, and her brokerage firm turned Wall Street upside down with its relentlessly successful insider trading. What about Carry Nation, whose husband was a drunk and who came to believe that her destiny was to destroy saloons across the nation with an axe? Many have heard of Sam Patch, who went over Niagara Falls, but what about Annie Taylor, the first woman to go over in a barrel and live? Taylor, nicknamed Queen of the Mist, lectured to increasingly diminishing crowds on her experience and left behind the following inscription on her tomb: "I did what no other woman in the world had nerve enough to do, only to die a pauper." Others, like Mae West (who, when asked "Haven't you ever found a man who could make you happy?" replied, "Sure I have. Lots of times.") and Tallulah

Bankhead take our breath away with their direct and unfettered appetites. Isadora Duncan's and Amelia Earhart's strange deaths still unsettle our imagination. (Duncan's scarf caught in the wheels of her splendid car and snapped her neck like a twig, while Earhart disappeared into the Pacific Ocean never to be seen again.) But the deeds of such women are only a small part of the story of great women in America.

Too often there appear to be two principal requirements for the creation of a cultural heroine in American folklore: first, the ability to do everything that the male hero can do (fight, shoot, build, etc.), and second, her willingness to move off the stage quickly once she has done it. Modesty, humility, and deference to the principal actors should mark her behavior. Look, for example, at the famous Revolutionary War heroine, Molly Pitcher. We know her story as the lady who dutifully followed her husband into battle, carried water to the soldiers during the fight, and who, upon seeing her husband overcome by heat and unable to continue firing his cannon, took his place and coolly fought on to victory. She binds her husband's wounds and retires into legend. Perfect American heroine.

Behind the chamber of commerce portrait of Molly Pitcher is the contentious, inspiring reality of the real woman. "Molly" was a young girl named Mary Ludwig, who worked as a servant in a prosperous Pennsylvania home. She married a local man named Hayes who, when war with England broke out, enlisted in the army. Childless, tough-minded, game for adventure and, like her husband, without anything better to do, Mary followed his regiment into war, washing clothes and cooking for the troops. She was unafraid of the hard and brazen quality of army life, and she came to be known not only for her astonishing stamina but also for her rough mouth and mocking humor. At the Battle of Monmouth, on a brutally hot, windless day, she did indeed carry the pitchers of water to the troops for which she would earn her immortal sobriquet, and many accounts testify to her steadiness under fire. When her husband was wounded, she took his place. She had seen the cannoneers in action countless times, and it was entirely within her combative nature to answer the enemy with a fire of her own. Far more real than the image of the brave lady in petticoats dirtying her delicate hands with gunsmoke is the sight of Hayes swearing with enthusiasm and joyfully firing the cannon without hesitation. The soldiers called her "Sargeant Molly" and she won a brief moment of appreciation before the army returned to the road that led to Yorktown.

Why leave the story there when the best part of it is yet to come? Why let the popularizers leave us a saccharine legend when she has so much more to give us? Life was not easy for Molly after the war ended. Her husband died and she toiled on as a washerwoman and domestic. She married again, unhappily. She didn't suffer fools gladly and her legendary toughness was unflagging. She believed her service had gone well beyond her role in the battle—after all, hadn't she fed, clothed, cleaned, and nursed the nation's soldiers?—and she repeatedly petitioned Pennsylvania for compensation. She argued with all comers that it was a matter of honor, that the state, the government itself, should do what was right. It would be more than forty years before she won her argument, becoming, in 1822, the first woman to receive a military pension from a state government—$40 plus an annual payment of the same. Molly Ludwig Hayes McCauley fought the British, she fought local bureaucrats, and she fought state authorities; she knew who she was and what she deserved. The mythmakers would have her pass across the stage as a marble maiden servicing a noble cause and, by doing so, make her less than she was.

Still, the question persists: If we know that the women have been there all along, working, fighting, building, why has the cavalcade of American folklorists and mythmakers and storytellers all too frequently passed these heroines by with barely a nod? It is unsettlingly easy to do—I know firsthand because throughout the writing of my previous book, *Great American Folklore,* I failed completely to account for the female dimension of American folk life. Women were present but, more often than not, they were simply foils for the adventures of men, counterweights to men's humor and folly. Women were gratefully acknowledged as the purveyors and gatherers of folklore; their songs and sayings were enthusiastically recounted, but they were not accorded their own voices, nor given their own characters. The failure was neither malicious nor intentional, which makes it even worse because ignorance is no excuse. I simply didn't know how to listen and I blindly passed by great stories, great women, one after the other. I might never have even noticed the oversight at all had not my young daughter, who lives with gusto and loves adventure, and who rightly believes she should be able to do anything a boy can do, asked me why, when it came to American folklore, "boys seemed to have all the fun?" The real origin of *Hearts of Fire* lies in the stories I want her to hear, the stories that would help her (and her siblings) realize that, indeed, women *were* there all along, living bold lives, challenging and audacious lives, spinning legends about themselves even if few took time to notice or celebrate them.

~

After reading many thousands of stories, tall tales, memoirs, letters, diaries, and historical portraits written by both men and women, I am drawn to a broad generalization that directly impacted the selection process for this collection. Men and women appear to have very different instincts about the way they tell stories. For men, a good story often seems something of a performance, rounding higher and higher towards a crowning point. They seem more concerned with the order and the pacing of the story because its primary purpose is the entertainment of the listener (with great credit paid to the teller). For women, the issue often seems less about performance than collaboration. Information, the *experience* of the story, seems to take precedence over the method of the telling. Women provide compelling details without so many sound effects.

The differences in narrative technique surfaced repeatedly in the research. The third-party stories so central to *Great American Folklore* were often utterly inadequate because too often the patronizing prejudices of gender, conscious or otherwise, diminished the basic narrative. Soon enough, the only trustworthy voices were those who spoke for themselves. Where interesting women have not left behind material that might shed light on their essential character or experience, I have tried to fill in the gap. Mary Read, the fierce pirate who sailed with Calico Jack Rackham, for example, was neither the "pirate in petticoats" (the nineteenth-century sentimental version) nor simply a cross-dresser with grit (the twentieth-century academic version). The real Read was interesting for who she was, the choices she made and the passionate conviction with which she directed her own life.

What follows then is an entirely subjective selection of stories that caught my imagination and inspired my spirit. Missing from this book are many great American women. Some have been excluded by design because their voices and stories are well known and much admired; still others have been overlooked through my own ignorance. To them all, I extend my apologies and plead the best of intentions.

A parting thought: Throughout the research for this book I returned again and again to Pocahontas, one of America's earliest folk heroines. Like many great women in American lore, Pocahontas is far more interesting than the brief cameo appearance she is routinely given by American mythmakers. What we learned about her as schoolchildren (as did a new generation, instructed by the cinematic storytellers at Walt Disney) was her generous, impetuous act of charity toward her father's captive, Capt. John Smith. Pocahontas—what have we done to you? We lost your true form in the bewildering mists of romantic legend and misplaced the meaning of your life in search of a folkloric sound bite. You should not be remembered for an act of girlish devotion but rather for your womanly faith in a profound and abiding truth: that vengeance is not as powerful a remedy as mercy. You should be remembered for your intense curiosity, your willingness to see the strange white settlers as messengers from another world, bearers of momentous tidings. Why else would you have volunteered—while only twelve years old—to act as your father's emissary and negotiate with the settlers for the release of hostages from your own tribe? Why else would you have braved a terrible winter storm to warn the settlement that their lives were in danger? You must have believed you could find the common tongue, the shared language of compassion, collaboration. You loved a white man, not the avuncular Smith, but John Rolfe, a man who was at first frightened of the feeling he had for you, fearful because he could not see, as you could, that what separated the two of you was not nearly as strong as what bound you to one another. You would convince Rolfe, as you would your father, that your love was a blessing, a gift (how he must have loved you, his exuberant daughter whose very name meant "playful"). Soon great with child, did you rejoice that your own body had become the sacred ground of mediation between two cultures? As for Rolfe, the love he finally offered you seemed bound by demands, rules: he asked you to change your name, take his religion, wear his costume, return with him to England to be paraded before the King and Queen, to serve as a celebrity for a gawking court. These things you did. Did he not see you start to sicken? Did he not recognize that your spirits ebbed as the coal-filled fogs of London withered lungs used to forest air and the wind off the ocean? The world you had been so curious to learn about was starting to kill you, and you were only twenty-two.

Dear Pocahontas, when you died thousands of miles from home, you became a legend, but what a price you paid for your wild, adventurous spirit! You defied your father in the name of justice, you risked your life to avoid war, you followed the passionate commands of your own heart and did not look back. We may honor your name, but we should not forget the costs involved: You did not see your home again; you did not grow old and touch the heads of your grandchildren; your body came to lie among strangers. No one even knows for certain where you were buried.

Strange how often the great women of American lore paid a steep price for voicing their deepest desires; strange, too, how blind some of us are to the messages their lives hold for us. Those of us who choose blindness, however, can be taught to see. In the twilight world of gender debates, where politics and oppression, instinct and biology, economics and cultural conformity are in a state of constant conflict, our first true teachers are those who are unafraid to speak their minds. They take our fingers to their hearts and we feel the heat. *Hearts of Fire* is filled with women who were believers in, sometimes even proselytizers of, a sure and unassailable right; that of moral, intellectual, and emotional self-determination. They knew that too often the coded message of American society reinforced the grim truth offered by Lois Wyse: "Men are taught to apologize for their weaknesses, women for their strengths." The women in the following pages make no apologies. They are not interested in debates or intellectually trumping their critics. They are concerned principally with the opportunity to live out the promptings of their own inner life. The succinct slogan of the early suffragettes suffices: "Men's rights and nothing more; women's rights and nothing less."

We need these heroines now more than ever. We need to tell different kinds of stories to our children, stories which reaffirm that the hard-won path or the bravely fought contest has nothing at all to do with gender. No more cartoons, no more fanciful inventions, no more patronizing stories. The debt we owe these women is to retell their stories or, better yet, listen to them as they tell us. Some shed light on the long march towards freedom; others illustrate the barriers and prejudices that made the march harder; still others are simply snapshots of women in motion, women on the move. We are likely to see in these snapshots something of ourselves. The determination of these women, come hell or high water, to be who they choose, to act and feel as they wish, is a breathtaking reminder that all of us, men and women alike, have the same audacious opportunity presented to us every day of our lives.

K.P.B.
Lawrenceville, N.J.

Give her of the fruit of her hands, and let her own works praise her in the gates.
                                    Proverbs 31:31

THE HEARTH

Oh, if instead she'd left to me
The thing she took into the grave!—
That courage like a rock, which she
has no more need of, and I have.

~Edna St. Vincent Millay
THE COURAGE THAT MY MOTHER HAD

B I R T H

*M*en know nothing about birth. Nothing at all. No man can truly grasp the thousand nameless moments when her body weaves within itself a new life, those long months of quiet, astonishing transformation. Even the male doctors, who routinely bring babies into the world and know everything about the medical procedures, cannot really know the pain and the joy of that one, startling moment when the baby comes. But women know. They speak to one another wordlessly about the pain, about the sacrifice, the bliss. Those who have made that journey take those who have not by the hand—*Do not be afraid. You can do it.*

Strange, then, how many stories of birth we know with men at the center—the country doctor who rides out and delivers the baby in the driving storm (remember his unflappable calm and steady wisdom?); the firemen and taxi drivers, called in as unexpected midwives, allowed for a moment to take part in the mystery (we applaud them for not flinching); the familiar figure of the husband pacing anxiously up and down the corridor, waiting for the doctor to come and tell him triumphantly "It's a boy!" American folklore anthologies are filled with the comical clichés of the birth story and, inevitably, they minimize the toil and the mystery of the event by making the birth itself something of a sideshow.

Such stories are not the ones women tell one another. They are not the narratives that women use to help one another. The best of them touch on the lonely and powerful journey that every woman takes in childbirth: the journey towards empowerment and solitude that often means leaving everyone else behind—the doctors, husbands, even the midwives—and climbing alone toward that place where one's child is waiting to be claimed, saved, born.

Increasingly in America, birth is being reclaimed by women. Midwifery is once again being viewed as economical, practical, and superior to the automatic interventions routinely authorized by a medical establishment long dominated by men. These midwives are part of a long and honored tradition, one in which women look upon birth as a natural event, not a medical one. The midwives are seasoned guides through the anxious and sometimes confusing landscape of birth. Like many mothers, midwives often find themselves at odds with male doctors intent on moving women in and out as quickly as possible. Midwives have traveled the road so many times, seen the mother's fear and her triumph—and they are among our best folklorists. Every midwife has a great birthing story to tell and each knows that a man, even a good, kind, and anxious one, must stand aside when the pain comes. *There is work to be done, honey,* the midwife tells him. *Hold her hand but let her concentrate.* And then she speaks to her woman as if the man were not there at all.

B I R T H

||||||||||||||||||||||||||||||||||||||||||||||||||||||||||||||||||||||||||||

Of the sadness or joy, good fortune or tragedy that awaits every mother and newborn child in this life, we can never know in advance. But the birth journey is and will always be nothing short of heroic, for every child and every mother, every time.

Ceremonies of Childbirth (Hopi)

The Hopi infant began life in a society where elaborate religious ceremonials dominated much of village life. Each new baby was immediately immersed in the rich, sacred traditions that would so fully shape its life experience. In the Hopi pueblos a young mother was often alone at the moment of birth, but as soon as the baby had slipped out of the birth canal onto the patch of warm sand, the newborn's maternal grandmother entered the room to tie and sever the cord and to make her daughter and new grandchild comfortable. After washing the baby she rubbed its body with ashes from the corner fireplace so that its skin would always be smooth and free of hair. Then she took the afterbirth and deposited it on a special placenta pile at the edge of the village.

Very soon the baby's paternal grandmother arrived and began to take up her duties as mistress of ceremonies for all the rituals that would be performed during the twenty-day lying-in period and for the culminating dedication of the baby to the sun. Her first task was to secure a heavy blanket over the door so that no sunlight could enter the room where the mother and baby lay. It was thought that light was harmful to newborn children, and so the baby began its life on earth in a room almost as dark as the womb from which it had just emerged.

For eighteen days the mother and baby lay at rest in the darkened room. Each day a mark was made on the wall above the baby's bed and a perfect ear of corn laid under each mark. On the nineteenth day the mother got up and spent the day grinding corn into sacred meal to be used in the special ceremony the next day.

On the next morning the new mother's female relatives arrived at her home well before dawn, dressed in their most colorful shawls and carrying gifts of cornmeal and perfect ears of corn. When all the guests had arrived, the solemn ceremony for the dedication of a new life was begun. First, the mother was ritually purified. Her hair and body were washed in suds made from the root of the yucca plant, and then she took a steambath by standing over a bowl of hot water. Next, all the grandmothers and the aunts each took a turn at bathing the baby in yucca suds and giving it a name.

While all this was taking place inside the home, the father, who since the birth had been living in his religious society's kiva, or underground ceremonial chamber, was stationed on the flat roof of the stone house watching for the sun. When the sacred Sun Father began to appear, the father alerted the women, who hastily took the child to the edge of the mesa. The grandmother who carried the baby crouched low so that no light would fall on the infant. Then, as the sun appeared over the horizon, the grandmother lifted the baby, turning her tiny bundle so the rays fell directly on the little face. Taking a handful of prayer meal, she sprinkled some over the baby while reciting a short prayer. She flung the rest of the meal over the edge of the mesa toward the sun. The baby, now a full member of the family, was taken home and allowed to nap while the rest of the family enjoyed a breakfast feast.

"Here's to the Mothers . . ."

"Here's to the mothers, who came hither by long, tedious journeys, closely packed with restless children in emigrant wagons, cooking the meals by day, and nursing the babies by night, while the men slept. Leaving comfortable homes in the East, they endured all the hardships of pioneer life, suffered, with the men, the attacks of the Dakota Indians and the constant apprehension of savage raids, of prairie fires, and the devastating locusts. Man's trials, his fears, his losses, all fell on woman with double force; yet history is silent concerning the part woman performed in the frontier life of the early settlers. Men make no mention of her heroism and divine patience; they take no thought of the mental or physical agonies women endure in the perils of maternity, ofttimes without nurse or physician in the supreme hour of their need, going, as every mother does, to the very gates of death in giving life to an immortal being!"

—*Elizabeth Cady Stanton*

Birth on the Trail (1853)

Virginia Ivins set off with her family for California while pregnant with her second child. Birth came, prematurely, at the foothills of the Sierra Nevada range. The following excerpt, from her memoir Pen Pictures of Early Western Days, *tells the story with classic nineteenth century understatement:*

The ascent of the Sierras began now in earnest. The road was very rough, in many places covered with round boulders which made it almost impassable. I was obliged to lie down most of the day. In the afternoon, as he usually did, Mr. Ivins went forward to look for a camping place. We often had to leave the

road to find good grass. . . . After he went away, the road becoming somewhat smoother, I went to sleep, not waking till quite late. . . .

It was dusk when we drove up to what seemed to be a small lake, and the
order was given to unyoke. The cattle were driven to the lake to drink but
turned away without tasting the water. What was our consternation to find it to
be an alkali lake, which looked like ashes and water mixed, not fit to be used at
all, and all together the outlook was most distressing. Carl made the fire and
cooked the supper by the light of a dim lantern, making the coffee out of a little
water which was left over in the cans, keeping about a quart to drink. I fixed my
"house" and Carl brought me my supper but I could not eat and spent the time
in tears. Little Charlie was put to bed and Mr. Ivins retired also. After all was
quiet I lighted my lamp and sat down to sew. I had been quietly at work making
a small wardrobe out of some of the clothes which were in the broken box, for I
realized that I might need it before we arrived in California, or very soon after.
There was only one more garment to finish and I thought that I had better get
it done. I sewed till about ten o'clock. Outside the poor, thirsty cattle lowed,
the coyotes barked and snarled, the owls hooted and the night hawks
screamed. It seemed as if we were deserted by God and man. I thought that I
would go to bed and sleep if possible, but found that I could not help myself;
that now, indeed, trouble was in store for us. I woke my husband and told him
the situation. He would not believe me at first, but soon was convinced, and
God only knows the fear and agony of that dreadful night. I tried to be brave
for the sake of my husband and child, and at three o'clock there came to us a
dear little daughter, with no one near to help, comfort or relieve.

After doing what he could for me, my husband wrapped the little one in a
blanket and laid her in my arm. It turned very cold and a dreadful chill came
on. My husband put warm covers over me and tried to warm me by holding me
in his arms. A bed had been made for Charlie on the spring seat. He was put
there and we watched for daylight with aching hearts. At the first faint glimmer
of dawn Mr. Ivins dispatched a man on horseback with a can for water to Pea
Vine springs. It was five miles and breakfast was late that morning. My husband inquired of the first [wagon] train that came past for some elderly woman
to come in and see me and the somewhat unexpected guest. About ten o'clock
a good Samaritan came in, looked at the baby, said a few kind words to me, and
left me to my fate.

Onnie Lee Logan: "This is the way I did it."

When Katherine Clark, a professor at the University of Alabama, sat down to listen to Onnie Lee Logan talk of her life as a midwife, she must have realized quickly that she was in the presence of a master storyteller. Logan, a black woman raised in rural Alabama, started delivering babies in 1931. By 1984, when the Alabama board of health refused to renew her permit (despite a superb record), Logan, then seventy-four, had assembled an astonishing body of knowledge. The following excerpt is from Clark and Logan's collaboration (called Motherwit: An Alabama Midwife's Story, *published in 1989):*

Now this is the way I did it. There was a beautiful setup with mother and daddy when their baby was conceived. They enjoyed it. When she get in labor—another beautiful setup. I think the husband and wife should be by themselves durin the first stage of labor. That mother and daddy is together quietly by themselves at her beginnin of labor until labor get so severe. Now this just comes from me. Even though some of em get kinda skittish and want me to come right on, I tells em this. "It was you and yo' husband in the beginning and it was fine. It's you and yo' husband should be in the beginning a the birth a the baby, quiet and easy, talkin and lovin and happy with one another. You don't need nobody there. Me nor nobody else until a certain length a time." That's the reason I tell my patients, "When you get in labor, you call me when you think you in labor"—especially the ones right here in the city.

"Let's have telephone conversations befo' I come cause that's beautiful for you and yo' husband to be together. Then every so often befo' I get there you call me and let me know how you're comin on." And she will call me. Call me back in thirty minutes. Time yo' pains and see how many you've had within the thirty minutes and if it be a good ways apart I says, "Well don't call me no mo' until they start pickin up." We stay in touch with each other through telephone conversations. And when their pains start gettin severe I say, "Well I better come on out so I can start gettin things ready." Once labor gets so severe that's when the two both wanna call somebody in that's experienced that knows what to do. I be prepared myself sittin ready at home so when they call and say they're getting rapid now, I'll be ready to just shoot out. . . .

I tell you one thing that's very impo'tant that I do that the doctors don't do and the nurses doesn't do because they doesn't take time to do it. And that is I'm with my patients at all times with a smile and keepin her feelin good with kind words. The very words that she need to hear it comes up and come out. And that means a lot. Most of the doctors when they do say somethin to em it's so harsh. They already had contractions, and then with a ugly word to come out not suitable to how they're feelin. Some of em say that if they wasn't strapped down there they would get down and come home. A lot a women are left totally alone. And plenty of em have had their babies right by themselves. Well see I don't leave my patient like that. I'm there givin her all the love and all the care and I be meaning it and they know I mean it. It's from my heart and they can feel me. You see what I mean? There's a lot of a certain lil black gal— they can feel that black gal. They can feel the love from her—the care from her. What she's goin through with I'm goin through right along with her.

Now I know how to stay away. In another room. Right. While I'm sitting right in here now, if you need me befo' I walk back here you call me. I be right here. That's what I tell em and that works. And they like it. I'm right there. The most impo'tant thing is that I'm with em givin em love and care the whole time. I'm there from beginnin to end with smile, good words, happy words. Keepin you happy. And that's a very happy experience for you. . . .

The contractions can leave awhile completely. That's God's way. That's what I love about it. Give mother time to rest between the contractions. This is a beautiful point about it. They gets so sleepy just befo' that baby is really fixin to crown on us yet, mother gets so sleepy. That's the anesthesia that God give em. I know that's true. They can rest. I don't care what no doctor say or nobody else say. That is the anesthesia that God give mother. He said He wouldn't put no mo' on em than they could bear. And befo' you think you're gonna give or it's gonna kill you, He take it completely away and make you sleepy. You cain't stay awake to save yo' life. That's anesthesia from God. Man had nothin to do with that. It's true. These thirty-eight years that I've been workin it's true. God have deal it with me. I have experienced it. I have looked it over and over and over and God give it to me. That is true.

Some of em say this. "Onnie, if these pains would just hold up so I could sleep just one minute I would feel better." God take it away. I don't care if they don't hold up for that lil length of time—they sleep just that quick. Just befo' it crowns they get those hard severe contractions that they're not gonna be able to do nothing but push. Befo' they get the urge to push that's when they get sleepy for a rest. That's true. Honey, when it get right to the last minute they think, Well, I done gone as far as I can go. But God give me new strength. He will take the contractions away from em and they get so sleepy. He gives em some anesthesia between time. I've told so many people that. They looks at me and say, "Where is it you get that from?" I said, "God gives that to me and tells me to tell you that and it's true." . . .

I let em walk until their baby get ready to come through the birth canal. You walk and sit down and you walk. Try to make mother comfortable from these contractions. Let her do mostly what she want to do. That's the good purpose of stayin at home havin a baby. If you got a good midwife or somebody that knows what she's doin and knows how to watch mother and knows how mother's comin on, she'll let mother do just exactly what she want to do. And say, "Now I'm gonna let you do yo' thing but now when it get to this point, I want you to do what I tell you to do." You tell her that between contractions. You don't tell her that when she's havin a contraction. And she'll pay strict attention. And it'll work out.

As I say, I let em do first one thing and then another. Sometimes they want to be first in the bed, first out the bed, in bed, out bed. Well I know the baby is not fixin to crown and that's good for mother and I just let her do it. Now don't get me wrong. I'm right there with her, watchin her, holding her. Right at her fingertips for her. When I get em up to walk, contractions slow down, and see usually when the contractions start they want to hurry back to bed. I say, "Don't do that. Right where yo' contractions start, a table or anything, just lean awhile until that contraction leaves. It's no use tryin to hurry back tryin to lay down cause yo' baby ain't comin yet." . . .

When they get in that last stage of labor they sometime get to cryin and start to say what they cain't do. "I just cain't—I done tried. I done all I could. There ain't no mo' I can do." That is the worst feelin for the mother at that stage of labor. Mostly those contractions is the worst. I just tell em to leave the rest to God. "All I want you to do is be calm and easy." Plenty times I say, "All you got to do is hush yo' mouth and you'll see it ain't worth the vibration you're makin, you'll be through." Plenty times I say, "You done had yo' baby. All you gotta do is hush yo' mouth and let me reach in there." They done had all the contractions it takes to bring that baby down comin through the birth canal. All they have to do is be a lil patient. Just a lil patient. You see who gonna handle the rest of it. I say, "Now right here is where God comes in. You say you done all you could. You done beared as much as you could. Leave the rest to God. He'll do it."

In the last stages of labor when the baby is fixin to crown, that's when really, you really get irritable. They don't want to be bothered and they easily gets furious. Just like I had one girl, I says, "Well, honey, you're doin fine." "Mrs. Logan, you don't know what you're talkin about. You ain't never had no babies." Well that wasn't her. That was the stage she was in at the time, see. When they get in that last stage of labor just most anything they say would come up. And all at the same time the baby was crownin, it was comin out. I stay cool and calm. Don't you get irritable like they are. You got to know better than that which I do know better than that. I know better and I just keep my calm. Smile and say somethin to em. Finally they get right along with you.

The Cows Mooed and the Horses Neighed

Annie Farrell assists a midwife in a rural area of upstate New York, which she describes as "a beautiful place of white houses and red barns and black and white cows." In fact, the land, the animals, and the people there would seem to live in a special harmony, as evidenced by the following account:

I believe in the right time and the right place for everything. I've been in births where the mother really had to work, where it was not easy. One mother whose birth I was assisting in really had to work hard to get that baby out. Her first baby had been born by caesarean section. She had attempted a home birth, but the midwife who worked with her that time was a passive midwife, someone who didn't get involved. A "hands-off" midwife, where you just let the lady do her thing, and whatever happens, happens. You don't really work with her. Whereas the midwife I work with is a "hands-on" midwife; she gets in there and works right with you, and it's just as if she were having the baby. She has pre-natals, and is equipped with fetal monitors and oxygen. If you're going to have a home birth, you should be prepared. And I think it's good to have someone there who knows even more than you do, to tell you if they think there's a good reason that you should transport to the hospital.

This lady, the first time—the time she'd had the caesarean—she'd worked and worked, and pushed and pushed, and couldn't get anywhere. Couldn't get that baby down. The midwife who was with her thought they ought to go to the hospital, and they did. And they did a caesarean on her right away. But this time she'd made up her mind that she was going to try again.

This woman was a very strong lady. She was in her late twenties, her husband a little older, and she happens to be a very religious person. She has a lot of faith—a very serious girl. She's not someone who would do anything lightly. So I trusted her judgment. And she is also very strong physically. She has a lot of animals, does her own butchering—very strong. Anyway, she was in labor for two and a half days, but not to the point where she couldn't work or walk around. She worked, she milked her goats, she did everything she normally does up until the last twenty-four hours. In fact they went to the movies Saturday night to try to get things relaxed.

By Sunday afternoon, however, things were pretty radical. She was having contractions very fast. She wasn't milking the goats anymore. And she pushed and she squatted and she made loud noises until about ten o'clock Sunday night when she just felt like she could not do it anymore. She just wanted to quit. And I thought that if she wanted to quit, she should. That she should feel she had that option. That she shouldn't feel obliged to stick with it if she didn't want to—that she could go any way she wanted. But the midwife was a little more aggressive. "C'mon, stick with it, you can do it!" Whereas my job—you know, "If you want to go to the hospital, you are welcome. Just say the word."

She decided to go. I got the car ready; everything was prepared for her to leave. We went outside with the bags and all, and it was a beautiful starlit summer night. Out she came into the yard, and suddenly all her animals—she has guinea hens, peacocks, goats, horses, chickens, turkeys, pigs, cows—all of them began to carry on. They just made every noise—it was like Noah's Ark, with all the honking and neighing and mooing. And she went to the fence and held on—it wasn't a conscious thing—and got her energy back. All the animals got so excited—maybe they thought they were going to get fed, I don't know. But it was as if they infused their energy into her. And she said, "Maybe I'll try a little longer."

So we went back inside, and she ended up down on the floor on a blanket in her living room. What finally happened was that her waters broke and showed some meconium stain, which means that the baby has pooped inside the womb. Then if the baby starts to come out, any kind of oxygen hitting the baby could make it take a breath; and if it began to breathe and breathed in some meconium, that could cause viral pneumonia which can be fatal in newborns. It was essential that that baby get out fast. At that point it was really too late to transport. There was no choice but to do it. I get tingles thinking about it, it was so heavy. I was not responsible, but I was there, and I was involved. In the end I actually pushed the baby out with my hands. I was braced with my feet against the wall, pushing. It took all my strength and it sounds brutal, but really you're just pushing the baby's fanny. There must have been a lot of praying going on, because her head came out finally, and once her head was out we were able to suction her, and then the rest of her came. We put her right up on her mother's belly and covered her up and rubbed her, and her mother rubbed her, and finally she began to turn pink. She opened her eyes and looked at everybody, and she was fine. Nine pounds.

Weighing the Baby (1848)

How many pounds does the baby weigh,
　Baby, who came but a month ago;
How many pounds from the crowning curl
　To the rosy point of the restless toe?

Grandfather ties the handkerchief's knot,
　Tenderly guides the swinging weight,
And carefully over his glasses peers
　To read the record, "Only eight!" . . .

Nobody weighed the baby's smile,
　Or the love that came with the helpless one;
Nobody weighed the threads of care
　From which a woman's life is spun.

No index tells the mighty worth
　Of a little baby's quiet breath!
A soft, unceasing metronome,
　Patient and faithful unto death.

Nobody weighed the baby's soul,
　For here, on earth, no weights there be
That could avail. God only knows
　Its value in eternity. . . .

Oh, mother, laugh your merry note,
　Be gay and glad, but don't forget
From baby's eyes looks out a soul
　That claims a home in Eden yet.

Ethel Lynn

"*He just ain't going to do it.*"

The following stories are grim reminders of the terrible price of slavery. The moment of freedom that birth represents for a child and its mother was often brutally severed by the will of the slaveowner. The following accounts from former slaves highlight two kinds of grief that could come to a mother and the precious baby she loved:

My mother told me that he owned a woman who was the mother of several children, and when her babies would get about a year or two of age he'd sell them, and it would break her heart. She never got to keep them. When her fourth baby was born and was about two months old, she just studied all the time about how she would have to give it up, and one day she said, "I just decided I'm not going to let Old Master sell this baby; he just ain't going to do it." She got up and give it something out of a bottle, and pretty soon it was dead. Course didn't nobody tell on her, or he'd of beat her nearly to death.

Diana and Her Baby

I heard the woman I lived with, a woman named Diana Wagner, tell how her mistress said, "Come on, Diana, I want you to go with me down the road a piece." And she went with her, and they got to a place where there was a whole lot of people. They were putting them up on a block and selling them just like cattle. She had a little nursing baby at home, and she broke away from her mistress and them and said, "I can't go off and leave my baby." And they had to git some men and throw her down and hold her to keep her from going back to the house. They sold her away from her baby boy. They didn't let her go back to see him again. But she heard from him after he became a young man. Some one of her friends that knowed her and knowed she was sold away from her baby met up with this boy and got to questioning him about his mother. The white folks had told him his mother's name and all. He told them, and they said, "Boy, I know your mother. She's down in Newport." And he said, "Gimme her address and I'll write to her and see if I can hear from her." And he wrote. And the white people said they heard such a hollering and shouting going on they said, "What's the matter with Diana?" And they came over to see what was happening. And she said, "I got a letter from my boy that was sold from me when he was a nursing baby." She had me write a letter to him. I did all her writing for her, and he came to see her. I didn't get to see him. I was away when he come. She said she was willing to die that the Lord let her live to see her baby again and had taken care of him through all these years.

Elizabeth Cady Stanton's Lesson in Self-Reliance

We will come across Stanton time and again in the following pages. Born in 1815, she is best known as a feminist who worked to organize the first women's convention in 1848 and led the women's movement with Susan B. Anthony in the decades after the Civil War. A gifted orator, she had the common touch and a tough, unflinching quality to her reasoning; she could silence a crowd with her eloquence and bring them to their feet with her humor. Stanton was convinced that modern women had two enemies to their progress: men (like the doctors in the following story) who think they know what is best for women, and women (like the nurse in the story) who accept that condition. Needless to say, Stanton was among those who argued persistently for more women doctors:

Besides the obstinacy of the nurse, I had the ignorance of physicians to contend with. When the child was four days old we discovered that the collarbone was bent. The physician, wishing to get a pressure on the shoulder, braced the bandage round the wrist. "Leave that," he said, "ten days, and then it will be all right." Soon after he left I noticed that the child's hand was blue, showing that the circulation was impeded. "That will never do," said I; "nurse, take it off." "No, indeed," she answered, "I shall never interfere with the doctor." So I took it off myself, and sent for another doctor, who was said to know more of surgery. He expressed great surprise that the first physician called should have put on so severe a bandage. "That," said he, "would do for a grown man, but ten days of it on a child would make him a cripple." However, he did nearly the same thing, only fastening it round the hand instead of the wrist. I soon saw that the ends of the fingers were all purple, and that to leave that on ten days would be as dangerous as the first. So I took that off.

"What a woman!" exclaimed the nurse. "What do you propose to do?"

"Think out something better, myself; so brace me up with some pillows and give the baby to me."

She looked at me aghast and said, "You'd better trust the doctors, or your child will be a helpless cripple."

"Yes," I replied, "he would be, if we had left either of those bandages on, but I have an idea of something better."

"Now," said I, talking partly to myself and partly to her, "what we want is a little pressure on that bone; that is what both those men aimed at. How can we get it without involving the arm, is the question?"

"I am sure I don't know," said she, rubbing her hands and taking two or three brisk turns round the room.

"Well, bring me three strips of linen, four double." I then folded one, wet in arnica and water, and laid it on the collarbone, put two other bands, like a pair of suspenders, over the shoulders, crossing them both in front and behind, pinning the ends to the diaper, which gave the needed pressure without impeding the circulation anywhere. As I finished she gave me a look of budding confidence, and seemed satisfied that all was well. Several times, night and day, we wet the compress and readjusted the bands, until all appearances of inflammation had subsided.

At the end of ten days the two sons of Æsculapius appeared and made their examination and said all was right, whereupon I told them how badly their bandages worked and what I had done myself. They smiled at each other, and one said:

"Well, after all, a mother's instinct is better than a man's reason."

"Thank you, gentlemen, there was no instinct about it. I did some hard thinking before I saw how I could get a pressure on the shoulder without impeding the circulation, as you did."

Thus, in the supreme moment of a young mother's life, when I needed tender care and support, I felt the whole responsibility of my child's supervision; but though uncertain at every step of my own knowledge, I learned another lesson in self-reliance. I trusted neither men nor books absolutely after this, either in regard to the heavens above or the earth beneath, but continued to use my "mother's instinct," if "reason" is too dignified a term to apply to woman's thoughts. My advice to every mother is, above all other arts and sciences, study first what relates to babyhood, as there is no department of human action in which there is such lamentable ignorance.

"For that crippled baby
I have kept an affection that is ineffaceable."

*Founder of the Frontier Nursing Service in Kentucky in 1925, Mary Breckinridge
was one of the great nurse-midwives in American history. She dedicated her life to the
service of the impoverished, working in cities and backwoods alike, and her unflinching vision of family health, her compassion, her medical skill, and her remarkable
stamina are hallmarks of her long, adventurous life. She told one particular story of her
student nursing years that reveals the sensitivity of her character and the challenge of
the work she did so well:*

Although the district nursing tore at my heartstrings, I suffered even more in
the nurseries. In the nursery to which I was assigned, both for day and night
duty, there were never fewer than twenty babies and sometimes as many as
thirty. The heat seemed to be turned on rather low at night and the east wind,
from over the river, penetrated through the cracks of the windows. Only one
thin cotton blanket was allowed to each bassinet. It was cold enough at night
for us to take sweaters to put over our uniforms, but I never had the heart to
wear mine. It was an extra covering for at least one baby. There weren't anything like enough diapers to keep the babies dry, the result, in part, of using
them for a lot of other things. The mothers had them for face towels, and the
ward maids used them for dust rags. I solved the diaper problem by taking
cotton and gauze out of the delivery and operating rooms, the only places
where there was a reserve of anything. While I had the nursery shift, both at
night alone and in the daytime with two other nurses, we started a system of
taking enough gauze and cotton to leave a narrow supply of diapers on hand for
the alternate shift as we went off duty. Although none of the student nurses on
my floor were known to me before I went there, I found that, unlike the head
nurse, most of them had the welfare of the patients at heart. We cooperated.

One fine thing about the nursery was that all the babies were breast-fed
except two who had been there for weeks, one with head injuries and one with
a malformed spine. The schedule of feeding in the daytime was every two
hours, and the babies were taken to their mothers in little carts. During the
night there was only one longer period during which the babies were not taken
to nurse. I think that this frequent contact with their mothers, whether they
were too sleepy to nurse or not, kept the breast milk stimulated. The wave of
bottle feeding of newborn babies came about with the lengthening of time

between feedings. This is only a speculation, but I do know from experience that hospital nursery babies in the first decade of this century were not only breast-fed but nearly always had enough milk to gain back their birth weight by the end of the first week. Since mothers were not sent home as early as they are now, breast milk was well established before the fatigue of tenement life had to be taken up again.

During my term of night duty, I was sometimes in despair over the two older bottle-fed babies. More than once the head nurse went off duty leaving no formula for them, nor even any milk in the refrigerators. One of the young doctors, on staff duty, went out on the streets to buy milk for me when this happened. I did not report the lack of milk to the night supervisor. Student nurses in my day were silent creatures. We compensated for the failure of a superior as best we could. However, after a couple of months at the Lying-In, I was fit to be tied and had to talk to somebody. During a half-day off duty, I sought out my girlhood friend, Nelly Morton, now married to Irving Brock. Nelly was not at home, so I poured out a lot of things to Irving and then said I would look up a respectable woman to whom I would tell the rest. When Nelly returned, Irving said he couldn't imagine what was left to tell the respectable woman!

One of the two bottle-fed babies in my nursery, the *spina bifida,* was paralyzed in both legs. Her name was Margaret. Never have I known so young a creature with the personality of this baby. Her eyes were luminous and her whole expression more mature than that of babies twice her age. She never fretted. When she was hungry, or wanted attention, she called out once, and then waited to give me time to get to her. During the weeks I attended her, both at night and in the daytime, she became dear to me. Her mother did not want her. When I saw her she readily gave the child to me. I arranged with St. Luke's Hospital to let me pay for Margaret's care in the infants' ward until I finished my training. Although this baby was crippled for life, the feeling I had for her was not one of pity. There were babies enough on the East Side to drain one's heart of pity. Margaret and I had become friends. I wanted her companionship, and I wanted to make life easy for her as long as she lived. I could well afford a baby, even a crippled baby.

When it came to the transfer from the Lying-In to St. Luke's, I thought I had it properly lined up. A physician on the Lying-In house staff, who had the authority to do so, gave Margaret a medical discharge. The Lying-In's own office staff gave her a hospital discharge and my friend Biddle, who was on night duty, took the baby up to St. Luke's for me before going to bed for the day. I was in the Out-Patient Department then, and on the district. When I came in at noon, I was met by the biggest cyclone that ever swept over my head. I found that not only was I suspended but the house staff physician and Biddle were suspended too, only Biddle was asleep and didn't know it. We had to go singly before a Board to explain why we had stolen a Lying-In baby. When the district supervisor let me go, she said, in her Irish brogue, "You were trying to do a good deed." But it wasn't that; I loved the baby.

Awkward as things were at the moment, I was struck by the realization that there was a Board, and that for once it had taken an interest in one of the patients. Although the plot was mine, as I freely admitted, my suspension was lifted, with the others', after only a few hours. The fact that the Lying-In's own office had cleared the papers to transfer the baby to St. Luke's made it difficult for the Board to raise a fuss. They got Margaret back. The curious thing to me in all of this storm was that I, the only person in the world who wanted Margaret, was not allowed to keep her.

Only two days after I had gone back to St. Luke's Hospital, they telephoned me from the Lying-In that Margaret was dead. They said I could have her body if I wanted it. Thus, the only thing I could do for my little friend was to save her body from a pauper's grave. I went back to the Lying-In to sign papers. I arranged with an undertaking firm to buy a grave in the Kensico Cemetery, and to meet me there with the casket on the first afternoon I could be off duty. I asked my Aunt Jane's minister to go with me and hold a brief service at the grave. He readily consented and was deeply kind. I have never been back to see Margaret's grave but I still own it. For that crippled baby I have kept an affection that is ineffaceable. I hope, and expect, to see her with my own two children when I have crossed through to the other side of death.

Wartime Birth (1966)

Vietnam was the first place I delivered a baby by myself. It seemed like a Saturday afternoon. It might have been, I don't know why, but for some reason it seemed like a Saturday afternoon. It was very quiet. There were no other patients around. I was feeling very depressed and this lady came in. I got pissed off at first, because we were supposedly there for taking care of military casualties. We were only supposed to take care of civilian situations if we possibly had the time. But this particular day, I got her onto a gurney and started leading her back to the OR because I could tell she was very close to delivery and I had already put in a call to one of the surgeons to come down and deliver it. He didn't have time to get there.

She looked over at me and said, "Baby come, baby come." I looked down and there was the head. I just grabbed myself a sterile towel and held it under, and that kid just popped his little head out and turned around on his side, and popped his little shoulders out, and there was this little squalling bundle of humanness. And the life came back again. It was the creation of life in the midst of all that destruction. And creation of life restored your sanity.

Those moments when we had a little baby around were very precious. I have a couple of slides of me sitting in the operating room with my foot up on the table, in my fatigues and combat boots, with a scrub shirt over the top of me, holding a little tiny bundle in my arms, feeding it. Those were the things that kept you going. That there was still life coming. There was still hope.

Birth and Infancy Superstitions

Birth is a great seedbed of superstition, and midwives are frequently the first and most powerful gardeners. Sometimes the superstitions are veiled ways to modify behavior: Isn't the admonition that tickling a newborn's feet will cause stammering just another way of keeping fathers and siblings from unduly annoying a newborn? Sometimes superstitions are offered by way of prophetic explanation: The mother of a mean boy had kicked a dog while pregnant. Most of the time, however, superstitions represented shards of a deeper medical or emotional truth. Just as we are discoving the medicinal properties of herbs that Native Americans routinely employed centuries ago, so are some of the oldest folk superstitions proving to be less silly than imagined. In any event, the selections throughout the book are offered more for their fun than their verity:

> If a married woman is the first one to see a newborn baby, that woman will become a mother.
> If one finds a baby pacifier, there is going to be an addition to the family.
> A bright star in the sky means there will soon be a birth.
> Conceiving under the increase of the moon or in the moonlight means the baby will be a girl.
> A woman with child is always lucky.

If a pregnant woman steps over a rope to which a horse is tied, she will be late delivering the child.

If a pregnant woman is frightened, her baby will bear a birthmark of the object that frightened the mother.

Heartburn while pregnant means your child will have a full head of hair.

Do not stand in front of a mirror and look at yourself while pregnant; it brings bad luck.

A daughter born with a closed hand will be stingy.

If she is born on Christmas Day, your daughter will be able to speak with animals and talk with the spirits.

A baby speaks with angels when it smiles.

A daughter will be lucky if she resembles her father.

Ugly in the cradle means she'll be pretty in the saddle.

If a baby teethes early, it is making way for a new baby.

If you cut off a baby's finger nails, it will die before it is six months old.

Rub rabbit brains, still warm, on her gums and the baby will cut teeth easily.

F A M I L Y L I F E

$\mathcal{H}$arry Crews, the American novelist, wrote a powerful portrait of family life of growing up poor in Bacon County, Georgia. He describes one particular windless summer day when he is two or three and watching his mother from his playpen. She is scrubbing the kitchen floor with homemade lye and occasionally looking out a screenless window at her husband who is out in the tobacco field, spraying for cutworms. Her husband is a driven man, exhausted by long hot days in the field but intent on saving the tobacco crop that will, upon its harvest, feed the family. Crews tells us that it has been a good year for his parents and that the two recently acquired yearling cows were the first livestock the family had ever owned. As Crews' mother watches her husband, she sees the two cows amble toward the bucket of poison her husband is using to spray on the crops. She knows that the cows are thirsty, realizes that they will drink from the bucket, and understands they will die. She calls out to her husband but he cannot hear her over the hissing of his pump. She runs toward the field but halfway is stopped by her child's terrified scream. Realizing at once why, she rushes back to her bleeding child whose hands, mouth, and tongue are now covered with lye. They carry the little boy to the hospital where his burns (less serious than feared) are treated and, upon coming home, they find the two yearlings dead by the fence.

For Crews it is understandably a salient memory—a story that touches on the hard and bitter struggle of the rural poor for survival. It also seems a vivid metaphor for the roles mothers and fathers sometimes play. Consider the father: he is consumed by the long, hot hours that are a necessary requirement for the economic well-being of his family. He loses himself in his work, and brings a single-minded focus that enables him to spray the fields, prime the tobacco, plough the ground, day after grueling day. His work—however difficult and demanding—is a powerful, unexamined assumption, a rationale for living. She, who is scrubbing the floor, is doing work no less vital to the health and safety of the family. But unlike him, lost in the hiss and spray of his poison, she must be aware of many things beyond her own work—her child, the food they will eat, the clothes they will wear, her exhausted man in the field, the cows moving toward death.

The dynamics of frontier life may well have demanded that men and women divide up the required chores, but once progress tamed necessity, the American mother began a juggling act that has not stopped. Her multiple responsibilities inevitably disrupt her ability to focus on one thing to the exclusion of all others, a luxury men assume as a birthright. The bleak humor mothers share with one another (and ultimately with their daughters) about the behavior of their husbands toward the duties of family life is passed like a generational torch. Mothers understand that much is demanded of them, that the margin for error while balancing their tasks will be slim and that the assistance they can expect is likely to be marginal.

In Steinbeck's *Grapes of Wrath*, Ma Joad gets to the heart of it: "Man," she says, "lives in jerks—baby born an' a man dies, an' that's a jerk—gets a farm an' loses his farm, an' that's a jerk. Woman, it's all one flow, like a stream, little eddies, little waterfalls, but the river, it goes right on. Woman looks at it like that."

Aunt Jane's Quilting (Kentucky, 1908)

"But there never was any time wasted on my quilts, child. I can look at every one of 'em with a clear conscience. I did my work faithful; and then, when I might 'a' set and held my hands, I'd make a block or two o' patchwork, and before long I'd have enough to put together in a quilt. I went to piecin' as soon as I was old enough to hold a needle and a piece o' cloth, and one o' the first things I can remember was settin' on the back door-step sewin' my quilt pieces, and mother praisin' my stitches. Nowadays folks don't have to sew unless they want to, but when I was a child there warn't any sewin'-machines, and it was about as needful for folks to know how to sew as it was for 'em to know how to eat; and every child that was well raised could hem and run and backstitch and gether and over-hand by the time she was nine years old. Why, I'd pieced four quilts by the time I was nineteen years old, and when me and Abram set up housekeepin' I had bedclothes enough for three beds.

"I've had a heap o' comfort all my life makin' quilts, and now in my old age I wouldn't take a fortune for 'em. Set down here, child, where you can see out o' the winder and smell the lilacs, and we'll look at 'em all. You see, some folks has albums to put folks' pictures in to remember 'em by, and some folks has a book and writes down the things that happen every day so they won't forgit 'em; but, honey, these quilts is my albums and my di'ries, and whenever the weather's bad and I can't git out to see folks, I jest spread out my quilts and look at 'em and study over 'em, and it's jest like goin' back fifty or sixty years and livin' my life over agin.

"There ain't nothin' like a piece o' caliker for bringin' back old times, child, unless it's a flower or a bunch o' thyme or a piece o' pennyroy'—anything that smells sweet. Why, I can go out yonder in the yard and gether a bunch o' that purple lilac and jest shut my eyes and see faces I ain't seen for fifty years, and somethin' goes through me like a flash o' lightnin', and it seems like I'm young agin jest for that minute."

Aunt Jane's hands were stroking lovingly a "nine-patch" that resembled the coat of many colors.

"Now this quilt, honey," she said, "I made out n' the pieces o' my children's clothes, their little dresses and waists and aprons. Some of 'em's dead, and some of 'em's grown and married and a long way off from me, further off than the ones that's dead, I sometimes think. But when I set down and look at this quilt and think over the pieces, it seems like they all come back, and I can see 'em playin' around the floors and goin' in and out, and hear 'em cryin' and laughin' and callin' me jest like they used to do before they grew up to men and women, and before they was any little graves o' mine out in the old buryin'-ground over yonder."

Why Not Save Mother?

The farmer sat in his easy chair
Between the tire and the lamplight's glare.
His face was ruddy and full and fair.
His three small boys in the chimney nook
Conned the lines of a picture book.
His wife the pride of his home and heart
Baked the biscuit and made the tart—
Laid the table and steeped the tea—
Deftly, swiftly and silently:
Tired and weary, weak and faint
She bore her trials without complaint,
Like many another household saint—

Content, all selfish bliss above
In the patient ministry of love.

At last, between the clouds of smoke
That wreathed his lips, the farmer spoke:
"There's taxes to raise and inter'st to pay,
And if there should come a rainy day
'T would be mighty handy, I'm bound to say,
T' have something put by. For folks must die
An' there's funeral bills and gravestones to buy
Enough to swamp a man, purty nigh;
Besides, there's Edward an' Dick an' Joe
To be provided for when we go
So, if I were you, I'll tell you what I'd do;
I'd be savin' of wood as ever I could—

Extra fires don't do any good.
I'd be savin' of soap, and savin' of ile,
And run up some candles once in a while;
I'd rather be sparin' of coffee and tea,
 For sugar is high,
 An' all to buy,
And cider is good enough drink for me;
I'd be kind o' careful about my clo'es
And look out sharp how the money goes—
Gewgaws is useless, nater knows;
 Extra trimmin'
 's the bane of women.
I'd sell the best of my cheese and honey,
An' eggs is as good, nigh 'bout as the money;
An' as to the carpet you wanted new—
I guess we can make the old one do;
And as for th' washer, and sewin' machine,
Them smooth tongued agents, so pesky mean,
You'd better get rid of 'em slick and clean.
What do they know 'bout women's work.
Do they calkilate women was made to shirk?"

Dick and Edward and little Joe
Sat in the corner in a row
They saw the patient mother go
On ceaseless errands to and fro;
They saw that her form was bent and thin,
Her temples gray, her checks sunk in;
They saw the quiver of lip and chin—
And then, with a wrath he could not smother,
Outspoke the youngest, frailest brother:
 "You talk of savin' wood an' ile
 And tea an' sugar all the while,
But you never talk of savin' mother!"

Health Tips in Colonial America

For Comforting the Head & Braine

Take Rosemary & Sage of both sorts of both, wth flowers of Rosemary if to be had, & Borage wth ye flowers. Infuse in Muscadine or in good Canary 3 dayes, drinke it often. The fat of a Hedg-hog roasted drop it into the Eare, is an excellent remedy against deafnes. Also a Clove of Garlick, make holes in it, dip it in Honey, & put it into the Eare at night going to bed, first on one side, then on the other for 8 or 9 dayes together, keeping in ye Eares black wooll.

For Hoarsness

Take 3 or 4 figs, cleave them in two, put in a pretty quantity of Ginger in powder, roast them & Eate them often.

To Kill Worms in Children

Take sage, boil it with milk to a good tea, turn it to whey with alum or vinegar, and give the whey to the child, if the worms are not knotted in the stomach, and it will be a sure cure. If the worms are knotted in the stomach, it will kill the child.

To Cure Hard Drinking

Take Roman wormwood, gather it in the full of the moon when it is in the blossom, and in the morning when the dew is on; dry it one day in the sun, then under cover until it is dry, roll it up in paper then put it into a tight place, and make a bitter of this by putting it into water—drink this frequently and when you are faint—so continue one year, and it will deliver you from the desire of ardent spirit. This is called Roman wormwood, because it cured the Romans of a stinking breath.

Treatment for Croup

Take goose oil, or olive oil, rub it up and down on each side of the nose, and round about the eyes. If the child is pressed at the stomach, take a portion of the goose oil, enough to puke it. If the child's difficulty appears to be that of the rattles, or is some like the quincy, take a great spoonful of goose grease and two spoonfuls of chamber lie (and in the same proportion for a larger quantity), and mix them by warming them on embers, and sweeten it with a spoonful of honey, if you can get it, if not, with molasses, and give it to the child forcibly and sufficiently, pausing now and then to prevent the child's strangling to death. This has caused them to strive and puke up the bladders, whereby the child was relieved. Repeat it if necessary.

Share and Share Alike (1825)

It happened in 1825 at the frontier village of Fredonia near Lake Erie. New York State was furiously playing host to the venerable Marquis de Lafayette—towing him up and down the Grand Canal, letting him shake the hand of every surviving veteran of the Revolution, and giving him a sight of Red Jacket, Niagara Falls, and all the other natural wonders. At Fredonia the citizens had prepared something special. A French explorer had named their creek *La Terre Puante,* "Stinking Shore,"—not without cause but now the village could and did boast that it was the first in America to be illuminated by natural gas. In honor of the Marquis, additional lights had been installed about a platform on the village green, to shine on the bright red hue of the only "boughten" carpet in the region, generously and anxiously lent by the Episcopal minister's wife. Her anxiety was well founded, for on that memorable night the carpet was damaged beyond repair by the stomp of hobnailed boots.

The expectation was that the General would arrive in the early evening. Long before dark, the five hundred citizens were assembled, their numbers augmented by other hundreds who had come from outlying farms to tread upon the store-carpet. Night fell, and the wonderful lights were turned on, but no Lafayette appeared. Nine, ten, eleven, twelve o'clock struck, and still the crowd waited. Then up to the common raced yelling boys with the news that the General's carriage was at the bridge. The great Reception began.

Now there was one lady in Fredonia who was expected to shine with special glory when she curtseyed to Lafayette. Mrs. Laurens Risley was the owner of a handsome Paisley shawl, presumably imported from Scotland, certainly the fairest article of feminine apparel in the county. Tradition derives the name Fredonia from an Indian one meaning Free Woman; that night Mrs. Risley proved herself free in the noblest sense of generous. No sooner had she greeted the French hero on the platform than she slipped back into the shadows and handed her shawl to a friend—and then to another, and to another, until the General's eyes were more dazzled by bright Paisley tints than by the illumination. Afterward he said: "Fredonia! It is a village of beautiful women, beautifully dressed. You would scarcely believe it of a frontier settlement, but I give you my word that in none of the large cities of America have I ever seen so many handsome shawls."

Lydia Maria Child's Household Hints (1832)

How to categorize Lydia Maria Child (1802–80)? Shall we call her a poet? A novelist? She was considered both by such writers as Walt Whitman and John Greenleaf Whittier. Shall we call her a newspaperwoman and a passionate reformer? William Lloyd Garrison certainly did and relied upon her stamina and dedication in the public crusade against slavery. Some remember best her career as a children's editor/writer (she authored the well-loved ditty: "Over the river and through the woods, to grandmother's house we go"). Her husband was a dreamer and, for all his charm, was not capable of securing a steady livelihood for his family. Child took up the burden and wrote like one possessed in order to generate the royalties she needed to keep her family out of poverty. Her first book, published a year after her marriage, was called The Frugal American Housewife *and was shrewdly "dedicated to those who are not ashamed of economy." The following excerpt from that book gives us a taste not only of Child but of the kind of homespun counsel she was to find so profitable in her long, illustrious career:*

The true economy of housekeeping is simply the art of gathering up all the fragments, so that nothing be lost. I mean fragments of *time*, as well as *materials*. Nothing should be thrown away so long as it is possible to make any use of it, however trifling that use may be; and whatever be the size of a family, every member should be employed either in earning or saving money.

"Time is money." For this reason, cheap as stockings are, it is good economy to knit them. Cotton and woollen yarn are both cheap; hose that are knit wear twice as long as woven ones; and they can be done at odd minutes of time, which would not be otherwise employed. Where there are children, or aged people, it is sufficient to recommend knitting, that it is an *employment*.

In this point of view, patchwork is good economy. It is indeed a foolish waste of time to tear cloth into bits for the sake of arranging it anew in fantastic figures; but a large family may be kept out of idleness, and a few shillings saved, by thus using scraps of gowns, curtains, &c.

In the country, where grain is raised, it is a good plan to teach children to prepare and braid straw for their own bonnets, and their brothers' hats.

Where turkeys and geese are kept, handsome feather fans may as well be made by the younger members of a family, as to be bought. The sooner children are taught to turn their faculties to some account, the better for them and for their parents.

In this country, we are apt to let children romp away their existence, till they get to be thirteen or fourteen. This is not well. It is not well for the purses and patience of parents; and it has a still worse effect on the morals and habits of the children. *Begin early* is the great maxim for everything in education. A child of six years old can be made useful; and should be taught to consider every day lost in which some little thing has not been done to assist others.

Children can very early be taught to take all the care of their own clothes.

They can knit garters, suspenders, and stockings; they can make patchwork and braid straw; they can make mats for the table, and mats for the floor; they can weed the garden, and pick cranberries from the meadow, to be carried to market.

Provided brothers and sisters go together, and are not allowed to go with bad children, it is a great deal better for the boys and girls on a farm to be picking blackberries at six cents a quart, than to be wearing out their clothes in useless play. They enjoy themselves just as well; and they are earning something to buy clothes, at the same time they are tearing them.

Advice to the Victorian Woman

Brooms

Always stand your brooms on the handle or hang them from a nail. Once a week give them a dip in boiling soap-suds, as a restorative.

Filling Jelly Glasses

Put a spoon in the jelly glass or jar before you pour the boiling fruit or syrup into it. The spoon acts as a conductor to the heat, and the glass is less likely to crack. The same end is gained by standing the jar or glass upon a thick, wet cloth.

Fingermarks

A piece of stale bread will often remove finger-marks from wall-paper. Rub with the inside of the crust.

Unguents and Powders

Cold cream is probably the best facial unguent. Cocoanut oil is recommended to increase the flesh and improve the skin, but this, as well as the oft-vaunted lanoline, in many cases stimulates the growth of superfluous hair. The same objection has been urged against vaseline, white or yellow. Glycerine, mingled with rose-water or bay rum, may generally be used successfully upon moist skins, but dry-skinned women cannot use it with comfort. For a thin neck and arms unctions of olive oil are sometimes advised. This is well rubbed into the parts that need filling out. A compound of albolene, a form of almond oil, and alcohol, in the proportion of two or three parts of the albolene to one of alcohol is also good for developing flesh upon the thin neck and arms.

Of powders the best is some form of talc. Powdered starch is also excellent. The cheap perfumed powders that contain bismuth are to be avoided, because of their bad effect upon the skin. Powder will clog the skin unless it is carefully removed by later applications of an unguent. It is almost indispensable to the possessors of greasy skins in hot weather, but it should be used so carefully that its presence will not be offensively apparent.

The Care of the Feet

Chilblains may sometimes be cured by persistent bathing, night and morning, with witch-hazel. A poultice of roasted turnip is recommended for obstinate cases.

The Care of the Hair

Once a month is generally often enough for a wet shampoo. In hot weather it may be taken more frequently. In this matter each woman is usually the best judge for herself. Under no circumstances use dyes or bleaches.

A fine comb should never be employed, as it irritates the scalp and produces dandruff. This may be removed by brushing or by shampooing. Lemon juice applied to the scalp, not to the hair, will sometimes remove dandruff. Soap is so hard to rinse from the hair that it is better to use something else in cleansing. A good wash is made by mixing the yolk of an egg with a little water.

The scalp is rubbed with this and then rinsed clean, first in warm and then in cold water. If no other preparation is used, add a little ammonia and borax to the water in which the hair is washed. This is better for oily than for naturally dry hair. The woman who has the latter should anoint the scalp after washing with a little vaseline or scentless pomatum.

The hair may be dried after a shampoo by fanning, and should be left hanging until it is quite dry. The ends should be clipped once a month. Eucalyptus is recommended to promote the growth of the hair. Sage tea is also used for this purpose, and rum and quinine or whiskey and quinine in the proportion of ten grains of quinine to half a pint of the liquor are said to have a tonic effect upon the hair and scalp. Frequent brushing with a moderately stiff brush also stimulates the growth of the hair.

Freckles

Scrape a teaspoon of horseradish into a cup of sour milk; let it stand six hours before using. Apply to the freckles twice a day.

Lemon-juice will sometimes cure freckles. Dip your finger-tip in the acid and touch the freckles with it. Buttermilk may be used in the same way.

A poultice of leaves boiled soft and washed and left on the face all night is said to remove freckles and whiten the skin.

Wrinkles

The best plan for keeping free of wrinkles is to avoid tricks of grimacing, raising the eyebrows, frowning, etc. A few minutes' absolute facial repose during the day is said to retard the approach of wrinkles.

A spray of cold water on the face night and morning is said to tone up the skin and prevent wrinkles. In washing the face, wipe it from the chin *up,* and from the sides toward the center.

Getting Rid of a Red Nose

A red nose, frequently a serious blemish in an otherwise charming face, is often caused by tight lacing or tight shoes; and with the removal of the cause of the impeded circulation, the trouble will vanish.

Aunt Weed's Rat Letter

From the hill country comes an extraordinary resourceful letter from Aunt Weed, whose descendants swear it worked and that no rats were ever seen again! (Did they all go to poor Ike Nute's house?)

I have borne with you till my patience is all gone. I cannot find words bad enough to express what I feel, you devils you, gnawing our trace corn while we are asleep! And even when we are awake you have the audacity to set your infernal jaws to going. Now, spirits of the bottomless pit, depart from this place with all speed! Look not back! Begone, or you are ruined! If you could know as much as I do, you would never take another thing from here. I will keep nothing to myself. You shall hear the whole. We are preparing water [to] drown you; fire to roast you; cats to catch you; and clubs to maul you. Unless you want your detested garments dyed in fire and brimstone, you satans, quit here and go to Ike Nute's! This is for cellar rats. Please give notice to those in the chamber. There are many of us in the garret plotting against you, when our eyes are open all but one poor female who is afraid of life. But the rest is not afraid I can tell you. There is our bill, and I leave if they get hold of you [you] would think you're in wire cage. A hint to the wise is sufficient.

To the biggest and most inventive rat.

Mrs. Weed

When Her Courage Failed Her

Sometimes in the narratives of women who are making their mark on a new frontier, their honesty heartens us. One story is told of a Mrs. Hyde, a Maine woman, who had endured great trials in the wilderness to lay the foundation for her family farm. First was survival—housing, barns, domestic shelters; next the basic amenities—crops, milk, eggs; and then, the pleasures of farm life— pies. Mrs. Hyde began digging about the stumps to plant some pumpkin seeds in anticipation of her favorite pies in the fall. Her only problem, a serious one for pies, was that she had not a single pie plate. During the summer her husband managed to find for her the much-coveted blue-edged plates; he brought them through the woods strapped upon his back. With great care, he built for her an oven of stones on the top of a large stump. It was made with two stories in order that she might bake as many pies as she had plates. The great day arrived; Mrs. Hyde and her family were thoroughly hungry for pumpkin pies. The oven was heated, the pies were placed in position—and then there came a terrible crash. The oven had caved in and every pie plate was smashed! Mrs. Hyde, in narrating the incident to her friend, said she had been threatened by Indians, surrounded by howling wolves and prowling bears; she had been exposed to many dangers, but her courage had never failed her till then. She went to bed and cried.

There's Many an Empty Cradle (1858)

Last June our rude cabin was blessed by two beautiful little ones. You never saw a more beautiful child than my little Mary Katherin. Her eyes made me think of my own dear father's. Every one exclaimed, soon as they saw her, what beautiful eyes! She was so fair, and she had such regular features, and her hair so dark, she was beautiful. Oh, how I loved her! How proud I was of her, yes too proud of her. He that knoweth all things saw it and called her home to himself, while she was yet pure and guileless. My little boy was not so handsome as his little sister, but he was smart, and after his little sister died I let all my affections center in him. My heavenly father saw the idolatry of my heart, and he sent the messenger for my little William Henry, and my heart was stripped of its idols. When I gazed on his little face cold in death, I realized how I had forgotten the giver in my mad worship of the gift. My little Mary breathed her last in my arms on the 16th of September last, and little Willie lingered along until the 14th of December. We laid him out in his little white dress, took his coffin into a wagon, and with one of our neighbors, who was on horseback, went to the burial. We opened the grave where little Mary lay and set Willie's coffin on the top of hers. They both rest in the same grave, and their little spirits on the other side to join our fast gathering band. For six months I had almost the entire care of these little ones, day nor night they were hardly out of my arms. I had not one good night's sleep after they were born until they were gone. And after we returned from the grave, I was sick for a week but am now quite well, and so are Sarah and Cephas and Celia. But there is a void in my heart, and the rocking chair that was their cradle is empty, and I often find myself repeating these lines:

> There's many an empty cradle,
> There's many a vacant bed,

There's many a lonesome bosom
Whose joy and light have fled.
For thick in every graveyard
The little hillocks lie,
And every hillock represents
An angel in the sky.

It is indeed a consolation to think they are angels. Oh, my sweet babes! I would not call you back to this world of troubles and trials of sickness and death. No, no, rest in peace! It will be but a short time before I shall join you in that happy land to which you have gone before.

The Doctor seems worn down, but it is not for himself that he cares, it is for his family, for there is not that one in the world that thinks more of his family than he. Last spring he put in a large crop of potatoes and has already harvested and sent to San Francisco 2000 sacks of them. We are in great hopes of the coming season. He is wearing himself out with toil and care. He is so proud of Cephas. God grant that the boy may be spared to him, but he misses little Willie so much. Thanks to my Heavenly Father I have been kept from murmuring and never gave a word of reproach that this or that might have been done. I have seen and known how he has struggled, and if I have not been able to render him that assistance I might wish, I have endeavored to make everything as cheerful and pleasant as I could, and I am now reaping my reward in his devotion to me. Oh, how I prize it! And is it not worth suffering patiently for? Adieu, my mother and my sisters.

San Leandro, Cal.
March, 1858

I feel I am in a strange land, and that the trials I have been called upon to pass through have never been few or far between. I often find myself saying, "All alone—all alone." Oh, my dear mother, if I could only have you with me, to lay my poor weary aching head upon your lap, and feel your dear hand upon my burning brow, and have your kind sympathy, it would take a great deal of the pain from my heart, but dear mother I much fear we shall never meet again except in the spirit land; not that my health is poor, for it never was better in my life, but dear mother, your wanderer is not yet at rest,

once more I fear I will have to take up my staff and travel on,
but whatever befalls me I shall hope for the best.

May God bless you all.

Adieu, Mary

Counting Your Blessings (1859)

1. bild fire in back yard to het kettle of rain water.
2. set tubs so smoke won't blow in eyes if wind is peart.
3. shave 1 hole cake lie sope in bilin water.
4. sort things. make 3 piles. 1 pile white, 1 pile cullord, 1 pile work briches and rags.
5. stur flour in cold water to smooth then thin down with bilin water [for starch].
6. rub dirty spots on board. scrub hard. then bile. rub cullord but don't bile, just rench and starch.
7. take white things out of kettle with broom stick handel then rench, blew, and starch.
8. pore rench water in flower bed.
9. scrub porch with hot sopy water.
10. turn tubs upside down.
11. go put on a cleen dress, smooth hair with side combs, brew cup of tee, set and rest, and rock a spell and count blessings.

"I am scareing the hogs out of my kitchen . . ." (1852)

The year is 1852, the location a mining camp in California. The letter from Mary Ballou to her son Seldên speaks for itself:

My Dear Seldên,

we are about as usual in health. well I suppose you would like to know what I am doing in this gold region. well I will try to tell you what my work is here in this muddy Place. All the kitchen that I have is four posts stuck down into the ground and covered over the top with factory cloth no floor but the ground. this is a Boarding House kitchen, there is a floor in the dining room and my sleeping room covered with nothing but cloth. we are at work in a Boarding House.

Oct 27 this morning I awoke and it rained in torrents. well I got up and I thought of my House. I went and looked into my kitchen. the mud and water was over my Shoes I could not go into the kitchen to do any work to day but kept perfectly dry in the Dining so I got along very well. your Father put on his Boots and done the work in the kitchen. I felt badly to think that I was destined to be in such a place. I wept for a while and then I commenced singing and made up a song as I went along. my song was this:

> *To California I did come*
> *and thought I under the bed*
> *I shall have to run*
> *to shelter me*
> *from the piercing storm.*

now I will try to tell you what my work is in this Boarding house. well sometimes I am washing and Ironing sometimes I am making mince pie and Apple pie and squash pies. Sometimes I am frying mince turnovers and Donuts. I make Biscuit and now and then Indian jonny cake and then again I am making minute puding filled with rasons and Indian Bake pudings and then again a nice Plum Puding and then again I am Stuffing a Ham of pork that cost forty cents a pound. Sometimes I am making gruel for the sick now and then cooking oisters and sometimes making coffee for the French people strong enough for any man to walk on that has Faith as Peter had. three times a day I set my Table which is about thirty feet in length and do all the little fixings about it such as filling pepper boxes and vinegar cruits and mustard pots and Butter cups. sometimes I am feeding my chickens and then again I am scareing the hogs out of my kitchen and Driving the mules out of my Dining room. you can see by the description that I have given you of my kitchen that anything can walk into the kitchen that chooses to walk in and there being no door to shut from the kitchen into the Dining room you see that anything can walk . . . into the Dining room so you see the Hogs and mules can walk in any time day or night if they choose to do so. sometimes I am up all times a night scareing the Hogs and mules out of the House. last night there a large rat came down pounce down onto our bed in the night. sometimes I take my fan and try to fan myself but I work so hard that my Arms pain me so severly that I kneed some one to fan me so I do not find much comfort anywhere. I made a Blue-berry puding to day for Dinner. Sometimes I am making soups and cranberry tarts and Baking a chicken that cost four Dollars a head and cooking Eggs at three Dollars a Dozen. Sometimes boiling cabbage and Turnips and frying fritters and Broiling stake and cooking codfish and potatoes. I often cook nice Salmon trout that weigh from ten to twenty pound apiece. sometimes I am taking care of Babies and nursing at the rate of Fifty Dollars a week but I would not advise any Lady to come out here and suffer the toil and fatigue that I have suffered for the sake of a little gold neither do I advise any one to come. . . .

now I will tell you a little more about my cooking. sometimes I am cooking rabbits and Birds that are called quails here and I cook squrrels. occasionally I run in and have a chat with jane and Mrs Durphy and I often have a hearty cry. no one but my maker knows my feelings. and then I run into my little cellar which is about four feet square as I have no other place to run that is cool.

October 21 well I have been to church to hear a methodist sermon. his Text let us lay aside every weight and the sin that doth so easely beset us. I was the only Lady that was present and about forty gentlemen. So you see that I go to church when I can. . . .

there I hear the Hogs in my kitchen turning the Pots and kettles upside down so I must drop my pen and run and drive them out. so this is the way that I have to write—jump up every five minutes for something and then again I washed out about a Dollars worth of gold dust the fourth of July in the cradle so you see that I am doing a little mining in this gold region but I think it harder to rock the cradle to wash out gold than it is to rock the cradle for the Babies in the States.

October 11 I washed in the forenon and made a Democrat Flag in the afternoon sewed twenty yards of splendid worsted fringe around it and I made whig Flag. they are both swinging acrost the road but the Whig Flag is the richest. I had twelve Dollars for making them so you see that I am making Flags with all rest of the various kinds of work that I am doing and then again I am scouring candle sticks and washing the floor and making soft soap. the People tell me that it is the first Soft Soap they knew made in California. Sometimes I am making mattresses and sheets. I have no windows in my room. all the light that I have shines through canvas that covers the House and my eyes are so dim that I can hardly see to make a mark so I think you will excuse me for not writing any better. . . .

Oh my Dear Seldên I am so Home sick I will say to you once more to see that Augustus has every thing that he kneeds to make him comfortable and by all means have him Dressed warm this cold winter. i worry a great deal about my Dear children. it seems as though my heart would break when I realized how far I am from my Dear loved ones this from your affectionate mother.

American Cooking, Frontier Style

How to Keep Eggs Fresh

All it is necessary to do to keep eggs through the summer is to procure small, clean wooden or tin vessels, holding from 10 to 20 gallons, and a barrel, more or less, or common, fine-ground land plaster. Begin by putting on the bottom of the vessel 2 or 3 inches of plaster. Then, having fresh eggs, with the yolks unbroken, set them up, small end down, close to each other but not crowding, and make the first layer. Then add more plaster and enough so the eggs will stand upright, and set up the second layer; then another deposit of plaster, followed by a layer of eggs, till the vessel is full. Finish by covering the top layer with plaster. Eggs so packed and subjected to a temperature of at least 85 degrees, if not 90 degrees, during August and September, came out fresh, and if one could be certain of not having a temperature of more than 75 degrees to contend with, I am confident eggs could be kept by these means all the year round. Observe that the eggs must be fresh laid, the yolks unbroken, the packing done in the small vessels, and with clean, fine-ground land plaster, and care must be taken that no egg so presses on another as to break the shell. Eggs may be kept good for a year in the following manner:

To a pail of water, put of unslacked lime and coarse salt each a pint; keep it in a cellar, or cool place, and put the eggs in, as fresh laid as possible. It is well to keep a stone pot of this lime water ready to receive the eggs as soon as laid. Make a fresh supply every few months. This lime water is of exactly the proper strength; strong lime water will cook the eggs. Very strong lime water will eat the shell.

How to Choose Eggs

In putting the hand round the egg, and presenting to the light, the end which is not covered, it should be transparent. If you can detect some tiny spots, it is not newly laid, but may be very good for all ordinary purposes except boiling soft. If you see a large spot near the shell, it is bad, and should not be used on any account. The white of a newly-laid egg boiled soft is like milk; that of an egg a day old is like rice boiled in milk; and that of an old egg, compact, tough, and difficult to digest. A cook ought not to give eggs two or three days old to people who really care for fresh eggs, under the delusion that they will not find any difference; for an amateur will find it out in a moment, not only by the appearance, but also by the taste.

C o o n   C a k e

Take what flour you have, mix with water, shorten with coon oil and fry in coon fat.

F r o n t i e r   C a k e s :   W h e n   A r e   T h e y   D o n e ?

Most cooks test a cake with a broom splint. Put it in quickly, and if it comes out dry and clean, the cake is done. If cleanliness is desirable, however, it might be suggested that a very good plan is to keep a knitting needle in the kitchen table drawer for testing cake. A sure way of testing cake in the oven is to draw it to the edge of the oven and put the ear close to it. When it is not sufficiently baked, a slight sputtering noise will be heard, but when thoroughly done there will be no sound.

F r i e d   S q u i r r e l

Rinse skinned squirrel in cold water and pat dry. Dip in buttermilk and then in seasoned flour and fry in hot fat. If the squirrel is young, steaming is not necessary. Otherwise, drain off excess fat, add 1 cup water, and steam covered. Make gravy in the frying pan by adding the leftover seasoned flour and milk or water. Serve with hot biscuits and wild plum jelly.

H o g s h e a d   C h e e s e

Use 1 small pig's head, or half a large head, and 4 pig feet (have cleaned and trimmed at the market). These make the cheese firmer, and less fat. Put in a kettle with water enough to cover; boil slowly until all the bones will slip out. Then set away. When cold, skim all the fat off the top. Then set the kettle back on the stove until it warms the meat. Set off, skim out the meat into a chopping bowl, and work through the hands to remove all the small bones. Season highly with pepper, salt, powdered thyme, summer savory, allspice, and cinnamon. Chop fine and add some of the liquor. Pack closely in deep dishes or pint bowls. Keep in cold place. Slice thinly. A weight will press it firmer.

Baked Raccoon

Boil 1 skinned and gutted coon in water for an hour to tenderize. Remove, dry, and rub skin with butter. Place 1 tart apple and 2 medium onions inside of coon. Season with salt and pepper. Place coon in roasting pan with a little water in bottom. Cover with fat meat. Bake in moderate oven until tender.

Barbecued Squirrel

Put some slices of fat bacon in an oven. Lay the squirrels on them and lay two slices of bacon on the top. Put them in the oven and let them cook until done. Lay them on a dish and set near the fire. Take out the bacon, sprinkle one spoonful of flour in the gravy and let it brown. Then pour in one teacup of water, one tablespoon of butter, and some walnut catsup. Let it cool, then pour it over the squirrel.

Corn Dodgers

(Will keep several days in a saddle bag.) About 2 cups cornmeal, $^{2}/_{3}$ tsp. salt, and enough boiling water so you can pick them up and make a patty (about like a mud patty you made as a child).

These may also be made on a clean shovel at the edge of a campfire. Be sure they are brown on both sides.

These cakes and black coffee made in a tin can on a fire kept many a weary cowboy going on the long trail rides to the railroad.

Army Coffee for One Hundred

Take 5 pounds of roasted coffee, grind and mix with 6 eggs; make small muslin sacks, and in each place a pint of coffee, leaving room for it to swell; put 5 gallons boiling water in a large coffee urn or boiler having a faucet at the bottom; put in part of the sacks and boil two hours; five or ten minutes before serving raise the lid and add one or two more sacks, and if you continue serving several times add fresh sacks at regular intervals. . . .

To make coffee for twenty persons, use 2½ pints ground coffee and 1 gallon of water.

Isabella Bird: "Epicures at home would have envied us."

She was born in England in 1831 and would live there most of her life, when she wasn't traveling. But we shall claim her as our own, if only because her solitary journey through the Rocky Mountains in 1873 was so thoroughly American. In the best American tradition, Isabella Bird did not take herself too seriously and did not hesitate to tell her readers of all the humiliations and humorous misadventures that befell her on her travels through most of what is now Colorado. She did not mind traveling alone, nor did she duck the pressures that came when falling in with mountain guides or fellow voyagers. As we see below, one of her strengths was her ability to master frontier cuisine on very short notice:

Thanksgiving day. The thing dreaded has come at last, a snow-storm with a north-east wind. It ceased about midnight, but not till it had covered my bed. Then the mercury fell below zero, and everything froze. I melted a tin of water for washing by the fire, but it was hard frozen before I could use it. My hair, which was thoroughly wet with the thawed snow of yesterday, is hard frozen in plaits. The milk and treacle are like rock, the eggs have to be kept on the coolest part of the stove to keep them fluid. Two calves in the shed were frozen to death. Half our floor is deep in snow, and it is so cold that we cannot open the door to shovel it out. . . . The snow may either melt or block us in. Our only anxiety is about the supplies. We have tea and coffee enough to last over tomorrow, the sugar is just done, and the flour is getting low.

It is really serious that we have "another mouth to feed." The newcomer is a ravenous creature, eating more than the three of us. It dismays me to see his hungry eyes gauging the supply at breakfast, and to see the loaf disappear. He told me this morning that he could eat the whole of what was on the table. He is mad after food, and I see that Mr. K. is starving himself to make it hold out. Mr. Buchan is very far from well, and dreads the prospect of "half rations." All this sounds laughable, but we shall not laugh if we have to look hunger in the face.

Now in the evenings the snow clouds, which have blotted out all things, are lifting, and the winter scene is wonderful. The mercury is 5 degrees below zero. Mr. Buchan can hardly get his breath; the dryness is intense. We spent the afternoon cooking the Thanksgiving dinner. I made a wonderful pudding, for which I had saved eggs and cream for days, and dried and stoned cherries supplied the place of currants. I made a bowl of custard for sauce, which the men said was "splendid"; also a rolled pudding, with molasses; and we had venison steak and potatoes, but for tea we were obliged to use the tea leaves of the morning again. I should think that few people in America have enjoyed their Thanksgiving dinner more. We had urged Mr. Nugent to join us, but he refused, almost savagely, which we regretted. My four-pound cake made yesterday is all gone! This wretched boy confesses that he was so hungry in the night that he got up and ate nearly half of it. He is trying to cajole me into making another.

November 29, 1873

Before the boy came I had mistaken some faded cayenne pepper for ginger, and had made a cake with it. Last evening I put half of [the cake] into the cupboard and left the door open. During the night we heard a commotion in the kitchen and much choking, coughing, and groaning, and at breakfast the boy was unable to swallow food with his usual ravenousness. After breakfast he came to me whimpering, and asking for something soothing for his throat, admitting that he had seen the "gingerbread" and "felt so starved" in the night that he got up to eat it.

The first day after he came while I was washing up the breakfast things he told me that he intended to do all the dirty work, so I left the knives and forks in the tub and asked him to wipe and lay them aside. Two hours afterwards I found them untouched.

Again the men went out hunting, and he said he would chop the wood for several days' use. After a few strokes, which were only successful in chipping off some shavings, he came in and strummed on the harmonium, leaving me without any wood with which to make the fire for supper. He talked about his skill with the lasso, but could not even catch one of our quietest horses. Worse than all, he does not know one cow from another. Two days ago he lost our milch cow in driving her in to be milked. . . .

I told him to fill up the four-gallon kettle, and in an hour afterwards found it red-hot on the stove. Nothing can be kept from him unless it is hidden in my room. He has eaten two pounds of dried cherries from the shelf, half of my second four-pound spice loaf before it was cold, licked up my custard sauce in the night, and privately devoured the pudding which was to be for supper.

He confesses it all, and says, "I suppose you think me a cure [pest]." Mr. K. says that the first thing he said to him this morning was, "Will Miss B. make us a nice pudding to-day?" This is all harmless, but the plagiarism and want of honor are disgusting, and quite out of keeping with his profession of being a theological student. . . .

November 30

This morning we came to the resolution that we must break up. Tea, coffee, and sugar are done, the venison is turning sour, and the men have only one month left for the hunting on which their winter living depends. I cannot leave the Territory till I get money, but I can go to Longmount for the mail. . . .

Yesterday I was alone all day, and after riding to the base of Long's Peak, made two roly-poly puddings for supper, having nothing else. The men, however, came back perfectly loaded with trout, and we had a feast. Epicures at home would have envied us. Mr. Kavan kept the frying pan with boiling butter on the stove, butter enough thoroughly to cover the trout, rolled them in coarse corn meal, plunged them into the butter, turned them once, and took them out, thoroughly done, fizzing, and lemon colored. For once young Lyman was satisfied, for the dish was replenished as often as it was emptied. They caught 40 lbs., and have packed them in ice until they can be sent to Denver for sale. The winter fishing is very rich. In the hardest frost, men who fish not for sport, but gain, take their axes and camping blankets, and go up to the hard-frozen waters which live in fifty places round the park, and choosing a likely spot, a little sheltered from the wind, hack a hole in the ice, and fastening a foot-link to a cotton-wood tree, bait the hook with maggots or bits of easily-gotten fresh meat. Often the trout are caught as fast as the hook can be baited, and looking through the ice hole in the track of a sunbeam, you see a mass of tails, silver fins, bright eyes, and crimson spots, a perfect shoal of fish, and truly beautiful the crimson-spotted creatures look, lying still and dead on the blue ice under the sunshine. Sometimes two men bring home 60 lbs. of trout as the result of one day's winter fishing. It is a cold and silent sport, however.

How a cook at home would despise our scanty appliances, with which we turn out luxuries. We have only a cooking-stove, which requires incessant feeding with wood, a kettle, a frying pan, a six-gallon brass pan, and a bottle for a rolling pin. The cold has been very severe, but I do not suffer from it even in my insufficient clothing. I take a piece of granite made very hot to bed, draw the blankets over my head and sleep eight hours, though the snow often covers me. One day of snow, mist and darkness was rather depressing, and yesterday a hurricane began about five in the morning, and the whole park was one swirl of drifting snow, like stinging wood smoke. My bed and room were white, and the frost was so intense that water brought in a kettle from the fire froze as I poured it into the basin. . . . Tomorrow, weather permitting, I set off for a ride of 100 miles, and my next letter will be my last from the Rocky Mountains.

All in a Day's Work

*I*t is now August. Orric is cutting his hay and is quite busy. He always eats cold dinner. But I left my daughter Helene home in the Fore noons to fix him something warm. On this occasion which I am going to speak of she came running to the school. . . . I was anxious to know what was the matter. She called to me to run quick. Mr Orric's team has ran away, and He is cut all to pieces. I told Tommy Smith to dismiss the school and come down to the house immediately. When I got home he was laying on the floor in the front room in a pool of blood. Tommy Smith was just coming. I told him to get me a lot of water, and I taken a large sheet which I used to give Mr Brittain wet sheet packs and put blankets on a lounge which was in the room, then diped the sheet in a tub of water. Tommy wrung it out lightly, placed it on the blankets. Then I cut what few cloths was left on him off but while Tommy was fixing the pack I was holding an Artery which was cut in the left arm above the elbow. I bandaged it tight—then put him in the pack, then put cold towel to his head, kept him in the pack with hot bottles of water to his feet. . . . In this time a lot of men and women came. One fellow said, Orric I would not let this woman put water on me that way. Orric told him he was in my Power. I told the fellow to go way, that I knew what I was doing. . . . The women said to me how could you take that mans clothes off. Oh I would be Ashamed if I were you. Yes, I said, you would let him die on account of a little false modesty. Well the doctor is here. He is going to give Orric Chloroform and dress his wounds and amputate a finger or two. There was not a man that would stay in the room to help the Dr, so I helped him. The next day was Saturday, and The Dr came and dressed the wounds. Orric thanked him. The Dr told him to thank me, that I saved his life. . . .

Dust Bowl Observations

"Now honey," the old woman from Oklahoma said to me, "you ever seen a dust storm?" "No Ma'am," I said, "I haven't." "Well now," she said with a slow shake of her head, "they was the worst. Sky-high walls of dust, darkening the noonday sun, pulling off the best soil, filling your eyes and clothes and closets with dust, driving you near crazy. You know the first thing my husband said when part of our farm blew off into Kansas? He said 'Martha Ann, we are going to have to pay taxes in two states now.' Yessir, that dust was so bad that once, when a drop of water fell on my brother, we had to throw two buckets of dust to revive him. And one time, I swear this is true, a traveling salesman stopped at our house for directions and asked my Ma, while looking at some clouds on the horizon, 'Think it'll rain?' 'Hope so,' my Ma said, 'not so much for my sake as my children's. I've seen rain before.' "

Culpepper's Pride

She died under an umbrella. . . .

It was a large umbrella of yellow and white, and as I recall it had an Italian's name stamped on it. "Musso," I think. It was a most ordinary umbrella, but it served its purpose. . . .

Do you see that little mound over there by the summer house? Well, that is a pile of shingles. It has been lying there for twenty years, and I suppose they are all rotten now. It does not matter any more.

You see, that was a proud family, and after all the old people died, Bessie was left with her bachelor son. Bessie and I were the same age, and the son was old enough to be your father. They lived pretty much to themselves and they were very poor. They were sensitive too, for they had always held their heads so high. The old house began to go to pieces and a bad leak developed in Bessie's bedroom. Because she was sick that winter, she was in her room a great deal. I remember going to see her and noticing that the rain had spotted the red silk on the tester of her big four-post bed. She laughed a little bit about it and said that all of the bedrooms were leaking, but that through great good luck they had found enough money to buy new shingles. The shingles had been ordered and would arrive any day. They had arranged that a carpenter come and put them on. She was very pleased about it, and we joked a little bit about hard times.

Well, the shingles arrived and were unloaded and piled up right there by the summer house, and the son, Culpepper—that was a family name on her mother's side—was very pleased that the leaky roof was to be renewed at last. The work was to begin the following day.

But the most unfortunate thing happened. One of the neighbors, really he was a man without any tact whatever, rode by on his horse, and began to tease Culpepper. "Well, it is high time you had a new roof," he said. "I understand that the water drips right through onto your piano in the parlor."

Now I told you that family held their heads high, and Culpepper was furious. He said, "There is no hurry about repairing the roof. I shall do it when I get damn good and ready, but not before." And with that he turned to the carpenter and said, "Don't come tomorrow. I've decided to delay the work until the comments of our impertinent neighbors have stopped."

Naturally, his neighbor was furious and never spoke to Culpepper again.

Well, time passed and the shingles lay there and the roof was not repaired. Culpepper would have none of it. I did not dare speak to him about it, but I felt sorry for Bessie up there in the damp. I don't know how she felt about it, but I think she agreed with him on general principles. It was not the business of anybody to comment on their domestic arrangements.

My, how it rained that summer! It was the wettest August I ever remember, and every time it rained I kept thinking about poor Bessie. Surely, I thought, Culpepper would have the roof fixed by Thanksgiving. But, All Saints' Day and Thanksgiving passed and the shingles lay there. We laughed a little bit about it at home and joked about it in a friendly fashion; but none of us said anything to Bessie or Culpepper. Christmas came, and I dropped over to take a fruit cake. Culpepper met me upstairs in the hall and said that his mother was really sick. And so I went up. There she was lying in that great bed with big stains on the pillow where the rain had dropped through that morning. The red stain on the top of the bed was soaking wet. I just didn't know what to do. I finally suggested that we get some Negroes in and move the bed, but Culpepper said that one part of the room leaked just as much as any other part. Bessie did not say anything. So I left the cake and went downstairs and talked to Culpepper. We sat in the parlor and I let him have a piece of my mind.

"Culpepper," I said, "it is none of my business whether you have the roof fixed or not, but Bessie is my girlhood friend, and I love her like a sister, and she is sick. I think you should get a trained nurse right away."

He agreed with me and he said that he would attend to it at once.

I went over that night and stayed with Bessie until the trained nurse could get there. None of us said anything about the roof, but it stopped raining about that time. The nurse came in the next morning, and I declare I never was so glad to see anybody in my life. It was really the most fortunate thing that ever happened, because as it turned out she was one of the Magee girls. They were another plantation family nearby. . . . I never saw such spirit in my life. She talked right sassy to Culpepper. "This is perfectly ridiculous—you and your pride. My father is just as proud and just as silly as you are, but by the good Lord, sir, if I am to take care of Miss Bessie, I am to have full charge." Now, nobody had ever talked to Culpepper like that in his life, and he just stood there looking at her. I knew those Magee girls and I knew she would get her way, no matter what he did. To tell the truth, I think he was beginning to feel pretty uncomfortable just through that stiff neck of his.

Along about four that afternoon it began to rain again, and Sally Magee was furious when the drops began to fall on poor Bessie's bed. It was just at that time that a fruit peddler drove up to the house. And do you know what that girl did? She went right downstairs without a word to Culpepper or anybody and she took Musso's big white and yellow umbrella right off his wagon and carried it inside along with a small bunch of grapes she had bought. She just left Culpepper to settle with the Italian. I don't know what arrangements he made, but he probably paid a good price for that parasol. Well, anyway, Sally Magee carried it upstairs and fastened it up in the top of the four-post bed, changed all the linens, and made her patient as comfortable as she could.

It was not much use though, because pneumonia had set in; and a few days later the umbrella was not needed any more.

Well, there is one comfort; Bessie died dry.

Billie Holiday Gets Her Start

Billie Holiday was one of America's greatest singers. She had soul and an emotional power that gave jazz a distinctive voice. Her death in 1959 from a long and tenacious drug addiction closed out her turbulent, even tragic life, but she left behind a body of work that will help define the age in which she lived. Though Holiday did not actually write her memoirs (they were ghostwritten for her), the memories,

*as well as the unique rhythm of her language and humor, seem, to those who knew
her, unmistakably Holiday. The excerpt below sounds the first notes of* Lady Sings the
Blues:

Mom and Pop were just a couple of kids when they got married. He was
eighteen, she was sixteen, and I was three.

Mom was working as a maid with a white family. When they found out she
was going to have a baby they just threw her out. Pop's family just about had a
fit, too, when they heard about it. They were real society folks and they never
heard of things like that going on in their part of East Baltimore.

But both kids were poor. And when you're poor, you grow up fast.

It's a wonder my mother didn't end up in the workhouse and me as a
foundling. But Sadie Fagan loved me from the time I was just a swift kick in
the ribs while she scrubbed floors. She went to the hospital and made a deal
with the head woman there. She told them she'd scrub floors and wait on the
other bitches laying up there to have their kids so she could pay her way and
mine. And she did. Mom was thirteen that Wednesday, April 7, 1915, in Baltimore when I was born.

By the time she worked her way out of hock in the hospital and took me
home to her folks, I was so big and smart I could sit up in a carriage. Pop was
doing what all the boys did then—peddling papers, running errands, going to
school. One day he came along by my carriage, picked me up, and started
playing with me. His mother saw him and came hollering. She dragged at him
and said, "Clarence, stop playing with that baby. Everybody is going to think
it's yours."

"But, Mother, it *is* mine," he'd tell her. When he talked back to his mother
like this she would really have a fit. He was still only fifteen and in short pants.
He wanted to be a musician and used to take lessons on the trumpet. It was
almost three years before he got long pants for the wedding.

After they were married awhile we moved into a little old house on Dur-
ham Street in Baltimore. Mom had worked as a maid up North in New York
and Philly. She'd seen all the rich people with their gas and electric lights and
she decided she had to have them too. So she saved her wages for the day. And
when we moved in we were the first family in the neighborhood to have gas and
electricity.

It made the neighbors mad, Mom putting in the gas. They said putting
pipes in the ground would bring the rats out. It was true. Baltimore is famous
for rats.

Pop always wanted to blow the trumpet but he never got the chance. Before he got one to blow, the Army grabbed him and shipped him overseas. It was just his luck to be one of the ones to get it from poison gas over there. It ruined his lungs. I suppose if he'd played piano he'd probably have got shot in the hand.

Getting gassed was the end of his hopes for the trumpet but the beginning of a successful career on the guitar. He started to learn it when he was in Paris. And it was a good thing he did. Because it kept him from going to pieces when he got back to Baltimore. He just *had* to be a musician. He worked like hell when he got back and eventually got a job with McKinney's Cotton Pickers. But when he went on the road with that band it was the beginning of the end of our life as a family. Baltimore got to be just another one-night stand.

While Pop was overseas in the war, Mom had worked in a factory making Army overalls and uniforms. When Pop hit the road, the war jobs were finished and Mom figured she could do better going off up North as a maid. She had to leave me with my grandparents, who lived in a poor little old house with my cousin Ida, her two small children, Henry and Elsie, and my great-grand-mother.

All of us were crowded in that little house like fishes. I had to sleep in the same bed with Henry and Elsie, and Henry used to wet it every night. It made me mad and sometimes I'd get up and sit in a chair until morning. Then my cousin Ida would come in in the morning, see the bed, accuse me of wetting it, and start beating me. When she was upset she'd beat me something awful. Not with a strap, not with a spank on the ass, but with her fists or a whip.

She just didn't understand me. Other kids, when they did something wrong, would lie their way out of it. But if I did anything wrong I'd come right out and admit it. And she'd have a fit, call me a sinner and tell me I'd never amount to anything. She never got through telling my mother I was going to bring home a baby and disgrace the damn family like she did. One time she heard me say "Damn it" and she thought this was so sinful she tossed a pot of hot starch at me. She missed, though, because I ducked.

She was always finding fault with whatever I did, but she never did pick up on Henry. He was her son and he could do no wrong. When I got tired of getting beaten because he wet the bed I got Elsie one night and convinced her we should both sleep on the floor. She was scared. It was cold and she thought we might freeze.

"All right," I told her, "so we might freeze. But if we ain't frozen to death in the morning, the bed'll be wet and we won't be in it."

It was and we weren't, so this time Cousin Ida beat me for being smart with her. "Henry's weak," she said.

You couldn't tell her nothing about Henry, why that boy used to give us girls a terrible time. He even tried to do what we called "that thing" to us while we were sleeping. Sometimes we would be so tired from fighting this little angel off all night, we wouldn't wake up in time for school. I used to try to plead with him because I knew it wouldn't do any good to talk to Cousin Ida.

"Henry," I'd say to him, "it ain't so bad with me. I'm only your cousin. But Elsie's your sister, and besides, she's sick."

Henry grew up to be a prize fighter and then a minister. But when he was little I had hell with that boy.

Cowgirls Carry On

At the time that Teresa Jordan was writing her colorful book on western American women called Cowgirls, *she interviewed Biddy Bonham, a successful rancher, who was, at the time, fifty-two years old. Bonham had grown up near Colorado Springs and her father and mother raised some of the best horses in the state. Her talk with Jordan included a description of her life after the death of her father; it is a striking portrait of a mother and daughter, and the choices that they made:*

Before Daddy got killed, we really didn't think about Mother very much. You know, daughters are very father-oriented. Daddy was very much a Southerner, and he had his idea of the role a woman should play—or rather, his wife should play. Mother was always supposed to be a lady. She was allowed to ride and she was allowed to buy horses, but she didn't work outside doing the everyday nitty-gritty.

I think I always respected Mother's horse judgment. I remember when she bought Beulah. Beulah was the mother of Gold Heels, which Daddy kept for stud. Gold Heels was the first champion Quarter Horse at the Denver Stock Show, so I think that gave us respect for Mother. But since she didn't work outside, she sort of got left out of our memories. She was definitely the underdog, if you stop and think about it.

[My older sister] Mary and I went with Daddy right from the start. Why he was so liberal as to let us ride, I don't know. There were definitely some things ladies didn't see. If we were moving cattle and a bull mounted a cow, Daddy made sure that we turned our heads. He always checked to make sure we were looking the other way. I still turn my head. It's funny the things you don't outgrow.

Daddy was such a hero to me. He was the greatest, outside of Paul Bunyan. Now, he told great Paul Bunyan stories. When we were little and we had been riding a long way and we'd see a pile of rocks, he'd tell a story about how Paul Bunyan dropped those rocks there. I thought Daddy was the closest to Paul Bunyan you could get.

When I was about sixteen, Mary and I decided we wanted to go into the cattle business. We each bought fifty heifers. Daddy financed us. We went through the whole process of drawing up the note and everything. Then we had to calve out those heifers. And that was shortly before Daddy died.

We had just moved to Colorado. We sold the place near Steamboat and bought a ranch near West Plains, northwest of Sterling. The new place didn't run the amount of cattle it was supposed to, and it was short-watered. We had to move cattle every day. The day Daddy died, he and I were putting the cattle out. There were two calves Daddy wanted to doctor.

The day before, the vet had been out to vaccinate our horses for sleeping sickness and he gave them bad vaccine. He didn't bring it out on ice. All our horses were sick except for two old, retired horses that weren't worth vaccinating. So that day, Daddy and I were riding these two old horses.

I was riding along, goofing off, and not paying attention. I was practicing heeling [roping a calf by its heels] and I heeled this calf and turned it loose. Daddy said, "Hey, that's the calf we're supposed to doctor!" So Daddy went after it to rope it. He caught the calf, but just then his horse hit a hole and fell, and that was it. Daddy hit his head when the horse fell down. It wasn't the horse's fault. He was old and retired, but he was the only horse we could ride that day.

I went to Daddy and I thought he was dead because he was so still. I turned the calf loose. We were about five miles from home and I rode home on the run. I came onto the hired man—he'd been moving cattle someplace else. I'll never forget that. I didn't have on a brassiere because I didn't have enough that I needed one. In some way, my shirt had come unbuttoned when I was running that horse. I rode up to the hired man and he kept looking at me so funny. I looked down and my whole front was open. I don't know why that sticks out in my mind. I still can't face that man. He went back to Daddy and I went on and told Mother.

I felt so guilty about Daddy's death, because I didn't see the calf. I had heeled it and turned it loose, and that meant that Daddy had to rope it again. I think I still probably feel bad, but it was terrible for a while. I'm sure that's one of the reasons I hate that vet so, because I don't want to have to take all the blame.

I was sixteen and I was very dramatic. I come from a dramatic family. My sister's horribly dramatic. I think my mother is a little bit too. I know the next time we had to rope I just went to pieces. Jack, our foreman, roped a calf to doctor it and I just fell apart. Of course everybody jumped all over me, and I couldn't figure out why. They thought I was mad because Jack roped the calf. But it all came back. And I couldn't rope for a long time after that. I still can't rope, not like I could before.

Mom and Mary babied me like mad because I started having these horrible sideaches right after the funeral. They didn't think it was appendicitis; the doctor kept saying it was in my mind. But within a month it got so bad that they finally operated, and they caught it just before it ruptured.

Now, that's the reason I got the mare, Margie. I was in the hospital for quite a while. I don't remember that I thought I was that bad, but they thought I was going to die. We had these three full sisters and Mother and Mary divided the horses. They gave me the best mare.

There was never any doubt that we would keep the ranch. That was almost automatic when we discussed it. We affirmed with each other how we felt. That's what Daddy would have expected us to do.

But it was hard. We had just bought the place and nobody knew the boundary lines except Daddy. And because Mother was so lost and we were new in the country, people weren't all that honest. Daddy had leased quite a bit of land and all the leases got snapped up immediately. The people took them back. So we had to buy all the land we ran on. We couldn't get enough land for all our cattle, so we had to sell down our herd.

Mother had to learn everything. But she said—probably even before the funeral—she said, "They're not going to run us off." No, she never was accepted into that neighborhood, and she never worked with many of the neighbors. They were just like vultures. They tried to run her off.

But we were *all* so mean to her. You look back, and even her daughters were mean to her.

Even as soon as they pronounced Dad dead, Mary and I looked at each other and said, "Jack's not going to be on this place." Jack had been our foreman in Steamboat. He was a very strong-willed man. Daddy could control him, but Mary and I didn't want him around because we'd worked with him before. We knew him well enough to know what he'd do to Mother and us.

But the first thing Mother did when we went back to Steamboat for the funeral was ask Jack to come work for us. He treated her like a dog because he thought he knew so much more than she did. And we were mean to her because we resented her getting him when we thought we were qualified to teach her how to run the ranch. It was hard on Mother, I know. And I don't even know all that went on 'cause I went to school. I missed a lot and I'll *never* know what all went on. . . .

Right from the moment Daddy died, Mother never went through that hand-wringing "Oh, what am I going to do?" stuff. You look back on it, and it's surprising. But Mother is bright, and she's awfully well read. She's interested in so many things. When I was younger and Daddy was alive, we didn't realize that she had this storage bin up here [in her head] and was always collecting more information. And she retains it. She can call up anything. And I think that's where her confidence came from. I think that deep down she knew she could handle anything. And she knew that from the beginning.

I think she also knew more about the ranch than anybody realized. Now, from things she says, I know that Daddy used to talk to her about the ranch, late at night. Because she has—well, it's kind of a photographic memory. So he would discuss things with her because he respected her memory and knew she would be able to recall it if he needed it. But Mary and I didn't know anything about this.

I don't really know when I realized that Mother was probably a lot smarter than I'd ever be. Maybe I realized it when Mary left, because it was hard to pay her off. I used to go in to see the banker with Mother, to borrow money. And Mother has this great way when she's doing business. She will put on the most stupid face and act dumb. She'd just let me do the talking and she'd sit there and bat her eyes like a bullfrog. But somewhere in there I realized that she was the power behind what I thought *I* was doing. She knew everything that was going on. When the final word came, she would mumble something in a stupid way, to make sure everything was right. But until you got out of there, you didn't realize what an important role she played.

There was an oil boom in that country. We didn't strike oil but we had an awful lot of dry holes on us, and a lot of leases. And Mother always got the best leases in the country. And that's probably when I really realized about that stupid bullfrog look, when I realized that it was an act. Mother knew exactly what she was doing, and she always had.

Really, I probably didn't get married 'til I was older because I always thought Mother had to have somebody to care for her. I realize now that she was always perfectly capable of taking care of herself, but I'm glad it worked out that way. I wouldn't have married Wayne if I hadn't waited.

Some Things My Ma Used to Say
(at one time or another . . .)

Now don't go trying to teach your grandmother to suck eggs;
That there knife wouldn't cut hot butter in June;
It sure beats a hen a-scratchin';
You ain't gonna get blood out of a turnip;
Now don't be kicking till you get spurred;
I guess that they'll be living at the top of the pot for a while,
*   now;*
Everything's lovely and the goose is hanging high;
She's as playful as a pup;
Yessir, she certainly lost her feathers when I told her that;
That gal rules the roost but she ain't got sense enough to get out
*   of the rain;*
Baby, you may as well eat sugar with a knitting needle;
She ain't got neither chick nor child;
That poor gal's been ridden hard and put up wet;
He's too lazy to scare the flies out of his mouth and too mean to
*   die;*
That boy sure thinks he's some punkins;
That man was lower than a snake in a wagon rut;
The Reverend's hat is just gettin' too small;
You know what the old woman said when she kissed the cow?
*   Everyone follows their own notion.*

$\mathcal{M}$y $\mathcal{M}$other, $\mathcal{M}$yself

Sara Lawrence Lightfoot is an accomplished sociologist; an admired author and educator; winner of the prestigious MacArthur Prize Award (1984); and daughter of Dr. Margaret Morgan Lawrence, a pioneer in child psychiatry. Lightfoot's stirring memoir of her mother (Balm in Gilead) *offers us a vivid portrait of the mind and memory of her mother, her family, and her African American heritage. In the excerpt below, however, we glimpse Lightfoot herself, vividly revealed by the sensitive questions she asks about the intersection between her mother's life and her own:*

By the time I was in my mid-thirties, with two children of my own, the identification with my mother was complete. Now I became a baker of "Maggie Bread," the hearty whole wheat variety, with my own embellishment of raisins. Now I wore colorful shawls like my mother always did, draped for warmth and drama. Now I plaited my daughter's brown braids and could feel the sensations of my mother's soothing hands on my head as I laid mine on my daughter's. Now I tried to put the pieces of my own too-busy life together, racing home to place bright napkins and candles on the dinner table, to create the appearance that I had been there all day. Now I heard my children's harsh complaints or watched their silent resignation when I flew off to distant places to deliver speeches, attend meetings—to do my version of the teaching/healing legacy. Now I could feel so keenly the mothering I was replaying, while being aware that the father in me had not disappeared.

This slow discovery of identification with my mother became intriguing to me. I recognized the ways I incorporated her style and her values, sometimes unknowingly, sometimes on purpose. I began to think of writing her story. If I could learn about her origins, her childhood, her dreams, her fears, I might have greater insight into my own life. If I could move beyond family myths—so static and idealized—to trace the actual events of my mother's life, I might uncover the historical patterns that give shape to my own.

My interest in telling my mother's story, however, was charged by more than my emerging identification with her. I wanted to explore beyond the myth of Margaret Lawrence. All families have elaborate tales that stand as models of courage, wisdom, strength, or loyalty for their members. The tales are told and retold, in long embroidered versions or in family shorthand. Everyone is comforted by their familiarity, the promised punch line, but no one would claim that these tales are the whole story. Bigger than life, they have turned into legends, morality plays. For as long as I can remember, my mother had been an idealized figure in our community, put on a pedestal, spoken of with awe and envy. Parents of my friends, neighbors, teachers, shopkeepers in town, would speak about my mother's serenity and quiet intelligence, about the way her very presence seemed to ease their pain. Sometimes their veneration made me wonder.

I remember the day my mother and I went to the Corsette Shop on Main Street to buy my first brassiere. I was twelve and "ample," as my father would say diplomatically. I had been walking around self-consciously for months, enduring my bobbing breasts as a horrible humiliation, and had begged my mother to let me get a bra. She had quietly, but stubbornly, resisted. My mother had never worn a bra, had refused to use the one thrust upon her at age fourteen, and seemed to regard them as nothing but sham and artifice. After weeks of my lobbying, she reluctantly gave in. I think she wanted me to avoid the abuse of my peers, several of whom had sported bras since the fourth grade. The two of us made a special trip to town to search for the most natural, least pointed kind. The Corsette Shop ladies greeted my mother with fanfare, oozing delight out of every pore. "Dr. Lawrence, we are so *thrilled* to see you!" The chatter continued while the ladies passed selections through the green curtains of the dressing room and I fumbled with snaps and straps and "cups." Occasionally one of them would come in unannounced to inspect the fit. During one of those unwelcome intrusions (my mother had gone out briefly to put a nickel in the parking meter), I remember waiting for the inevitable refrain— "Your mother is the loveliest woman I've ever met . . . she's as good as gold." I could be anywhere, even here in this underwear shop, under these embarrassing conditions, and I'd be treated to this familiar litany.

The worshipful praise always seemed genuine, but even as a child I recognized that it came at some cost. People did not always like the image that they had created of Margaret Lawrence. It made them feel inadequate or graceless in contrast. For some, the image of her goodness led to resentment. "How does your mother do it all?" asked the mother of one of my fellow Girl Scouts. "And she always looks so good." Each word of praise bore an edge of cynicism, and I could hear both, having learned early to catch these double-edged inflections.

The world's image of my mother never squared with mine. Yes, I knew she was different, even special, an achiever. I knew of no other mother who seemed to put so many pieces together, whose work seemed to require so much passion, who managed all her competing commitments. But rather than the serenity the world perceived, I saw my mother on the move, beads of sweat above her upper lip, her fingernails filled with paint and clay, brow furrowed, muscles sore, and eyelids drooping by days' end. When I bothered to look, I saw a grown-up life that was hard and demanding, that left no time for frivolity. What others saw as peacefulness, I saw as my mother's chief survival strategy—complete concentration. I am sure that the dissonance between the idealized perceptions of Margaret and a daughter's nonheroic view must also have fueled my interest in exploring her life. I mistrusted the legend that seemed, in its grandeur, to diminish me.

Years later, having written other books that tried to get beyond surface and stereotypes, I felt the impulse to look at my mother's life more deeply, to tell of her grace against odds, of the pain that accompanied achievement, the loss of laughter that came with single-minded pursuits. Not only would the story focus on her triumphs, it would also show how her life was filled with very ordinary twists and turns, with moments of traumatic defeat . . . and slow, purposeful recovery. I wanted to explore the family silences, the breaks in family stories that emerge because people have simply forgotten, because memories have faded with time, because images have had to be repressed in order to move on with life, because people have chosen to hide a piece of the truth for their own peace of mind. In tracing my mother's development, I wanted to undo the caricatures that never wholly fit my view of her.

E D U C A T I O N

$\mathcal{K}$nowledge is power. The taming of the mind through education, moral training, and disciplined reflection is an essential
part of the journey toward the fullest realization of the self. Political acuity and cultural leadership are powerful by-products of
the books we read, the teachers who teach us. So it is, that ever
since Adam and Eve stumbled into the hard glare outside Eden's
gate, women have had to wrestle men for the right to learn. And
America is no exception; if the country's foundations were laid
on a firm faith in intellectual freedom, American women were
among the first to recognize the daunting gap between theory
and practice.

In the early months of the American republic, no one saw
more clearly than Abigail Adams that American women's right to
a full education was at risk. She knew that the tyranny most
women feared was not from governments or religious zealots but
from within their own homes, coiled around their hearths like a
serpent—the tyranny of husbands and fathers. It was not that
she believed men and women were enemies or essential adversaries, but rather she knew that most men took their wives and
daughters for granted and failed to consider what these women

might themselves want or need in any given situation. As John Adams and his colleagues debated the future laws of the new government (with no women present), she wrote to him not as a wife but as a wary constituent without representation: "Do not put such unlimited power into the hands of the husbands. Remember, all men would be tyrants if they could. . . . That your sex are naturally tyrannical is a truth so thoroughly established as to admit of no dispute. . . ." She wanted the new American laws to recognize the rights of women as individuals capable of pursuing their own happiness, and she knew that education was essential to that process. She also realized that after the great debates that framed the Constitution and the Bill of Rights had concluded, the opportunity to afford women an equal chance had been lost. She recognized that what the women were going to have to win would not come from the beneficence of the men but from a determined political struggle.

We have seen the theme over and over—in the workplace, in politics, even in the dynamics of the American family—men think they know what's best for women. The classroom was one of the best and easiest places to establish that premise, but all too often the home was little better. Enlightened mothers and fathers were rare, and too often the hardest lessons for young women were self-taught. A common theme throughout the following stories is the making of one's own way despite the barriers of prejudice or neglect.

Throughout the nineteenth century, the debate raged over women's right to learn as men did. Some women framed their arguments within the ideal of the divine spark—that access to education would lead to a new and unexpected crop of enlightened and valuable citizens. These women were heartily applauded at the women's conventions but generally ignored in the bustle and politics of daily life. Others, looking to offer what they thought would be a moderate, sensible rationale, suggested (half in jest) that as mothers were the first and best educators of young men, shouldn't they be afforded a suitable education to do their job effectively? Interestingly, such arguments won the attention of many distinguished men who could not dispute the role their own mothers had had on their lives. In the end, however, the most effective women were the most outspoken, the least compromising. Theirs was a call for equal rights, the basic and unambiguous assertion that men and women should be treated the same and that the right to pursue her own passions and interests should not be denied any woman. Women like Abigail Adams, Elizabeth Stanton, Ernestine Rose, and others were considered dangerous, not only by many men in positions of power but also by many women who feared the audacity of their resolve.

Coming of age in eighteenth- and nineteenth-century America was much tougher on girls than boys. Young women swam into the bewildering and formidable currents of expectation and restraint, and in contrast to their brothers, their ambitions were not endorsed, their desires not accommodated. So it was that neglect and indifference became powerful catalysts in maturing proud young girls who recognized that if they did not take their own lives seriously, no one else would either. Some of the most able leaders in the nineteenth-century women's-rights movement learned that weak mothers (uncertain or timid allies) or overbearing fathers (strong-minded or opinionated adversaries) had to be challenged if a sense of self were to be protected.

Policy platforms and public exhortations aside, however, the truth is no different in America than anywhere else in the world: The best place for daughters and sons to gain a sense of purpose and identity is a home where the careful attention of a good father and the steady nurturing of a loving mother are offered without condition, day after day.

What Happens When Women Read
Too Many Books (1645)

The following was written on April 13, 1645, by John Winthrop the elder as a warning to those husbands who mistakenly thought their wives' mental development was as important as their own:

Mr. Hopkins, the governor of Hartford upon Connecticut, came to Boston, and brought his wife with him, (a godly young woman, and of special parts,) who was fallen into a sad infirmity, the loss of her understanding and reason, which had been growing upon her diverse years, by occasion of her giving herself wholly to reading and writing, and had written many books. Her husband, being very loving and tender of her, was loath to grieve her; but he saw his error, when it was too late. For if she had attended her household affairs, and such things as belong to women, and not gone out of her way and calling to meddle in such things as are proper for men, whose minds are stronger, etc., she had kept her wits, and might have improved them usefully and honorably in the place God had set her. He brought her to Boston, and left her with her brother, one Mr. Yale, a merchant, to try what means might be had here for her. But no help could be had.

Abigail Adams: "We should have
learned women." (1776)

You remark upon the deficiency of Education in your Countrymen. It never I believe was in a worse state, at least for many years. The Colledge is not in the state one could wish, the Schollars complain that their professer in Philosophy is taken of by publick Buisness to their great detriment. In this Town I never saw so great a neglect of Education. The poorer sort of children are wholly neglected, and left to range the Streets without Schools, without Buisness, given up to all Evil. The Town is not as formerly divided into Wards. There is either too much Buisness left upon the hands of a few, or too little care to do it. We daily see the Necessity of a regular Goverment.—You speak of our Worthy Brother. I often lament it that a Man so peculiarly formed for the Education of youth, and so well qualified as he is in many Branches of Litrature, excelling in Philosophy and the Mathematicks, should not be imployd in some publick Station. I know not the person who would make half so good a Successor to Dr. Winthrope. He has a peculiar easy manner of communicating his Ideas to Youth, and the Goodness of his Heart, and the purity of his morrals without an affected austerity must have a happy Effect upon the minds of Pupils.

If you complain of neglect of Education in sons, What shall I say with regard to daughters, who every day experience the want of it. With regard to the Education of my own children, I find myself soon out of my debth, and destitute and deficient in every part of Education.

I most sincerely wish that some more liberal plan might be laid and executed for the Benefit of the rising Generation, and that our new constitution may be distinguished for Learning and Virtue. If we mean to have Heroes, Statesmen and Philosophers, we should have learned women. The world perhaps would laugh at me, and accuse me of vanity, But you I know have a mind too enlarged and liberal to disregard the Sentiment. If much depends as is allowed upon the early Education of youth and the first principals which are instilld take the deepest root, great benefit must arise from litirary accomplishments in women.

"*The end and aim of a woman's being.*" (1827)

Freedom's Journal *was the first African American newspaper in America and offered black men and women a needed forum for their views and opinions. On August 10, 1827, the newspaper carried a letter, anonymously signed "Matilda"; it was one of the early calls for a woman's right to an education:*
Messrs. Editors:

Will you allow a female to offer a few remarks upon a subject that you must allow to be all-important? I don't know that in any of your papers you have said sufficient upon the education of females. I hope you are not to be classed with those who think that our mathematical knowledge should be limited to "fathoming the dish-kettle," and that we have acquired enough of history if we know that our grandfather's father lived and died. It is true the time has been when to darn a stocking and cook a pudding well was considered the end and aim of a woman's being. But those were days when ignorance blinded men's eyes. The diffusion of knowledge has destroyed those degrading opinions, and men of the present age allow that we have minds that are capable and deserving of culture.

There are difficulties, and great difficulties, in the way of our advancement; but that should only stir us to greater efforts. We possess not the advantages with those of our sex whose skins are not colored like our own, but we can improve what little we have and make our one talent produce twofold. The influence that we have over the male sex demands that our minds should be instructed and improved with the principles of education and religion, in order that this influence should be properly directed. Ignorant ourselves, how can we be expected to form the minds of our youth and conduct them in the paths of knowledge? How can we "teach the young *idea* how to shoot" if we have none ourselves? There is a great responsibility resting somewhere, and it is time for us to be up and doing.

I would address myself to all mothers, and say to them that while it is necessary to possess a knowledge of cookery and the various mysteries of pudding making, something more is requisite. It is their bounden duty to store their daughters' minds with useful learning. They should be made to devote their leisure time to reading books, whence they would derive valuable information which could never be taken from them.

I will not longer trespass on your time and patience. I merely throw out these hints in order that some more able pen will take up the subject.

MATILDA

"Ah, you should have been a boy!"

From Elizabeth Cady Stanton's memoir, we hear the brave, sad words of a daughter determined to win her father's loyalty:

When I was eleven years old, two events occurred which changed considerably the current of my life. My only brother, who had just graduated from Union College, came home to die. A young man of great talent and promise, he was the pride of my father's heart. We early felt that this son filled a larger place in our father's affections and future plans than the five daughters together. Well do I remember how tenderly he watched my brother in his last illness, the sighs and tears he gave vent to as he slowly walked up and down the hall, and, when the last sad moment came, and we were all assembled to say farewell in the silent chamber of death, how broken were his utterances as he knelt and prayed for comfort and support. I still recall, too, going into the large darkened parlor to see my brother, and finding the casket, mirrors, and pictures all draped in white, and my father seated by his side, pale and immovable. As he took no notice of me, after standing a long while, I climbed upon his knee, when he mechanically put his arm about me and, with my head resting against his beating heart, we both sat in silence, he thinking of the wreck of all his hopes in the loss of a dear son, and I wondering what could be said or done to fill the void in his breast. At length he heaved a deep sigh and said: "Oh, my daughter, I wish you were a boy!" Throwing my arms about his neck, I replied: "I will try to be all my brother was."

Then and there I resolved that I would not give so much time as heretofore to play, but would study and strive to be at the head of all my classes and thus delight my father's heart. All that day and far into the night I pondered the problem of boyhood. I thought that the chief thing to be done in order to equal boys was to be learned and courageous. So I decided to study Greek and learn to manage a horse. Having formed this conclusion I fell asleep. My resolutions, unlike many such made at night, did not vanish with the coming light. I arose early and hastened to put them into execution. They were resolutions never to be forgotten—destined to mold my character anew. As soon as I was dressed I hastened to our good pastor, Rev. Simon Hosack, who was always early at work in his garden.

"Doctor," said I, "which do you like best, boys or girls?"

"Why, girls, to be sure; I would not give you for all the boys in Christendom."

"My father," I replied, "prefers boys; he wishes I was one, and I intend to be as near like one as possible. I am going to ride on horseback and study Greek. Will you give me a Greek lesson now, doctor? I want to begin at once."

"Yes, child," said he, throwing down his hoe, "come into my library and we will begin without delay."

He entered fully into the feeling of suffering and sorrow which took possession of me when I discovered that a girl weighed less in the scale of being than a boy, and he praised my determination to prove the contrary. The old grammar which he had studied in the University of Glasgow was soon in my hands, and the Greek article was learned before breakfast.

Then came the sad pageantry of death, the weeping of friends, the dark rooms, the ghostly stillness, the exhortation to the living to prepare for death, the solemn prayer, the mournful chant, the funeral cortège, the solemn, tolling bell, the burial. How I suffered during those sad days! What strange undefined fears of the unknown took possession of me! For months afterward, at the twilight hour, I went with my father to the new-made grave. Near it stood two tall poplar trees, against one of which I leaned, while my father threw himself on the grave, with outstretched arms, as if to embrace his child. At last the frosts and storms of November came and threw a chilling barrier between the living and the dead, and we went there no more.

During all this time I kept up my lessons at the parsonage and made rapid progress. I surprised even my teacher, who thought me capable of doing anything. I learned to drive, and to leap a fence and ditch on horseback. I taxed every power, hoping some day to hear my father say: "Well, a girl is as good as a boy, after all." But he never said it. When the doctor came over to spend the evening with us, I would whisper in his ear: "Tell my father how fast I get on," and he would tell him, and was lavish in his praises. But my father only paced the room, sighed, and showed that he wished I were a boy; and I, not knowing why he felt thus, would hide my tears of vexation on the doctor's shoulder.

Soon after this I began to study Latin, Greek, and mathematics with a class of boys in the Academy, many of whom were much older than I. For three years one boy kept his place at the head of the class, and I always stood next. Two prizes were offered in Greek. I strove for one and took the second. How well I remember my joy in receiving that prize. There was no sentiment of ambition, rivalry, or triumph over my companions, nor feeling of satisfaction in receiving this honor in the presence of those assembled on the day of the exhibition. One thought alone filled my mind. "Now," said I, "my father will be satisfied with me." So, as soon as we were dismissed, I ran down the hill, rushed breathless into his office, laid the new Greek Testament, which was my prize, on his table and exclaimed: "There, I got it!" He took up the book, asked me some questions about the class, the teachers, the spectators, and, evidently pleased, handed it back to me. Then, while I stood looking and waiting for him to say something which would show that he recognized the equality of the daughter with the son, he kissed me on the forehead and exclaimed, with a sigh, "Ah, you should have been a boy!"

My joy was turned to sadness. I ran to my good doctor. He chased my bitter tears away, and soothed me with unbounded praises and visions of future success. He was then confined to the house with his last illness. He asked me that day if I would like to have, when he was gone, the old lexicon, Testament, and grammar that we had so often thumbed together. "Yes, but I would rather have you stay," I replied, "for what can I do when you are gone?" "Oh," said he tenderly, "I shall not be gone; my spirit will still be with you, watching you in all life's struggles." Noble, generous friend! He had but little on earth to bequeath to anyone, but when the last scene in his life was ended, and his will was opened, sure enough there was a clause saying: "My Greek lexicon, Testament, and grammar, and four volumes of Scott's commentaries, I will to Elizabeth Cady." I never look at these books without a feeling of thankfulness that in childhood I was blessed with such a friend and teacher.

An Early Attempt at Coeducation in Hartford (1846)

That short bench of boys who have entered college, I wonder why they don't go there. Why need they be studying a year at home? It would be much more agreeable to us if they were away. Their room would be vastly better than their company. Mighty grand are they, because they happen to be in the fourth book of the *Eneid*. It will not be long ere we catch up with them, I trust. But the worst of it is, that every time we open our mouths to recite, they watch, and carp, and criticize. I only hesitated once to-day in a long lesson in Philosophy, and yesterday in the conjugation of a French verb, and heard them whisper to each other, "There! That's a'most a mistake." It was not, neither. I knew what to say, and should have said it as glib as ever, if they had not been looking straight at me with lynx eyes. Judges, indeed, they set themselves up to be, without any jury. I wish they had to wear wigs and sit upon a wool sack.

I studied all my lessons thoroughly last evening. I repeated them after I lay down in bed. While I was dreaming, Memory showed me that she had got the whole all right and clear. So now I will go bravely to school, and that bench of Scribes and Pharisees shan't have a chance to whisper again, "There! there! ain't that a'most a mistake?"

Overdressing of Unmarried Females (1837)

Our unmarried girls are entirely overdressed. They are allowed to wear such suits as are never worn by modest maidens in Europe, and are hardly seen in public upon the most matronly persons. The young miss, flauntingly costumed, is sure to attract a notice in the streets which should not be agreeable to, and is not safe for, virgin modesty. Overdress leads to false expectations. It has more to do than any other single cause with the fall of woman. Its effect in destroying female reserve, especially that of the young, as it thus takes away one of the best safeguards of virtue, makes it very pernicious. The excess of dress is certainly the cause of much of the vice of the day; and with the general adoption of a more modest attire, there would be less temptation to that part of the prevalent ill doing.

Mrs. Ernestine Rose:
"Sisters, you have a duty to perform . . ."

How did Siismund Potowski, born in Poland in 1810, become one of the great leaders of the American suffrage movement in the nineteenth century? Her wonderful story begins in a Polish court where at sixteen years old, Siismund is not only pleading for her rightful share of her mother's inheritance but against the marriage her father has arranged for her. She won on both counts, immediately moved to Paris and then to London, and took the name Ernestine Louise. A beautiful woman (in America she would be known as "the Queen of the Platform"), she was also very resourceful. She supported herself by selling her own invention: a room deodorizer. After her marriage to William Rose, she moved to America where she took up the cause of married women's right to property. After the Seneca Falls convention in 1848, she was drafted by the movement's leaders as a leading speaker. Charismatic, bold, and persuasive, she served the women's rights movement well. Susan B. Anthony always maintained that Rose was one of the true believers who sustained the long struggle for women's suffrage. The speech below, an exhortation on education, is typical of Rose's infectious, inspiring spirit:

. . . I am told that woman needs not an education as man, as her place is only the domestic sphere; *only* the domestic sphere! Oh, how utterly ignorant is society of the true import of that term! Go to your legislative halls, and your Congress; behold those you have sent there to govern you, and as you find them high or low, great or small, noble or base, you can trace it directly or indirectly to the domestic sphere.

The wisest in all ages have acknowledged that the most important period in human education is in childhood—that period when the plastic mind may be moulded into such exquisite beauty, that no unfavorable influences shall be able entirely to destroy it—or into such hideous deformity, that it shall cling to it like a thick rust eaten into a highly polished surface, which no after-scouring shall ever be able entirely to efface. This most important part of education is

left entirely in the hands of the mother. She prepares the soil for future culture; she lays the foundation upon which a superstructure shall be erected that
shall stand as firm as a rock, or shall pass away like the baseless fabric of a
vision, and leave not a wreck behind. But the mother can not give what she
does not possess; weakness can not impart strength.

Sisters, you have a duty to perform—and duty, like charity, begins at
home. In the name of you poor, vicious, outcast, down-trodden sister! in the
name of her who once was as innocent and as pure as you are! in the name of
her who has been made the victim of wrong, injustice, and oppression! in the
name of man! in the name of all, I ask you, I entreat you, if you have an hour to
spare, a dollar to give, or a word to utter—spare it, give it, and utter it, for the
elevation of woman! And when your minister asks you for money for missionary
purposes, tell him there are higher, and holier, and nobler missions to be
performed at home. When he asks for colleges to educate ministers, tell him
you must educate woman, that she may do away with the necessity of ministers, so that they may be able to go to some useful employment. If he asks you
to give to the churches (which means to himself) then ask him what he had
done for the salvation of woman. When he speaks to you of leading a virtuous
life, ask him whether he understands the causes that have prevented so many
of your sisters from being virtuous, and have driven them to degradation, sin,
and wretchedness. When he speaks to you of a hereafter, tell him to help to
educate woman, to enable her to live a life of intelligence, independence,
virtue, and happiness here, as the best preparatory step for any other life. And
if he has not told you from the pulpit of all these things; if he does not know
them; it is high time you inform him, and teach him his duty here in this life.

This subject is deep and vast enough for the wisest heads and purest hearts
of the race; it underlies our whole social system. Look to your criminal
records—look to your records of mortality, to your cemeteries, peopled by
mothers before the age of thirty or forty, and children under the age of five;
earnestly and impartially investigate the cause, and you can trace it directly or
indirectly to woman's inefficient education; her helpless, dependent position;
her inexperience; her want of confidence in her noble nature, in her own
principles and powers, and her blind reliance in man. We ask, then, for
woman, an education that shall cultivate her powers, develop, elevate, and
ennoble her being, physically, mentally, and morally; to enable her to take care
of herself, and she will be taken care of; to protect herself, and she will be
protected. But to give woman as full and extensive an education as man, we

must give her the same motives. No one gathers keys without a prospect of having doors to unlock. Man does not acquire knowledge without the hope to make it useful and productive; the highest motives only can call out the greatest exertion. There is a vast field of action open to man, and therefore he is prepared to enter it; widen the sphere of action for woman, throw open to her all the avenues of industry, emolument, usefulness, moral ambition, and true greatness, and you will give her the same noble motives, the same incentives for exertion, application, and perseverance that man possesses—and this can be done only by giving her her legal and political rights—pronounce her the equal of man in all the rights and advantages society can bestow, and she will be prepared to receive and use them, and not before.

Lillian Hellman:
"The stubborn, relentless, driving desire
to be alone . . ."

Lillian Hellman was an accomplished American playwright who wrote, among other things, The Little Foxes *(1939) and* Watch on the Rhine *(1941). In her memoir* An Unfinished Woman, *she takes us back to the tree where her life really began:*

There was a heavy fig tree on the lawn where the house turned the corner into the side street, and to the front and sides of the fig tree were three live oaks that hid the fig from my aunts' boardinghouse. I suppose I was eight or nine before I discovered the pleasures of the fig tree, and although I have lived in many houses since then, including a few I made for myself, I still think of it as my first and most beloved home.

I learned early, in our strange life of living half in New York and half in New Orleans, that I made my New Orleans teachers uncomfortable because I was too far ahead of my schoolmates, and my New York teachers irritable because I was too far behind. But in New Orleans, I found a solution: I skipped school at least once a week and often twice, knowing that nobody cared or would report my absence. On those days I would set out for school done up in polished strapped shoes and a prim hat against what was known as "the climate," carrying my books and a little basket filled with delicious stuff my Aunt Jenny and Carrie, the cook, had made for my school lunch. I would round the corner of the side street, move on toward St. Charles Avenue, and sit on a bench as if I were waiting for a streetcar until the boarders and the neighbors had gone to work or settled down for the post-breakfast rest that all Southern ladies thought necessary. Then I would run back to the fig tree, dodging in and out of bushes to make sure the house had no dangers for me. The fig tree was heavy, solid, comfortable, and I had, through time, convinced myself that it wanted me, missed me when I was absent, and approved all the rigging I had done for the happy days I spent in its arms: I had made a sling to hold the school books, a pulley rope for my lunch basket, a hole for the bottle of after-noon cream-soda pop, a fishing pole and a smelly little bag of elderly bait, a pillow embroidered with a picture of Henry Clay on a horse that I had stolen from Mrs. Stillman, one of my aunts' boarders, and a proper nail to hold my dress and shoes to keep them neat for the return to the house.

It was in that tree that I learned to read, filled with the passions that can only come to the bookish, grasping, very young, bewildered by almost all of what I read, sweating in the attempt to understand a world of adults I fled from in real life but desperately wanted to join in books. (I did not connect the grown men and women in literature with the grown men and women I saw around me. They were, to me, another species.)

It was in the fig tree that I learned that anything alive in water was of enormous excitement to me. True, the water was gutter water and the fishing could hardly be called that: sometimes the things that swam in New Orleans gutters were not pretty, but I didn't know what was pretty and I liked them all. After lunch—the men boarders returned for a large lunch and a siesta—the street would be safe again, with only the noise from Carrie and her helpers in the kitchen, and they could be counted on never to move past the back porch, or the chicken coop. Then I would come down from my tree to sit on the side street gutter with my pole and bait. Often I would catch a crab that had wandered in from the Gulf, more often I would catch my favorite, the crayfish, and sometimes I would, in that safe hour, have at least six of them for my basket. Then, about 2:30, when house and street would stir again, I would go back to my tree for another few hours of reading or dozing or having what I called the ill hour. It is too long ago for me to know why I thought the hour "ill," but certainly I did not mean sick. I think I meant an intimation of sad-ness, a first recognition that there was so much to understand that one might never find one's way and the first signs, perhaps, that for a nature like mine, the way would not be easy. I cannot be sure that I felt all that then, although I can be sure that it was in the fig tree, a few years later, that I was first puzzled by the conflict which would haunt me, harm me, and benefit me the rest of my life: simply, the stubborn, relentless, driving desire to be alone as it came into conflict with the desire not to be alone when I wanted not to be. I already guessed that other people wouldn't allow that, although, as an only child, I pretended for the rest of my life that they would and must allow it to me.

A Business Woman's Advice to Her Daughter (1907)

New York, *February 22, 192—*

My dear Sally:

So Beatrice is more thorough than you are. A comparison of your chatty essay with the imposing thesis she offered for the prize contest convinces you that you have no chance whatever. She worked for hours and hours in the library, turned over tons and tons of authorities, had lots of footnotes and a bibliography a mile long. Such a monumental work, you feel sure, must impress the members of the jury. And probably it will bore them too.

I do not say that this thoroughness may not be just the quality which will win in this particular case. But you may console yourself that there are many other unofficial contests in which quite different qualities will be decisive of victory. The world likes to look solemn and admire solid work, while it does its reading elsewhere. There is seldom a lecturer on English literature who does not refer to the splendors of Shakespeare. But do you often see your friends eagerly snatching up his plays at the beginning of a long winter evening? The *North American Review*, you know, is very highly respected. But I seem to have noticed that it is not the magazine which has the widest circulation.

It is not that I wish to undervalue thoroughness. But you know that every error is a truth abused. Every virtue has its corresponding vice, while its opposite has a compensating virtue. Thoroughness too often leads to diffuseness and lack of clearness. In the effort to present all the information available the writer loses proportion. It is the same in other affairs. The conscientious, thorough worker is so anxious to perform every last detail of his task that he is incapable of neglecting the unessential and seizing the essential opportunity.

Poor old Anna Davis was a sad example of too much thoroughness. I say old, though she was only thirty-five at the time I am thinking of. She lived a few doors from me in Medway, before I was married. I went to call on her after her husband ran away with that pretty silly Travers girl. There she sat in the midst of her spotless parlor, her workworn hands folded in her lap. It was terrible to see her cry—it made her uglier than ever. "I can't see why he did it," she repeated. "I can't see why he did it. I worked early and late to have everything nice and make him a home!" Well, I could see why he did it, but it was too late to tell her. I looked at the immaculate curtains, through the door at the shining silver and back again at her straggling hair, her ill-fitting dress, her bent shoulders and gaunt hands. Poor Mrs. Davis had thought keeping the house in order was making a home. A little less thoroughness, a little more intelligent neglect—and three lives would not have been torn and broken.

But another disadvantage for the thorough type of mind is the unwillingness to present anything but a completed work. Life is never complete; and it cannot wait. If you must find your way down cellar, you would rather have a candle tonight than a complete lighting system a year hence. Anyone running for the doctor will feel more grateful for a lift in a truck than for the offer of a limousine the next day.

You remember the evening you came from an automobile trip with a crowd of your friends. As it happened I had just returned from Baltimore an hour before. The whole famished horde of girls burst into my apartment just as I was eating a dropped egg and a cup of coffee from the kitchen table. In three hours I could have prepared a full dinner for you. But how glad you all were that instead I put on my apron, mixed griddle cakes and was serving them piping hot from the stove in ten minutes.

So anyone in a business crisis would rather have a suggestion on the moment than a complete report after the emergency is past. Because you have an abundance of ready ideas, you are inclined to distrust them. No one is so easily dissuaded from an idea as a person who has plenty of them. Another who has but one idea in a lifetime can afford to spend a lifetime in elaborating it. It receives all the loving care to which the only child is destined.

You are weak on thoroughness, but strong on makeshifts. Perhaps you will resent having your work described as a makeshift. You need not. A makeshift is better than an anachronism. Moreover, makeshifts are the special province of women, who frequently offer illuminating suggestions superior to any of their finished ideas. In that sense the hairpin, with which women are reputed to meet any emergency, is symbolic; it is the original makeshift. Not that I think the hairpin can be a key to unlock all doors. You must recognize when the makeshift is essential and when you had better go home for your toolbox.

Love from your pedagogical and preachy

Mother

Daddy, Teach Me Something

We know a great deal about Margaret Mead and Gregory Bateson, world-class anthropologists whose influence has been felt around the world. Their daughter Catherine Bateson's childhood memoir (With a Daughter's Eye) *captures the heady freedom of a most unorthodox kind of parenting. In the excerpt below, we catch a glimpse of the intense dynamic between Bateson and her father and, in the process, are offered profound insights about the way children want to learn and the way some of us can instruct them:*

I used to fly out there to visit him in his bachelor digs. Those were early years in the emergence of patterns of visiting for the children of separated and divorced parents. In San Francisco, puzzled by the question of what to do with a little girl, he took me to restaurants and amusement parks, amazing me by the disorder in which he lived, stacks of unanswered mail and a single frying pan in which everything was cooked, with layers of lingering tastes. We spent most of our time as a twosome, although there were several years when I went to a camp in Marin County where he could visit intermittently over a longer period, and he would come and travel with the camp on our pack trips. Occasionally we visited friends of his and people with whom he was working—Joe and Janie Wheelwright, Erik and Joan Erikson—and occasionally other children were found for me to play with, but my sense of those times was of being alone with him all day for several days, no one else involved, no structure or household rhythm to shape the time.

After a day or so, we would make plans and shopping lists on the back of an envelope and then pack up the trunk of his old Mercury convertible and head for the Sierras. We camped with very little equipment, a small tent in case of rain, a stove that worked with white gas, and sleeping bags on a tarp on the ground—two for him, zipped together.

The insoluble problem was my hair, which I wore in two long plaits with French braids at the sides, almost long enough to sit on. No one had taught me to care for it myself, and there was always my mother or someone else to braid it and Aunt Marie to comb it out after washing until I had it cut when I was

eleven. In those days we did not have the rinses we have today, and my hair
was fine and full of tangles. When I was with my mother, combing it took
twenty minutes every morning and was our most intimate time of the day. She
had a special stool I sat on at the foot of her bed, identifying each pull and
tangle with an animal of the appropriate size and ferocity: "Ouch, that was a
rhinoceros!" . . . "Sorry, darling." "Okay, Mummy, that one was just a wood-
chuck." My father tried and gave up, for the braids he constructed would
hardly last half a day. Instead, we simply left it braided for a week at a time
while we camped, letting it gradually escape into a halo of tangles around my
head, full of pine needles, and then for the day of reckoning he took me to a
beauty parlor to have it washed and combed.

We drove and I sang, songs I'd learned at school and songs I made up. I
came home from my first trip to California with a song of many verses:

> We'll not be together in the mountains,
> Nor in the forests you fear,
> We'll not be together in the desert,
> But we'll be together here.

I varied the places but always in the same framework, and my mother wept as I
dictated it to her to put in the notebook of my poetry, and I looked at her
amazed, saying, "But it says we *will* be together." Gregory would sometimes
sing hymn tunes, horribly off key, "Rock of Ages" or "Jerusalem." For the first
few years I used to carry a supply of comic books but he had a real revulsion for
the idea of my sitting there reading them, and eventually I put them aside.
Wind in our faces and escape to the hills where there was no need to embody a
social institution.

Sometimes we would camp in one place for several days, and then we
would always pursue natural history. We would find a side road with many
trails leading off from it, and make a lure with bacon or sardines, dragging it
along the trails for a mile or so, hoping to interest night visitors, and then we
would put out bait and sit up most of the night in the car with a thermos of hot
soup, ready to switch on the headlights or trigger the flash camera if there was
any pull on the string. We pored over a book of California mammals and
longed, more than anything, to see a spotted skunk, the kind that does a
courting dance standing on its front legs, but we never did. We went to an area
of salt marshes along the coast—I no longer know where—and waited all day

in a blind with a camera, photographing the water birds, and we sat for hours in Monterey watching the sea otters.

It was early in that period that Gregory became interested in the question of the nature of play and filmed the otters in the San Francisco zoo as they recovered and then lost their playfulness. The intellectual question was the question of the metamessage, the signal that identifies a particular segment of communicative behavior as "play" or "courtship" or "threat" even though the behaviors might be very much the same. We ranged up and down the coast finding the activities that might carry the metamessage that would identify them as expressions of love and closeness. The tastes of the meals we improvised stay with me, especially lunches, a loaf of sourdough bread, Genoa salami cut with a hunting knife into jagged slices, butter grown soft from carrying in the car, and pungent cheese, spread out on a few sheets of newspaper by the roadside. Gregory believed in looking at plants but was not much interested in eating them.

Sometimes in a public campground in a state park we would strike up a conversation and someone would ask and learn that he was an anthropologist and then often enough start talking about my mother, the only anthropologist they had heard of, as often with hostility as with admiration. I remember feeling him beside me, wrestling with the question of whether and how to acknowledge the connection, and when we might escape. Once, just over the border into Nevada, we stopped at a place that looked like a country fair but was devoted to gambling. He got suckered into a game, throwing good money after bad until all the cash he had brought for the trip was lost and we had to head back for the city, while he analyzed the psychology and mathematics of the game on the way. Once when we came down from the Sierras and into the central valley the flatness made me uneasy and we drove all night to get back into the coastal range, to a place where we knew how to be. For all the informality and makeshift, we did best when we avoided "civilization" and shared a narrow place and a way of being together where the keys were "teach me something" or "let's do some natural history."

"*It took the bigness out of my head in a hurry.*"

I have seven kids and every one of them rodeos, right down to the little baby. Tye is five and he rides calves and he's in barrel racing. He's been doing that for three years. They all started young. They've all come right up with it. I try to encourage them. Anytime I can help them in any way, I do. We'll take off from work if we have to. If there's a rodeo, we'll get there.

When I was a kid, I had encouragement from my daddy. I grew up working on the ranch, and if I worked really hard my daddy would always take time off to take me to the rodeos. That's the way we did it. My mother used to say, "There's nobody works harder than your dad, and nobody plays harder either."

I had been rodeoing for nearly twelve years before I ever went to a rodeo without my dad. He'd just always take me. One time I asked him to take me to a rodeo and it was just before hunting season. He was an outfitted guide at the time and he said, "Boy, babe, I don't really have time." So I said, "Daddy, if you will come to the rodeo, I'll be sure and help you." So he took me.

I had a real nasty cow. Cows are real bad in the chute. You know, bulls can't compare with a cow for just being stupid in the chute. They bang you around; they won't hold still.

My dad's always been one to just drop right down on their head in the chute and hold them still for you. He'd do this not just for me, but for all the girls up and down the line.

Well, this old cow I had, she was jumping all over. He just sits on her head and she runs forward and falls down. Bent both of his knees backward and we had to pack him out, put his knees back in.

I'd told him I'd help him, you know. So I had to go with him and shoe fifteen head of horses that next week, pack out camps, and everything else. But that was part of the deal. He'd help me if I'd help him.

I'll tell you about my first rodeo. As you can well see, I think an awful lot of my daddy. And this was the first [all-girl] rodeo my dad was producing. He went and leased some of this stock from a friend of his. Then he rode every one of them out because he wasn't going to put the girls on them until he knew what they did for sure.

I was twelve. I rode my first bareback horse at that rodeo. Name was Meathead. And Meathead went out there and he just kind of crow-hopped out across the arena. I rode him and there was only four of us covered [rode the required eight seconds]. Well, I was setting third and, boy, I was proud as punch. Real big head, you know. First horse I ever rode and I was winning third place on him.

I went down to the other end of the arena and I was untying calves and this girl come along and said, "Jan, you got a re-ride." Course, I'd been raised around rodeo. I knew what a re-ride was. And I thought, "Oh, good. Now I'll win first."

Before I rode, I had a little time and I told Momma I had a re-ride. I imagine I was playing pretty hotshot, pretty big stuff. I told her I was going to ride Basher Boy. I didn't know the horses, 'cause I hadn't been with Dad when he tried them out, but Momma had. Basher Boy was one of the top horses, and he was rank. Momma said, "Your dad better not put you on that horse." I said, "Oh, Mom, I can ride him!"

I went up and Daddy had my rigging on this big, stout sorrel horse. I got on and Dad said, "Now, watch this horse, babe. Don't let him get you back off that riggin'. He's pretty stout." Well, if my dad will warn me about anything, it's time to look out, but it still didn't put a dent in me. I just came out on that old horse and about the second jump, I'll tell you, he popped me back off that rigging. I ploughed a furrow in that arena you could have planted corn in. I couldn't close my eyes, couldn't close my mouth, they were so full of dirt.

What had happened when I'd rode old Meathead, somebody back behind said, "Oh, that's the producer's daughter. She gets an easy horse." Well, Dad wasn't going to have them say nothing like that, so he put me on the roughest horse he had! That's the way he is. It helped. It took the bigness out of my head in a hurry. I found out right quick I couldn't ride just anything.

"*I'd rather dig ditches than go to school.*"

I've ranched all my life. I never wanted to do anything else. My mother was a schoolteacher, and I think she was a little disappointed that my sister and I didn't want to teach. She sent us to school over in Ouray. When I was twelve I was there in town and a neighbor pulled his team up and unhitched them. I asked him, "When are you going back?"

"Oh, not for a couple hours, anyway."

"Well, I'm going with you."

"No, you're not. Your mother would kill me if I brought you home."

"Well, I'm either going with you, or I'll walk over that mountain myself. I know the way all right. And I'll make it in a third the distance!"

"All right. But you'll have to deal with your mother yourself." So he took me home. And then he cleared out quick, 'cause I think he thought something was going to happen.

I walked in and my mother was in the kitchen. There were about ten men at the table. She looked at me and said, "Marie, where did you come from?"

"I graduated," I told her, "and tomorrow I'm going to work in the hayfields, or I'll go down the road and get a job on my own." I knew I could do that, you see, 'cause I could irrigate and dig post holes and all that. Whatever a man could do, I could do. I knew I could do it, and I knew I could get hired. And I'd rather dig ditches than go to school.

"No, you're not," my mother said. "Tomorrow you are going back to Ouray and go to school."

"I am not. I've never told you I won't do something before, but this time I'm telling you. And you can do what you want. Because I'm either going to work in the hayfield or I'm going out on my own. I've graduated from school."

So the next morning, I went to work in the hayfield. It was hard work, but it was what I wanted to do. And it's what I've always wanted to do, and it's what I've always done.

This is good country, and you can make a living here if you are willing to put twelve hours a day on the business end of a shovel or a pitchfork. Sometimes sixteen hours, sometimes twenty. But it's good country here, just so you're willing to work.

COURTSHIP

There are those of us who remember the coming of new love; there are those who still wait. The luckiest ones are those for whom the dazzling possibilities of courtship are close, emerging, radiant. Do we ever know one another again as well as we do in those first mesmerizing days, when everything we are and want to be is laid out for the other like a pearly string of hopes? The sharp longing, the resurgent faith, the sudden disappointment; whether rising or plunging, the passions of courtship are breathtaking. Even when those whom we love do not love us or those whom we do not love seek us out with a relentless determination, courtship's absolute promise is that the intensity will never end. Leave it to the bitter scolds to assure young lovers that wild promises would be unbearable if kept; the best in us wants them to dance on and on to a wondrous and transforming music.

Courtship tales, however, often have little to do with the lovers themselves. We may be moved by the demonstrations that pass between Romeo and Juliet, but we are transfixed by the machinations of those outside love's magic, the ones determined to break love's will. The Native Americans, the first great storytellers in North America, knew too well that where the heart leads, society is often loath to follow. Every tribe had stories about brave young women who refused unwelcome suitors or the commands of their fathers to obey the dictates of their own hearts. The penalty for such independence was customarily grim—typically death—and the message was always clear: Romance was dangerous because of its unpredictability, a river that would not hold its banks. Sometimes, the woman's choice for a lover eclipsed her father's authority; other times, as with *Woman in the Moon,* the heart's desire was simply to be alone. These tribal tales suggest that the right of a woman to choose the one she loved, the right to her own pleasure and passion, would never be granted without a steep price. Later society was no different, although it offered a new and vicious penalty for the independent heart: the threat of a living death, the unforgiving community's promise that inappropriate choices in love would lead to isolation and shame. Didn't Hester Prynne endure the penalty for letting her hair down in a secret wood?

In America, we like to think our young men and women can approach one another largely free of class or custom or caution, and that courting is unbiased, uncomplicated, even raucous. We want to believe that the American right for self-invention includes the ability to love whomever we choose. Our history is no different from the rest of the world, however, and courtship has always had purposes that tried to render individual passion powerless. For fathers, the daughter has been a valuable mechanism for social advancement and the ambitious alliance of formidable families in America. Even as American society expanded its range in the eighteenth and nineteenth centuries, (de Tocqueville admired the independence and directness of the American woman), the oppressive social choreography of the European salons still prevailed on the East Coast. The great cities of New York, Boston, Philadelphia, and Savannah were hotbeds of appropriate civility, and the burden fell, as usual, on the American woman. She was to look and act as one contained; she was reserved for the man who would one day become her husband, and her emotional health had nothing to do with the behavior expected of her. She was first a daughter and then a wife—anything else would evoke a neighbor's pity and scorn. While social instructions may seem ludicrous to us today (look at *Directions for Fainting Elegantly)*, they were serious enough to make or break a young woman's fortunes. The social hypocrisy, expressed in what women could and could not do or wear or think was deeply vexing to women of spirit. Should a man fail in his role of gallant, for example, he was labeled (not without admiration) something of a rogue. But should a woman stray—should she love the wrong kind of man, or, heaven forbid, profess the cravings of her heart—she was as branded as one fallen, unredeemable. How much have we changed?

Suffice it to say, however, that after the arguments with stubborn fathers are over, when the demands of society matrons no longer hold, when local gossip has lost its sting, there is still the essential passion that belongs solely to the heart that feels it. Not all of it is sorrow, of course. In the following chapter Bette Davis's regrets are minimal; Mammy Wise meets her destiny without complaint; young Ann Rainey, a frontierswoman from Texas, tells a marvelously frank and straightforward story of her courtship; her resolve is no less compelling than Ellen Glasgow's poignant question: Is it a miracle or an illusion? In America, as across the rest of the world, courtship tales are part of a great folkloric tradition, an extravagant, unceasing parade. So let's listen to the changing notes of a song that has been sung everyday by American lovers since the Mayflower dropped anchor.

The Woman Who Fell from the Sky (Iroquois)

Once upon a time, long ago so far, a young woman was told by her dead father to go and marry a stranger. Being a strange woman, she did as he said, not taking her mother's counsel in the matter as she should have done. She journeyed to the place where the dead father had directed her to go, and there found the man she was to marry.

Now this man was a renowned magician, a sorcerer. He heard her proposal that they marry skeptically. He said to himself, "This woman is but a girl. It would be more fitting for her to ask to be my servant rather than my wife." But he only listened silently to her; then he said, "It is well. If you can meet my tests, we will see if I will make you my wife."

He took her into his lodge and said, "Now you must grind corn." She took the corn and boiled it slightly, using wood he brought her for the fire. When the kernels were softened, she began to grind them on the grinding stone. And though there were mounds and mounds of stuff to be ground, still she was done with the task in a very short time. Seeing this, the sorcerer was amazed, but he kept silent. Instead he ordered her to remove all her clothing. When she was naked, he told her to cook the corn in the huge pot that hung over the fire. This she did, though the hot corn popped and spattered scalding, clinging mush all over her. But she did not flinch, enduring the burns with calm.

When the mush was done, the woman told the sorcerer it was ready. "Good," he said. "Now you will feed my servants." He noted that her body was covered with cornmush. Opening the door, he called in several huge beasts who ran to the woman and began to lick the mush from her body with their razor-sharp tongues, leaving deep gashes where their tongues sliced her flesh. Still she did not recoil but endured the torment, not letting her face lose its look of calm composure.

Seeing this, the sorcerer let the beasts back out, then said she and he would be married, and so they were. After four nights that they spent sleeping opposite each other with the soles of their feet touching, he sent her back to her village with gifts of meat for the people. He commanded her to divide the meat evenly among all the people, and further to see to it that every lodge had its roof removed that night, as he was going to send a white corn rain among them. She did as she was told, and after the village had received its gifts, the meat and the white corn rain, she returned to her husband's lodge.

Outside his lodge there grew a tree that was always filled with blossoms so bright they gave light to his whole land. The woman loved the tree, loved to sit under it and converse with the spirits and her dead father, whom she held dear in her heart. She so loved the light tree that once, when everyone was sleeping, she lay down under it and opened her legs and her body to it. A blossom fell on her vagina then, touching her with sweetness and a certain joy. And soon after she knew she was pregnant.

About that time her husband became weak and ill. His medicine people could not heal him, but told him that his sickness was caused by his wife. He was certain they were right, for he had never met anyone so powerful as she. He feared that her power was greater than his own, for hadn't she been able to withstand his most difficult tests? "What should I do?" he asked his advisors. They did not advise him to divorce her, because that kind of separation was unknown to them. They did not advise him to kill her, because death was unknown among them. The only death that had occurred was of the woman's father, and they did not understand what had happened to him.

After deliberating on the matter for four days, the advisors told the sorcerer that he should uproot the tree of light. Then, lying beside it, he should call his wife to come and sit with him. He should by some ruse get her to fall over the edge of the hole the uprooted tree would leave, and she would fall into the void. When she had fallen, they said, he was to replace the tree and he would recover his health and power.

That afternoon he went outside his lodge and pulled up the tree. He peered over the edge of the hole it left, and he could see another world below. He called his wife to come and see it. When she came, he said, "Lean over the edge. You can see another world below." She knelt beside the hole and, leaning over the edge, looked down. She saw darkness, and a long way below she saw blue, a shining blue that seemed filled with promise and delight. She looked at her husband and smiled, eyes dancing with pleasure. "It looks like a beautiful place there," she said. "Who would have thought that the tree of light would be growing over such a place!"

"Yes," her husband agreed. "It surely seems beautiful there." He regarded her for a moment carefully, then said, "I wonder what it is like there. Maybe somebody could go down there and find out."

Astonished, the woman looked at her husband. "But how would someone do that?"

"Jump." The husband said.

"Jump?" she asked, looking down through the opening, trying to calculate the distance. "But it is very far."

"Someone of your courage could do it," he said. "You could jump. Become the wind or a petal from this tree." He indicated the tree lying fallen next to them. "A petal could fall, gently; on the wind it would be carried. You could be a petal in the wind. You could be a butterfly, a down-gliding bright bird."

She gazed for a long time at the shining blue below her. "I could jump like that. I could float downward. I could fall into the shining blue world below us."

"Yes," he said. "You could."

For another long moment she knelt gazing downward, then taking a deep breath she stood, and flexing her knees and raising her arms high over her head, she leaned into the opening and dove through.

For some time the sorcerer watched her body as it fell downward through the dark, toward the blue. "She jumped," he finally said to the council as they made their way slowly toward him. "She's gone."

And they raised the tree and placed it back firmly in its place, covering the opening to the other world with its roots.

The Sun and the Moon (Cherokee)

The Sun was a young woman and lived in the east while her brother the Moon lived in the west. The Sun had a lover who used to come every month in the dark of the moon to court her. He would come at night and leave before daylight, and although she talked to him she could not see his face in the dark and he would not tell her his name. The Sun was wondering all the time who her lover was.

At last she had an idea how she could discover her lover's identity. The next time he came, as they were sitting together in the dark, she slyly dipped her hand into the cinders and ashes of the fireplace and rubbed her fingers over his face, saying, "Your face is cold; you must have suffered from the wind." After a while he left and went away again. The next night when the Moon came up in the sky his face was covered with spots, and then his sister knew he was the one who had been coming to see her.

He was so ashamed to have her know it that he kept as far away as he could at the other end of the sky. Ever since he has tried to keep a long way behind the Sun, and when he does sometimes have to appear near her in the west, he makes himself as thin as a ribbon so he can hardly be seen.

The Woman in the Moon (Chippewa)

An Indian tale from North America. The "big water" in the story is Lake Superior:

Many snows in the past, before the White Man came to take the Indian lands, the Chippewa were great and strong. They were as many as leaves upon the maple tree; their tents were as thick as the stars up in the sky. They were feared by their foes and loved by their friends. The Good Spirit smiled upon the People, and the People were content.

In those long-ago years, on the shores of the big water there lived an Indian maid, Lone Bird. She was the only child of She Eagle and Dawn of Day. And no daughter of the tribe was so proud and strong as she. From all the camps of the Chippewa nation young braves would come to seek her favor. But she stared coolly at them all. In vain they sang to her of their skill as hunters, of their daring in war. In vain they brought gifts to the lodge of She Eagle and Dawn of Day.

The maiden's heart was, they said, like winter's ice.

Her father tried to breathe some warmth into his daughter's heart. He praised the skill and courage of the braves he knew; he told her that no maid of the tribe had so noble a band of suitors from whom to choose.

But Lone Bird took his hand in hers. She smiled as she said, "Do I not have my parents' love? What need have I to wed?"

Dawn of Day made no reply. He did not understand. How could he? Next day he went from his lodge, summoned young braves of the camp, and told them of his plan.

"All you who want my daughter as your squaw should gather on the shore. A race will be run. He who is fleetest of foot shall have her as prize."

At these words, the young men's hearts were filled with joy. Each eagerly made ready for the race, and each hoped for the deer's nimbleness of foot.

News of the contest spread through the Chippewa camps, and braves came from far and near. On the morning of the race, a great throng gathered upon the shore.

The elders were there to strut and judge the race.

Mothers were there to give comfort to their sons and cast an eye on future brides.

Fathers came to seek sons worthy of their daughters.

Daughters were there to see the braves and be noticed in return. And, of course, the braves were there, painted in the finest hues and plumed with feathers of the eagle and the turkey cock.

Only one member of the tribe was missing—Lone Bird. She sat in her parents' lodge alone, in tears.

When all was ready for the race, the braves lined up, bronze muscles rippling in the sun and hearts pounding like war drums. At the signal, they all dashed forward in a jostling throng.

Soon two runners had broken free of the chasing pack. They were Bending Bow and Hunter of Deer. Both had loved Lone Bird for many moons. Each was as fleet-footed as a deer, as swift as the rushing wind. Neither could outstrip the other, and when they reached the finishing line, the judges could not tell which brave had won.

So Bending Bow and Hunter of Deer raced again. And once more they came in side by side. A third time they ran, and no victor was declared.

"Let them jump against each other," someone said.

Yet when they jumped, neither could beat the other by a hair.

"Let them display their hunting skill," the elders declared.

So next day at dawn, Bending Bow and Hunter of Deer set off across the plain. On their return, each threw down the skins of ten bears and twenty wolves.

The elders muttered amongst themselves and an anxious buzz went around the tribe: It was clear that the Good Spirit had been at work. Lone Bird's father, Dawn of Day, returned to his lodge with a troubled mind. There sat his daughter, head bowed, eyes red with weeping, knuckles white upon trembling hands. His heart was moved, for he dearly loved his only child.

Lifting her head, he spoke gently to her. "You must not weep, daughter. Every man must have a wife, every wife a man."

"Dear Father," she replied, "but what if I do not wish it to be so?"

Sadly he returned to the elders gathered beside the lake.

"The race is at an end," he said. "Bending Bow and Hunter of Deer have done well, but it seems the Good Spirit's will is against our plan. My daughter shall remain unwed."

And so, dismayed, the braves returned to their camps.

Summers passed; leaves of autumn fell; cold winter winds blew across the lake. And then one spring, as the snows began to melt, Dawn of Day went to Maple-Syrup Hill to make sugar from the sap of maple trees. As always, Lone Bird went along to gather the sweet liquid in birch-bark bowls. By and by, as smoke was curling slowly from her father's fire, she sat upon a rock and glanced around. The sun was warm and bright, the air was filled with the scent of fir and pine, yet somehow Lone Bird felt sad. Her thoughts were of her parents, of their silver hair and stumbling steps; their journey to the spirits was not far off.

"What will become of me when they are gone?" she thought. "I have no brother or sister, no children of my own, no one to share my tent."

And for the first time she felt the chill hand of loneliness grip her heart. As she gazed down the slope at the early snowdrops, pushing their frail heads through the margin of the snow, she saw that they grew in clusters, like small families. As she watched the birds busily building nests, she saw that they too did not live alone. Just then she heard the whirring of a flock of wild geese swooping across the lake; they landed in a furrow upon the water and glided away in pairs.

"No flowers, no birds, not even wild geese live alone," she murmured to herself.

Her lonely thoughts made her sadder still. She recalled her coolness to the braves who used to court her; no longer did they come. She recalled her father's efforts to find her a husband; he had long since let her be.

"Yet still I am glad I did not wed," she sighed. "No one understands that I have no love in my heart for men."

For a long time she sat upon the rock above the lake, wrapped in her gloomy thoughts. When she rose to go it was already dusk, and the full round moon made a silvery path across the lake. Lone Bird gazed up longingly at the bright moon in the sky and, stretching forth her arms, she cried, "Oh, how beautiful you are. If only I had you to love, I would not be lonely."

The Good Spirit heard the cry of the lonely maid and carried her up to the moon.

Meanwhile, her father finished his work upon the slopes and, not seeing her anywhere about, he went back home. Yet when he did not find her in the lodge he returned to Maple-Syrup Hill. From there he called his daughter's name. "Lone Bird! Lone Bird!"

Time and again he called.

No answer came.

His worried eyes searched the trees, the slopes, the surface of the lake. Then in despair he looked up to the sky towards the brightly shining moon. Could it be? Yes, there was no doubt. He clearly saw his daughter smiling down, held in the moon's pale arms.

She seemed to say she was content.

No longer did he grieve. No longer did She Eagle or Dawn of Day worry about their daughter's fate. They knew she would be cared for tenderly by the loving moon.

Many, many snows have passed since the days of Lone Bird and her Chippewa tribe. Their people have become weak and few; their tents are scattered to the winds. White strangers occupy their hunting grounds and the graves of their dead go unmourned.

But the flowers still bloom in springtime; birds still build their nests; wild geese fly and stars still shine. And if you look up to the moon, you can still see the face of Lone Bird smiling down. She gives hope to her people as they tell her story by their fading fires.

She understands. And so do they.

Sarah Winnemucca Hopkins: Life Among the Paiutes

Published in 1883, Hopkins's Life Among the Paiutes: Their Wrongs and Claims was originally intended as an autobiography. Soon enough Hopkins, who had come east to tell her story and draw attention to the plight of her tribe, turned her narrative into a more general treatise on the life of her people. Recognizing that her own experiences wove a deeper meaning into the depictions of tribal life, Hopkins was able to balance her narrative beautifully between the personal and the descriptive. The excerpt below reminds us of the tender days in the lives of young women who are, at last, coming of age:

Our young women are not allowed to talk to any young man that is not their cousin, except at the festive dances, when both are dressed in their best clothes, adorned with beads, feathers or shells, and stand alternately in the ring and take hold of hands. These are very pleasant occasions to all the young people.

Many years ago, when my people were happier than they are now, they used to celebrate the Festival of Flowers in the spring. I have been to three of them only in the course of my life.

Oh, with what eagerness we girls used to watch every spring for the time when we could meet with our hearts' delight, the young men, whom in civilized life you call beaux. We would all go in company to see if the flowers we were named for were yet in bloom, for almost all the girls are named for flowers. We talked about them in our wigwams, as if we were the flowers, saying, "Oh, I saw myself today in full bloom!" We would talk all the evening in this way in our families with such delight, and such beautiful thoughts of the happy day when we should meet with those who admired us and would help us to sing our flower-songs, which we made up as we sang. But we were always sorry for those that were not named after some flower, because we knew they could not join in the flower-songs like ourselves, who were named for flowers of all kinds.

At last one evening came a beautiful voice, which made every girl's heart throb with happiness. It was the chief, and everyone hushed to hear what he said today.

"My dear daughters, we are told that you have seen yourselves in the hills and in the valleys, in full bloom. Five days from today your festival day will come. I know every young man's heart stops beating while I am talking. I know how it was with me many years ago. I used to wish the Flower Festival would come every day. Dear young men and young women, you are saying, 'Why put it off five days?' But you all know that is our rule. It gives you time to think, and to show your sweetheart your flower." All the girls who have flower-names dance along together, and those who have not go together also. Our fathers and mothers and grandfathers and grandmothers make a place for us where we can dance. Each one gathers the flower she is named for, and then all weave them into wreaths and crowns and scarfs, and dress up in them.

Some girls are named for rocks and are called rock-girls, and they find some pretty rocks which they carry, each one such a rock as she is named for, or whatever she is named for. If she cannot, she can take a branch of sage-brush, or a bunch of rye-grass, which have no flower.

They all go marching along, each girl in turn singing of herself; but she is not a girl any more—she is a flower singing. She sings of herself, and her sweetheart, dancing along by her side, helps her sing the song she makes.

I will repeat what we say of ourselves. "I, Sarah Winnemucca, am a shell-flower, such as I wear on my dress. My name is Thocmetony. I am so beautiful! Who will come and dance with me while I am so beautiful? Oh, come and be happy with me! I shall be beautiful while the earth lasts. Somebody will always admire me; and who will come and be happy with me in the Spirit-land? I shall be beautiful forever there. Yes, I shall be more beautiful than my shell-flower, my Thocmetony! Then, come, oh come, and dance and be happy with me!" The young men sing with us as they dance beside us.

Our parents are waiting for us somewhere to welcome us home. And then we praise the sage-brush and the rye-grass that have no flower, and the pretty rocks that some are named for, and then we present our beautiful flowers to these companions who could carry none. And so all are happy, and that closes the beautiful day.

My people have been so unhappy for a long time they wish now to *disincrease,* instead of multiply. The mothers are afraid to have more children, for fear they shall have daughters, who are not safe even in their mother's presence.

The grandmothers have the special care of the daughters just before and after they come to womanhood. The girls are not allowed to get married until they have come to womanhood; and that period is recognized as a very sacred thing, and is the subject of a festival, and has peculiar customs. The young woman is set apart under the care of two of her friends, somewhat older, and a little wigwam, called a teepee, just big enough for the three, is made for them, to which they retire. She goes through certain labors which are thought to be strengthening, and these last twenty-five days. Every day, three times a day, she must gather, and pile up as high as she can, five stacks of wood. This makes fifteen stacks a day. At the end of every five days the attendants take her to a river to bathe. She fasts from all flesh-meat during these twenty-five days, and continues to do this for five days in every month all her life. At the end of the twenty-five days she returns to the family lodge, and gives all her clothing to her attendants in payment for their care. Sometimes the wardrobe is quite extensive.

It is thus publicly known that there is another marriageable woman, and any young man interested in her, or wishing to form an alliance, comes forward. But the courting is very different from the courting of the white people. He never speaks to her, or visits the family, but endeavors to attract her attention by showing his horsemanship, etc. As he knows that she sleeps next to her grandmother in the lodge, he enters in full dress after the family has retired for the night, and seats himself at her feet. If she is not awake, her grandmother wakes her. He does not speak to either young woman or grandmother, but when the young woman wishes him to go away, she rises and goes and lies down by the side of her mother. He then leaves as silently as he came in. This goes on sometimes for a year or longer, if the young woman has not made up her mind. She is never forced by her parents to marry against her wishes. When she knows her own mind, she makes a confidant of her grandmother, and then the young man is summoned by the father of the girl, who asks him in her presence if he really loves his daughter, and reminds him, if he says he does, of all the duties of a husband. He then asks his daughter the same question, and sets before her minutely all her duties. And these duties are not slight. She is to dress the game, prepare the food, clean the buckskins, make his moccasins, dress his hair, bring all the wood—in short, do all the household work. She promises to "be himself," and she fulfills her promise. Then he is invited to a feast and all his relatives with him. But after the betrothal, a teepee is erected for the presents that pour in from both sides.

At the wedding feast, all the food is prepared in baskets. The young woman sits by the young man, and hands him the basket of food prepared for him with her own hands. He does not take it with his right hand, but seizes her wrist, and takes it with the left hand. This constitutes the marriage ceremony, and the father pronounces them man and wife. They go to a wigwam of their own, where they live till the first child is born. This event also is celebrated. Both father and mother fast from all flesh, and the father goes through the labor of piling the wood for twenty-five days, and assumes all his wife's household work during that time. If he does not do his part in the care of the child, he is considered an outcast. Every five days his child's basket is changed for a new one, and the five are all carefully put away at the end of the days, the last one containing the navel-string, carefully wrapped up, and all are put up into a tree, and the child put into a new and ornamented basket. All this respect shown to the mother and child makes the parents feel their responsibility and makes the tie between parents and children very strong.

Dirty Dancing (1684)

In 1684, Boston was a tough place to be for the young at heart. What better illustration than the following admonition from the treatise An Arrow Against Profane and Promiscuous Dancing Drawn out of the Quiver of the Scriptures:

Concerning the controversy about dancing, the question is not whether all dancing be in itself sinful. It is granted that pyrrhical or polemical saltation, i.e., when men vault in their armor to show their strength and activity, may be of use. Nor is the question whether a sober and grave dancing of men with men or women with women be not allowable; we make no doubt of that, where it may be done without offense, in due season and with moderation. The Prince of Philosophers has observed truly that dancing or leaping is a natural expression of joy; so that there is no more sin in it than in laughter or any outward expression of inward rejoicing.

But our question is concerning gynecandrical dancing, or that which is commonly called mixed or promiscuous dancing, viz., of men and women (be they elder or younger persons) together. Now this we affirm to be utterly unlawful and that it cannot be tolerated in such a place as New England without great sin.

A Christian should do nothing wherein he cannot exercise grace or put a respect of obedience to God on what he does. This in lawful recreations may be done. . . . But who can seriously pray to the Holy God to be with him when he is going to a promiscuous dance? It is that which hinders religious exercises, especially for persons to go immediately from hearing a sermon to a gynecandrical dance. It is a high degree of profaneness, an impudent contempt put upon the Gospel. The devil thereby catches away the good seed of the Word, and the former religious exercise is rendered ineffectual. . . .

Directions for Fainting Elegantly (1782)

The eyes grow dim, and almost closed; the jaw fallen; the head hung down; as if too *heavy* to be supported by the neck. A general inertia prevails. The voice trembling, the utterance through the nose; every sentence accompanied with a groan; the hand shaking, and the knees tottering under the body. Fainting eventually produces a sudden *relaxation* of all that holds the human frame together, every sinew and ligament unstrung. The color flies from the vermilion cheek; the sparkling eye grows dim. Down the *body drops,* as helpless, and as senseless, as a mass of *clay,* to which, by its color and appearance it seems hastening to resolve itself.

Female Stocking Supporters

Girls, I do not blame you for wishing to keep your stockings smooth. How shall they be kept smooth? The means, usually employed, is to apply a ligature just below the knee. If the calf of the leg be very large, the knee small, and the circulation vigorous, I suppose an elastic garter may be used without *serious* injury. But, as most American girls have slender legs, as there is but little enlargement at the calf, the pressure of the garter required to keep the stocking in position is very injurious. It produces absorption of important muscles, and, therefore, weakness of the legs and cold feet. The stockings must be drawn up and held. How shall it be done?

Let me illustrate. In attaching a horse to a load, we never draw a strap about its body and attach to that for draft purposes, but we seek some part of the body where the draft may come at right angles. When we wish to support the several pounds of skirts, the stockings, or any other garment, we look over the woman's body. To apply it about her legs, or about her waist, is precisely the same mistake that would be made if the draft were attached to the girth of the harness. There is only one point of support. In this place it is only necessary to say that a strap should be fastened to the skirt-band at the side, to run down over the hip, and on the outside of the leg, above the knee to divide into two straps, one of which is to be attached to the stocking on the front of the knee, and the other on the back of the knee. This sort of support has been very much used. It has now been adopted by thousands of women. . . .

She Loves Me, She Loves Me Not (1839)

Dear Miss Hawley:

You will, I trust, forgive this abrupt and plainly spoken letter. Although I have been in your company but once, I cannot forbear writing to you in defiance of all rules of etiquette. Affection is sometimes of slow growth, but sometimes it springs up in a moment. I left you last night with my heart no longer my own. I cannot, of course, hope that I have created any interest in you, but will you do me the great favor to allow me to cultivate your acquaintance? Hoping that you may regard me favorably, I shall await with much anxiety your reply. I remain

Yours Devotedly,

Benson Goodrich

Unfavorable Reply

Mr. Goodrich:

Sir: Your note was a surprise to me, considering that we had never met until last evening, and that then our conversation had been only on commonplace subjects. Your conduct is indeed quite strange. You will please be so kind as to oblige me by not repeating the request, allowing this note to close our correspondence.

Marion Hawley

Favorable Reply

Mr. Goodrich:

Dear Sir: Undoubtedly I ought to call you severely to account for your declaration of love at first sight, but I really cannot find it in my heart to do so, as I must confess that, after our brief interview last evening, I have thought much more of you than I should have been willing to have acknowledged had you not come to the confession first. Seriously speaking, we know but very little of each other yet, and we must be very careful not to exchange our hearts in the dark. I shall be happy to receive you here, as a friend, with a view to our further acquaintance. I remain, dear sir,

Marion Hawley

How to Pick a Husband (1849)

If a man wipes his feet on the door-mat, he will make a good domestic husband. If a man in snuffing a candle puts it out, you may be sure he will make a stupid husband. If a man puts his handkerchief on his knee while taking tea, you may be sure he will be a prudent husband. The man who wears rubbers and is careful about wrapping himself up before venturing in the night air not unfrequently makes a good invalid husband, that mostly stops at home, and is easily comforted with slops. The man who watches the kettle, and prevents its boiling over, will not fail in his married state in exercising the same care in always keeping the pot boiling. The man who does not take tea, ill-treats the cat, takes snuff, stands with his back to the fire, is a brute whom I would advise you not to marry upon any circumstances, either for love or money—but most decidedly not for love.

The Woman and the Silver Box

"Now the historians will tell you this ain't true," old Mrs. Adams said as we sat on her front porch looking out on the windy Carolina coast, "but I know it is." She leaned forward and rapped her cane twice and fairly shouted. "I know this to be true.

"Blackbeard was a vicious pirate. He robbed and killed and took whatever he pleased. And like most greedy men, it was the wantin' that made Blackbeard go after women and gold, not the gettin'. Now folks were scared of him. Really scared. My grandaddy used to say that his shadow could kill a cat with cold fear, so no matter how much you think you had, you had nothing when that pirate walked the streets. Well one day he chanced upon a beautiful young woman—she was the daughter of a wealthy man—and that old wantin' got started. Blackbeard followed her home and asked her father with great cere-mony if he could have his daughter (remember, even the baddest man will try good manners before he takes what he wants) and the father said yes. What kind of father says something like that? A scared one, for sure. He certainly didn't deserve the daughter he had though because she was proud and dark and beautiful. She stood before the two men when they came to tell her the news and said that most marvelous word, the second best word in the English language: she said no. Her father argued with her but she didn't budge. I won't, she said, I love another. Well Blackbeard (they also called him Teach around here) got mad and demanded to know who the man was: Tell me, he hissed, or your father will hang like a flag on a windless day. She smiled. Don't tempt me so to withhold his name (she was angry herself by then, I expect), but pride commands me to tell you for I am not ashamed. Old Teach had heard of the man and said he'd be back. He put out to sea but he kept his eye out for the young woman's lover. One night, the unfortunate man was caught and brought out to Teach's ship. The pirate did not come by his reputation through talk so he wasted no time giving speeches or making plans. He cut off the man's right hand and tossed him into the sea. He then placed the hand in a silver box, beautiful it was. My granddaddy saw that box when he was a boy (the hand was long gone) and said it was the brightest silver he ever saw. It shown like a mirror on a bright day. Well, you know what happened. He sent the box with his compliments to the young woman. Folks will tell you she opened the box, swooned and died, but that's cause folks love to think a girl's only option when her lover's gone is to up and die. But I'll tell you what this woman did. She cut off her left hand and sent it back to the pirate in the box. There's the hand you so wanted, she wrote him, suit yourself. She got mighty sick after that, nearly died, but she didn't because the tough ones never do, you know. They live because that's what's required of 'em. She took a house on a hill by the sea and gardened until she was an old woman. And that's a fact."

The Real Truth

*W*ell, a fella stayed with a girl, and by and by he went to his father and he said, "Father, I'm going to marry that girl." He says, "John, let me tell you—I'se fast when I was young, and that girl's your sister."

Well, he felt bad and he left her. By and by, he picked up another one, and he stayed with her for a while, and he went to his father and he said, "Father, I'm going to marry that girl." He said, "Johnny, I was fast when I was young— that girl's your sister."

Felt awful bad, and so one day he's setting up by the stove with his head hung down, and his mother said, "What's the trouble, John?" "No nothing." She says, "There's something, and I want to know what it is. Why did you leave that girl, the first one you stayed with, and you left your second one?" "Well," he said, "Father told me he was fast when he was young, and they's both my sisters." She says, "Johnny, I want to tell you something, I was fast when I was young, and your father ain't your father at all."

Mother Knows Best

A young man told his mother that he would like to marry but feared that he might not choose a good wife, and he would like to have his mother's counsel.

His mother said to him, "Saddle your horse and ride to the home of the girl that you have in mind. When close to her home, dismount and tie your horse to a tree. Then, go towards the house, and when the girl appears, as she will, say to her, 'My horse has been suddenly taken with colic. Would you kindly give me a handful of the scrapings of the kneading trough for him.' "

The son did as directed. He rode until he came close to the home of a girl whom he knew fairly well. Then he dismounted, tied his horse to a tree, and walked towards the house. The girl came out on the porch, and he asked her for a handful of scrapings of the kneading trough.

She answered, "That I shall gladly give you."

She went into the house, and came back with two heaping handfuls saying, "If this isn't enough, I can get more."

The young man thanked her and left. He returned to his mother and recounted to her his experience. She shook her head, and said, "Try again."

On the following day, the son rode forth again. To his request, the second girl replied, "When we are through baking, we clean our kneading trough, and there are no scrapings to be gotten."

When his mother heard his account, she shook her head, and said, "Try again."

He rode forth the third day, and went towards the home of a girl of whom he had heard but whom he had never met. To his request, she answered that she didn't know whether she could get any scrapings for him but she would try.

After a while she came out with a small handful and said, almost apologetically, as she gave them to him, "This is all I could get out of the corners of the trough. I am sorry that I cannot give you more."

He thanked her and rode back to his mother, who smiled when she heard his story. "That," she said, "is the one for you. Seek no further."

Four Winds

"Four winds blowing through the sky,
You have seen poor maidens die,
Tell me then what I shall do
That my lover may be true."
Said the wind from out the south,
"Lay no kiss upon his mouth,"

And the wind from out the west,
"Wound the heart within his breast,"
And the wind from out the east,
"Send him empty from the feast,"
And the wind from out the north,
"In the tempest thrust him forth;
When thou art more cruel than he,
Then will love be kind to thee."

Courting, Frontier Style (Texas)

To modern lovers, courting should be a spontaneous drama of shifting intrigues and impulsive passions. For frontier men and women, however, courting had a more serious purpose. Marriage was an economic necessity, and the deals that couples struck with one another reflected the hard and challenging circumstances of frontier life. A man without a woman was considered a prospect (by single women), an oddity (by married women), or even a drifter (by married men); a woman without a man was considered a prospect (by single men), dangerous (by married women), or irrelevant (by married men). Courtship was everyone's business, a sober game of musical chairs, which led to tough choices and the fear of being left with no place to sit. If, as in the excerpt below from the Texas diary of Ann Coleman, the courtship seems a bit on the dry side, we should not judge too harshly. In this self-proclaimed age of uninhibited emotion, we may not like to think that we make the same bargains with necessity as Miss Coleman and Mr. Thomas, but the cool reasonings of courtship are with us more often than we think:

T he Doctor came home and said, "Miss Ann, I wish you to put on your best attire this evening. I am going to bring home a beau for you. He is a rich bachelor and wishes to get married very much. You must set your cap for him; he will be a good husband for you." I laughed and told him I believed he was getting tired of me and wished to get rid of me by marrying me off to some old bachelor. "Not so, Miss Raney," he said, "unless you could do well for yourself; and I know you would if you should get Mr. Thomas. He is a man well known in the country, out of debt, and has a good home to take a wife to."

That evening after supper he came, and to my surprise, I found him the same little consequential fop I saw going into the billiard room in the morning.

Mr. Thomas was a man about thirty years of age, black hair and eyes, good complexion, good-looking, and a good address, a pleasant smile upon his features, and very communicative. He had one of his arms broken, which turned a little out of its natural position. This gave his arm a swagger that I took for conceit of his own personal dignity. A game of whist was proposed; we went to play one, but were soon compelled to quit as Mr. Thomas was not sufficiently acquainted with the game to play.

I retired to the other end of the room to get my sewing. The Doctor and Mrs. Counsel left the room for a short time, which seemed a long time to me. Mr. Thomas drew his chair up to the table where I sat and commenced the following conversation. "I think I have been introduced to you before, Miss Raney, about six months ago at Mr. Bell's who kept the ferry across the river Brazos. I was crossing a yoke of oxen. Do you remember me? Captain Brown was with you, and I understood from Mr. Bell that you were to be married to Captain Brown." I told him I recollected the time. "I see you are not married yet, Miss Raney." "No, sir," I replied, "it isn't quite soon enough for that event." He then remarked, "How do you like this country, Miss Raney?" I replied, "I like it well enough, but we have been very unfortunate in losing our parents in a foreign land, without relations or home." "As far as home is concerned," he replied, "Miss Raney, I think I can offer as good a one as any man in the country, if you will accept it. I am not like a terrapin that carries all upon my back. I have plenty at home to make you comfortable. I know you have a great many suitors who can make many flattering speeches to you, which I cannot. I am plain as a book."

This speech brought the color to my face, and I would have given anything to have left the room. He seeing me silent, proceeded by saying, "I live thirty miles from here and the water courses are difficult to pass. If I come often to Brazoria, I shall make no crop, as I have no overseer. I should like, Miss Raney, if you could let me know if it is worth my while to come and see you again and pay my respects to you. I expect to leave town tomorrow morning, but will come back and see you before I leave." . . .

Before we had finished breakfast next morning, in walked Mr. Thomas. I was again caught for another day's courtship. I tried to excuse myself by saying I had to go and meet a friend, but he would not let me off and made himself as agreeable as possible. When evening came I could hardly believe I had been sitting all day in his company. Next day I was in hopes he would go home, but I was disappointed. He stayed this day also. He had been three days in town, notwithstanding he came in such a hurry and said he must leave the next day. He had appointed to return in one week from the time he left. I thought I would be absent, but he came in before breakfast and left me no chance to escape. It was during those visits he had been seen by Mr. McNeel coming to the house. Now Mr. Thomas had proposed marriage to me and waited my answer. . . .

After many a debate in my own mind I determined to accept Mr. Thomas's proposal. He had visited me about half a dozen times; he was well known in the country; everyone spoke well of him. This was satisfactory to me. He had given me several references as to his standing as a man in society. . . .

It was on returning from seeing [a friend] and his family one evening, I was called in the street by someone. On looking around I saw Mrs. Smith who was now keeping the same hotel as Mrs. Long used to keep, Mrs. Long having retired into private life with her daughter into the country. Mrs. Smith said, "I wish to see you a little while." I went in, took off my bonnet when Mrs. Smith remarked, "I hear you are going to be married to Mr. Thomas." "Who told you so?" I replied. "Mr. Thomas himself." "He is rather too communicative," I said. She replied, "You need not be ashamed of him. He is one of the finest men in the country. He will make you a good husband." She then went on to tell all his good qualities and said nothing about the bad ones. I came out of her house to go home when I was met by Mrs. A, another friend of Mr. Thomas and one of mine also. She got hold of my arm and said, "Come take a walk with me up the street." I complied. She commenced with, "I hear you are going to be married to Mr. Thomas. Is it so?" I was silent. "If you marry him you will get a close stingy husband; and he has got a woman at home, one of his servants that will turn you out of doors before you have been home a month. He has lived a bachelor so long, he knows every grain of coffee that goes into his pot."

I listened patiently to this unpleasant news and said little in return. We did not stay long; or rather, I made my walk as short as possible without seeming rude, and bid her good evening. I was determined to tell Mr. Thomas of what his friend Mrs. A had said the next time we met, for he was a constant visitor at their house. I was looking for him to come in town daily. Had my death knell been going to be sounded, I could not have dreaded it more. I was trying to summon up all my fortitude for the occasion when in walked Mr. Thomas. He came up to myself first and shook my hand and then passed on to the rest of the family. As soon as breakfast was finished Mr. Thomas and myself were left alone in the breakfast room.

He first broke the silence by saying, "I hope, Miss Ann, you have made up your answer to make me happy. It is to receive your answer I came to town today. I came near getting drowned crossing Linnville's Bayou, but I shall be repaid for the dangers I have passed if you consent to be my wife." My silence seemed to give consent, and he took my hand in his and pressed it warmly, while I burst into an agony of tears. "You shall never have cause to repent being my wife. I will do everything in my power to make you happy." I now told him what his friend Mrs. A had said. He seemed surprised and said, "Everyone is jealous of my expected happiness. You may pay no attention to anything you may hear against me. If you do not find strict obedience from every servant I have got, I will sell the first one that dares to insult or disobey you. I have a woman called Minerva who I raised from a child. She is a smart field hand and in cotton picking time she picks 300 pounds a day. In my absence she is my overseer, and though she is sometimes saucy she knows better than to give my wife any insolence." I told him I should expect perfect obedience from every one of his servants, and should they prove otherwise, he must sell them, which he said he would do. I told him I wished my sister to live with us. He said it would give him great pleasure to offer her a home.

He then went into town to make arrangements for our wedding. He was determined that no expense should be spared to make a handsome supper, which was to be provided at the hotel, Doctor Counsel's house not being large enough to entertain all that were being invited. Mr. Thomas left for home next day, and a week from that day was the one appointed for our wedding day. Mr. Thomas gave me an order on Mr. Mill's store to get anything I wanted for the occasion. I was now as busy as a bee making up my wedding suit, which was of rich white satin with blond lace, white silver artificial flowers, silver tinsel belt, black kid shoes with white satin rosettes and a gold bracelet, gold chain, and no veil. This was all of my wedding dress. I had been in a fever of excitement all week, and with no appetite.

The day arrived. It rained in the morning so hard the streets were one sheet of water. Mr. Thomas arrived early in the morning bringing the girl Minerva, who I understood was such a high-minded piece of humanity. He brought a boy to wait upon himself. At three o'clock in the evening I left Dr. Counsel's house for the hotel on horseback with Mr. Thomas. The streets were muddy from the recent rain. The sun shone out with all its brightness. There was a possibility that before night the water would dry up sufficiently to admit of visitors to attend our marriage. The amphibious race, the frogs, were silenced by the subduing melody of the winged tribes; all nature was bespangled with smiles. I alone seemed sad. Everyone else seemed cheerful. My intended tried to cheer me, as he saw me look thoughtful, and never left my side only when obliged to. We had a private room to ourselves, and when it was time to dress he left me and went to dress also. Crowds of persons began to flock in from the country, and by seven o'clock in the evening the hotel was filled to overflowing by two hundred persons.

Ours was the first public wedding given at the town of Brazoria. At eight o'clock my bridesmaids arrived, one a Miss Anderson, the other a Miss Bailey with whom we found our father on our arrival in Texas. Mr. Thomas had two groomsmen, one Mr. Edmond St. J. Hawkins, the other a gentleman whose name I have forgotten. At eight o'clock we entered the ball room to be married, it being the largest room in the house. The bridesmaids and groomsmen went first into the room, myself and Mr. Thomas last. I felt much abashed at the presence of so many people, and my eyes which on first entering had been cast to the ground were now raised to the face of Mr. Smith, the presiding *alcalde,* who was going to perform the marriage ceremony. A breathless silence pervaded the room whilst the ceremony was performed. The alcalde himself was so much excited that he paused once or twice while performing the ritual. I looked at the bridesmaids who were tastefully dressed. They looked like marble statues. As for myself, I trembled from head to foot, and when the ceremony was finished and the *alcalde* told Mr. Thomas to salute his bride, I saw no motion made by him to do it. At last, feeling for his embarrassment, I turned my cheek to his so that he might more easily salute me, which he did. The same was done by the bridesmaids and groomsmen, the groomsmen kissing me first, then the bridesmaids. We then went out as we came in until tea and coffee were ready. Then we all assembled in the dining room where tea, coffee, and cakes were handed around.

I saw a multitude of people, half of whom I was unacquainted with. The ladies were dressed very gay and in good taste and might have vied with city belles. After tea our congratulations commenced. I stood up with my husband until I was nearly exhausted, receiving one after another. At last a chair was brought me, and I sat down and only rose when obliged to. The dance had commenced and not more than half of the company had been presented to us. About ten o'clock that night I got liberty to dance for a short time. My engagements were too many to fill, so I danced but a little that I might give offense to none. About twelve o'clock at night supper was announced by our hostess, Mrs. Smith, and we retired to the supper room. Everything was tastefully arranged and the table laden with every delicacy that could be procured. Fruit from Orleans was in abundance, the cake delicious, fowl and meats plentiful, plenty of wine, also coffee. All eyes were on my husband and myself, so I ate but little; a cup of coffee was grateful to me, as it had always been my favorite beverage.

I hurried to retire where I would not be so closely observed. Everyone praised my dress, which I made myself, and said I looked charming but sad. This was a truth. I masked the feeling of my heart on this night that I might make him who I had chosen for my husband feel happy. At one o'clock I went up to my room with my servant Minerva, who, I had forgotten to state, was all obedience. I dismissed her shortly afterwards and I was left alone. My bridesmaids insisted on waiting upon me to disrobe me and see me in bed, but I would not permit them to and told them to go and enjoy themselves in the ball room. I had been sitting in one position half an hour before a looking glass that reflected my form to my view, when I thought, "I am dressed and adorned for a sacrifice." I had been sitting in one position without a motion to undress. My thoughts were on my native land with my dear brother and Henry, who I never expected to forget; my love was still his, and parted only by force of circumstances. I was disappointed in not seeing that beloved face, my sister, at my wedding.

In the midst of these reflections, someone opened the door and the *alcalde* put in his head. "My dear, are you not in bed? Your husband wishes to retire for the night, and it is my business, according to the Spanish law, to see you both in bed." I felt indignant to this method of the Spanish law and promised to go to bed directly. With that promise he closed the door. My face, if anyone could have seen it, was crimson with blushes. And my husband came in and I was still sitting there with all my clothes on. He was surprised at seeing me still up, and taking my hand and kissing it, he said, "My child, I will be a father as well as a husband. Do not sit there, but go to bed and take some rest, for you have need of it. Tomorrow you have a long and tiresome journey to take. The roads are bad, and without rest, you will be unfit for it. I want to start as soon as we get breakfast."

I hid my face in my handkerchief and wept bitter tears. Would he fulfill all he had promised? I had need of a father's and a husband's care. I was fifteen years younger than Mr. Thomas and a child in appearance to himself. Without saying any more he went to the other end of the room, my back being turned to him, and in a few minutes he was in bed. I slipped off my dress and all my ornaments, blew out the light, and in a few minutes I was also in bed. Shortly afterwards in came my evil genius with a light in his hand, opened a part of the [mosquito] bar and looked at us both the space of a minute and was gone without speaking. My husband laughed and so did I, though no one saw me do so for I hid my face with the cover.

Ellen Glasgow: Love at First Sight

Strong-minded, self-educated, author of her first novel at the age of seventeen, Ellen Glasgow nevertheless carried a kind of doom in her. Born in Virginia (where she was to set most of her novels) in 1873, she lived with a sense that the past held more promise than the future. What was coming, she seemed to say, was a loud and relentless age; what had passed was a nobility and grace that would not come again. For Glasgow, love, as she describes it below (in an excerpt from her autobiography The Woman Within, *published years after her death in 1945), seemed to have something of that doom about it too; we feel it even at the moment when its joy seems most radiant:*

Without warning, a miracle changed my life. I fell in love at first sight. Though I had had my casual romances, and even a rare emotional entanglement, I had not ever been in love with my whole being. One major obstacle was a deep conviction that I was unfitted for marriage. Loneliness had exercised a strange fascination; and I felt that I could not surrender myself to constant companionship, that I could not ever be completely possessed. It is true that I was both temperamental and imaginative, lightly disposed to cherish unreal and airy romances; but, apart from the lack in me of what people call the maternal instinct, I felt that my increasing deafness might be inherited, and that it would be a sin against life to pass on an affliction which, even while it was scarcely noticeable, had caused such intense suffering. . . .

It was the winter after our return from abroad, and Cary, Rebe, and I were spending a few weeks in New York, in order that I might talk with my new publishers, Doubleday, Page and Company. While we were there we went often to the play and the opera; and, among our friends, one we loved very much would ask us to drop in for tea on our way home from a matinee. It was in her charming drawing room (how vividly I can still see it!) that the flash came from an empty sky, and my whole life was transfigured.

Like all other romantic episodes, great or small, in my life, this began with a sudden illumination. Or, rather, it did not begin at all; it was not there, and then it was there. One moment the world had appeared in stark outlines, colorless and unlit, and the next moment, it was flooded with radiance. I had caught that light from the glance of a stranger, and the smothered fire had flamed up from the depths. And this first love, as always, created the illusion of its own immortality. When I went out into the street, after that accidental meeting, I felt that I was walking, not in time, but in eternity. I moved amid values that had ceased to be ephemeral, and had become everlasting.

I remember shrinking back, as I entered the room; and when we were introduced, I scarcely distinguished him from the man with whom he was talking. Then, gradually, I noticed that he kept his eyes on me while he was speaking to someone else, and, in my shyness, I became faintly uncomfortable. Still, however hard I tried, I could not keep my glance from turning in his direction. I felt my gaze drawn back to him by some invisible thread of self-consciousness. I was aware of his interest, and I was aware, too, of his tall thin figure and his dark keen face, with hair which was slightly gray on the temples. What I did not know, at the time, for his name meant nothing to me, was that he had been married for years, and was the father of two sons, already at school or at college. What I knew, through some vivid perception, was that the awareness was not on my side alone, that he was following my words and my gestures, that a circle of attraction divided us from the persons around us. Most women, I suppose, have lived through such moments, but with most women this emotional awakening, as intangible as air, and as life-giving, must come, I think, earlier in youth. For I was twenty-six, and my twenty-seventh birthday would come in April. In the years before my youth was clouded by tragedy, I had known an attraction as swift and as imperative; but not ever the permanence, and the infallible certainty, as if a bell were ringing, "Here, now, this is my moment!"

Looking back, over the flat surface of experience, the whole occurrence appears incredibly wild and romantic. It does not belong to life; yet it remains, after all the years between, intensely alive. It is the one thing that has not passed; for not ever again, in the future, could I see my life closing as if it had not once bloomed and opened wide to the light.

After a little while, he broke away from the group, and crossed the room to join me by the window. I remember the window, the street outside, the carriages that went by; and I remember, too, the look of the room behind him, and even the shadows of firelight on his face, as he paused for an instant on his way toward me. We talked first of my two books, and, crude as they were, he liked them, because he said, "there is something, I don't know what, but there is something." While I listened to him, not wondering whether I could hear his voice, I found, with a shock of pleasure, that his clear, crisp tones were distinct, without straining, without effort. The one tremendous obstacle to a natural association did not exist at all, or existed but slightly, when I was with him. Even when, as occasionally happened, I had to ask him to repeat what he said, he replied as if this touch of dependence were an added attraction. Out of the whole world of men, I had met the one man who knew, by sympathy, or by some other instinct, the right way of approach, who could, by his simple presence, release me from my too sensitive fears. I shall call him Gerald B——, because this name will do as well as another.

Of this, I knew nothing at that moment. All I felt was a swifter vibration, a quivering joy, as if some long-imprisoned stream of life were beginning to flow again under the open sky. His eyes were gay, searching, intensely alive. Though I felt, or found, that we had scarcely an intellectual interest in common, the difference seemed only to increase his imperative charm over my heart and my senses. For, through that difference, he had recognized something in me—that mysterious something—which was akin to his own nature.

Months afterwards, an unsuspecting friend said to me: "One miracle in life I have seen, without knowing the cause. I saw your whole life change in a single spring. Everything about you, even the way you looked, came to life. I saw radiance stream under your skin. I saw the stricken look leave your eyes. I saw the bronze sheen return to your hair. No one could miss it who watched you. A month before you had been cold and reserved. Then suddenly, you bloomed again, and everyone felt your charm. I used to see people look at you, and think to myself, 'They feel something about her.'"

If these were not her exact words, they are near enough to express her meaning and her surprise. What she did not know was that this passionate awakening to life had restored my lost faith in myself. Love had proved to me that my personality, or my charm, could overcome, not only my deafness, but the morbid terror of that affliction, and, especially, of its effect upon others. . . . But of the many ties between us, I think the strongest was a kind of intimate laughter. It began at that first meeting, and it endured until the end of his life, seven years later. This laughter, springing from a kindred sense of humor, with a compelling physical magnetism, was to thrust itself, as a memory, between me and the fulfillment of any future emotion. . . .

Mammy Wise

For a certain, Mammy Wise was the most seeingest woman in the Valley or that ever lived.

She was a big woman, a tall woman, and had white hair as coarse as so much rope. She had black beady eyes and looked dark as an Injun. Nobody didn't know how old she was, because she was already living when everybody in the Valley was borned and she couldn't tell nobody her age because she didn't know it her own self.

Folks come for miles around for her to blow in the mouths of their young'uns to cure the rash. Mammy claimed she was borned after her pappy died was the reason she could do that. Nor curing rash wasn't all she could do. Folks come from clear over in the next county to git Mammy Wise to sooth up something that was troubling them. And she always spelled up the truth too. Like the time before the Civil War when she went into a fit and spelled up the whole dang war. Said she seen a star from the north sky travel clean acrost the heavens and run smack dab into a star in the south end of the sky.

"They is shore trouble a-brewing betwixt the North end of America and the South end of America," she said. "I done spelled it up and what I spell up always happens for a fact."

And that war *did* come for a fact, just like old Mammy Wise said.

People got to pestering her so about going into a trance to spell up something that was bothering them that Mammy got to charging. Not money, because folks in the Valley most never had none, but they fotched over maybe a gallon of lasses or a peck of taters or a turn of meal, and Mammy's cupboard was always fat with vittles on account of it.

Mammy always meant good when she spelled up things, but even the truth will hurt somebody sometimes. Like when Hog Bittle come from acrost the Valley a far piece to see Mammy and says, "I shore been hard hit, Mammy. I need yore seeing help the worst kind."

"Signs is right for soothing," says Mammy. "What lays on yore brain, Hog?"

"Well," says Hog, "I had nigh onto forty dollars of money tied up in a yarn sock and it sticking in under the old shuck bed me and Ida sleeps on. Now it's gone. See if you can spell up where it went to. I know I ain't spent it."

Well, old Mammy's eyes begun to git set in her head like as if she was dead and ripe to bury. Then her hands begun to shake and pretty soon, when she quit shaking and was almost as stiff as a corpse, she begun to mutter something nobody but a soothsayer knowed what it was.

Then she speaks out loud, "I see a woman with yeller hair a-going to a shuck bed. She gits the money, but it ain't forty dollars. No it ain't but twenty-five there in the first place. It's a dark night. This yeller-hair woman puts the money in her bosom, sock and all. She slips down to the barn and gives it to a raggedy young feller with yeller hair, and he shore is lean looking too. And that's just where yore money went to for a certain."

Then Mammy shaked herself just like a dog a-shaking water and her eyes come back to their natural place. She says, "Did I help you out any, Hog?"

"Help me!" says Hog. "You shore did! I aim to go home and whup that woman of mine. I doggies, I'll frail her with a limb for handing out my money to that yeller-headed hossthief of a fugitive from justice of a son of hers!" And Hog he went off a-spitting fire.

Wasn't nothing Mammy could say that would tame him down neither, and the very next day when Old Lady Allen went santering over to the Bittles' to borry some lard or whatever, she found that Ida was some stove up.

So after that old Mammy tried to be keerful what all she spelled up. "It's like as if I'd done the flogging myself," says she. "But what I see—I see!"

And folks noticed she did sort of ease up on things after that. She started spelling up mostly good things and trying to help them that was troubled in mind.

Like when Miss Ruthie Bottoms went over calling on Mammy. Miss Ruthie was one of the old-maidest old maids ever was. So Mammy seen her ambling towards her shanty in the cove and knowed she was in for a evening of listening to griping and complaining.

"I aim and intend," says Mammy, "to put a little hope in that old maid's heart. No harm in that, surely now. Just pretending so as she'll sort of have something to live for."

Well, Miss Ruthie Bottoms come a-walking in the house as stiff like as if ever joint in her body was about to crack in two, which was the way she always walked.

Mammy Wise says, "What's on yore brain today, Ruthie?"

Ruthie says, "Just worry and lonesomeness is all. I know I'm the lonesomest person ever lived. All the other gals got men but me. Not a mortal soul to be my company since Ma and Pa died off. Guess it's the Lord's will for me to live and die alone."

"Now, Ruthie," says Mammy, "who's the best soothsayer in this Valley? Who, I ask you, who?"

"Why you are, Mammy, for a certain," says Ruthie.

Mammy she then says, "Set right where you are and I'll see what I can spell up." So Mammy Wise went through all her doings of blinking her eyes and them setting in her head and her a-shaking all over.

Miss Ruthie was just aching for her to start telling her about a man, and she done it, Mammy did. She says, "Go alone of a dark night when they ain't no moon to Lovers' Leap where the Injun lovers jumped off once, and set there until a man comes along. He's yore man for shore."

Then Mammy blinked her eyes and unstiffened herself. Her fit was over and wasn't no use in gitting her to trance on that matter no more. When she was done, she was done.

"Mammy," says Miss Ruthie, "I'm afeard to go to Lovers' Leap of a dark night by myself."

"You want you a man, don't you, Ruthie?" says Mammy.

"I mighty well do, Mammy," says Miss Ruthie.

"Well, go after him then," says Mammy. "Just take him unawares. After all, the other wimmen just surprise the men into marrying up with them. Many's a man unwakened to find his self wedded. It's the same thing."

So Miss Ruthie went away right pert. She didn't mosey along like always. And she got a almanac from the store man to see when the first dark unmoonless night was due.

Now, truth to tell, Mammy thought Miss Ruthie would just sort of wish she had the nerve to go to Lovers' Leap of a dark night. Miss Ruthie never had the nerve to do nothing of a dark night, much less go out on the wild mountainside. Mammy figgered it would keep her hopes going and do no harm.

But come the plumb pitch-dark night and Mammy Wise was wrong for once and not much wrong neither as you will see. Miss Ruthie put on her prettiest bonnet and did for shore start to Lovers' Leap. She was so scared she'd run awhile and then stop and listen if anybody was about or any varmint. When she got near to the rock that stuck away out over the Valley and that folks called Lovers' Leap, she runned faster than ever before. And then Miss Ruthie seen a shadder on the rock which hadn't ought to be there. It was a man-shape shadder and pretty soon hit lit up a pipe and Miss Ruthie knowed it was a flesh and blood living man.

Now, it happened that when this here dark unmoonless night settled down, Mammy Wise got uneasy. "Reckon that feather-headed Ruthie would go out yan to Lovers' Leap?" she says to herself. And finally she knowed she wouldn't have no peace about it. So Mammy just put on her shawl and hurried over to Miss Ruthie's. Sure enough Miss Ruthie was gone.

"If that don't just beat the old hen a-loping!" says Mammy. So Mammy Wise cut through the backtracks and cross-timbers to Lovers' Leap to bring Miss Ruthie back before the night air give her her death.

And just as the old lady got near to Lovers' Leap, she heared Miss Ruthie scream and a man beller and a mule *he-honker*. And then there was the sound of hoof-tracks a-flying down the mountainside.

Mammy was too dumbfoundered to holler out anything to stop Miss Ruthie from being kidnapped. She was the most took back she had ever been in her whole life and tried to follow which way Miss Ruthie and that man went but they was too fast for her and got clean out of hearing.

She went back to the Valley settlement right fast for an old woman that didn't even know how old she was and pounded on ever door anywheres until she roused up the biggest posse that ever ganged up to git man or beast.

"Can't you tell us nothing more than that, Mammy?" the men says. "How come her to go over there noways? Sounds like some of yore funny work, Mammy."

The looks they give her was enough to kill her dead. Mammy was scared to tell the folks she had been just making like she had spelled up a man for Miss Ruthie. She knowed they might flog her like they done to witches years ago, specially if Miss Ruthie was any harmed. She said she didn't know a thing. But she rid out with the posse.

Well, that posse combed them mountains from the far side to the back side. And no Miss Ruthie.

"Pore Miss Ruthie," Mammy said. "She always wanted a passel of men chasing after her and she's shore got them doing it now. But, pore thing, she can't enjoy it. Most likely she's dead and throwed in some lonesome hole by now."

Mammy and the posse tracked mule tracks here and yon and still never found no tall lanky lean pore skinny figger of pore Miss Ruthie stretched out somewheres with her brains battered out with a rock like they was looking for.

Mammy was feeling sorrier and sorrier that she had tried to help up Miss Ruthie's heart.

Well, the posse and Mammy they hunted the rest of the night and till near midday the next day and then frazzled out and decided to go back in towards the Valley and git a bite to eat.

"Maybe she's broke loose from that thieving woman-grabber," they said, "and got home herself footback." But wasn't much hope and it was shore a sorrowful bunch that rid back up to Miss Ruthie's cabin.

"Smoke's coming out of the chimney like it was last night, like as if the fire is a-waiting for her," Mammy says sort of absent-minded to herself.

So some of the posse heard her. "Like last night, Mammy?" they says. "Was you over to her house last night?" And Mammy just decided to tell it all.

"Let's go inside and set a spell," she says. "I'm about winded now, and hungry, too. Then I got something to say, folks. A sorry mess I've made of things. A mighty sorry mess."

Then Mammy opened the door to Miss Ruthie's cabin and let out a screech like a painter and looked like as if she'd seen a ghost. For there set Miss Ruthie on the sparking chair she'd owned all them years without nobody to spark with.

Leastways a man set on the sparking chair and Miss Ruthie in his lap.

"Land a-living!" says Mammy. "If you knowed how we been scouring the woods for yore dead body and you here a-carrying on with a man like this! It's a double twisted shame, that's all!" And Mammy would've said some more but Miss Ruthie aimed to have *her* say.

Just sassy as can be, she says, "You can call me Miz Ab Lingle, Mammy. I've a right good right to set on this here man's lap. Him and me got wedded over at the county seat just like you said, Mammy. You shore spelled up a man for me, for a certain! We rid all night and all morning to git back here and we aim to have a house-warming tonight for shore."

"Well!" says Mammy. "Well! Make us acquainted with your man, Miz Ab Lingle."

"Wouldn't do no good," says Ruthie. "He's deaf and a mite nearsighted and he's still a little drunk. But that's his name, all right, because he had a letter in his pockets. He sobered up a little after we got hitched and said he losted his way is why he was at Lovers' Leap. Course, he don't know it was really you, Mammy, that spelled him to be there."

So Mammy Wise just drawed herself up proud-like and says, "I might've knowed it! Might've knowed this power of mine was too strong to be trifled with. It just taken the bit between its teeth and spelled up that man anyhow!"

Everybody in the whole Valley said it *was* a *mighty* power. It just *had* to be, they said, to sooth up a man that would marry Miss Ruthie Bottoms, drunk or sober.

And nobody couldn't deny Mammy Wise had done it.

Bette Davis on Desire

Most women have a special sexual fantasy. Mine was to make love on a bed covered with gardenias. Once I was involved with a man famous in the music world, a composer and orchestra leader. He was, I suppose, what I had once hoped Ham Nelson would be. We were both married, not very happily, and my marriage was soon to end. His went on. He was one of those who would not leave his wife. I did not expect him to do otherwise.

As we were both famous, our affair had to be a discreet one. Discretion is tiring, often nerve-wracking, and therefore such affairs usually are of limited duration. He wrote a song for me.

One day at the height of our romance, he reserved a suite at the Waldorf-Astoria in New York. To my delight and amazement, the bed was covered with gardenias. When the maids were tidying up the room next day, what did they think of a wastebasket filled with very wilted gardenias?

Long after the affair had run its course, I was in a nightclub where his orchestra was playing. He danced with me and told me that he had written the song the orchestra was playing about our romance. To this day, whenever I hear that song or see a gardenia I think of him.

On my seventy-fifth birthday, I came home after a working day. When I walked into my *salle de bain*, to my utter amazement there was champagne, caviar and a bathtub full of floating gardenias. I counted them. There were seventy-five. There was a note inside one of the champagne glasses saying, "Happy Birthday. See you shortly."

I promised myself years ago that when I was old and gray and looked back on my life, I would have no regrets in the romance area. I have kept that promise. When I fell in love and felt romantically inclined I did not ignore my desires.

There is a song, "Someone to Watch over Me." This, I felt, was the perfect kind of man for me to marry. I never found him. I imagine no man ever felt this way about me, because I was and still am capable of managing my own life and could not imagine I would like to be "watched over." I'm still hoping one day I'll find him. I am the eternal optimist, always have been.

Tallulah Bankhead on Courting

Her staggering eccentricities would become part of her legend; she was blunt, self-made, shrewd and full of life. As an actress she could be very good and very bad. As a woman, she could be unpredictable, tortured, and downright venomous—as a Hollywood legend, she may have been one of the greats of all time. Daughter and granddaughter of U.S. Congressmen, she had little interest in either tact or diplomacy. She did, however, have a dangerously sharp wit, and soon enough audiences would love her for it. First on the stage, later on radio and television, Bankhead developed her public image of the wealthy sophisticate, impatient with niceties and etiquette. Her memoir Tallulah, *though ghostwritten by a man, speaks to that image better than anything she left behind on screen or television. Whether she tells us of love or marriage or life, we are bound to get her point straight on—she was not one for nuance:*

The curious may be muttering, "What about your love life, honey chile? If you were as beautiful as your partisans insist, as magnetic as you hint, as provocative and heretic as you boast, why, at seventeen, weren't you head over heels in love, with a queue of blades panting behind you?"

It's a fair question. Burning with ambition, scorched with the desire to please at whatever cost, why hadn't I capitulated to some ardent young man on his promise that surrender would validate my womanhood, endear me to such Bohemians as scorned conventional sex taboos, add both to my sophistication and my experience?

The truth is that while curious, even eager, I was scared, too. My family, without laying undue stress on penalties, had hinted that New York was booby-trapped with enticements for young girls, particularly young girls who sought advancement in so loose a profession as the theater. I had been hedged in with chaperones, with a grandmother and aunts who still looked upon me as a child—as indeed I was. One false step and I might be withdrawn from the tournament.

I am pleased, as you may be disappointed, to say that at seventeen I was a virgin. I certainly didn't look like one. The screen's sirens and seductresses, those vixens whose physical charms and brazen displays reduced strong men to putty, fascinated me. A virgin at seventeen, I was a technical virgin at twenty, when I took to the deep and London. I use the phrase "technical virgin" advisedly. I had my share of necking. More than once I trembled on the brink of compliance. More than one night I lay in my bed rejoicing in thoughts of conquests, the scandal and stir that would erupt did I bring a great warrior or a great poet whimpering to my couch, desolated because I had denied him my favors.

Don't think from this that I had been baited by any barons, that I had been challenged by any knights. I had been pawed in taxicabs, even found this agreeable. Faced with the great sacrifice, I retreated at the last split second. Later I was to scrap my scruples, indulge myself in my desires, think no less of myself for giving way to a primitive urge. I was a hedonist, long before I knew what a hedonist was.

Amelia Earhart Spells It Out

Relentlessly courted by G. P. Putnam, the well-known publisher and socialite, Amelia Earhart finally agrees to marry him. With her characteristic honesty, she writes him a letter on the eve of their wedding that stands as a succinct manifesto from an independent woman:

Dear GP;

There are some things which should be writ before we are married. Things we have talked over before—most of them.

You must know again my reluctance to marry, my feeling that I shatter thereby chances in work which mean so much to me. I feel the move just now as foolish as anything I could do. I know there may be compensations, but have no heart to look ahead.

In our life together I shall not hold you to any medieval code of faithfulness to me, nor shall I consider myself bound to you similarly. If we can be honest I think the difficulties which arise may best be avoided. . . .

Please let us not interfere with the other's work or play, nor let the world see our private joys or disagreements. In this connection I may have to keep some place where I can go to be myself now and then, for I cannot guarantee to endure at all times the confinements of even an attractive cage.

I must exact a cruel promise, and that is you will let me go in a year if we find no happiness together.

I will try to do my best in every way. . . .

A.E.

Katharine Hepburn on Love

Now I'm going to tell you about Spencer.

You may think you've waited a long time. But let's face it, so did I. I was thirty-three.

It seems to me I discovered what "I love you" really means. It means I put you and your interests and your comfort ahead of my own interests and my own comfort because I love you.

What does this mean?

I love you. What does this mean?

Think.

We use this expression very carelessly.

Love has nothing to do with what you are expecting to get—only with what you are expecting to give—which is everything.

What you will receive in return varies. But it really has no connection with what you give. You give because you love and you cannot help giving. If you are very lucky, you may be loved back. That is delicious but it does not necessarily happen.

It really implies total devotion. And total is all-encompassing—the good of you, the bad of you. I am aware that I must include the bad.

I loved Spencer Tracy. He and his interests and his demands came first.

This was not easy for me because I was definitely a *me me me* person.

It was a unique feeling that I had for S.T. I would have done anything for him. My feelings—how can you describe them?—the door between us was always open. There were no reservations of any kind.

He didn't like this or that. I changed this and that. They might be qualities which I personally valued. It did not matter. I changed them.

Food—we ate what he liked.

We did what he liked.

We lived a life which he liked.

This gave me great pleasure. The thought that this was pleasing him.

Certainly I had not felt this way with my other beaux. I was looking for them to please me. It is a very different relationship. It's like a wonderful cocktail party. But it ain't love.

Luddy loved me—in my sense of the word. He did everything he possibly could to make me happy.

Luddy took care of me and gave me confidence.

I took care of Spencer and gave him confidence.

I shared the two best types of relationships.

I loved Dad and Mother. They always had the last word with me. If they wanted it—I did it. And happily—also they loved me—and I felt this and it made me very happy.

There is an enormous difference between love and like. Usually we use the word "love" when we really mean like. I think that very few people ever mean *love*. I think that like is a much easier relationship. It is based on sense. A blind spot—love.

What was it about him that fascinated me? Well, that is not a difficult question to answer. He had the most wonderful sense of humor. He was funny. He was Irish to the fingertips. He could laugh and he could create laughter. He had a funny way of looking at things—at some things, I should say.

There was a group—Spencer Tracy, James Cagney, Pat O'Brien, Frank Morgan, Frank McHugh. They had a weekly meeting on Thursdays. It was called Irish night. It was at Romanoff's. Sometimes at Chasen's. And *finally* it was at my house when I lived in the Boyer house. I used to go to bed—or clear out and go to another house to sleep. I had a wonderful cook—a great projection room. I'd order the food—get the movie—and there was Irish night. I think it sort of came to an end. Well, we all do just that, don't we? I know that finally I moved out of the Boyer house and down to Spence's tiny house, which we rented from George Cukor. Spence wasn't all that well and it was better to have me there. And there were no more Irish nights.

~

People have asked me what was it about Spence that made me stay with him for nearly thirty years. And this is somehow impossible for me to answer. I honestly don't know. I can only say that I could never have left him. He was there—I was his. I wanted him to be happy—safe—comfortable. I liked to wait on him—listen to him—feed him—talk to him—work for him. I tried not to disturb him—irritate him—bother him—worry him, nag him. I struggled to change all the qualities which I felt he didn't like. Some of them which I thought were my best I thought he found irksome. I removed them, squelched them as far as I was able.

When he was sort of toward the end of his life—his last six or seven years—I virtually quit work just to be *there* so that he wouldn't worry or be lonely. I was happy to do this. I painted—I wrote—I was peaceful and hoping that he would live forever.

What was it? I found him—totally—totally—total! I really liked him—deep down—and I wanted him to be happy. I don't think that he was very happy. I don't mean that he did anything or said anything which would indicate that he was. How can I say—well, who is happy?—I am happy. I have a happy nature—I like the rain—I like the sun—the heat—the cold—the mountains, the sea—the flowers, the— Well, I like life and I've been so lucky. Why shouldn't I be happy?

I don't lock doors. I don't hold grudges. Really the only thing I'm not mad about is wind. I find it disturbing. I mean wind in the heavens.

Spence didn't like cold—he didn't like too much heat—he—well, he liked comfort. I think that states it.

He was a great actor—Simple. He could just do it. Never overdone. Just perfection. There was no complication. The performance was unguarded. He could make you laugh. He could make you cry. He could listen.

Someone once asked me why I said that Spencer Tracy was like a baked potato. I think it is because I think that he was very basic as an actor. He was there skins and all—in his performances. He was cooked and ready to eat. The only person to whom he could be compared is Laurette Taylor.

Now I must add that the baked potato description only refers to the incredible perfection of their performances. In his *life,* Spencer was as far from a baked potato as possible. He was as complicated as a human being could be.

I've just had a thought. He did not—he *could not* protect himself.

How can I explain what I mean? I think most of us have a sort of shell of self-protection. We can hide behind it even when we are acting. Whatever the circumstance, we can protect ourselves. Spence couldn't. He had no shell.

Maybe that is why at his most vulnerable age he liked to drink—and he drank too much at times. He had a strong character. He could stop. And then sometimes he wouldn't have a drink for a long time—a year or two or three. And then—but he'd stop, and finally he didn't do it anymore. He didn't allow himself to get into situations which tormented him.

We made nine pictures together.

Woman of the Year
Keeper of the Flame
Without Love
The Sea of Grass
State of the Union
Adam's Rib
Pat and Mike
The Desk Set
Guess Who's Coming to Dinner

Never rehearsed together at home. Almost never used to discuss the script. It was curious. I always loved to work on the script. Not Spence. He'd read something. Say yes or no. And that was it.

Someone asked me when I fell for Spencer. I can't remember. It was right away. We started our first picture together and I knew right away that I found him irresistible. Just exactly that, irresistible.

His father died before I knew Spencer. I never met his mother. I don't know much about either of them. His father was a heavy drinker. I do not think that he was very close to either of them. Certainly not like my relationship with my parents. He had his brother Carroll, who took care of all the business end of Spencer's career. But they were not really—well, they were entirely different in personality. Carroll was married to a woman whom he had known back home in Wisconsin—Dorothy. I now have a good friend in Spence's daughter Susie. She is quite like him but with an easier nature.

Someone asked me what about Spence and Mother and Dad. Well of course they met. He went to Hartford several times and to Fenwick. But they were never close. I think that they liked him—but Spence felt a bit uncomfortable with them. After all, he was a married man. I don't think that Dad and Mother were bothered too much by this. But there it was as far as Spence went—and he felt uncomfortable—unrelaxed. So we seldom were together when I went home.

I have no idea how Spence felt about me. I can only say I think that if he hadn't liked me he wouldn't have hung around. As simple as that. He wouldn't talk about it and I didn't talk about it. We just passed twenty-seven years together in what was to me absolute bliss.

It is called LOVE.

Tried and True Courtship Superstitions

After you stub your toe, kiss your thumb and face the opposite direction and you'll see your sweetheart.

The person who winks at you with the right eye loves you.

Think of your sweetheart when you have the hiccups. If they stop immediately, he loves you; if they continue, he doesn't love you.

Swallow the heart of a wild duck and you may have whom you want for a husband.

A girl will be an old maid if she is struck by a broom while someone is sweeping.

On seeing a new moon, look over your left shoulder and say:

> New moon, true moon,
> All dressed in blue,
> If I should marry a man,
> Or he should marry me,
> What in the name of love,
> Will his name be.

Then wait patiently. The next name that someone mentions will be the one you're looking for.

Taking cod-liver oil will make a man passionate.

In New Orleans they say that if you want a man to love you always, draw blood from your left hand, write his name and your name in blood. Circle the names with blood. At nine o'clock bury the paper and don't tell a soul and he will always love you. But be sure that is what you want!

If a woman's first toe is shorter than her second toe, she will be the ruler in her future household.

M A R R I A G E

Did you ever hear the story about the patient wife from Texas who was married to a mean rancher? He drank and cursed and stayed out all night and made her life nearly impossible. Folks wondered how she could put up with him but she did for twenty years and, when he turned up in a ditch one day dead of a heart attack, her neighbors breathed a sigh of relief on her behalf. She saw to the details of the funeral and the town turned out to see him go under the ground. On the way to the local cemetery, the hearse hit a bump on the road and jarred the casket loose from the back. It burst through the door and hit the road with a heavy thump; a moment later everyone in the procession was startled to hear the old rancher swearing and pounding on the coffin lid. It appeared that the jolt had got his heart beating again! Well, it seems that coming back from the dead did the rancher no good at all because before long he was worse and meaner than ever. It was another decade before he turned up dead in the ditch again, and again the coroner confirmed that a heart attack was the cause. Once more the patient wife prepared for the funeral and once more readied for the drive to the local cemetery. Just before the procession got under way, however, the wife paused at the window of the hearse and signaled for the driver to roll his window down. "Sam," she told the driver quietly, "This time, let's be sure to take the drive nice and easy." Grim marriage humor, some might say, but even happily married wives will recognize in the patient wife a similar desire to safeguard any opportunity to begin living for themselves, no matter how long in coming.

"The economy, stupid"—a political slogan in the 1990s—has been a truth for American women since Plymouth Rock. From the beginning of American life, marriage was one of the few havens afforded the single woman who otherwise had precious few ways to survive economically in the brave new world. All too often, men controlled the cash and the jobs. It is no heresy to suggest that marriage in America often had less to do with love than with the contracts that men and women made with one another to fend off loneliness, social isolation, or economic deprivation. American men have long struggled with the idea that though marriage was a necessary part of a woman's economic well-being, the institution was by no means the sum of her achievement in life. Throughout American folklore there are countless stories by men about their wives that seem to celebrate qualities more appropriate to a mother than a life partner. Stories abound of the nagging wife, the impatient, scolding, curious, critical, and talkative women who cost a fortune to maintain and leave their husbands little room to pursue their own pleasures. Many wives, on the other hand, must endure these stereotypes before recognizing a woman who might actually represent their own experience of marriage. The following stories are about the challenge of mastering the expectations of others while keeping alive one's own. Consider the enthusiasm of nineteenth-century readers for the account of Ann Eliza Young's defiance of her husband Brigham Young (leader of the Mormon church) as the only woman—after eighteen wives—to divorce him. Over and over again we see a common theme in the stories American wives told one another in letters, diaries, and memoirs: the wish for a life outside the confines of marriage, a life where another self, which had nothing to do with being a wife, a mother, a daughter, or a mate, could be explored and celebrated.

De Tocqueville, the often quoted observer of early American culture, summarized what he thought was the American wife's greatest virtue: "She knows beforehand what will be expected of her, and she herself has freely accepted the yoke. She suffers her new state bravely, for she has chosen it." Not likely. Many American wives are more likely to recognize the truth of Gertrude Atherton's succinct reply to a journalist who asked her opinion of the ideal husband. Atherton is reputed to have said: "Why, no husband at all." Despite the cultural gulf between them, Atherton and our patient Texas wife appear to have much in common.

The Faithful Wife and the Woman Warrior (Tiwa)

A long time ago a band of Apache lived in a place called Namtsuleta, or Yellow Earth. In the band were two young men: Blue Hawk, son-in-law to the tribe, who was married to the daughter of the head chief, and Red Hawk, his friend.

Their tribe was fighting with a fearful and dangerous tribe that lived far away, and the two young men meant to go there and get some scalps. One day they packed their horses and started out. When they camped that night, they talked of what was ahead and what they had left behind.

Red Hawk, the unmarried boy, said to his friend, "As women do, your wife is probably sleeping with another man tonight."

"You may think that, but I never would," said Blue Hawk. "My wife is true to me."

"I'll bet I could go back tonight and sleep with your wife!"

"My friend, you can go back, but she won't accept you."

"I bet she will."

"Well, go and try!" And they bet their pack horses, their food, everything they had with them, and everything they had at home.

So Red Hawk returned to the village and hung around Blue Hawk's tipi. He saw his friend's wife sitting outside, but she never looked at him. Though he kept smiling at her, she ignored him so completely that he was afraid to speak to her.

"She must be as true as my friend said," the boy thought. When he realized that he was going to lose the bet, he went to an old woman in the village. He told her everything—about the two friends' journey and their wager, then about the wife's coldness and his shame.

"Is there any way I can see the girl unclothed?" he asked. "Or if not, can you find out what her body looks like? I'll pay well."

"Yes my grandson, I will find out for you."

Limping along with a cane, her toes sticking out of her shoes, the old woman shuffled past the wife's tipi. "Poor old grandmother!" said Blue Hawk's wife, looking out. She had someone bring the woman inside and fix her a bed of skins in the corner. It was from there late at night that the old one, watching through a hole in her blanket, managed to see the girl undressing.

Blue Hawk's wife had a long golden braid in the center of her abdomen which she unplaited, brushed out, braided up again, and wound around her body five times. As the girl bent and turned, the old one saw that she had a kind of black mark on her backbone.

At daybreak the old woman got up. "Granddaughter, I am going home to feed my turkeys," she said. And she returned to her own house, where Red Hawk had spent the night, and reported all she had seen.

Red Hawk rode back to his friend's camp. "I slept with your wife!" he said, but Blue Hawk would not believe it. "Well, she has long golden hair on the center of her abdomen and a black mark on her backbone."

Silently Blue Hawk dropped his head.

"My friend, you gave your word, and the words of a man are worth a great deal," Red Hawk said.

Then Blue Hawk spoke. "There are my pack horses and my money and everything I was carrying. Take all. We will go back and I will give you everything, money, horses, cattle, and house."

So they returned to the village, and Blue Hawk presented his friend with all his possessions, as one would when making funeral offerings. His wife kept asking, "What are you doing? Why are you giving everything to that boy?" He did not reply but went quietly to work making a huge rawhide trunk. In it he put money, food, and cooking gear.

At last Blue Hawk spoke to his wife. He was going to take a trip on the plains, he said—a long pleasure trip to the water. He asked her to dress in her finest clothes, and then he put her into the trunk too. "I made this case to keep you from the heat of the sun, so you won't get burned," he said.

Blue Hawk hitched a cart to the horses, set out on the trip, heaved the trunk into the first large river they came to, and went back to the tribe. Everyone asked where he had taken his wife and why he had given all his property to Red Hawk, but he would not say.

His silence was not pleasing to the girl's father, the head chief. He worked to make a hole down to the underworld, and then he arranged for his son-in-law to fall into that hole.

On the large river into which Blue Hawk had thrown the trunk, there was a fisherman who hooked something heavy. "A big fish," he said as he slowly pulled. He drew it to the edge of the river, dragged it out, and found that it was a rawhide trunk. To his amazement, a very pretty girl lay inside. He wanted to take her to his camp, but before she would go, the girl insisted on switching clothes with him.

The fisherman's band of Apaches were preparing to go to war, and the girl, dressed in the man's clothes, joined the warriors when they started off early the next morning. On the journey the young men talked among themselves about the handsome, well-dressed stranger. "His eyes look like a girl's," one said. "He moves like a girl," another said. That night when they made camp, a boy finally said, "I'll make friends and see if he is a boy or girl."

Now, the woman had told them that she was a medicine man, and she put her tent apart from the others. She said her medicine was the sun, which is why she carried a white eagle feather. The boy who wanted to make friends went over to her tent and asked if he could sleep there. After they went to bed, the boy stayed awake all night waiting for the stranger to fall asleep, but she never did. Whenever he moved slowly toward her and put his arm over her, she would say, "Don't do that!" After a while he would try again, and she would say, "Why don't you go to sleep?" That way they passed the night. In the morning the boy confessed his failure to the other warriors, and the next night another young man made the same unsuccessful attempt. Every night of the journey, a different boy tried fruitlessly to discover the stranger's true sex.

Finally the band of warriors reached enemy country. The medicine man ordered his tent pitched apart from theirs and warned them to stay inside their tents and be silent. Once she was alone, the girl spat medicine in the direction of the hostile tribe and in this way, with no assistance, killed off all their enemies.

She gave a war whoop, at which all the young men emerged from their tents. "I fought a big battle and killed them all," she announced. "Now I will go to the dead and cut off their ears, every one, and take their shields, bows and arrows, and war clubs." She did, and took their scalps too. When the war party returned home with the scalps, the grateful chief picked out a young warrior to escort her back to her home, but she refused a guard and asked only for a good horse.

At last she took off her man's clothes, and there she was, the faithful wife whose husband had thrown her into the river. "Though I am a girl," she said, "I did all the fighting for your young warriors. I killed your enemies—here you have their scalps and ears and weapons. My husband was once Blue Hawk, but you shut him up in the dark because of the trick that Red Hawk played on him. Now bring him to me!"

When they brought Blue Hawk, his wife embraced him and cried, because he looked so thin and sad. "You were beaten," she said, "by letting Red Hawk convince you that he knew my body. He deceived you. You know I love you honestly, truly. Now go and get Red Hawk and the old woman!"

The wrongdoers were brought before the couple and the head chief. The girl said to her father, "Tell your boys to get the wildest ponies in the camp!" They fetched the two wildest horses, and she ordered them to tie Red Hawk to the tail of one and the old woman to the tail of the other. Then they turned the horses loose. Off they went, kicking and jumping, and tore Red Hawk and the old woman to pieces, away from the camp.

The Crushed Lily (Chippewa)

A Chippewa woman, the daughter of a chief, and the wife of a warrior, had been cruelly treated by her faithless husband. She was not beautiful, but young and proud, and the mother of a lovely daughter-child. Goaded to the quick by repeated wrongs, she finally resolved to release herself from every trouble, and her child from evil friends, by departing for the Spirit Land, and the Falls were to be the gateway to that promised heaven. It was an Indian summer evening, and nature was hushed into a deep repose. The mother and her child were alone in their wigwam, within sight and hearing of the Falls, and the father was absent on a hunting expedition. The mother kissed and caressed her darling, and then dressed it with all the ornaments in her possession, while from her own person she rejected every article of clothing which she had received from her husband, and arrayed herself in richer garments, which she had made with her own hands. She then obtained a full-blown lily, and crushing its petals and breaking its stem, she placed it on a mat in the center of her lodge, as a memorial of her wrongs. All things being ready, she seized the child, hastened to the river, launched her frail canoe, and in a moment more was floating on the treacherous stream. According to a universal Indian custom, she sang a wild death-song—for a moment her canoe trembled on the brow of the watery precipice, and in an instant more the mother and child were forever lost in the foam below.

"I do."

Two outspoken objections to the time-honored wedding vow. The first is by Elizabeth Cady Stanton, who voiced her eloquent critique a century before it became commonplace to do so. The second is by Amelia Bloomer, a feminist reformer whose determination to wear trousers became a rallying cry for women tired of being confined in traditional female clothing. She edited The Lily, *a nineteenth-century journal dedicated to women's rights and the cause of temperance where "Golden Rules for Wives" was first published. An excerpt follows the Stanton "lesson":*

The Episcopal marriage service not only still clings to the word "obey," but it has a most humiliating ceremony in giving the bride away. I was never more struck with its odious and ludicrous features than on once seeing a tall, queenly looking woman, magnificently arrayed, married by one of the tiniest priests that ever donned a surplice and gown, given away by the smallest guardian that ever watched a woman's fortunes, to the feeblest, bluest-looking little groom that ever placed a wedding ring on bridal finger. Seeing these Lilliputians around her, I thought, when the little priest said, "Who gives this woman to this man," that she would take the responsibility and say, "I do," but no! there she stood, calm, serene, as if it were no affair of hers, while the little guardian, placing her hand in that of the little groom, said, "I do." Thus was this stately woman bandied about by these three puny men, all of whom she might have gathered up in her arms and borne off to their respective places of abode.

But women are gradually waking up to the degradation of these ceremonies. Not long since, at a wedding in high life, a beautiful girl of eighteen was struck dumb at the word "obey." Three times the priest pronounced it with emphasis and holy unction, each time slower, louder, than before. Though the magnificent parlors were crowded, a breathless silence reigned. Father, mother, and groom were in agony. The bride, with downcast eyes, stood speechless. At length the priest slowly closed his book and said, "The ceremony is at an end." One imploring word from the groom, and a faint "obey" was heard in the solemn stillness. The priest unclasped his book and the knot was tied. The congratulations, feast, and all, went on as though there had been no break in the proceedings, but the lesson was remembered, and many a rebel made by that short pause.

—Elizabeth Cady Stanton

Golden Rules for Wives

. . . *F*augh! on such twaddle! "Golden rules for wives"—"Duty of wives"—how sick we are at the sight of such paragraphs! Why don't our wise editors give us now and then some "golden rules" for husbands by way of variety? Why not tell us of the promises men make at the altar, and of the injunction "husbands love your wives even as your own selves?" "Implicit submission of a man to his wife is disgraceful to both, but implicit submission in a wife to the will of her husband is what she promised at the altar." What nonsense!—what absurdity!—what downright injustice! A *disgrace* to a man to yield to the wishes of his wife, but an *honor* to a wife to yield implicit obedience to the commands of her husband, be he good or bad—just or unjust—a kind husband, or a tyrannical master. Oh! how much of sorrow, of shame and unhappiness has such teachings of the above occasioned. Master and slave! Such they make the relationship existing between husband and wife;—and oh! how fearfully, cruelly has woman been made to feel that he who promised at the altar to love, cherish, and protect her, is but a legalized master and tyrant. . . .

Ah! that little word *"obey"*—how much mischief has it done!—how much wrong and injustice has it sanctioned!—how many lives has it embittered!—to how many joyous, happy, confiding women has it brought a life of trial suffering and wretchedness—and finally an early grave! It is the great cause of domestic bickerings and unhappiness—of quarrels and separations—of undutiful, immoral and vicious children. . . .

Oh! it should be a shame to a man to admit that he regards his wife as his inferior, and that he requires submission from her to his will. And the day will come when men will blush to own that they have wives whom they can treat like children, or slaves; and when woman will blush—yea utterly refuse to promise obedience to the man with whom she unites her destiny, and scorn to be treated as an inferior and subject. . . .

Let men be to their wives, what they would that their wives should be to them.—This is the only "golden rule" worthy to be observed, and the only one that will guide to esteem and true happiness.

—*Amelia Bloomer*

Lucy Stone's Horror of Being a Legal Wife
(1854)

Judge for yourself whether Lucy Stone is any less significant than Elizabeth Stanton and Susan Anthony, her better known comrades in the suffrage movement. A leader in the crusade for the right to vote, Stone broke with Anthony and Stanton over the Fifteenth Amendment. Both argued correctly that with no reference to gender, the amendment would give the vote only to African American men. Stone pointed out, however, that the passage of the amendment was a good start, and she believed the republicans who promised that after giving the black man the right to vote women were to be next. Stone misjudged the politics, and the leadership of the suffrage movement broke into two competing camps. It would be 1890 before the break was mended.

Born into a large Massachusetts family, Stone first had to fight for a right her brothers took for granted: the right to a college education. She was the first woman in the history of Massachusetts to receive a college degree (which she actually got at Oberlin in Ohio). Dedicated to the cause of anti-slavery, Stone soon earned a reputation as a persuasive and entertaining public speaker, and she traveled across the nation giving lectures. She was avidly pursued by Henry Blackwell (brother of the first female physician in America, Elizabeth Blackwell, also an extraordinary woman). Blackwell was much younger and did not rest until she agreed to marry him. They married and protested the marriage at the same time by publishing their manifesto on the prohibitive commandments of the ceremony. Stone also retained her own name, a bold decision that shocked many people of the time. She also refused to pay property taxes (arguing, in the best American tradition, that "taxation without representation" was a guiding principle) and much of her property was impounded. The letter below to the man she would marry speaks to her independence.

Lucy wrote the following letter to Henry, whom she called Harry, from Zanesville, Ohio:

> Tuesday evening 10 o'clock P.M.
>
> My last lecture is over, until the 10th of May. And I am so glad! I have dreaded these lectures, more than I can tell. But they are past, and very well too. Thank fortune! Now, Harry dear, I wish you were here, for an hour, & I would tell you

why, in *this* letter, I ask you to come east, and in the *last,* said I did not think it best. I said to myself, "it will cost Harry $50. to come east. It is not likely that he will get that value in return, for however much I love him, (and he is very dear to me,) the horror of being a legal wife, and the suffocating sense of the want of that absolute freedom which I now possess, together with the revulsions of feeling which continually re-cur, and the want of certainty that we are adapted, will never allow me to be his wife. And if he were sure that I would not be, he would not desire to come."

Now Harry, I have been all my life alone. I have planned and executed, without counsel, and without control. I have shared thought, and feeling, and life, with myself alone. I have made a path for my feet which I know is very useful; it brings me more intense & abundant happiness by far, than comes to the life of the majority of men. And it seems to me, I cannot risk it by any change. And when I ask, *"can I dare* to change," it rings an everlasting *"no."* And then I do not think it best, for you to spend time, and money, in vain. And so say, "don't come." I have lived alone, happily and well, and can still do it. I have always been superior to circumstances, and can con-tinue so. My life has never seemed to me, a baffled one, only in hours that now and then come, when my love-life is con-sciously unshared. But such hours are only as the drop to the ocean. The great whole of my life is richly blest. Let it remain so. And then again, I say, "don't come." But when I know by your letters that you do not understand me, I long for *one more* talk in freedom, and blame me, for desiring it, at so much cost to you. If there were any way, to see you, without scandal, before I leave, but there is not. So do as you please. Come east, or not.

I sympathize most fully with you dear Harry, in your struggle, and desire to make your life wholly beautiful. What we earnestly strive after, we *can* attain. "All things are possible to him that *wills."* We sometimes succeed in the *great* matters and fail in the lesser. "The *little* foxes spoil the vines." But I *expect,* that as you cultivate steadiness of purpose and deliberation, and love of & *trust in* the Truth, *without regard* to *conse-quences,* that you will find your life, most beautifully sphering itself about the Central Life, finding *all* its *true* relations, and in each, blessing, and being blessed. Good night and may all the good which a noble life deserves, be abundantly yours. . . .

> With love to the household,
> Yours truly,
> Lucy

Georgia Marriage Ceremony (With a Southern Accent)

By the authority vested in me as an officer of the State of Georgia, which is sometimes called the Empire State of the South; by the fields of cotton that spread out in snowy whiteness around us; by the howl of coon dogs, and the gourd vine, whose clinging tendrils will shade the entrance to your humble dwelling place; by the red and luscious heart of the watermelon, whose sweetness fills the heart with joy; by the heavens and earth, in the presence of these witnesses, I pronounce you man and wife.

Female Ingenuity under Pressure (1832)

A young lady, newly married, being obliged to show her husband, all the letters she wrote, sent the following letter to an intimate friend:

> *"I cannot be satisfied, my Dearest Friend!*
> *blest as I am in the matrimonial state,*
> *unless I pour into your friendly bosom,*
> *which has ever been in unison with mine,*
> *the various deep sensations which swell*
> *with the liveliest emotions of pleasure,*
> *my almost bursting heart. I tell you my dear*
> *husband is one of the most amiable of men.*
> *I have been married seven weeks, and*
> *have never found the least reason to*
> *repent the day that joined us; my husband is*

in person and manners far from resembling
ugly, cross, old, disagreeable and jealous
monsters, who think by confining to secure;
a wife, it is his maxim to treat as a
bosom-friend and confidant, and not as a
plaything or menial slave, the woman
chosen to be his companion. Neither party
he says ought to obey implicitly;—
but each yield to the other by turns—
An ancient maiden aunt, near seventy,
a cheerful, venerable, and pleasant old lady,
lives in the house with us—she is the de-
light of both young and old—she is ci-
vil to all the neighbourhood round,
generous and charitable to the poor—
I know my husband loves nothing more
than he does me; he flatters me more
than the glass and his intoxication
(for so I must call the excess of his love,)
often makes me blush for the unworthiness
of its object, and wish I could be more deserving
of the man whose name I bear. To
say all in one word, my dear,—and to
crown the whole, my former gallant lover
is now my indulgent husband, my fondness
is returned, and I might have had
a Prince, without the felicity I find with
him. Adieu! may you be as blest as I am un-
able to wish that I could be more happy."

N.B. The key to the above letter is to read the first, and then every alternate line.

On Behalf of Women Abused (1852)

"Though woman needs the protection of one man against his whole sex, in pioneer life, in threading her way through a lonely forest, on the highway, or in the streets of the metropolis on a dark night, she sometimes needs too, the protection of all men against one."

"I'd salt his coffee . . ." (1853)

"If your husband looks grave, let him alone; don't disturb or annoy him."

~

Oh, pshaw! when I'm married, the soberer my husband looked, the more fun I'd rattle about his ears. *"Don't disturb him!"* I guess so! I'd salt his coffee—and pepper his tea—and sugar his beefsteak—and tread on his toes—and hide his newspaper—and sew up his pockets—and put pins in his slippers—and dip his cigars in water—and wouldn't stop for the Great Mogul, till I had shortened his face to my liking. Certainly he'd "get vexed," there wouldn't be any fun in teasing him if he didn't, and that would give his melancholy blood a good healthful start, and his eyes would snap and sparkle, and he'd say, "Fanny, *will* you be quiet or not?" and I should laugh and pull his whiskers, and say, decidedly, *"Not!"* and then I should tell him I hadn't the slightest idea how handsome he looked when he was vexed, and then he would pretend not to hear the compliment—but would pull up his dickey, and take a sly peep in the glass (for all that!) and then he'd begin to grow amiable, and get off his stilts, and be just as agreeable all the rest of the evening *as if he wasn't my husband,* and all because I didn't follow that stupid piece of advice, "to let him alone." Just as if *I* didn't know! Just imagine *me,* Fanny, sitting down on a cricket in the corner, with my forefinger in my mouth, looking out the sides of my eyes, and waiting till that man got ready to speak to me? You can see at once it would be—be—. Well, the amount of it is, I *shouldn't* do it.

Fanny Fern

"Drive on."

In Virginia, when folks talk of a stormy marriage, they often talk of Colonel John Custis and his wife Frances Parke who resided in the beautiful mansion called Arlington (one day to be owned by Robert E. Lee). Legend has it that they would go for weeks at a time without speaking to one another—often passing messages between them via their servants. It got so bad that they had to go to court—she to get more property and allowance from him, he to keep her from stealing things from the beautiful estate of Arlington where they lived together. They both swore before a judge not to call each other "vile names" and to "behave themselves." The best story from their marital furies was the time that he asked her to take a Sunday drive with him. Wary that in the midst of a silent feud he should seek her company at all, she nevertheless climbed aboard the carriage in her elegant gown with her dainty parasol. After a brief ride, Custis drove the carriage off the road and out into the Chesapeake Bay without a word. "Where are you going, Mr. Custis," Parke asked as the water rose over the axle. "To hell, Madame," he answered. "Drive on," she is reputed to have said coolly. "Any place is better than Arlington." As the carriage went still deeper into the Bay (the poor horse finally having to swim), Custis said, "I believe you would just as soon meet the Devil himself, if I should drive to hell." "Quite true, Sir," came Parke's immediate reply, "I know you so well I would not be afraid to go anywhere you would go." He turned the horse back towards the shore.

My Opinions (1873)

Little known now, Marietta Holley was one of America's celebrated humorists in the late nineteenth century. The most famous character she created was "Samantha Allen" or "Josiah Allen's Wife," and this nosy, morally indignant and outspoken woman is a character in the best tradition of Mark Twain and Artemus Ward. In fact, the American Publishing Company, Twain's own publisher, immediately recognized that Holley's comic inventions were sharp and on the mark. Women's rights and temperance were the two themes Samantha Allen lived by, though her wit took her far afield and left many a public figure ridiculed. Interestingly, Holley would become fabulously successful with a series of Samantha books, but as the new century dawned, her comic techniques would lose their luster. She died in 1926.

The preface below is to her first book, My Opinions and Betsy Bobbet's, *and renders the voice of Samantha in its richest humor:*

Preface

Which is to be read, if it haint askin' too much of the kind hearted reader.

In the first days of our married life, I strained nearly every nerve to help my companion Josiah along and take care of his children by his former consort, the subject of black African slavery also wearin' on me, and a mortgage of 200 and 50 dollars on the farm. But as we prospered and the mortgage was cleared, and the children were off to school, the black African also bein' liberated about the same time of the mortgage, then my mind bein' free from these cares—the great subject of Wimmen's Rites kept a goarin' me, and a voice kept a sayin' inside of me,

"Josiah Allen's wife, write a book givin' your views on the great subject of Wimmen's Rites." But I hung back in spirit from the idea and says I, to myself, I never went to school much and don't know nothin' about grammer, and I never could spell worth a cent."

But still that deep voice kept a 'swaiden me—"Josiah Allen's wife, write a book."

Says I, "I cant write a book, I don't know no underground dungeons, I haint acquainted with no haunted houses, I never see a hero suspended over a abyss by his gallusses, I never beheld a heroine swoon away, I never see a Injun tommy hawked, nor a ghost; I never had any of these advantages; I cant write a book."

But still it kept a sayin' inside of my mind, "Josiah Allen's wife write a book about your life, as it passes in front of you and Josiah, daily, and your views on Wimmen's Rite's. The great publick wheel is a rollin' on slowly, drawin' the Femail Race into liberty; Josiah Allen's wife, put your shoulder blades to the wheel."

And so that almost hauntin' voice inside of me kept a 'swaidin me, and finally I spoke out in a loud clear voice and answered it—

"I *will* put my shoulder blades to the wheel!"

I well remember the time I said it, for it skairt Josiah almost to death. It was night and we was both settin' by the fire relapsted into silence and he—not knowin' the conversation goin' on inside of my mind, thought I was crazy, and jumped up as if he was shot, and says he, in tremblin' tones,

"What is the matter Samantha?"

Says I, "Josiah I am goin' to write a book."

This skairt him worse than ever—I could see, by his ghastly countenance—and he started off on the run for the camfire bottle.

Says I, in firm but gentle axcents, "camfire cant stop me Josiah, the book will be wrote."

He see by my pale but calm countenance, that I was not delirious any, and (by experience) he knows that when my mind is made up, I have got a firm and almost cast iron resolution. He said no more, but he sot down and sithed hevily; finally he spoke out in a despairin' tone, he is pretty close (but honest),

"Who will read the book Samantha? Remember if you write it you have got to stand the brunt of it yourself—I haint no money to hire folks with to read it." And again he sithed two or three times. And he hadn't much more than got through sithein' when he asked me again in a tone of almost agony—

"Who will read the book Samantha after you write it?"

The same question was fillin' me with agonizin' apprehension, but I concealed it and answered with almost marble calm,

"I don't know Josiah, but I am determined to put my shoulder blades to the wheel and write it."

Josiah didn't say no more then, but it wore on him—for that night in the ded of night he spoke out in his sleep in a kind of a wild way,

"Who will read the book?"

I hunched him with my elbo' to wake him up, and he muttered—"I wont pay out one cent of my money to hire any body to read it."

I pitied him, for I was afraid it would end in the Night Mair, and I waked him up, and promised him then and there, that I never would ask him to pay out one cent to hire any body to read it. He has perfect confidence in me and he brightened up and haint never said a word sense against the idea, and that is the way this book come to be wrote.

The Tale of the Wedding Ring

A woman clothed in black sat on a rock beside the road, waiting for the stagecoach. She was young and beautiful, though her eyes were red with weeping over the death of her mother. The funeral had been held, she had said farewell to her father, she was returning to her husband and children—a three-day journey. A man stopped his team and buggy beside her, an old friend of her youth, more than friend once. The stage, he told her, had been rerouted on account of swollen streams. But he would be glad to help her catch it. She climbed into the buggy and sat beside him. Before long they came to a stream whose usually sluggish waters had been whipped by the spring rains into a raging torrent. Bravely the horses plunged through it—only their heads above water. The buggy tipped dangerously. Water splashed around its occupants. At last, wet and cold, they were on the other side. A few miles farther the man turned off the road toward the gleaming white pillars of his plantation home. He would get dry clothes there for them both. Then they would continue their journey—there was plenty of time.

No one knows exactly what happened then behind the white walls of that Big House. All the slaves were away at a baptizing. The man and the woman were alone in there. The woman never came out alive. Most people believe that the man attacked her and that she resisted so strenuously that he killed her. The only certainty is that he hid the woman's corpse. The new shed room behind the house had not yet been completed. He dragged her there and buried her in a shallow grave beneath the unfinished floor. And that very night he got word that the stage had overturned in midstream and all its occupants were drowned. He jumped on his horse and rode over to help in the search for the bodies. His companions said that he worked like a madman.

Everyone believed that the woman had been drowned with the other occupants of the stage, though her body was not recovered. And so her murderer lived on peacefully in his Big House for three years. Then came a season of bad crops, his investments were unfortunate, and he sought to sell his home. When his victim's husband bought it in order that his children might be near their mother's father, he went west. A report came, a few months later, that he had died there.

More years intervened. Then one night old black Aunt Sophie, caring for her young master who had a cold, bore a lighted lamp into the shed room to find an iron, which she would warm and place at his feet. A screech owl hooted outside and, perhaps frightened by the sudden glare, dashed against the window. Down went the lamp as Aunt Sophie screamed and fled. When the fire had been put out a big hole had been burned in the shed room floor. But the shallow grave had not yet been betrayed.

Early's raiders were responsible for the uncovering of the gruesome secret. Word flashed through the Black Belt that the Yankee cavalry were coming and the planters rushed to hide their gold and silver. One of them, remembering the hole burned in his shed room floor, crawled through it and began to dig a cache for his treasures. He unearthed a skeleton and on one ghastly, bony finger he saw a wedding ring—his wife's!

A Joke Only a Wife Could Understand

Scene: A private investigator's office
She: I want you to follow my husband and his girlfriend.
Private Eye: You want a complete report?
She: I certainly do! I want to find out what she sees in him!

The Mountain Man and the Mirror

One time a mountain man found a small mirror—the first one he'd ever seen. He looked in it and said with surprise, "By cracky, it's a pitcher of my old pappy!"

Sentimentally, he hid the mirror under the bed. His wife saw him hiding it. When he went to work the next morning she went under the bed, took the mirror out, looked into it, and snorted, "So that's the old bag he's been chasin'!"

"Pack down the big chest!"

This is one of them step-husband tales. The step-husband, you know: He's the one that steps in when the real husband steps out.

One time there was a woman and she did have her a man, but they were pretty sorry kind of folks—*she* was anyhow. And one day her husband had to go off somewhere. Told her he'd be gone several days. So time he was good-and-gone—that very night, here come a step-husband. That woman she let him in the house, and they went to playin' around and one thing and another. But in a little while they heard somebody walk up on the porch. "Lord-'a-mercy! There's my man!"

That feller jumped out on the floor, says, "What'll I do? Where'll I get? Where'll I hide at?"

She ran up the stairs and he headed right in behind her. She opened a big chest and he rolled in it quick. She let the lid down on him and mashed it shut. Latched it fast. That old chest was half full of quilts and that feller nearly smothered.

So she went traipsin' down again and unbuttoned the door. But it wasn't her man. Hit was another feller had heard her husband was off from home. He was younger and stouter than the first one; so she let him in. Just left that poor feller up there in the chest. And she and the other man they went to playin' around and one thing and another. The one in the chest he kept right quiet. He didn't know no different and he was scared to death it *was* her husband.

Well, there was a window there right at the bed. And the next thing they knew somebody went to tappin' easy-like on a window-light. That man pulled the covers up over his head and laid right still. She opened the window a little crack. Hit was, you might say, step-husband number three. But she didn't care much for this one. He was snag-toothed and baldheaded. "What ye want?"

"I want in."

"Oh law me, no! My man'll be back in tonight."

He kept on beggin' her to let him in and she kept on tellin' him No, till directly he asked her, says, "Well just stick your face out the winder and let me have a big kiss."

That feller inside poked her like he wanted to tell her somethin'. So she told the one outside, says, "Wait just a minute then."

And shut the window to.

The other man whispered to her, says, "Let me over there by the winder. I'll fix him."

Now it was awful thick-dark that night and there was a shade tree had a lot of branches right over that window. So that feller he slipped over there and backed up against the window-sill, pulled up his shirt-tail. Then she opened the window right wide, and he got fixed there. "All right," she says. "Kiss me quick now."

So he did—And the man inside hopped off the sill and she slammed down the window.

The man outside he went off just a-spittin'—and he was mad as time.

Well he went and hunted him up an old pot. Built a fire there just out of sight of the house, and it wasn't long till he had him a pot full of boilin' water. Then he got hold of it with a piece of thick rag and back he went. Tapped on the window again. "What ye want now?"

"I just got to have me another kiss."

"No. Go on now or my man'll be liable to catch you here."

"Aw just give me one more big kiss."

Well that other feller had eased over by the window. He was plumb tickled about makin' a fool of him twice. So he got fixed again and then she says, "All right, honey."

And—Kerslosh!—he let that scaldin' water fly.

That poor feller inside he went to jumpin' up and down and tearin' around knockin' over chairs and a-hollerin', "Fire! I'm on *fire!*"

The man upstairs heard all the racket, and he thought the house had caught on fire. So he hollered out, "Pack down the big chest! Don't forget the big chest! Some of ye run up here and pack down the big chest!"

The man that got burnt he thought it was a ha'nt [ghost] and he left there in his shirt-tail a-goin' *whippity-cut!*

Number three he went on about his business I reckon. And after that woman had got done laughin' she went and unlocked the big chest. She told that'un what-'n-all had happened, and they both had to sit there on the loft floor and laugh some more.

Well, they fin'lly went back downstairs and got to playin' around and one thing and another—and they're at it yet, I reckon.

𝑀other 𝒥urgenson: 𝒯he 𝒬ueen of the 𝐵ull-𝒲hackers

She was a huge, raw-boned, muscular woman, homely enough to excite pity; as untidy as a Sioux squaw and as fond of chewing tobacco as any woman is of drinking her tea—every inch a queen if these be our standards. Such was Mother Jurgenson, and she was the only woman who ever drove a bull team hauling freight for pay; perhaps this is the reason why she was called Queen.

Nearly all of the freight shipped into the Black Hills before the advent of the railroad was hauled by bull teams. Certainly no more forlorn and pitiable looking animals were ever seen on the face of the earth. The animals grazed their own subsistence when they should have been resting, and could thus transport goods for much less cost than horses and mules that had to be fed. When the grass was short the poor animals were almost starved, and it required all the encouragement of those cruel black-snake whips to keep them moving and pulling their share of the heavily laden wagons. The drivers were of the lowest order of humanity, dirty, rough, and cruel.

Now, as I said, Mother Jurgenson drove a bull team, and Mother Jurgenson's husband also drove a bull team. He was no handsomer than she, and only more cleanly because, not having her inches, there was less space to be grimy.

He had moods when it was his most agreeable pastime to beat the partner of his daily toils. She must originally have belonged to that class of peasantry in Europe who, travelers tell us, are trained to believe in the supremacy of man, and that it is a husband's privilege as well as duty to chastise his wife. At times the other bull-whackers had noticed a dangerous gleam in Mother Jurgenson's eyes when, at the close of a hard day's work, her husband had whipped her.

On the arrival of the teams in Deadwood, Jurgenson would slip off to the saloon and leave his wife to unload the freight from his wagon as well as her own. Occasionally when very heavy lifting was required, Jurgenson, between drinks, would give his wife valuable advice or hurry her with the work.

One evening, after a very wearisome day's work, Mother Jurgenson was slower than usual about the final unloading. Jurgenson concluded that a little conjugal discipline might quicken her movements, but as it happened, he struck her just one too many times; like a tigress she sprang upon him and rained blow upon blow and fairly wiped the earth with him, while the crowd cheered her on. Jurgenson's astonishment was soon followed by pleas for mercy, but mercy was not for him. Finally, from sheer exhaustion, she ceased, and gathering what remained of her liege lord, and holding him at arm's length, said: "Old man, henceforth I'm boss; you play me for meeks again and I'll break every bone in your cowardly body."

After this there was a great change in the financial condition of the Jurgenson family. Mother Jurgenson collected all the freight bills; she allowed her husband a limited allowance to spend in the saloons, while she unloaded the freight, bought needed supplies, and did the banking. When all the business was transacted, and she was ready to start on the overland trip, she would go to the saloon where Jurgenson had been enjoying himself as best he could on his now limited means, and say, "Come, old man, git a move on you"; and he would go at once to his place and drive his bull team right behind hers. She saved money and bought a good ranch, and is now among the prosperous farmers of Dakota.

Tootie Brocker: "Everything we do is half and half."

I was always a tomboy. There wasn't any boy that I couldn't beat up. I kicked football for the football team because I was the only one—including the guys on the team—who could kick half the football field. The football players talked about the girls, how they didn't like the girls, but they never included me with the girls.

I didn't wear dresses to school. Not me. For a long time I was very faithful and wore dresses to weddings and funerals, but that was it. Any more, I don't always wear a dress to those! I was a cheerleader for six years, and I wore skirts for that. And I was prom and homecoming queen. You wore the formals, but you still could be the tomboy.

The first prom I went to, I had just started going with Gordon. It was during calving time and one of their cows was having a caesarean. I'd never seen one, so Gordon and his cousin and this other girl and I all went out to the barn in our formals and watched the operation.

I always thought the biggest thing in my life was to marry somebody who had a ranch. I always said I would never live in town. Gordon had a ranch, and we were in school together. He was really good-looking and he was really popular, so it was a super challenge to see if I could get him. I didn't chase him. I was just always there and always around in the same group. It seemed to work out. We went together six years before we were married. We bought our ranch, though. It wasn't given to us.

Everything we do is half and half. I can do anything on the ranch, and so can Gordon. We each have our areas of expertise, but we can both do everything. There's no hard feelings, there's no bitterness over the fact that it's half and half. Of course, maybe this is a little different here, because I am half owner of this—not because I'm married to him, but because I invested in it. Anything that is signed, or anything that's done, has to be both of us.

It wasn't important to me that I owned half the ranch. It was important that I got to do the work. As far as owning half, I couldn't care less. I always said that if something ever did happen and we didn't get along or got divorced, I didn't want any more than I started with. If I could leave with the horses and the cats, that's all I'd need.

I'm a very stubborn, determined person. I have a mind of my own. Gordon has his ideas and I have mine. Gordon's Irish and I'm Scotch, so one's as stubborn as the other, you know. We have our running battles. Like, we both went to AI school [Artificial Insemination] and I breed cattle one way and he breeds them another. It's best if only one of us goes to the corral at a time. Lots of things like that. But everybody has their say and maybe it's an argument at the time, but the best comes out of it.

I can't imagine a woman living on a ranch and not wanting to know how it runs. If something happened to your husband, you're in for a big surprise and a long ride if you don't know the business. I know from a good example—Gordon's mother. Her husband did everything. He took care of the books, he made all the deals. She never got out of the house. She was a good mother, a good cook, a good housewife. But when he died, she was lost. She had no idea what to do. Consequently, the lawyers took her for a ride and the bankers took her for a ride.

If something happened to Gordon, I know I could run the ranch. I'm a firm believer that you'd better know how to take care of yourself. You better know how, in this day and age. And if you don't, you're out of luck.

Don't Call Him, He'll Call You . . .

Edie and Frank Jones had been happily married for years. They lived on the upper East Side in a stylish New York apartment. When Frank took off on a business trip to Dallas, Edie lamented his departure. She missed him and, since it was one of the first times she had been alone since their marriage, she didn't sleep well. She paced the floor restlessly, read, watched TV, and then counted sheep until early into the morning hours. Finally she arose and decided she would call him at his Dallas hotel. "I'm sure my man misses me as much as I miss him," she thought.

"May I speak to Mr. Frank Jones?" she said to the hotel operator.

Edie waited for some time before the operator came back and said, "I'm sorry, but Mr. Jones doesn't answer . . . and, for that matter, neither does Mrs. Jones."

Don't Move In on My Man

The young screen actress Lauren Bacall was a presence. Her lidded eyes, the gruff whisper, the flirtatious and menacing smile, her intelligence coiled like a snake in the sun. An unforgettable image of a young woman sure of herself and her place in a dangerous world. Yet Bacall acknowledged that the screen persona was based on the woman who "discovered" her, a charismatic socialite named Slim Keith. Keith was a dazzler. Pal of Hemingway, wife at one time to filmmaker Howard Hawks, Broadway's Leland Hayward, and finally Sir Kenneth Keith in London, Slim moved through the high times of the twentieth century with confidence, a touch of abandon, and a shrewd guile. Her memoir (Slim) is filled with steamy vignettes and memorable scenes, including the one below, where Mary Hemingway vividly demonstrates what some wives will do to protect their position:

So there I was, going along with everything, and having, if truth be told, a pretty good time. Betty Bacall was making a film in Granada, so I went and spent a couple of days with her. Ernest was in Málaga for a week or so with a cuadrilla of friends, following the mano a mano between the two great matadors of the day, Luis Miguel Dominguin and Antonio Ordóñez, which resulted in the book *The Dangerous Summer.* At this point he was staying with his dearest friends, Bill Davis and Bill's wife Annie. Betty, who had wanted to meet Hemingway ever since she made *To Have and Have Not,* suggested that we join them. So off we went.

Long experience had taught me to take Miss Mary's temperature immediately; this time, I knew from the moment we arrived that she wasn't too pleased. Not only did she have me to contend with, but I had one of the world's most provocative, witty, and lively women in tow. And that was when Betty wasn't working at it. Here in Spain, invigorated by sun and fresh air, she was looking as handsome as a golden palomino. Any man would fall for her—and Papa did.

Give this to Mary: she didn't crack until our last night in Málaga. We went to dine at the Davises', where we spent a long time at the table, chatting, making jokes, and consuming a lot of rough Spanish wine. No one really noticed when Mary excused herself.

After ten minutes or so, Mary returned. She walked over to Betty, who was seated beside Ernest, and held out two closed fists. "Which hand do you want?" she growled.

Betty, always up for some fun, missed the hostility completely. "I'll take that one," she said merrily, and pointed to the left hand.

Mary turned it over and slowly opened her fingers. In the palm of her hand was a bullet. "That is for anyone who moves in on my man," she said.

There was a deafening silence for what seemed like the longest minute on earth.

"Betty," I said at last, "I think we'd better be going."

Betty readily agreed. I can only imagine what ensued after our departure.

The Eye of the Beholder: Part I

The darkness or the light that comes forth from the one we have chosen to love is our own. We choose our own colors, we paint boldly here, timidly there—we love as we ourselves were loved. The following are two versions of love, one man seen through the eyes of two women who loved him. The man is F. Scott Fitzgerald, American novelist, author of The Great Gatsby, *and the women are his wife Zelda and the companion at the end of his life, Sheila Graham. In the first piece, the transcripts of a meeting between Scott, Zelda, and her doctor, we see that the grim links they forged now bind them both; in the second piece, from Graham's own memoir, we see a different man and a different kind of affection altogether:*

Their confrontation came to a head in one of the clinical conversations that Fitzgerald thought were "barren" and unfair to him. This one was conducted at La Paix between himself and Zelda, with Dr. Rennie serving as a moderator. It was recorded by a stenographer.

Fitzgerald claimed that he was a different sort of person from Zelda, that his equipment for being a writer, for being an artist, was different from hers. . . . He knew she was a drunkard the first time he met her. . . . She was spoiled. She was made the pet of the family and was told she had no obligations. Like all women, she ceased being the prettiest person in the world, ceased to be so at twenty-five, though she still was, to him, the most sexually attractive woman in the world. . . . Writing is a struggle; it was a struggle for him. He was aware that nobody cared about anything anymore. But it was a perfectly lonely struggle that he was making against other finely gifted and talented writers. She was a third-rate writer and a third-rate ballet dancer. . . . He was a professional writer with a huge following. He was the highest paid short story writer in the world.

She said that he was making a rather violent attack on a third-rate talent. . . . Why in the hell was he so jealous? If she thought that about anybody, she wouldn't care what they wrote.

He said that she was poaching on his material at all times. It was as if a good artist came into a room and found that some mischievous little boy had drawn on his canvas.

Well, she said, what did he want her to do?

He said he wanted her to do what he told her to do. That was what he wanted her to do. The doctors and he had agreed that it was extremely inadvisable for her to write any novels that dealt with her insanity or discussed insanity. But one day he had given her a clipping about Nijinsky, and immediately she had decided to write a novel about insanity. She had been sneakingly writing it for several months. It was for her sake that he didn't want her to write a book on the subject and because she knew there was certain psychiatric stuff in his books. She picked up the crumbs that he dropped at the dinner table and stuck them into books. She wanted to write a novel against everybody's advice. . . . Everything that they had done was his—if they made a trip, it was his material. He was the professional novelist and he was supporting her. It was all his material. None of it was her material. . . .

He said that these were bad times, things were hard and tough. . . . He had all the worries that everyone else had—of making a living—and he found that he had an enemy in the family, treachery behind his back, or what he considered treachery.

She said that he thought it was personally all right for him to feel that way, for him to accuse her of everything in the world—with having ruined his life, not once, but over and over again.

And when, he asked, did that first happen?

She said that it was last fall. That he had sat down and cried and cried. That he had been drunk and said that she had ruined his life and that he did not love her, that he was sick of her and wished he could get away. He said it again when he came back from New York, drunk again—and that, she said, was the kind of life she was expected to live with him, making whatever adjustments she could.

What, he asked, did she think had caused those two episodes?

She said it was impossible to live with him. She would rather be in an insane asylum—where he would like to put her.

What, he repeated, did she think caused those episodes?

She said that it was his drinking. That was what she thought was the cause. She was perfectly willing to put aside the novel, but she would not have any agreement or arrangements, because she would not submit to his neurasthenic condition and be subjected to these tortures all the time. She could not live in that kind of a world and she would rather live in any insane asylum. That was her last word on the subject.

He said that their sexual relations had been very pleasant until he got the idea that she was ditching him. They were all very nice till then, weren't they? he asked her.

Well, she said, she was glad he considered them satisfactory.

He said he wanted her to stop writing fiction. . . . Whether she wrote or not did not seem to be of any great importance.

She said that nothing she did seemed to be of any great importance.

Then why, he asked, didn't she drop it?

Because, she said, she didn't want to live with him. Because she wanted to live some place where she could be her own self.

Would she like to go to law about it? he demanded.

She said, Yes, she would. . . . The only thing was to get a divorce, because there was nothing but ill will on his part—and suspicion.

He said that he was perfectly determined to take three or four drinks a day. . . . If he should stop drinking, her family would always think that he was acknowledging that he was responsible for her insanity—and so would she. And it was not so.

She said that the problem was that he had not written his book and that if he would ever get it written, then he wouldn't feel so miserable and suspicious and mean toward everybody else.

He said that it had to be unconditional surrender on her part. That was the only promise he could accept. Otherwise he would rather go to law, because he didn't trust her. . . . The unconditional surrender was that she would have to give up the idea of writing anything. . . . She was only to write when, under competent medical assistance, he said that she could write. That might sound awfully egotistical, but that was the only way he could ever organize his life again.

She said that she wanted to write and she was going to write. She was going to be a writer—but she would not do it at his expense if she could possibly avoid it. She would agree not to do anything he did not want—a complete negation of self—until his book was out of the way, because the thing was driving her crazy as it was. . . .

He told the doctor that she always claimed that she was working to get away from him. That was the thing that stuck with him.

She told the doctor that it wasn't true. . . . The truth of the matter was that she always felt some necessity for the two of them to be on a more equal footing than they were. . . . She simply could not be completely dependent on him, when he did not care anything about her and reproached her all the time. . . . When he said something that was not so, then she wanted to do something so good that she could say, That is a goddamned lie—and have something to back it up. . . .

Now, he said, we have found rock bottom.

What is our marriage anyway? she asked. It had been nothing but a long battle ever since she could remember.

He said he didn't know about that. He said, We were about the most envied couple in America around 1921.

She said, I guess so—we were awfully good showmen.

He said, We were awfully happy.

The Eye of the Beholder: Part II

I did not hear Scott return. "I'm going to Schwab's for cigarettes," he had said, twenty minutes before. It was a Thursday afternoon in November, a dull, gray day, and I was curled up on the sofa, listening to the massed voices lifted in the stirring chorus of Bach's cantata *Singet dem Herrn*. Then I looked up. Scott was there, gray and trembling, letting himself slowly into his easy chair. Alarmed, I asked, "Is anything the matter, Scott?" I hurried to turn down the music. He lit a cigarette carefully before he spoke. "I almost fainted at Schwab's," he said. "Everything started to fade." He had never felt quite like that before. "I think I'd better see Dr. Wilson in the morning."

"Scott, I wish you would," I said, thinking, *Scott and his hypochondria.* I tried never to comment on his aches and pains because he was so quick to resent my concern.

In the morning he drove downtown to Dr. Wilson's office. He was back an hour later, his face solemn. He said, "I had a cardiac spasm."

A great pang of fear shot through me. "Is that a heart attack?"

Scott was vague. "No—"

"Did he say you must stay in bed?"

"No," said Scott. He lied, and I did not know. "But I must take it easy. Stairs are out."

I was relieved. Dr. Wilson had not put him to bed. I had read about heart attacks. If you had one, you were sent to bed at once and kept there, flat on your back. Yet Scott must take care of himself. His apartment was on the third floor, mine on the first. "All right," I said. "You move in with me right away." Frances and I would look for a suitable ground-floor apartment nearby. Until then, he would stay with me.

Scott was a difficult patient. As had been the case in New York, he made me promise I would not talk to the doctor alone. "I don't want him telling you anything he wouldn't tell me," he explained. On Dr. Wilson's visits, I was not to take him aside. I never questioned Dr. Wilson about the condition of Scott's heart.

In late November we attended a preview at Metro. As Scott brought his little car to a halt in the parking lot, I suddenly recalled that Metro's projection room was at the top of a long flight of steps. Scott, I knew, would disdain any show of weakness: I had to do something—and I did it. As I got out of the car I cried sharply, "Oh!" and almost fell. I held my ankle. "I've turned it, Scott," I groaned. I played my role well. He helped me as I limped to the stairs and I went up them slowly, one at a time, Scott holding my arm as I rested on each step. We took about five minutes to reach the top. If Scott knew that I pretended for his sake, he never let me know.

Most of the day he took it easy, remaining in bed, writing steadily, keeping Frances busy typing his material. Then he labored over the typed pages with infinite care, revising, rewriting, polishing. He was in excellent spirits. At night I lay awake, thinking. If only the novel could go on forever! I had never seen him so content before. And then I worried. If it was a success, would he drink, to celebrate? If it was a failure, would he begin to drink again, to forget?

Sometimes, however high in spirits, he became unexpectedly, unpredictably, irritable. Once a week I brought fresh flowers to the apartment, filling the vases industriously as I had done at Malibu. One afternoon, as I came in with an armful of flowers from the florist, Scott said, sharply, "Take those flowers away!"

I stared at him. He said, still sharply: "I hate cut flowers!"

"But at the beach—" I began.

"I couldn't stand them there, either."

I was perplexed, but I said nothing. I thought, and all that time at the beach he never said anything.

One afternoon, two weeks before Christmas, I returned from a shopping spree ecstatic over three dresses I had bought. "They're so heavenly!" I described them in detail. "Of course, they're terribly expensive, but they're worth every penny—" I prattled on and he snapped, "Oh, stop talking about it! I don't want to hear about your dresses and what they cost!"

I was taken aback. A moment later he apologized but I had begun to think. I had bought the dresses with my own money. Why should he be annoyed? There had been such anguish in his voice—the words seemed to burst forth despite himself. I asked myself, was it money? Was Scott in financial difficulties? Until he became completely well again, he could not accept any screenwriting jobs. Had he enough money to keep going until he finished his novel? I questioned Frances. And Frances, who paid all of Scott's bills, admitted reluctantly that he had only enough funds to carry him for three months. He would have been in even greater straits had he not had several weeks' work on *The Light of Heart*.

That night I made notes for a letter I would send, when the time came, to Maxwell Perkins, Scott's editor at Scribner's. I had nearly $3,000 saved. I would give $2,000 to Scott, but in such a fashion that he would not know it came from me. I would give it on condition that Scribner's advance $3,000, making $5,000 in all, the entire sum to come from Scribner's in the form of an advance to Scott so that he could finish the first draft of his novel.

My notes for the letter to Perkins read:

Scott never to know, even if book brings back millions. He would never forgive me. If book a success, naturally I'll be happy to get the money back; if not, that is all right, too. Important thing is for him to finish this book. No mention ever to be made of this correspondence—he'd be too humiliated, and might take to drink again, just to prove something. No drinking since last December—more than 12 months now. Been working steadily on book for five months, in addition to what done last year. It would be criminal for him to be forced to go back to a studio which destroys his confidence and may mean he'll never finish book. But all money must come from you. Query: Is it best to wait until Scott asks you for an advance? Or offer it before, in case he doesn't ask? Some tactful way of giving him $1,000 a month for five months. This is better than a lump sum. Use my $2,000 first, so if anything goes wrong, I inform you and you needn't send the rest. At worst I lose two, you lose three. At best, a good novel, Scott reclaims his position as writer and person, and we get our money back. My honest conviction this will be best of all his writing.

Scott struggled with *The Last Tycoon*. He was in the middle of a difficult chapter. The solution he sought would not come. He had been in bed all morning, it was mid-afternoon, he wanted to dictate, and Frances was not there. He was fretful.

I sat on the edge of his bed and stroked his forehead and pushed the hair out of his eyes. "You go to sleep now, and I promise you that when you wake up, Frances will be here and things will seem a lot better." I sat there talking quietly until he became drowsy and fell asleep. I tiptoed out and closed the door behind me.

I phoned Frances. "Please come over. Scott needs you."

He slept for about two hours while I worked on my column. "Sheilo—" he called. When I came into his room he was like a new man, yawning and stretching. "I've had a wonderful sleep," he said. Frances had arrived and waited, ready for dictation.

They were closeted about half an hour; then she left. Scott set up his writing board and began to write energetically. Dr. Wilson was due in an hour to take a cardiogram. Would I telephone him, Scott called, and tell him to come tomorrow? His work was moving too well to be interrupted now.

Not until seven o'clock did Scott rise and join me for dinner. He read me the last paragraph of what he had written. "I've solved it," he said with satisfaction. He was elated, almost exhilarated.

I said, "You see, by just not fretting and taking it easy, you work better."

He kissed me. "Let's celebrate." He was in high spirits. "Let's go out."

I had tickets to a press preview of *This Thing Called Love,* a comedy starring Rosalind Russell and Melvyn Douglas. I hadn't gone to a preview in weeks. A comedy would be just the thing.

Scott dressed. He stood before the mirror fixing his bow tie. He gave it a final tug at both ends and threw a puckish glance at me. I was waiting at the door. "I always wanted to be a dandy," he said, with a grin. That night, Friday night, December 20, we went to the Pantages Theatre and saw *This Thing Called Love.*

When the film was over and the house lights came on, Scott stood up to let me by him into the aisle. I looked back just in time to see him stagger, as if someone had struck him off balance. He had to lean down and grab the arm rest for support. I thought he had stumbled. I hurried back and took his arm. He said, in a low, strained voice, "I feel awful—everything started to go as it did in Schwab's." I held his arm tightly. He said, "I suppose people will think

I'm drunk." I said, "Scott, nobody saw it." I held him under his arm, supporting as much of his weight as I could without drawing attention, and we moved slowly up the aisle. A chill went through me as I realized that he had not pushed my hand away as he had done each time I had tried to help him in the past. I tried to appear in animated conversation with him as we made our way. I thought, furiously, he hasn't taken a drink in a year and now they'll all think he's drunk again.

We walked slowly to his car. The air revived him and he breathed deeply. "How do I look?" he asked. In the powerful lights of the Pantages, I could see him clearly. I said, "You look very pale. Shouldn't we call the doctor?"

Scott said no. Dr. Wilson was coming tomorrow, anyway. Let's not make any fuss.

He drove home slowly and by the time we had arrived, he felt better. He took his sleeping pills, went immediately to bed, and fell asleep.

I went into his room, later, and looked at him. He slept very peacefully, like a tired child.

I did not know that he would die the next day.

Billie Holiday: "Every broad for herself."

A man can leave home one morning and come home that night whistling and singing to find there ain't nobody there but him. I left two men like that.

But John Levy had that hammer at my head. I was tied up a thousand ways. Leaving him had to be the kind of production that would make Liza crossing the ice look easy. He could always turn me in, get me busted, or hit me or something. There were bookings he had made, contracts he had signed for weeks or months in advance. Even if I could have split out I'd have been in a snowstorm of lawsuits and union charges that might have washed up my career. So I had to try to keep my head and untangle myself piece by piece, whittle down the backlog of bookings, keep him happy enough so he didn't kill me.

I was on my own. Nobody could help me.

Weeks later, while fulfilling a booking in the Brown Derby, Washington, D.C., my luck was running bad in one way, good in another. The management of the joint went bankrupt, during my run; when it came time to pay off, they couldn't make both the band and me.

This was a drag. I needed that two thousand dollars as bad as I needed any week's salary I ever made. It was my freedom money. But I couldn't take it and leave the cats of the band all hung. So I told the management to pay the band. They gave me a check that's still bouncing to this day. All the district attorneys have never been able to collect on it.

Mr. Levy had said he had business in New York, so he had left. But I couldn't be sure he wouldn't turn up in the lobby of the Charles Hotel in Washington any minute.

It was cold and there was snow up to your panties over the capital. I had two thousand dollars in the hotel safe downstairs, but I didn't dare touch it. If I did I was sure someone would notify Mr. Levy. He had it locked up where I couldn't touch it. He had taken one other precaution to keep me a prisoner. He had taken my mink coat and hidden it under the mattress. He was sure I wouldn't leave without that.

But I found it, put it on, put my last few dollars in a bag, put my dog under my arm, and walked out in my stocking feet down the fire escape of the Charles Hotel. I didn't have a thing except what I had on my back and that bouncing check. I split for New York with my dog looking over my shoulder.

I thought I was through with men—for sure, forever, and for keeps.

I moved into the Hotel Henry on 44th Street. I was so sure I was going to live the rest of my life there, I wanted it fixed up to suit me. It cost me $450 just to paint the joint. Then I put up drapes, got a few Chinese lamps, and kept buying things to turn that place into something that was mine—my home.

I knew I might have an affair or two here and there maybe, but anything serious—never.

My only company was a cat I liked who sometimes used to help me in and out of my gowns before I went on stage. When he wasn't doing that, he was helping himself in and out of them. We took to calling him Miss Freddy and he was always good for a laugh. He was close enough to my size, too, so a fitter or a dressmaker could work on him and not bug me. He was crazy for a lynx cape I had. It looked better on him than it did on me, too. Although the police didn't always think so. They're so narrow-minded they were always picking on him for being overdressed. I'd have to go down to the station and bail him out—and whatever part of my wardrobe he had on him.

One time I loaned him my mink coat when he was going to that big annual Halloween Ball. Mrs. Sugar Ray Robinson loaned her coat to a girl friend of his for the same ball. After the ball was over and they were supposed to be off the street, these two Cinderellas were hanging out in a bar someplace when the cops spotted them. They made a stand and started throwing garbage-can lids at the cops, so I had to go down again and get my mink coat out of police storage.

But Miss Freddy was good for a million laughs and never hurt anybody except himself—especially when he tried to wear my pumps.

Leonard Averhart used to come around a lot and be my handsome escort. He would stay with me for hours and keep me from being bugged.

Joe Glaser had installed Billy Sharp, the well-known band manager, as my personal and road manager. We played a few tours together, my first date in Miami at Mother Kelly's and other places. While we were playing in Canada I got sore at Sharp. We were due to fly direct to Detroit for an engagement at the Club Juana when I fired him on the spot at the airport.

I didn't have a soul I could get to take care of the endless details of these tours that drag me so. So I finally persuaded a close friend, Maely—who later married Bill Dufty—to come to Detroit with me. She went with me on Billy Sharp's ticket. She had handled other musicians, had been Charlie Parker's personal manager at one time, and she knew the ropes.

It was in Detroit at the Club Juana that I met Louis McKay again. I hadn't seen him since I was sixteen and he wasn't much older and I was singing at the Hotcha in Harlem. But during that date at the Juana, one night Louis was late getting there and I cried like a baby. So I knew my resolutions with men were going down the drain.

It got to be that way, every time I'd give up on him and cry, he'd arrive. So I finally quit fighting it, got a divorce, and we got married.

Sarah Vaughan was unlucky enough to be in an afterhours joint in Detroit that week I was there when the police raided it. With anybody else, this doesn't matter too much. So the joint is behind in its payments for protection, it can happen to anybody.

But all the cops have to do is find a celebrity, and it's page-one stuff. When I heard about it, I happened to see Jimmy Fletcher, a U.S. Treasury agent. I went on my knees to the man.

"You're so big," I said, "you know everybody, do something for that girl. She's clean, she's never been in jail before. Neither have you, and you don't know what it's like. Tonight is Friday, and unless you do something she'll have to stay all weekend in the place waiting for the judge to come to work Monday morning."

Finally Jimmy went downtown and he got her out at nine in the morning. I had Maely call George Treadwell, Sarah's husband and manager, to find out if she'd gotten out. All I wanted to know was if Sarah was all right. George said, "Tell Billie not to worry about Sarah."

It's the easiest thing in the world to say, "Every broad for herself." Saying it and acting that way is one thing that's kept some of us behind the eight ball where we've been living for a hundred years.

Louis and I came back to New York together, and we've been together ever since. I'm not going to try and say we walked off into a storybook sunset. We lived in a hotel for a while. Then we settled down at our own little place in Flushing, where we have our fights just like everybody else.

Ida Tarbell: On the Business of Being a Woman (1914)

Not infrequently she is loath to encourage free expression because it seems to her to disturb the peace. Certainly it does disturb fixity of views. It does prevent things becoming settled in the way that the woman, as a rule, loves to have them, but this disturbance prevents the rigid intellectual and spiritual atmosphere which often drives the young from home. Peace which comes from submission and restraint is a poor thing. In the long run it turns to revolt. The woman, if she examines her own soul, knows the effect upon it of habitual submission to a husband's opinion. She knows it is a habit fatal to her own development. While at the beginning she may have been willing enough to sacrifice her ideas, later she makes the painful discovery that this hostage to love, as she considered it, has only made her less interesting, less important, both to herself and to him. It has made it the more difficult, also, to work out that socialization of her home which, as her children grow older, she realizes, if she thinks, is one of her most imperative duties.

A woman is very prone to look on marriage as a merger of personalities, but there can be no great union where an individuality permits itself to be ruined. The notion that a woman's happiness depends on the man—that he must "make her happy"—is a basic untruth. Life is an individual problem, and con-sequently happiness must be. Others may hamper it, but in the final summing up it is you, not another, who gives or takes it—no two people can work out a high relation if the precious inner self of either is sacrificed.

Tallulah Bankhead on Marriage

I'm given to explosive rages. Three or four times a day I'm irritated to the point I want to commit murder. Shrinking from the penalty, I fall back on my tongue. I'm something of a hellion when I lash out. In these spasms I may get obnoxious. Later I suffer pangs of repentance, save when convinced my opponents have deliberately tried to upend me. Then I go all out—an eye for an eye and a tooth for a tooth. . . .

I doubt I'll ever marry. It's too late for me to adjust myself to the compromises necessary for such a union. I'd be frantic did I have to face the same man over the table every morning. Besides, I always eat breakfast in bed. Aggressive males get up and thresh about and snort under the shower. For a good half of my professional life I didn't know where my next magnum was coming from. I've always been a free agent, aware that whatever my lot, whatever my problem, I was the author. On me the guilt! A husband might have problems of his own. A lot of confusion might ensue when his trials intruded on mine. I've lived for too long, stage center, to submit to second billing. No man worth his salt, no man of spirit and spine, no man for whom I could have any respect, could rejoice in the identification of Tallulah's husband. It's tough enough to be bogged down in a legend. It would be even tougher to marry one.

Besides, I can't cook. I'll settle for that couplet from Kipling: "Down to Gehenna or up to the Throne, he travels the fastest who travels alone." I'm too opinionated, too consuming and demanding a person, to abide by domestic house rules. Those within my sphere of influence are likely to suffer if long exposed. The brave will revolt, the timid crumble. Where would that leave me? That's why I shun permanent attachments, that's why my romantic life is a paradox. The men for whom I have the greatest respect could not long condone my excesses. Those who could would only gain my scorn.

All's Well That Ends Well (1773)

*C*oleman Theeds and Elizabeth, his Wife, having this Day parted by mutual Consent, and given Bond each to the other, the Subscribers being Witnesses to their Agreement, that they will not interfere with any Estate which shall hereafter accrue to either Party, this Notice is given to the Gazette, that no Person, after this Date, may credit the Wife on the Husband's Account, or the Husband upon that of the Wife's. Given under our Hands, this 12th Day of June, 1773.

Richard Beasley

John James

Miss Manners: Weddings the Second Time Around

Your second wedding may be a daytime (informal or formal) affair, or a black tie evening affair. If you wish to get married after six in a floor-length gown with your groom in a black dinner suit, then the invitations should spell it out to the guests by including the words "Black tie," meaning the guests are to come attired in evening dresses and tuxedos. (This is no time for that odious phrase "Black Tie Optional"!)

When a bride is being married for the second time, a full-fledged formal white tie wedding, held at eight o'clock or later, is simply never held.

For a very informal daytime wedding, you would wear a street-length silk dress or dressy suit (a strictly man-tailored style of suit is not appropriate) in an off-white or pastel color (not red or black).

For a more formal, larger afternoon wedding, you might wear a dress of a rather formal fabric (silk, crêpe, chiffon, organza, velvet, brocade, or whatever, according to the season) and in any length you desire, including floor length. For a six-o'clock-or-after wedding, you would wear a long evening dress.

You may carry a bouquet of the flowers of your choice—or a white prayer book with flowered ribbon streamers. You may wear a hat, bandeau, bow, or flowers in your hair, but forget the veil. It is a nice touch if your shoes match your dress. What is inappropriate is to be married in a house of worship wearing a backless dress that is cut extremely low in front, even if you have a great shape and the dress bears the label of the number-one dress designer.

Although the wardrobe departments of Hollywood and TV-land often don't seem to realize it, a woman marrying even for the fourth time should exude a sense of dignity appropriate to the occasion.

Marriage Superstitions

Bury your husband's shoes in the front yard and be sure to point the toes towards the door and he is sure never to leave you.

It is lucky to be married at home.

Brides! Don't look into a mirror on the way to your wedding; it is very unlucky.

Get married in green and it will bring you bad luck.

A bride can get good luck if she jumps over a broom on her wedding day—only after the ceremony!

A bride must not have an uneven number of guests at her wedding.

If your husband leaves the house angry go to a friend's house and eat apple sauce. It works every time—your husband will come home happy.

If your first husband dies, choose your second at his grave and you will have good luck.

A NEW ORDER ARISING

*I am glad that a new order of women is arising
. . . who are evidently sufficient unto themselves,
both as it regards love and bread and butter; in
the meantime, there are plenty of monosyllabic
dolls left for those men who, being of small mental
stature themselves, are desirous of finding a wife
who will "look up to them."*

—Fanny Fern (1857)

F R O N T I E R
J O U R N E Y S

The diaries and journals of the adventurous women who set off into the wilds of Michigan, over the Rockies, or out onto the wide Pacific sea are often quite different from the narratives of the men who accompanied them. Indians, inclement weather, raging rivers, wild animals were not, as they often were for the men, feared forces to be overcome, subdued, before a new life could begin. If men looked to the experience of settling the frontier as a measure of their own success and to the communities they created as the emblem of their victory over a hostile environment, not so the women. Rarely do we find in women's narratives, for example, the tone of the victor over the vanquished; rather we see in their poignant accounts a passion for the details that render the essence of the landscape in all its fearful, mysterious, and surprising aspects.

Here's what we have long known about the journey west, for example: between 1840 and 1870, more than 250,000 people crossed the prairies. On the same day in July, 1863, that the Union and Confederate armies faced each other on the hot, tense field at Gettysburg, more pioneers were heading to California than ever before. The trip lasted from late April or early May to September or October. The timing was crucial: Earlier there would be no grass for the cattle; later winter blizzards would slow their progress or, worse, kill them. The practical costs were high—$500–$1000 for the wagon alone, and the supplies required were daunting: 200 pounds of flour, 150 pounds of beef, 10 pounds of coffee, 20 pounds of sugar, 10 pounds of salt. At the beginning of the journey, the wagon was piled high with baggage and hopes, but the trail's hardest lesson—take only what you need and keep only what you use—exacted an unflinching sacrifice. The trail was awash with the discarded remnants of families, their worldly goods, utensils, and supplies melting away as they pushed west.

For men, the route west was more a political map through mountain passes, across rivers and wide plains; the journey's incidents and adventures had a colorfully generic quality—near misses with death, astonishing incidents in hunting or war—locker-room tales. For women the map was no less precise, but often more internal—there was the place where young Jonathan was buried, where Mother took sick, where we burned the precious belongings we could no longer carry. Details abound that made her journey vivid, immediate: the way that food was cooked or the clothes were washed; how the sick were cared for or the dead were buried; how the children were taught and the families kept together within those fragile wagon trains; the ways in which the religious, cultural, and social links to the world they had left behind would connect with the new world fast approaching. Women shared the perils and jubilation of frontier life with one another, understood the humiliation associated with the lack of privacy on the trail, as well as the backbreaking expectations to maintain an orderly family life in a chaotic, changing environment. As a result, the pioneer experience sparked a profound sisterhood and forged a link among women that made female strangers instantly accessible to one another.

Initially, the frontier woman's tasks accorded her an equal place with her husband. He knew that she was as imperative to the survival of the family as he was, and while her burdens were different, they were respected. The wilds demanded that she look for ways to accommodate herself and her family; thus, every spring was a chance to get her children clean, every rest stop an opportunity to assess the health and fortunes of her neighbors. Encounters with strangers were viewed as a chance for information, connection, or, best of all, news from home. Women, more often than men, felt their obligations to the community they had left behind and carried longingly within themselves the place from which they had come. How typical is the story of Mary Lawrence, the wife of a ship's captain, who, while anchored in a foreign port as her husband was off swapping stories with other sailors, eagerly read an old newspaper from home, only to see a notice of the death of her father (see "Alone on a Wide, Wide Sea"): "It seems as if it could not be," she wrote in her journal, "the thought that he is no more, that he died when I his eldest daughter was far away. . . ."

Once the journeying was over, however, the balanced accord between men and women seemed to slip. The work, the drudgery, the uncertainty, the isolation, the fear, the powerlessness, the waiting, the suffering, and the demands of her children were forces that the frontier woman faced every day while her husband still ranged beyond their new home in search of links to the outside. There is the old, doubtless true, story of the rancher who said: "I can't figure out why my wife went crazy. Why, she ain't been out of the kitchen in twenty years!"

The journey out into the frontier was long and hard and unspeakably sad in places. But women learned that moving on was neither sound advice nor a prescription for survival; it was a gift that led you past what you knew, through what you feared, beyond what you thought you longed for. The following stories touch on the varieties of experience that women faced on the frontier—seeing new sights, surviving great trials, traveling, burying, becoming.

Anna Howard Shaw:
Moving to the Frontier

Though born in England, Anna Howard Shaw (1847–1919) would live out a remarkably American life. She would educate herself and become one of the nation's leading crusaders for women's rights. Her father, who had brought his family to America in 1850 in search of better times, quickly demonstrated that, among other things, he was neither a good businessman nor much of a father. "Like most men," remembered Anna Shaw, his youngest daughter, "my dear father should never have married." Following her father's acquisition of 350 acres of land in Michigan, Shaw became a child of the American frontier. The following is her account of the family's journey to their new home in the wilds of Michigan, made all the more daunting by the absence of her father who had stayed behind to tend to more important matters! "He gave no thought to the manner in which we were to make the struggle and survive the hardships before us," she later wrote. "He had furnished us the land and the four walls of a log cabin." It is no wonder that Anna Shaw became so skilled at carving her own path in life—she had learned hard lessons well:

The move to Michigan meant a complete upheaval in our lives. In Lawrence we had around us the fine flower of New England civilization. We children went to school; our parents, though they were in very humble circumstances, were associated with the leading spirits and the big movements of the day. When we went to Michigan we went to the wilderness, to the wild pioneer life of those times, and we were all old enough to keenly feel the change.

My father was one of a number of Englishmen who took up tracts in the northern forest of Michigan, with the old dream of establishing a colony there. None of these men had the least practical knowledge of farming. They were city men or followers of trades which had no connection with farm life. They went straight into the thick timber-land, instead of going to the rich and waiting prairies, and they crowned this initial mistake by cutting down the splendid timber instead of letting it stand. Thus bird's-eye maple and other beautiful woods were used as firewood and in the construction of rude cabins, and the greatest asset of the pioneers was ignored.

Father preceded us to the Michigan woods, and there, with his oldest son, James, took up a claim. They cleared a space in the wilderness just large enough for a log cabin, and put up the bare walls of the cabin itself. Then father returned to Lawrence and his work, leaving James behind. A few months later (this was in 1859), my mother, and two sisters, Eleanor and Mary, my youngest brother, Henry, eight years of age, and I, then twelve, went to Michigan to work on and hold down the claim while father, for eighteen months longer, stayed on in Lawrence, sending us such remittances as he could. His second and third sons, John and Thomas, remained in the East with him.

Every detail of our journey through the wilderness is clear in my mind. At that time the railroad terminated at Grand Rapids, Michigan, and we covered the remaining distance—about one hundred miles—by wagon, riding through a dense and often trackless forest. My brother James met us at Grand Rapids with what, in those days, was called a lumber-wagon, but which had a horrible resemblance to a vehicle from the health department. My sisters and I gave it one cold look and turned from it; we were so pained by its appearance that we refused to ride in it through the town. Instead, we started off on foot, trying to look as if we had no association with it, and we climbed into the unwieldy vehicle only when the city streets were far behind us. Every available inch of space in the wagon was filled with bedding and provisions. As yet we had no furniture; we were to make that for ourselves when we reached our cabin; and there was so little room for us to ride that we children walked by turns, while James, from the beginning of the journey to its end, seven days later, led our weary horses. To my mother, who was never strong, the whole experience must have been a nightmare of suffering and stoical endurance. . . .

Our first day's journey covered less than eight miles, and that night we stopped at a farm-house which was the last bit of civilization we saw. Early the next morning we were off again, making slow progress due to the rough roads and our heavy load. At night we stopped at a place called Thomas's Inn, only to be told by the woman who kept it that there was nothing in the house to eat. Her husband, she said, had gone "outside" (to Grand Rapids) to get some flour, and had not returned—but she added that we could spend the night, if we chose, and enjoy the shelter, if not food. We had provisions in our wagon, so we wearily entered, after my brother had got out some of our pork and opened a barrel of flour. . . . When the meal was eaten she broke the further news that there were no beds.

"The old woman can sleep with me," she suggested, "and the girls can sleep on the floor. The boys will have to go to the barn." She and her bed were not especially attractive, and mother decided to lie on the floor with us. . . .

At dawn the next morning we resumed our journey, and every day after that we were able to cover the distance demanded by the schedule arranged before we started. This meant that some sort of shelter usually awaited us at night. . . .

In that fashion we made our way to our new home. The last day, like the first, we traveled only eight miles, but we spent the night in a house I shall never forget. It was beautifully clean, and for our evening meal its mistress brought out loaves of bread which were the largest we had ever seen. She cut great slices of this bread for us and spread maple sugar on them, and it seemed to us that never before had anything tasted so good.

The next morning we made the last stage of our journey, our hearts filled with the joy of nearing our new home. We all had an idea that we were going to a farm, and we expected some resemblance at least to the prosperous farms we had seen in New England. My mother's mental picture was, naturally, of an English farm. Possibly she had visions of red barns and deep meadows, sunny skies and daisies. What we found awaiting us were the four walls and the roof of a good-sized log-house, standing in a small cleared strip of the wilderness, its doors and windows represented by the square holes, its floor also a thing of the future, its whole effect achingly forlorn and desolate. It was late in the afternoon when we drove up to the opening that was its front entrance, and I shall never forget the look my mother turned upon the place. Without a word she crossed its threshold, and, standing very still, looked slowly around her. Then something within her seemed to give way, and she sank upon the ground. She could not realize even then, I think, that this was really the place father had prepared for us, that here he expected us to live. When she finally took it in she buried her face in her hands, and in that way she sat for hours without moving or speaking. For the first time in her life she had forgotten us; and we, for our part, dared not speak to her. We stood around her in a frightened group, talking to one another in whispers. Our little world had crumbled under our feet. Never before had we seen our mother give way to despair.

Night began to fall. The woods became alive with night creatures, and the most harmless made the most noise. The owls began to hoot, and soon we heard the wildcat, whose cry—a screech like that of a lost and panic-stricken child—is one of the most appalling sounds of the forest. Later the wolves added their howls to the uproar, but though darkness came and we children whimpered around her, our mother still sat in her strange lethargy.

At last my brother brought the horses close to the cabin and built fires to protect them and us. He was only twenty, but he showed himself a man during those early pioneer days. While he was picketing the horses and building his protecting fires my mother came to herself, but her face when she raised it was worse than her silence had been. She seemed to have died and to have returned to us from the grave, and I am sure she felt that she had done so. . . .

That night we slept on boughs spread on the earth inside the cabin walls, and we put blankets before the holes which represented our doors and windows, and kept our watch-fires burning. Soon the other children fell asleep, but there was no sleep for me. I was only twelve years old, but my mind was full of fancies. . . .

T o-night that which I most feared was within, not outside of, the cabin. In some way which I did not understand the one sure refuge in our new world had been taken from us. I hardly knew the silent woman who lay near me, tossing from side to side and staring into the darkness; I felt that we had lost our mother. . . .

We held a family council after breakfast, and in this, though I was only twelve, I took an eager and determined part. I loved work—it has always been my favorite form of recreation—and my spirit rose to the opportunities of it which smiled on us from every side. Obviously the first thing to do was to put doors and windows into the yawning holes father had left for them, and to lay a board flooring over the earth inside our cabin walls, and these duties we accomplished before we had occupied our new home a fortnight. . . .

We began by making three windows and two doors; then, inspired by these achievements, we ambitiously constructed an attic and divided the ground floor with partitions, which gave us four rooms. . . .

Steamboat Life: Fighting the Bedbugs (1848)

I was fatigued, and requested the chambermaid to prepare my berth as early as possible. She offered me a very disinterested piece of advice in reference to it, which I shall give here for the benefit of such as may be similarly situated, without the like kindness to direct their choice. It was, that I had better abandon the little pen, otherwise state-room, which I had chosen beside the cabin, and take my berth in the latter apartment, " 'Kase," to use her own elegant language, "the bugs ain't a touch in *hyur* to what they be in *yander*." Here was another volume of misery opened to my already oppressed senses. Seeing my consternation, she added, "O, you needn't dread 'em so powerful; I broomed the berths to-day, and shook the 'trasses, so they won't be so mighty bad."

"Make my berth where you think best," I said.

"There ain't no clean sheets, but I can tear off a pair, and you can sleep in 'em, you know, if they ain't hemmed, and I'll give you my pillow."

"No, thank you," I replied; "just tear off a third sheet, and I'll make a pillow-case of it for myself."

At last the berth was prepared, and the vermin made a night of it. They had evidently not been treated for some time, and brought vigorous appetites to my reception. After a contest of four or five hours, I was fain to yield possession to them. Making such limited ablution as the place allowed, I dressed myself and sat down on the stern of the boat to wait the coming day, and speculate on the distance we had made. When the light came up over the heavy forest . . . I saw that the waters were still muddy, and knew, therefore, that we could not have passed the mouth of the Missouri. Nine hours' running had brought us twenty-two miles! . . .

On the spine of a sand-bar which was just visible . . . the currents met, and the waters of the Missouri rose into a circling wave which toppled an instant and ran on, eager to mingle with the purer element that glittered and danced beyond. But the Mississippi, as if disdaining the foul alliance thus tumultuously sought, stole angrily away beneath the dark forest on the opposite shore. . . .

This, then, was the junction of these two streams! . . . When the child's geography had first been put in my hands, I read of these great rivers and put my feeble powers to their utmost task to conceive them. . . . I had taken the eagle's wing, and, perched upon the mountain pine, had seen the little rivulets . . . bending towards each other, and swelling as they united, till their march became resistless. I had followed them where the dim wood and towering cliff reëchoed to their tread, and where they cut the verdant bosom of the sunny plain like threads of molten silver. Vast, illimitable journey! . . .

While I was contemplating this scene, wrapt in silence, a little window close beside me opened, and a hand was thrust forth which I immediately recognized to be the solitary member belonging to the body of our chamber-maid. She drew back with a scream, and an exclamation not of the most feminine character; but the next moment her eyes relieved her trepidation, and after muttering some apology, she expressed her opinion that I "must feel *right peart* to be out that *airly."* I had no little difficulty in convincing her that there was sufficient activity in my nerves of sensation to render the insects that shared my berth somewhat troublesome.

"I reckon," said she, "thar must have been a mighty small chance of the varmints about you, 'kase I swep' up about a pint of 'em yesterday and throw'd 'em overboard; so it's impossible you could ha had a great many."

I yielded the point, and afterwards observed that whenever they were alluded to on board this boat, it was by measure!

No Rest for the Weary: Frontier Lodgings (1856)

A classic account from a frontier diary—its details typical of a thousand travelers all across frontier America:

On the fifth of June, we pursued our journey toward the southeastern part of the territory, intending to take a look at Lake Michigan from the mouth of the St. Joseph's River. Our way lay through forests and openings similar to those through which we had passed for days, but afterwards we struck into the more heavily timbered land, which the growth of the advancing season had clad with cumbrous garments of foliage, closing up the vistas of beauty and light; in places denying the summer sun its right to rest upon the flowers and shrubs it had but lately warmed into being. At nearly noon, we came upon the edge of a large prairie, the largest in the Territory, which although much smaller than those spread farther westward, had still all the distinctive features of those vast and undulating plains. The landscape was expanded and beautiful, and yet one can scarcely make intelligible the penetrating sentiment of its beauty. Perhaps the first influence consisted in the sense of relief from the pent-up feeling we had experienced in the close pressure as it were, of the deep, dark forest from which we emerged. In the centre of this plain was a collection of "innumerous boughs" like an island in the midst of circling waters. The prairie was begirt by a belt of timbered land, though the outline was so dim in the distance, as rather to look like a lazy cloud resting for support upon the verge of the horizon. We gave our horses the reins, and they cantered merrily across the rich plain, the whole covered in this early summer with short and close grass. Innumerable flowers raised their variegated heads between the tiny meshes of network woven by the wild pea, while the butterflies, with their bright tints and quick fluttering wings, were perpetually upspringing, startled by our approach. After crossing the prairie we again struck into the forest, having previously stopped at the island inn for some refreshment.

Towards evening, as was our wont, we felt that we must look along our way for some lodging for the night. Our custom had been, except in the villages, not to seek accommodation at the inns scattered at irregular distances along the road. The new settlers continually moving in toward their purchases, and the number of speculators in pursuit of locations on which to raise, not dwellings, but future fortunes, so completely filled them up, as to render it an impossibility to find for a lady even momentary seclusion, much less repose. Our practice was as soon as we found the shadows beginning to lengthen, to stop at the first decent log house and ask for a drink of water. Getting the water afforded time and opportunity for reconnoitering; and if the tin cup or basin in which the draught was offered looked clean, and the premises in any way inviting by comparison, we made the request that we could be accommodated for the night. We had not on this evening seen any houses, the tract of country through which we had been passing for some hours being without settlement.

On coming up to some woodmen whose gleaming axes told that their whereabouts was near at hand, we stopped, and after exchanging mutual glances of inquiry, my husband asked if they could tell us where we could find a tavern? They looked at each other and then askance at us. The question was repeated again; they looked bewildered, when my husband thoughtfully changed his phrase and said—"Where can I stay to-night, and have good care taken of my horses?" The answer then came quickly—"Oh, at Nicholas B—'s, the Hooshier's, he has a first-rate place, and takes in every night a great many folks." We made two or three further inquiries and passed on, with our expectations considerably raised in prospect of the promised accommodation.

Just after sunset, we reached the place designated by the woodmen, and peering through the gloaming, I espied a good-sized frame barn, with an enclosure, and all the appearance of a well stocked barn and rick. I fairly screamed with delight, so important to our further journey was the welfare of our horses, and so certain did the indication seem of a comfortable resting place for my own wearied limbs. We soon came out of the forest, upon the edge of a small prairie; there stood the barn in very truth, but I looked around in vain for the house which I had pictured in such glowing colors to myself, as presenting some comparison in size and comfort to the barn. A sudden chill of loneliness came over us. There lay the prairie, about three hundred acres in extent, shrubless and bare, except the patches of recent cultivation, which, however, in the dim light, gave but little indication of richness or growth. The trees shut us in completely, and after traversing the deep forest as we had been for hours, we could not even let imagination picture a livelier or brighter scene beyond. Night came rapidly on, while we stood baffled, without a present sign of human existence. Our horses had for a mile or two been lagging, perhaps in memory of the morning scamper and noon-day refreshment; and now the whole group seemed peculiarly sensible of the influence of solitude, which in us soon resolved itself into utter dreariness. A fresh glance of scrutiny, however, enabled us to descry a very small hut jutting into the woods, as uninviting a log house as we had seen in all our wanderings. We both looked at it for some moments without speaking, so completely paralyzed were all our high raised expectations. I then exclaimed, "We cannot stay in that hovel." But fastidiousness was soon displaced by eagerness with me, when my husband calmly said—"We must find shelter there or in the barn, for no further can we go tonight." We urged our horses to the door; a well stood directly in front of it, a rare and great treasure in a new settlement, and after grateful notice of this, my husband entered the dwelling. He asked the woman civilly, "if she could accommodate us for the night." Her answer came quick in utterance and shrill in tone. "I suppose I shall have to, any way." Such was our welcome. But necessity here giving no scope to pride, or even wonted self-respect, obliged me to dismount and receive the favor so grudgingly bestowed. The woman was perhaps about thirty years of age, plain in feature, and old-fashioned beyond my memory in attire. Her dress was a thick striped material, woven to defy time and its ravages. It was unlike any fabric to which I had been accustomed. It fitted the figure almost closely, low in the neck, with sleeves just coming below the elbow. The dress was extremely short-waisted, without a particle of fulness in the skirt, save the ordinary plaiting just behind essential to convenience. She had on no shoes or stockings, and a faded bandana handkerchief was tied in a loose knot around her neck. Her hair was bound straight about her head, and fastened with some sort of a metal comb, just large enough to perform its office.

On my entrance a wooden chair was handed me, after being hurriedly dusted; it was low and rickety, but it instantly bestowed the promise of rest, which I so much craved after sitting so many hours in the saddle. My husband, without entering the hut, went on the woman's vague direction to find the landlord, that our horses, whose prospects of accommodation were so far beyond ours, might speedily receive attention. As soon as he was gone, I essayed an acquaintance of my hostess, and soon believed that her want of courtesy at our reception proceeded more from a fear of not being able to make us comfortable, than from vexation at the present trouble. Two children, the eldest of them not more than two years of age, divided her care with the present bustle of preparing a meal and entertaining me by rapid talking. Her face became almost pleasant with the interest it soon showed in transforming me into a newspaper, from which she could extract without much trouble the information desired by woman, let her nook of the world be ever so obscure, or her connection with the things without ever so slight. I had in my daily progress become quite used to this sort of questioning, and in some instances had to make my tarrying a lasting memorial of usefulness, by drawing patterns of certain garments, collars, caps, etc., with a coal on the floor or table, where paper could not be had, so that when cloth could be procured the latest mode might be used in its fashioning. While thus engaged in conversation, growing in self-importance every moment, and quite forgetting that I was an unwished-for guest, I took a survey of the house. It was, of course, built of logs, fourteen feet by sixteen; its sides five feet six inches in height, and the roof covered with strips of bark. A few scattering boards made the floor. It had not the ordinary stick and round chimney common to log houses, but a sort of box was made of split logs at one end of the room; this was filled in with dirt and ashes, and the fire built in the centre of it. An opening in the ill-made roof permitted the smoke to find egress, though occasional puffs during the process of getting supper, advised us of its loitering presence. After my survey of the room itself, I began to take notice of the furniture, and more especially of its sleeping facilities. Two bedsteads, each sustained by *one* post—quite an anomaly in my previous experience of cabinet furniture; a large chest, which had evidently borne journeying when the essay at house-keeping was made away from the paternal home; a small box of home manufacture, and some other absolute essentials to the wants of even the poorest dwelling, constituted its wealth. I must add a note of description of the bedsteads. Two sides were formed by the projection of the logs of which the hut was made into the room; the *one* post supported the other two pieces, which were on the other ends inserted into the sides of the house. Feather-beds were heaped high upon them, and these were covered with blue and white woollen coverlids, doubtless part of the portion brought by the young wife to her husband. Small pillows, with clean-looking cotton pillow-cases, completed their decoration.

I had noticed that my hostess, during her bustle and constant chat with me, had gone frequently to the door, and looked anxiously into the increasing darkness, I of course supposed from no other motive than a desire to find out whether my husband had found hers, and secured attention for our horses. But not so interested was she in her stranger guests. At another visit to the low door, her anxiety could not be restrained, and she exclaimed, "I wonder where my children can be! They ought to have been here more than an hour ago; they are always out of the way when I want them." I looked aghast. More children! How many—how old! What could be done with them! I had been puzzling myself to know how *six* of us could be accommodated in the two beds, and in this tiny room; and now an indefinite number to be expected, how could we be made even tolerably comfortable? Speculation—quiet though it was—was soon to be ended by more precise apprehension, when *four* children, three boys and a girl, came rushing from the woods into the house, animated by all the buoyancy of hungry little mortals just liberated from a day's confinement and control. It being quite dark without, the light, small as it was within the dwelling, formed a strong contrast, and the little urchins were so suddenly arrested upon perceiving a stranger, that they stood like so many statues, incapable of thought or movement. The remonstration of the mother quickly restored them, and then began importunate demands for something to eat. Thus there were six children, the father and mother, with ourselves, to be stowed away for the night. It was in vain for me to speculate upon the probable disposition of these numbers, so trusting as I had often done before to the elastic capabilities of these log houses, I determined to bide my time.

Our host came in with my husband, both bending low in passing through the door. My husband gave a wistful glance at me, and seemed reassured when a *widened* rather than a *lengthened* face was turned upon him. Truth to tell, I was almost convulsed with laughter at some of the previous proceedings of my hostess. The ill-jointed planks which served for our floor, were quickly brushed hither and thither with an Indian broom (made of wood finely splintered); the flying dust seeming to have no particular destination, save to seek new places of deposit. The children were repeatedly hushed and pushed into sundry nooks and corners, while the cooking of the supper went on. The little urchins peered at the stranger, and anon played tricks with each other, when a sudden burst, caused by outbreaking mischief, would occasion a new effort at quieting. In process of time our supper was served, and ere long we gathered to the meal.

The table was an oaken plank, supported by three stout sticks put into bored holes, for legs. A table-cloth being altogether a superfluous luxury, we dispensed with it; some bread, baked in an open kettle, pork fried in the same utensil, and tea with maple sugar, formed the variety presented to us. Neither milk nor butter were afforded, and yet we were at a regular house of entertainment, kept by a large landed proprietor. Strange to say, the meal was quite palatable, eaten with a healthful appetite after a day's ride on horseback of some thirty-five miles. Soon after tea, the children being fed by pieces into their hands during the time we were supping, I ventured to hint, that as I was very tired I should like to go to bed. The woman went to the chest which I had before noticed, took out two clean sheets, spread them upon one of the feather-beds, and again put on the woollen coverlet, although it was a June night, a fire burning briskly, and ten persons were to inhabit the small apartment. Immediately after the bed was prepared, the hostess said in an authoritative tone to her husband, "Nicholas, the lady wishes to go to bed; turn your face to the wall." Nicholas, as if accustomed to this nightly drill, wheeled swiftly about, and stood as still as if suddenly become one of the scanty articles of furniture.

This said Nicholas looked somewhat like a barbarian, his bushy head and unshaven beard presenting quite a wild appearance. He however seemed intelligent enough for his locality and business, and took most excellent care of our horses. My toilet for the night was very speedily made, and I threw myself on the bed, having first removed the odious coverlet. Still no new developments were made in reference to the accommodation of the youthful group; ere long, however, sundry signs of sleepiness appeared, betokened by fretfulness and some quarrelling, and then the mother proceeded to lift out two trundle beds made of pieces of board nailed together. The absence of rollers made the operation rather laborious, but the husband and father vouchsafed not his aid. It was finally done by the woman alone, and into these five of the little ones were speedily placed. Very soon after, the dim, flickering light was put out, and we were left utterly abandoned, as I feared, to suffocation. I remonstrated decidedly against the shutting of the door, but was told there was fear of wolves; and indeed before morning our ears were saluted with the shrill, though somewhat smothered howl of these prowlers of the forest. I bore the heat and bad air for several hours, and then in desperation for want of a pure breath, I commenced picking the chinking out from between the logs at the side of the bed, and in this way secured for myself a breathing place, amid the enjoyment of which I fell asleep, and awaked not until the broad sunbeams were laughing in my face.

Stagecoach Across the Prairie (1859)

I fell asleep [on the stagecoach], and when I was awakened at dawn this morning, by my companion, that I might not lose the scene, I started with surprise and delight. I was in the midst of a prairie! A world of grass and flowers stretched around me, rising and falling in gentle undulations, as if an enchanter had struck the ocean swell, and it was at rest forever. Acres of wild flowers of every hue glowed around me, and the sun arising from the earth where it touched the horizon, was "kissing with golden face the meadows green." What a new and wondrous world of beauty! What a magnificent sight! Those glorious ranks of flowers! Oh that you could have "one glance at their array!" How shall I convey to you an idea of a prairie. I despair, for never yet hath pen brought the scene before my mind. Imagine yourself in the center of an immense circle of velvet herbage, the sky for its boundary upon every side; the whole clothed with a radiant efflorescence of every brilliant hue. We rode thus through a perfect wilderness of sweets, sending forth perfume, and animated with myriads of glittering birds and butterflies:

> *"A populous solitude of bees and birds,*
> *And fairy formed and many colored things."*

It was, in fact, a vast garden, over whose perfumed paths, covered with soil as hard as gravel, our carriage rolled through the whole of that summer day. You will scarcely credit the profusion of flowers upon these prairies. We passed whole acres of blossoms all bearing one hue, as purple, perhaps, or masses of yellow or rose; and then again a carpet of every color intermixed, or narrow bands, as if a rainbow had fallen upon the verdant slopes. When the sun flooded this mosaic floor with light, and the summer breeze stirred among their leaves, the iridescent glow was beautiful and wondrous beyond anything I had ever conceived. I think this must have been the place where Armida planted her garden, for she surely could not have chosen a fairer spot. Here are

"Gorgeous flowrets in the sun light shining,
Blossoms flaunting in the eye of day;
Tremulous leaves with soft silver lining
Buds that open only to decay."

The gentle undulating surface of these prairies prevent sameness, and add variety to its lights and shades. Occasionally, when a swell is rather higher than the rest, it gives you an extended view over the country, and you may mark a dark green waving line of trees near the distant horizon, which are shading some gentle stream from the sun's absorbing rays, and thus, "Betraying the secret of their silent course." Oak openings also occur, green groves, arranged with the regularity of art, making shady alleys, for the heated traveller. What a tender benevolent Father have we, to form for us so bright a world! How filled with glory and beauty must that mind have been, who conceived so much loveliness! . . .

"All aboard" cries the driver, and we were again upon our course, our horses prancing gaily as if refreshed by their breakfast. A tree appeared against the horizon, looking exactly like a sail in the distance—others followed it, and soon beautiful groups of forest trees were sprinkled over the prairie in front. This was the token of the vicinity of water, and in a short time we found ourselves upon an elevated bank from which we looked down upon a verdant valley through the center of which ran a silver stream. This was the valley of the Des Plaines—having every appearance of being the bed of a broad and deep river. Many geologists, among them Prof. Sheppard, thinks this and the valley of the Illinois have been scooped out by a vast torrent from Lake Michigan. Upon the opposite shore of the river and in this vale, at the foot of the ancient banks, stands the pretty town of Joliet, improperly spelt Juliet. The whole scene was one of great beauty. We descended the banks, which is nearly one hundred feet high, and is composed of yellow water-worn pebbles. Winding down the road upon the high bank opposite was a long train of covered wagons, filled with a household upon its way to "a new home" upon the prairies. After fording the stream, now rendered shallow by the summer heats, passing over the green sward we found ourselves before the door of the principal hotel in the town.

Sister Blandina Segale:
"The cowboys were constantly in my mind."
(1872)

The following incident occurred in Trinidad, New Mexico:

I ordered the stage for the morning of the 9th. Mrs. Mullen was very attentive. She had new clean hay put in the stage to keep my feet warm, and after I got in she wrapped a large comfort around me, remarking that "traveling on the plains and in winter was not a pleasant prospect." . . . For the first time I had indefinable fears. The cowboys were constantly in my mind. I expected there would be a number traveling with me on the plains. . . .

At noon the driver came to the stage door and said: "We take dinner here." I thanked him and said: "I do not wish any dinner."

"But lady, we will not have another stopping place to eat until six o'clock this evening."

I thanked him again, "But I do not wish any dinner." The jolting of the stage and my thoughts had taken all appetite away. Though I could see nothing from the stage (every flap was fastened), it seemed that the driver aimed to drive over every stone and make the wheels go into every rut. It was nothing but a jerk up and down all the way—in a stage that had no springs and traveling at the rate of twelve miles an hour!

At six o'clock we arrived at the station for supper. At every station the mules were changed. The driver came to ask me to supper. I thanked him, but said; "I do not wish any supper."

"There will not be another chance for a meal until twelve o'clock tonight, and you have not tasted anything to-day, so come now and take it if only a cup of black coffee."

"No, thank you, I have no desire for anything."

The poor man was quite distressed. He could not think I was trying to save traveling expenses, because of the price of stage traveling included meals. Here is the mental attitude I was in: If the driver could surmise the grave fear that is preying on me he would know I have no appetite.

He went in to supper and presently returned. "Lady, if you do not want to eat—come in and let me have my supper. The woman who runs this station will not give me a drink of muddy water unless I fetch you in to supper—I told her how you are dressed and she goes off wild and says: 'Bring her in or you will get nothing to eat to-night, no' any other time you come.' "

I went into an adobe, log-raftered, mud-floored, mud-plastered hut. The sight of the red checkered tablecloth and black coffee only added to my repugnance for food. The person who kept the station was an Irish woman of the good old stamp. I made an effort to sip some coffee, but not a drop would pass my lips. The cowboys were in my mind. I tried to ascertain if there were any in the vicinity; the answers I received were indefinite.

At midnight: "Now lady, you will have a good meal."

"No, thank you, I desire nothing."

"What will Otero and Sellar say to me when they find out you did not take a meal during this journey? They gave me more orders about you than I ever got since I'm staging, and that's ten years."

"Say I wished for nothing. I will write the firm my thanks."

Oh, the lonely, fearful feeling! The night was dark. No passengers to allay my turbulent thoughts. Footsteps drew near the stage. My heart was thumping. The driver opened the stage door and said:

"You will have a traveling companion for some miles."

In the open door, by the light of the lantern, I saw a tall, lanky, hoosier-like man, wearing a broad brimmed hat. On one arm he had a buffalo robe. While I sat riveted, he got in—asked me if I would take part of his "kiver." And before my fright permitted me to speak, he placed part of the buffalo robe over the comfort that enwrapped me, and sat beside me on the rear seat. The driver closed the door and we were in utter darkness. By descriptions I had read I knew he was a cowboy! With crushing vividness—"No virtuous woman is safe near a cowboy" came to me. I made an act of contrition—concentrated my thoughts on the presence of God—thought of the Archbishop's blessing, "Angels guard your steps," and moved to such position as would put my heart in range with his revolver. I expected he would speak—I answer—he fires. The agony endured cannot be written. The silence and suspense was unimaginable. Suddenly from the darkness I heard:

"Madam!"

"Sir!"

"What kind of a lady be you?"

"A Sister of Charity."

"Whose sister?"

"Everyone's Sister, a person who gives her life to do good to others."

"Quaker like, I reckon?"

"No, not quite."

By this time I learned from his tone of voice that I had nothing to fear. He asked me a number of questions, all prompted by a conversation he had had with the driver before he came into the stage. In my turn I asked him why he became a cowboy. He said he had read of cowboys and ran away from home to become one.

"Is your mother still living?"

"Yes, I allow she is—leastwise she was when I left home six years ago."

"Have you written to her?"

"No madam, and I allow that's beastly."

"It is certainly unkind to one whom you can always trust and who, I am sure, loves you as much now as she did when you were a little fellow."

His voice got husky. "What do you say I otter do?"

"Write; do so as soon as you get off this stage. Tell her you will soon make her a visit, and see to it that you keep your word."

"I will, so help me God! I was mighty feared to speak to you when I got in, because the mule driver said you was more particular than any lady he ever seen. I allow I am powerful glad I spoke to you."

To think that this lubberly, good-natured cowboy had made me undergo such mortal anguish. He got off on the outskirts of Trinidad where the driver stopped to point out to me dugouts at the side of the foothills. "This, lady, is Trinidad."

Learning on the Job

*B*orn *in Sacramento in 1872, Grace Thompson-Seton followed her mother back East after her parents' divorce. She took her studies seriously and came of age as an active suffragist. While traveling abroad she met and married a naturalist and began to camp and hunt with him on his expeditions. She developed a passion for the outdoors and went on to co-found the Campfire Girls in 1912. Ever resourceful and possessing incredible stamina, she would eventually travel the world. During World War I, while many of her comrades stayed home and watched from afar, this remarkable woman went to the front lines where she delivered food and hope to the American soldiers. Her first memoir,* A Woman Tenderfoot, *carried the marvelous excerpt below:*

Nimrod and I were on a hunting trip in the Canadian Rockies, and as the government map said there was a road, though not a good one, we decided to carry our belongings in a four-horse wagon, in which we could also ride if we liked, and to have saddle horses besides.

Green, a man of the region, was the driver and cook, and we had as guest a famous bear hunter from the Sierra Nevadas. On the first two days out from the little mountain town where we started, we saw many tracks of black bear, which encouraged the hunters to think that they might find a grizzly (which, by the way, they did not).

The dust was thick and red, enveloping us all day long like some horrible insistent monster that had resolved itself into atoms to choke, blind, and strangle us. Nimrod looked like a clay man—hair, eyebrows, mustache, skin, and clothes were all one solid coating of red dust. We were all alike. Even the sugar, paper-wrapped in the bottom of a box, covered by other boxes, bags, and a canvas, became adulterated almost past use.

On the fourth day this changed, and we camped at the foot of a granite mountain. It made one think of the Glass Mountain of fable, with its smooth stretches of polished rock shining in the sun. That a human being should dare to take a wagon over such a place seemed incredible. Yet there the road was, zigzagging up the rocky slope, while here and there the jagged outlines of blasted rock showed where the all-powerful dynamite had been used to make a resting place for straining horses.

That morning excitement surrounded our out-of-door breakfast table. We had had strange visitors during the night, while we slept. A mountain lion, the beautiful tan-coated vibrant-tailed puma, had nosed within ten feet of me and then, not liking the camp-fire glow and unalarmed by my inert form, had silently retreated.

It made me feel creepy to see how easily that lithe-limbed powerful creature might have had me for a midnight meal. But I was not trying to do him harm, and so he granted me the same tolerance. Then, too, not far away was a bear track, and the canned peaches were fewer than the night before.

All of this caused Nimrod and the bear-hunter to saddle their horses early; and agreeing to meet us at night on the other side of the mountain, where the map showed a stream, they set out for a day's hunt. Nimrod's horse having gone slightly lame, I offered mine, a swift-footed intelligent dear, and agreed to ride in the wagon.

It was the same old story. Virtue is somebody else's reward. I never had a worse day in the mountains. Green and I started blithely enough by nine, which had meant a 5:30 rising in the cold gray dawn. The horses had been worked every day since the start, and were jaded.

We went slowly along the only level road in our journey that day; but the load did not seem to be riding well, and at the beginning of the ascent Green got out to investigate. He said the spring was out of order. The wagon was what is known as a thorough-brace, which means that there are two large loopy steel bands on which the wagon box rests; the loops are filled in with countless strips of leather, forming a pad for the springs to play on. (The Century Dictionary will please not copy this definition.) The Deadwood stage coach was a thorough-brace, I believe.

Another interesting out-of-date detail in the construction of this wagon was that the brake had no mechanical device for holding it in position when it was put on hard, and the driver had to rely upon his strength of limb to keep it in place. It seems that Green, in pounding these bits of leather in the spring, had badly crushed his left hand. He said nothing to me, and I did not notice that, contrary to custom, he was driving with his right hand, which he usually reserved for the whip and the brake.

We crossed the shallow brook and started up the very steep and very rocky road, when everything happened at once. Two of the horses refused to pull and danced up and down in the one spot, a sickening thing for a horse to do. This meant the instant application of the brake. We had already begun to slip backward (the most uncomfortable sensation I know, barring actual pain). Nimrod's horse, tied on behind, gave a frightened snort and broke his rope. Green attempted to take the reins with his left hand. They dropped from his grasp, and I saw that his fingers were purple and black.

"Grab the lines, can you?" he said, as he seized the whip and put both feet on the brake. The leaders were curveting back on the wheelers in a way which meant imminent mix-up, their legs over traces and behind whiffle-trees. On the right of us was solid rock up, on the left solid rock down, one hundred feet to the stream, and just ahead was the sharp turn the road made to a higher ledge in its zigzag up the mountain.

I had always intended to learn to drive four-in-hand, but this first lesson left me no pleasure in the learning. There were no little triumphs of difficulties mastered, no gentle surprises, no long, smooth, broad, and level stretches with plenty of room to pull a rein and see what would happen. I had to spring into the situation with knowledge, as Minerva did into life, full grown. It was no kindergarten way of learning to drive four-in-hand.

I grabbed the reins in both hands. There were yards of them, rods of them, miles of them—they belonged to a six or sixteen horse set. I do not know which. I sat on them. They writhed in my lap, wrapped around my feet, and around the gun against my knee, in a hopeless and dangerous muddle. Of course the reins were twisted. I did not know one from the other. I gave a desperate jerk which sent the leaders plunging to the right, where fortunately they brought up against the rock wall. Had they gone the other way nothing but our destiny could have saved us from going over the edge. *Crack* went the whip in the right place.

"Slack the lines!" Green cried, as he eased the brake. A lash of the whip for each wheeler, and we started forward, the horses disentangling themselves from the harness as by a miracle, just as the rear wheels were hovering over the bluff. Green dropped the whip (his left hand was quite useless) and straightened out the reins for me.

"Can you do it?" he asked, grasping the whip, as the horses showed signs of stopping again. To attend to the brake was physically impossible. Green could not do it and drive with one hand.

"Yes," I said, "but watch me"—an injunction scarcely necessary.

If ever a woman put her whole mind to a thing, I did on that four-in-hand. There was no place for mistakes. There was no place for anything but the right thing, and do it I must or run the risk of breaking my very dusty, very brown, but none-the-less precious neck.

A sharp turn in a steep road with rocks a foot high disputing the right of way with the wheels, a heavy load, horses that do not want to pull, and a green driver—that was the situation. If it does not appeal to you as one of the horribles in life, try it once.

"Run your leaders farther up the bank—left, left! *Get up, Milo! Frank, get out of that!* Now sharp to the right. *Whoa! Steady!* Left—left, I say! *Milo, whoa!* Now to the right, quick! Let 'em on the bank more. *Nellie, easy—whoa! Steady, George!*" Crack went the whip on the leaders.

"Hold your lines tighter. Pull that nigh leader. *Get out of that, Frank! Now steady, boys!* Don't pull—there!"

Down went the brake; we were safely round the turn, and all hands rested for a moment.

Thus we worked all that morning, Green with the brake, the whip, and his tongue; I with the lines, what strength I had, and mother wit in lieu of experience.

There were stretches of two hundred feet of granite, smooth and polished as a floor, where the horses repeatedly slipped and fell, and where the wheels brought forth hollow mocking rumbles.

There were sections where the rocky ledges succeeded one another in steps, and the animals had to pull the heavy wagon up rises from a foot to eighteen inches high by sheer strength—as easy to drive up a flight of brownstone steps on Fifth Avenue. There were places between huge boulders where a swerve of a foot to the right or to the left would have sent us crashing into the unyielding granite.

When we got to the top there was no place to rest—only rock, rock everywhere. No water, no food for the exhausted horses, nothing to do but to push on to the bottom—and such going! Have you ever felt the shuddering of a wagon with brake hard on, as it poised in air the instant before it dropped a foot or two to the next level, from hard rock to hard rock? Have you ever tried to keep four horses away from under a wagon, and yet sufficiently near it not to precipitate the crash? Have you ever at the same time tried to keep them from falling on the rocks ahead and from plunging over the bank as you turn a sharp curve on a steep down grade? If you have, then you know the nature of my first lesson in four-in-hand driving.

We got to the bottom at dusk. I was too tired to speak. Every muscle set up a separate complaint and I had had nothing to eat since morning, as we had expected to make camp by noon. The world seemed indeed a very drab place. We found the hunters careering around searching for us. They thought they had missed us—as they had done the bear.

I have driven, and been driven, hundreds of miles since, but there never was a ride like those twelve, cruel, mocking, pitiless miles over Granite Mountain, when necessity taught me a very pretty trick, which, however, I have not yet been tempted to display at the Madison Square Garden in November.

Frontier Mother's Lament

But I am often sad at heart when I think of my dear brother and my dear little baby boy being laid to rest beneath Nevada's soil, and Oh how lonely they seem to be. This is the only thing causes me to regret to leave Nevada. But I presume it will be my lot to be laid in some lonely grave without a board to mark the spot.

Eleanor Brittain, a pioneer woman, from her diary

"*Oh, what dreadful places . . .*"

Yesterday we had to camp soon after starting, for a cow calved, and today we have come about eight miles, and have again stopped for same cause, but suppose we shall go in two or three hours. The calves are to be carried in the wagons for two or three days. We crossed the bridge built by the men who had gone ahead of us some time ago. William paid for our wagon going over, as Mr. Holly was going to ferry the stream, using one of the wagon beds for a boat, but as that leaked so much and such risk of our clothing getting wet, we preferred paying the toll of the bridge, which was very reasonable, the ferryman charging us but $1, as we paid it ourselves, the usual toll being $3. Mr. Holly gave William 75 cents towards it. He also had to treat his men with $5 worth of whiskey for going in the water, and they dropped a sack of sugar, 100 pounds, so he would have done better had he paid the toll and gone on without delay of a day's time.

There were a number of Indians around at this place, and I had a good chance to trade for a fur or two. I swapped one of my small blankets for a pretty robe of prairie dog skins. I think there are ten in it, all nicely sewed together. My blanket was considerably worn. I wonder the Indian was willing to trade. But they always seem so glad to get hold of a blanket. Another Indian had some beautiful mink skins tied over his shoulder and under his arm, with some kind of a bag for his arrows. It took my fancy (the skins, I mean) as being just enough to make a nice flat boa. William at the time had on an old flannel shirt, and being a warm day, he was in his shirt sleeves. I called him to me whilst the Indian stood by, and I went through the sign language intimating my desire to trade the shirt for the skins. He seemed to consent, so I made William strip off his shirt then and there and pass it over to the Indian, and I got the skins.

Well, a young man in our company, seeing my desire for furs presented me with a very fine wildcat skin, he having just traded for several, so I have a nice collection and am quite proud of them. I found on looking them over that vermin were quite plenty in them, so I could not have them inside our wagon. I tied them in sacks underneath, and thus they passed through several creeks or streams, and were finally cleansed. The catskin will make a pretty muff, as it's such beautiful, long, soft fur. I suppose the squaws do the tanning.

Oh, what dreadful places we have had to go through lately. The mud at the banks of the forks of the Humboldt was so deep that at one place nine yoke of our cattle had to be put on one wagon, and then it was a dreadful pull, and chains broke pretty fast. Yesterday William called me out of my wagon to come and see an ox down in the mud. Nothing was visible but the top of his back and head; his nose even was covered. Almost every week and sometimes twice we have to put boards across on the projections and put all the loading on them, for the streams we cross come quite a piece up our wagon box. But every stream we cross brings us nearer our journey's end, and we all are getting tired of the trip. Oh, what a loss I am at for amusement as I ride along. I could knit, but I have only some red yarn, which I bought for Sis, but it's too near summer to commence woollen socks. If I only had some muslin, how nice I could be preparing for our underclothes, for we each are quite destitute. I have no nightdress at all, so sleep in a colored sacque. Sissy now wears a little red flannel dress I made out of that piece you saw. She also wears that green quilted skirt, and on warm days they are too heavy. But I have no fears for the future, as Pa will see we have all we need when we reach him. It seems quite providential he went on to California last season, as we feel we have a home and something to expect.

Oh, if I could but see you, my loved sister, and have a long talk together, how happy I should feel. I shall look forward to such a season as not unlikely. My earnest desire is that we may end our days near each other, and I think we shall.

We are now over the desert, the forty-mile desert of which we had heard much, consequently we dreaded it. The evening before we reached it we camped very early, and had supper and let the cattle feed good, and toward night all was started again, as we were to cross it in the night for the sake of coolness. Every one filled their tin canteens with water at the last camping place, but the water was very poor (brackish); but there was no other well. Sis and I went to bed at dark, as usual, but the men folks were all walking, and expected so to do most of the night. The sand was very deep, and the wagons dragged along slowly. Toward midnight it began to rain, and the oxen showed signs of exhaustion, and what little water we carried was given to those most in need. Mr. Holly began to fear our wagon, which was the largest and heaviest in the crowd, could not be hauled any farther, and that some change must be made or he would get stuck on the desert. A consultation was held, and William came and awoke me, telling me that I would have to get out and go in one of the other wagons, as Holly would haul ours no farther. I was just all broken up at this bad news, for our roomy wagon had been our pride and comfort. But as we had given it to Holly in part payment for our passage, it was his, and he must do as suited him best. So I bundled up myself and baby, and the men gathered up the bedding and all the traps and threw them in other wagons, wherever there happened to be any room, and I tumbled in anywhere. No more good bed for us, but just a chance to exist in among the pork barrels and all the dirt of men's old clothes. But there was no help for us, and I had to suffer the inconvenience of the change. Perhaps I did not cry, but I think I did. But there was this comfort, we should soon reach the Carson River.

Well, our good wagon was left on the desert. But such was the prevailing custom on the Plains, to destroy anything that you might not then need, and so prevent the next one from benefiting by your discarded property, whatever it might be. Perhaps I ought not to write that this custom was general, for it was not; but some would do so, and Holly was of that class. He therefore had our nice good wagon set fire to, and when we left there was a big bonfire blazing. It did seem a "burning" shame, for surely some emigrant might have benefited by its use.

We reached the Carson River in the early forenoon, having traveled the whole night.

Plains Burial

The following diary entry from a pioneer woman is typical of the practical sorrows of the trail west:

Deer Creek North Platte Bridge

19th Came to Deer creek, crossed came up it half a mile and camped last night. It is quite a pretty stream. A great many camped on it last evening. To day is Sunday. We do not travel this forenoon. We came to the N. Platte a little while before coming to Deer creek. it is much narrower and far more meandering than before the Larimee Fork emptied into it. A few clumps of pretty trees are scattered along its banks which gives it quite a romantic appearance. We have travelled about five days since leaving Fort Larimee, and before coming on to the river have had, most of the way, rough hilly road, but good water and plenty of wood. I have been delighted with the flowers. We find new varieties almost every day, none very large or gaudy, but pretty, delicate mountain flowers, ever cheering and welcome to the heart of the weary traveler. There are quite enough to afford interest, and pleasure for many a leisure hour. We are just going to see a tree, in the top of which is an indian buried. Our tree proved not to have an indian in it. There were only buffalo skins and sticks fastened up in the tree. Some thought one had been buried and others not.

North Platte bridge

21st We had not travelled far yesterday before word came to us, from the back, that Louisa was worse. We supposed was fainting, but they soon said she was dying, and before we could get back from our wagons to the buggy she was gone. Poor girl! She hoped to get to California before she should die, but it was her lot to have to lie alone on these sandy plains, a sad lot indeed, and a hard thing for her parents to bear. We prepared her for the cold grave. Came on to the bridge where Mr. King had come to prepare a coffin. We could only get a rough one made as there were no tools to work with. This morning a grave was dug on the opposite side of the river where we followed her to her lonely resting place. A dreary place, to one of her sensitive feelings. She has often remarked that she wondered why people did not bury their friends under a tree when they could, or in some prettier place than by the roadside or where it was sandy & barren, but, poor girl! we were obliged to lay her where there is no tree or flower to shade her grave from the scorching rays of the sun. The ground was too low this side the river where there were a few trees, and her father thought it best to bury her near the bridge where there is a small cluster of huts, and tents. We wished to procure some rose bushes or cedar to plant on her grave, but cannot get any cedar and roses would hardly grow in so sandy a spot. She was very fond of roses. I carried her a bunch the night before she died, when she said, "O! I do like them so well." This was the last time I saw or spoke with her. We little thought she would die so soon. She had time to speak only with her father who was with her. Her last words were, "O! Pa, what does hurt me so?" Her pain only lasted a moment for she ceased to breathe. We cross the river in the morning.

North Platte

Thursday 23 Crossed the North Platte yesterday morning. Some got out to look at Louisa's grave. The men had brought from the mountains a spruce bush which the girls placed at the head of the grave. We had to leave her in her lonely resting place, where no friend will ever be near to look upon her grave, perhaps, again. Her father had promised her that if she died on the plains he would send a tombstone to mark the place of her repose.

Life Goes On

The intrepid Isabella Bird wrote the following account during her travels through the Rocky Mountains in 1873. She too understood that the frontier code of survival was as pitiless as the noonday sun:

After fording a creek several times, I came upon a decayed-looking cluster of houses bearing the arrogant name of Colorado City, and two miles farther on, from the top of one of the Foot Hill ridges, I saw the bleak-looking scattered houses of the ambitious watering place of Colorado Springs, the goal of my journey of 150 miles. I got off, put on a long skirt, and rode sidewise, though the settlement scarcely looked like a place where any deference to prejudices was necessary. A queer embryo-looking place it is, out on the bare Plains, yet it is rising and likely to rise, and has some big hotels much resorted to. It has a fine view of the mountains, specially of Pike's Peak, but the celebrated springs are at Manitou, three miles off, in really fine scenery. To me no place could be more unattractive than Colorado Springs, from its utter treelessness.

I found the ——s living in a small room which served for parlor, bedroom, and kitchen, and combined the comforts of all. It is inhabited also by two prairie dogs, a kitten, and a deerhound. It was truly homelike. Mrs. —— walked with me to the boarding-house where I slept, and we sat some time in the parlor talking with the landlady. Opposite to me there was a door wide open into a bed room, and on a bed opposite to the door a very sick-looking young man was half-lying, half-sitting, fully dressed, supported by another, and a very sick-looking young man much resembling him passed in and out occasionally, or leaned on the chimney piece in an attitude of extreme dejection. Soon the door was half-closed, and some one came to it, saying rapidly, "Shields, quick, a candle!" and then there were movings about in the room. All this time the seven or eight people in the room in which I was were talking, laughing, and playing backgammon, and none laughed louder than the land-lady, who was sitting where she saw that mysterious door as plainly as I did. All this time, and during the movings in the room, I saw two large white feet sticking up at the end of the bed. I watched and watched, hoping those feet would move, but they did not; and somehow, to my thinking, they grew stiffer and whiter, and then my horrible suspicion deepened, that while we were sitting there a human spirit untended and desolate had passed forth into the night. Then a man came out with a bundle of clothes, and then the sick young man, groaning and sobbing, and then a third, who said to me, with some feeling, that the man who had just died was the sick young man's only brother. And still the landlady laughed and talked, and afterwards said to me, "It turns the house upside down when they just come here and die; we shall be half the night laying him out." I could not sleep for the bitter cold and the sound of the sobs and groans of the bereaved brother. The next day the landlady, in a fash-ionably-made black dress, was bustling about, proud of the prospective arrival of a handsome coffin. I went into the parlor to get a needle, and the door of *that* room was open, and children were running in and out, and the landlady, who was sweeping there, called cheerily to me to come in for the needle, and there, to my horror, not even covered with a face cloth, and with the sun blazing in through the unblinded window, lay that thing of terror, a corpse, on some chairs which were not even placed straight. It was buried in the after-noon, and from the looks of the brother, who continued to sob and moan, his end cannot be far off.

"My last Indian story . . ." (From Fannie Beck's Journal)

It was a night in early summer. John was home from Austin, where he had been attending school, and after supper, Pa announced that John and I should stay with the children while he and Ma went to church. So they left about dusk for the Masonic Hall. This was quite a distance from our house and stood on a hill east of town. This building . . . was used for a schoolhouse, also, for several years. In fact, it was the only place we had for public gatherings of any kind, until a more commodious schoolhouse was built several years later. (A cyclone destroyed the old hall several years ago.) Our house was a double log house, with a wide hall running down the center and separating the four rooms; there was a porch (or gallery) the entire length of the house, and there

was a large yard enclosed with cedar pickets. We used the hall for many purposes, especially in warm weather. The four rooms opened onto it from the sides, and it was open to the gallery in front, with a back door leading into the kitchen. We had the dining table in the hall and ate all our meals there.

On this particular Sunday night, after the others had gone to bed, John and I took the lamp and our books and writing materials to the dining table in the hall. The night was so still that we could hear the least little noise outside. It was pitch dark, too, and we could not distinguish anything beyond the faint light from the lamp. We worked with our writing and reading a little while, and John got up to let the dog, a pup just a few months old, out of the room. As soon as it got outside the door, it began to growl and bark. It would run to the edge of the porch and then come tearing back. It kept that up until I was scared and John was provoked. So we shut the pup back in the room and went to bed. Pretty soon the folks came in. Pa insisted on putting his bed on the porch and sleeping there, as was his custom on hot nights. I heard all the commotion of his dragging the mattress out, Ma's protests, the little dog's continued tearing back and forth and barking his head off, and Pa's threats to "wring its neck." I had tried to tell John, earlier in the evening, that I could see something just beyond the rays of light from the lamp and near the porch. I *did* see several forms, indistinctly, of course, but he hooted at the idea. He said there was nothing out there to be afraid of, and the pup probably smelled some wild animal. Well, we slept a few hours that night when the dog quit barking. Pa always slept like a baby, and he probably dropped off while the pup was still yapping, but Ma said she lay trembling for hours, for she fancied she could see something moving around in the yard, and from the way the dog behaved, she felt that danger lurked out there in the darkness. It is a blessed thing that we are often spared the knowledge of the nearness of danger and death. When daylight came, we realized that we might all have been killed and scalped. We wondered why we were spared, for the yard was full of moccasin tracks, crisscrossed all over the place, and thickest near the porch where Pa and Ma had slept. I had some flowers growing in an old stump in the corner of the yard; they were pulled up and scattered on the ground. The mystery about the pup was cleared up by some of the men, who came as soon as the alarm was given that Indians had been to see us again. Indians have a satanic humor, and when the pup would run to the edge of the porch and bark they would try to catch him; then he would run back. Judging from the number of moccasin tracks, there were about sixty Indians in the raiding party that had chosen our place to reconnoiter. They had held a "caucus" in the calf pasture at the back of the stable, as was evidenced by the places in the sand where they had squatted for their powwow. They did not steal anything. They could have killed us all, for they had been around the place for several hours. A number of men got out after them as soon as they could the next morning, but the Indians had several hours' start and were never overtaken. This is my last Indian story, and this is the last time we ever heard of the Indians.

Incidents on the Frontier (1873)

In the summer of 1871, young Frances Roe set off for Colorado as the new bride of a West Point officer. Her subsequent letters home (gathered in a memoir called Army Letters from an Officer's Wife) *record in detail the daily challenges of life on the frontier. In particular, her eye for vivid particulars (consider the barking dog during the gunfight below) offers us a picture of the country as it was—free of exaggeration or sentiment. Clear, sober portraits of a wild country:*

When we got out about fifteen miles on the road, an Apache Indian appeared, and so suddenly that it seemed as if he must have sprung up from the ground. He was in full war dress—that is, no dress at all except the breech clout and moccasins—and his face and whole naked body were stained in many colors in the most hideous manner. In his scalp lock was fastened a number of eagle feathers, and of course he wore two or three necklaces of beads and wampum. There was nothing unusual about the pony he was riding, except that it was larger and in better condition than the average Indian horse, but the one he was leading—undoubtedly his war horse—was a most beautiful animal, one of the most beautiful I ever saw.

The Apache evidently appreciated the horse, for he had stained only his face, but this had been made quite as frightful as that of the Indian. The pony was of a bright cream color, slender, and with a perfect head and small ears, and one could see that he was quick and agile in every movement. He was well groomed, too. The long, heavy mane had been parted from ears to withers, and then twisted and roped on either side with strips of some red stuff that ended in long streamers, which were blown out in a most fantastic way when the pony was running. The long tail was roped only enough to fasten at the top a number of strips of the red that hung almost to the ground over the hair. Imagine all this savage hideousness rushing upon you—on a yellow horse with a mane of waving red! His very presence on an ordinary trotting pony was enough to freeze the blood in one's veins.

That he was a spy was plainly to be seen, and we knew also that his band was probably not far away. He seemed in very good spirits, asked for "tobac," and rode along with us some distance—long enough to make a careful estimate of our value and our strength. Finally he left us and disappeared over the hills. Then the little escort of ten men received orders from Faye to be on the alert, and hold themselves and their rifles ready for a sudden attack.

We rode on and on, hoping to reach the Cimarron Redoubt before dark, but that had to be given up and camp was made at Snake Creek, ten miles the other side. Not one Indian had been seen on the road except the Apache, and this made us all the more uncomfortable. Snake Creek was where the two couriers were shot by Indians last summer, and that did not add to our feelings of security—at least not mine. We were in a little *coulée,* too, where it would have been an easy matter for Indians to have sneaked upon us. No one in the camp slept much that night, and most of the men were walking post to guard the animals. And those mules! I never heard mules, and horses also, sneeze and cough and make so much unnecessary noise as those animals made that night. And Hal acted like a crazy dog—barking and growling and rushing out of the tent every two minutes, terrifying me each time with the fear that he might have heard the stealthy step of a murderous savage.

Everyone lived through the night, however, but we were all glad to make an early start, so before daylight we were on the road. The old sergeant agreed with Faye in thinking that we were in a trap at the camp, and should move on early. We did not stop at the Redoubt, but I saw as we passed that the red curtains were still at the little window.

It seems that we are not much more safe in this place than we were in camp in an Indian country. The town is dreadful and has the reputation of being one of the very worst in the West since the railroad has been built. They say that gamblers and all sorts of "toughs" follow a new road. After breakfast this morning we started for a walk to give Hal a little run, but when we got to the office the hotel proprietor told us that the dog must be led, otherwise he would undoubtedly be stolen right before our eyes. Faye said: "No one would dare do such a thing; I would have him arrested." But the man said there was no one here who would make the arrest, as there certainly would be two or more revolvers to argue with first, and in any case the dog would be lost to us, for if the thief saw that he could not hold him the dog would undoubtedly be shot. Just imagine such a thing! So Hal was led by his chain, but he looked so abused and miserable, and I was so frightened and nervous, our outing was short, and here we are shut up in our little room.

We can see the car track from the window, and I wonder how it will seem to go over in a car, the country that we came across in wagons only one year ago. From Granada we will go to the post in an ambulance, a distance of forty or more miles. But a ride of fifty miles over these plains has no terrors for me now. The horses, furniture, and other things went on in a box car this morning. It is very annoying to be detained here so long, and I am a little worried about that girl. The telegram says she was too sick to start yesterday. . . .

~

It has been impossible for me to write before, for I have been more than busy, both day and night, ever since we got here. The servant for whom we waited at Dodge City, and who I had hoped would be a great assistance to me in getting settled, came to us very ill—almost too ill to be brought over from Granada. But we could not leave her there with no one to take care of her, and of course I could not remain with her, so there was nothing else to be done—we had to bring her along. We had accepted Mrs. Wilder's invitation to stay with them a few days until we could get settled a little, but all that was changed when we got here, for we were obliged to come directly to our own house, unpack camp bedding and the mess chest, and do the best we could for ourselves and the sick girl.

The post surgeon told us as soon as he had examined the girl that she had tuberculosis in almost its last stage, and that she was threatened with double pneumonia! So you can imagine what I have been through in the way of nursing, for there was no one in the garrison who would come to assist me. The most unpleasant part of it all is, the girl is most ungrateful for all that is being done for her, and finds fault with many things. She has admitted to the doctor that she came to us for her health; that as there are only two in the family, she thought there would be so little for her to do she could ride horseback and be out of doors most of the time! What a nice arrangement it would have been—this fine lady sitting out on our lawn or riding one of our horses, and I in the kitchen preparing the dinner, and then at the end of the month humbly begging her to accept a little check for thirty dollars!

We have an excellent soldier cook, but the care of that miserable girl falls upon me, and the terrible experience we passed through at Dodge City has wholly unfitted me for anything of the kind. The second night we were there, about one o'clock, we were awakened by loud talking and sounds of people running; then shots were fired very near, and instantly there were screams of agony, "I'm shot! I'm shot!" from some person who was apparently coming across the street, and who fell directly underneath our window. We were in a little room on the second floor, and its one window was raised far up, which made it possible for us to hear the slightest sound or movement outside.

The shooting was kept up until after the man was dead, many of the bullets hitting the side of the hotel. It was simply maddening to have to stay in that room and be compelled to listen to the moans and death gurgle of that murdered man, and hear him cry, "Oh, my lassie, my poor lassie!" as he did over and over again, until he could no longer speak. It seemed as though every time he tried to say one word, there was the report of a pistol. After he was really dead we could hear the fiends running off, and then other people came and carried the body away.

The shooting altogether did not last longer than five or ten minutes, and at almost the first shot we could hear calls all over the wretched little town of "Vigilante! Vigilante!" and knew that the vigilantes were gathering, but before they could get together the murderous work had been finished. All the time there had been perfect silence throughout the hotel. The proprietor told us that he got up, but that it would have been certain death if he or anyone else had opened a door.

Hal was on the floor in a corner of our room, and began to growl after the very first scream, and I was terrified all the time for fear he would go to the open window and attract the attention of those murderers below, who would undoubtedly have commenced firing at the window and perhaps have killed all of us. But the moans of the dying man frightened the dog awfully, and he crawled under the bed, where he stayed during the rest of the horrible night. The cause of all the trouble seems to have been that a colored man undertook to carry in his wagon three or four men from Dodge City to Fort Dodge, a distance of five miles, but when he got out on the road a short distance he came to the conclusion, from their talk, that they were going to the post for evil purposes, and telling them that he would take them no farther, he turned his team around to come back home. On the way back the men must have threatened him, for when he got in town he drove to the house of some colored people who live on a corner across from the hotel and implored them to let him in, but they were afraid and refused to open the door, for by that time the men were shooting at him.

The poor man ran across the street, leaving a trail of blood that streamed from his wounds, and was brutally killed under our window. Early the next morning, when we crossed the street to go to the cars, [a] mule was lying on the ground, dead, near the corner of the hotel, and stuck on one long ear was the murdered man's hat. Soon after we reached Granada a telegram was received giving an account of the affair, and saying also that in less than one half hour after the train had passed through, Dodge City was surrounded by troops of United States cavalry from Fort Dodge, that the entire town was searched for the murderers, but that not even a trace of one had been discovered. . . .

Mary McNair Matthews Feeds Virginia City (1877)

It was about the 1st of April, the year '77, that business in Virginia City came to a state of stagnation, hundreds of men being out of employment. . . . Nearly all the mines were shut down. . . .

In the meantime the streets were filled with starving men, women and children . . . and still the people kept pouring in from the East. Men could not go to and from their places of business without being importuned to give "two bits" for a lunch, or "four bits" for a square meal. . . .

Mrs. Beck was at my house one day, and we were speaking of the amount of poor people on the streets, when she said she was afraid the city would go some night, and she had heard many express the same opinion.

While we were yet speaking, a man came out of the kitchen of Mr. Ryan's restaurant carrying a barrel of dry bread, and put it on his swill cart for the milk ranch.

"Look!" said she, "at those loaves of dry bread being dumped into that cart. How the hungry would like to have them! Just see the stuff that is wasted from one house, and it is just so all over the city! Why could not some one go around and gather it up, nice and clean, and spread it in some place, and let the hungry go and eat what they wanted."

I said it would be a good plan, but some would keep others away, while they carried all off themselves. If it could be gathered and nicely sorted, and served up properly on plates, it would do a vast deal of good. For instance, have a soup-house, like they have in Chicago. . . .

She sat thinking very seriously for a moment, then turning to me, said: "Well, why can't you and I do it, if no one else will?"

"All right," said I. "Where will we have it?"

"Well," said Mrs. Beck, "there is my carpenter shop on B Street, and the man is just using it temporarily. I will tell him I want it; I only get $15 a month for it, and I can afford to lose that much for two or three months. . . ."

I told her . . . I was ready to go. . . . I put on my things and we started out.

"Let us first get us a book, and then go around to the restaurants and take down the names of all who will give us their cold victuals," said Mrs. Beck. "After that we will go to the merchants and get them to give us their wilted vegetables."

We did this, and nearly every restaurant promised to save us its provisions in baskets, which we were to leave for the purpose.

The merchants also agreed to save us their vegetables, and some searched over their stores and gave us all their broken packages of pepper, tea, soda, spices, and other groceries.

"Now," said Mrs. Beck, "let us go to Mr. Beck and tell him we want him to send a good large stove, seven or eight tables, and all the odd chairs he can spare; and while we're there we will look out the dishes and have them sent down."

"You talk as if you were sure of the whole thing; perhaps your husband will not let us have them."

"Oh, yes he will! Beck is the best man in town about any such thing. He always gives me all the cracked dishes I want to give to any poor person. You know nicked plates are just as good to bake on, and saves the better ones."

After we had selected the dishes . . . we took down the names of all parties who were willing to donate towards the lunch house. We received subscriptions all the way from "two bits" to $4, and two or three of $5 each. . . .

The most of our subscriptions were of 50 cents each, consequently did not count up very fast. . . .

All the merchants with whom we traded let us have goods at reduced rates. We bought a firkin of butter and a half-barrel of sugar to commence on. But the most liberal of all . . . were the butchers of Virginia City. Each and all extended a liberal hand. They furnished us with more meat than we could possibly use in the lunch house; but we . . . knew plenty of poor people in town who needed it. . . .

We managed to feed four and five hundred people three times a day from our lunch house.

The Captain's Wife: Alone on a Wide, Wide Sea (1859)

The decision to go to sea was not always so easy for a Captain's wife—solitude was as certain a reward as adventure and often a good deal harder to take. The diaries kept by these women are often filled with everyday details that numb us with their regularity, and only the weather offers any dramatic change in pace. We know little of Mary Chipman Lawrence, author of the following, except that from her diary we see her as a keen observer, quick to catch a sure detail and willing to speak of her heart. Though her diary is often filled with exuberance, it is in the following extract that we see the hard loneliness of a woman who must keep the connections with family and community going while far, far away:

Arrived at Honolulu the next morning. Mr. Richmond, a nephew of our agent who is clerk with Wilcox and Richards, came on board and kindly offered to procure a boarding place for us, which he did at Mr. Whitney's. We found several letters at Lahaina and a number more awaiting us at Honolulu. Letters from Sandwich informed us that my dear father's health had been very poor throughout the summer, but that it had been improving for the last few weeks, and they thought as the weather became cooler he would continue to improve. How anxious I shall be on his account for the remainder of the voyage. Not one word more shall I hear, unless we should receive letters by the next mail, which I do not expect, until we arrive home. Oh that he may live until our return. Our other friends were all well. Received Willie's daguerreotype in a letter. He has grown very much and changed much in his looks since I saw him. From his picture I should judge that he was a fine-looking young man.

On our arrival at Mr. Whitney's found that Mrs. Whitney's niece Emmie Cutts, who arrived while we were there last fall, was married two nights previous to Charles Judd, a resident of Baker Island. They left for that place on the next week after our arrival.

We were pained to hear of the death of Captain Palmer of the *Kingfisher.* Mrs. Palmer arrived from Hilo a few days after our arrival, where she had been stopping through the season with her two children (one born since her husband left her), on her way home by way of California, a poor broken-hearted widow. My heart aches for her as it has seldom ached for anyone. It is hard to be thus bereft when one is at home, surrounded by loving friends, but to a stranger in a strange land it is desolate indeed. Oh, what a sad going home was that from what she had been fondly anticipating. May He who kindly tempers the wind to the shorn lamb deal so gently with her.

It was my painful duty to attend her on board the *Kingfisher,* then to overlook and pack up the clothing of her dear departed husband, and a trying duty it was to me. What must it have been for her.

Two other captains died in the Okhotsk Sea this last season, Captain Tallman of the *Midas* and Captain Waterman of the *J. D. Thompson,* both of them leaving families at home. Reports came by the Okhotsk fleet confirming the loss of the *Ocean Wave* and the *Phoenix,* about which there had been so much anxiety. The *Ocean Wave* was lost at the same time within a very short distance, and all were saved. We were also pained to hear of the death of Mr. Baxter, who came out with us as second officer. He left us a year out, then went a short cruise south in the *Ocean Wave,* procured his discharge from that ship, went to Fraser River, returned again to the Islands, sailed for home in the *Trident,* and was washed overboard in a gale of wind off the River La Plata.

We passed the time of our sojourn in port very pleasantly for the most part. Went to the theater building one evening to see Professor Anderson perform and again to hear the Swiss bell ringers. Saw many acquaintances while in port, some being home friends and others acquaintances of the voyage, especially captains and their wives, of whom there were many in port. We would generally meet at some boarding place, five or six couples, and after spending an hour or two very pleasantly, would adjourn to an ice-cream saloon.

The last November the *Yankee* arrived from California, and I with many others was anticipating news from home, although I did not really expect letters. We received one, however, from sister Sarah written from the first to the tenth of September. The only sad news it contained was the death of our minister, who has been settled since we left home. That evening we went out to make calls. On our way home called at Captain Wilcox' to get some New Bedford papers. After we arrived home I sat down, as I usually do on the receipt of home papers, to look over the deaths and marriages. Samuel had stepped out, and I was left alone. Shall I ever forget my sensations when the first paragraph on which my eyes rested was the death of my dear father. What a shock and how unexpected! Can it be that I have seen him for the last time? Oh, how fondly I have anticipated meeting Father, Mother, brothers, and sisters once more. It has been the great wish of my heart. Oh, it is so hard that I could not have heard one word in connection with his death. It seems as if it could not be, the thought that he is no more, that he died when I his eldest daughter was far away, that I never more shall see him. Oh, it almost overpowers me, and my poor mother, I fear that the blow was too heavy for her to bear. With what a sad heart shall I return home. I feel as if his vacant place would be more than I can bear.

Dorothea Balano: "Just so long as we go." (1910–12)

Born in 1882, Dorothea Moulton grew up in Minnesota, far from the open sea she would come to know and love so well. She was a spirited young woman who, upon graduation from college, was determined to travel the world. Her desire was facilitated by meeting and falling in love with Fred Balano, a lifelong seafaring captain. Her diaries aboard Fred's ship from 1908 to 1913 (where she began her journey as a passenger and ended as the "skipper's wife") were lovingly published by her son James Balano in The Log of a Skipper's Wife:

Sunday Morning—July 3, 1910

When we arrived on board, the awning was down as the crew prepared the ship for an early sailing in the morning. I got sea fever and couldn't think of sleeping. Such a night! Even the little stars were out, and there was a small new moon on the horizon. Wrote letters for the States mail, telling my poor family of the venture their wayward daughter is undertaking.

All sails set and we look like a great, white, winged bird as we roll stately over a sapphire sea along a dim outline of hazy mountains. It was a memorable experience to wake from a short nap at four in the morning to the sound of creaking rigging. Barely did we rush into a few clothes and scurry on deck when the mizzen sail majestically lifted and straightened. The gray darkness slowly lightened, and we watched the fore and main sails rise against the little, low moon. Halyards loosened and slackened, finally taking their proper lengths. Great booms swung into position with the breeze. With the coming of dawn and a great ball of sun, Captain Balano whistled for the pilot to hurry aboard. He spoke only the King's Spanish, and I was happy to translate a bit, although I found that seaman's talk is neither English nor Spanish but a code of grunts, pointing, and gesticulation.

To avoid the mud shoals in the narrow channel and lift the ship on her way, the spanker had to be partly hoisted for a few minutes. That extra power did the work and soon we were free, the prow, *proa,* pointing west. With a lazy majesty and billowing grace, the good ship *R. W. Hopkins* put to sea as though some stately creature had communed with the moon and stars and then bowed to their master, the sun, who would now lead the way. . . .

A man is always at the wheel. The mate eats at our table; the second mate and the engineer eat at the second table. I ate a hearty breakfast, but poor Betty did not. I don't know how much more I can eat without letting out a few seams. And I'm ashamed to be seen enjoying food so much in front of Betty. She told the Captain that her stomach was weak, and he didn't help matters at all by telling her she must have a strong stomach by the way she was throwing food over the side farther than anyone he had ever seen. The brute!

Eight bells is either four, eight, or twelve o'clock. Each half hour is marked by lovely bells.

After the buoys and the pilot became ancient history, the crew hoisted the jibs, outer, flying, main, and forestay-sail, and finished raising the largest sail on board, the spanker. Then the topsails were loosened and set, all four. We plowed past Caja de Muertos at eight when the watch was changed. Betty still seasick and the Captain scrubbing the dirt of land off his white paint. I'd take a bath but am sure this sea would toss me out of the tub. The wind is dead aft and breezing up. I'll tell my farmer-father that it comes from the rear. I hope that if I do get sick it won't be until Betty is better. The Captain asked me to help him stand the evening watch on deck. He seems every inch a man, a handsome one at that. I wonder; I wonder how it will all come out. *Dios sabe.*

Monday, September 25, 1911

Hemmed my suit skirt in the dense fog and mended my red gown. My boy is out, renewing old acquaintances and telling them lies, no doubt, of the big world about which they care nothing. Most of them have seen it anyway. But few of them know where they were, beyond remembering the docks and the waterfront ginmills. Cousin Watson, the family no-good, went to sea with his older brother, Captain J. W., until set ashore off the entrance to Chesapeake Bay in the pilot boat for having insulted Mother B., has been to Rio, pronounced Rye-oh, to Cuba, spoken of as Cubee, and I couldn't make him understand that he had been to Cienfuegos until I spelt it, and he said, "o'course, Signphugos!" He might as well have stayed back home with his lobsterpots. Mother B. is bright and smart and jolly. She was the favorite of her father's ten children, the tom-boy who would help him launch vessels, and she can still row a boat so well that she made Fred give her the oars to the dory yesterday when he was setting her on the island to visit her brother Orrin. Still she wouldn't eat the famous strawberries in Rio in December, because at home they were out of season, and she still can't understand why sailing south from the equator isn't easier than sailing the other way because it's downhill all the way. I do believe, though, that she's joshing me, and I'd better be a bit less proud of my brilliance in the company of these people, who like to act ignorant when they really are quite adept, in their own way, at things that matter to them.

Drove up the old road through Turkey to Glenmere in the enchanting autumn woods, and in came the river at several delightful coves.

Tuesday, October 31, 1911 (Boston)

Sailing tomorrow for Rio, I've had such a sea fever since my last entry, weeks ago, that I just couldn't burden you, my poor diary, with such stuff as who baked what apple pie. Maine was exquisitely beautiful, and the people so warm and kind; but it's not Rio de Janeiro. It's more jolly to have Fred tacking the ship instead of the auto, rain doesn't seem strange at sea as it does on land, food tastes better, even the lobsters we brought with us on board. Good-bye to great Aunt Katie Seavey, who, having been a sea widow for fifty-seven years, will hardly miss us. Farewell to Aunt Phronie and her misbegotten Civil War as well as to Grandmother Sarah, who still doesn't know whether I'm "from here or from away." Adios to Mother B., who showed me the island where she roved and ranged along the shore, picking lobsters out of the eel grass, Indian trinkets from the old Indian garden, and spent her girlhood as a better sailor and fisher than her sea-going brothers, and came "ashore" as soon, no sooner, as she was betrothed to Captain J. W., who was smart enough to marry the owner's daughter. *Au revoir* to the Pinkhams and to Mary Davis, who jumped from the frying pan of teaching in Puerto Rico to marrying a lobster fisherman at Port Clyde, a situation not to be described so much as a leap into a fire as into a cold douche. *Aufwiedersehen* to naughty cousin Perce and his proclivities for raunchy stories and raunchier women, whose nastier aspects he held up before Fred to try undermining the holy knot, which no man should rip asunder, damn him. Short shrift to the damnable auto, which caught fire one morning and had a collision the same afternoon. Even an impatient shrug to the Columbus Day procession, and I used to love parades. Miles of Italians marching past the Governor's pavilion and sixteen other lands represented with gaudy banners and silly streamers as I clung with boredom to an iron fence and longed for the open sea and its perfume of good salt, some of which the marchers should have used for a bath. I may miss the Keith Theatre, but not until I'm at sea awhile, because the tumbling, dancing, singing, and joking was good, but it might be more appreciated after a long passage at sea, which I now look forward to so long as my skipper, in his skipping, doesn't get his feet caught too often in his mouth. Shall really miss Tremont Temple and its splendid paintings by Sargent in the Public Library, the Law and the Prophets, Moses in bas-relief. Can take with me fond memories. . . .

Thursday, November 2, 1911 (4 A.M.)

Rushed into a few clothes and scurried on deck, awakened by the creaking rigging. The mizzen sail majestically lifted in the gray darkness to the sound of rough voices. Then appeared the main and foresails. The great booms swung into position. Next the stately great spanker and, as if staged, a great red ball of sun. Below the fort we hoisted forestay-sail and outer jib. Flying jib still tied up.

Sailing out of bay all day in company with many schooners and steamers. Passed Cape Cod Light at sunset. Put a whole basket of clothes to soak. Fred spent most of the evening buying a farm—the last thing I, brought up on a farm, want to hear about. I'll take *Two Years Before the Mast*. Fred says he's going to have the crew build a gangway so I won't have to use the ladder. Told him that was very thoughtful of him. I want a child and he presents me with a gangway!

Friday, December 13, 1912

I told Dr. North, a wonderful physician, to go back to Bowdoin College and study some psychology in order to learn that the best cure of a woman is to go and meet her husband. He laughed and said he guessed Captain Fred could find his way home without my navigation. So I read *Daddy Longlegs* by the lovely fire, about a girl who wrote letters to a man she didn't know but later married. Very bright but quite dangerous for her.

A letter from Puerto Rico tells me that my good old friend, Mr. Benedict of Hatillo, has passed away, leaving a pregnant widow who has gone to her brother's in Mississippi. Little Bernard has been shipped off to his sister, Mabel, my old teaching comrade at Utuado, who now lives in Oneonta, N.Y., and whom I shall visit if I can make the trip to meet Fred at the dock in New York City. But Dr. North says my convalescence still needs inactivity for a month of Sundays. No news from the *Hopkins,* temporarily commanded by another, or from Fred or from the Royal Mail about the ship on which Fred is supposed to arrive from Barbados. I'd convalesce faster if Jim Wilson and his rushing horses would get me something in the mail instead of magazines, advertisements, and bills. Why doesn't Fred telegraph me? Why doesn't he take the French steamer from Fort-de-France? Has he the typically English and American distaste and distrust of French ships? I'd love wine with my meals and a dish of bouillabaisse before my filet mignon and crepes suzettes to top it off, with a bit of Camembert to boot. It would be a welcome and far cry from Mother B.'s menu of cold porridge for breakfast, stale ham for lunch, and crackers with milk, sour milk at that, for supper. Her penny-pinching affects my health also, with the lack of heat. Captain J. W. installed a hot-water system for heating, radiators, and a new coal-burning furnace, but she won't use it because the price of coal is greater than the cost of cutting wood from her own woodlots. That would be reasonable, I suppose, if she allowed the cutters to cut more than what is needed for her kitchen stove and a bit for the fireplace, but she doesn't. The radiators must be frozen because there's no heat in the upstairs bedrooms. To keep from freezing, I must nap by the fireplace. Although some days she's not so vexing as usual, I do wait for Fred to straighten her out. Childbirth was not the cure-all for me that she claims it was for her (why did she have just the one child?), and I am in pain so often that I can't fight, especially in her own home.

To escape for a short while, I attended the Sewing Circle at the Advent Church and tonight will go to the annual sale at Mrs. Marshall's Bazaar. Shall have the Tibbetts girl in to care for Wilfred. She is so attentive and sweet with him and would never let him come to any harm.

At Mrs. Marshall's, I bought little Dutch bonnets made by Lena Harris. They are so fetching and make lovely presents. The center part is blue and pink muslin with white embroidery in matching colors. I shall send one to Eva Boyden, who is spending the year at Fajardo in a spendid position as principal. Awfully glad for the wondrous girl. Must get baby's photos from Rockland. Must get together a group interested in having a village library. There's so much to do that I shouldn't let Mother B. bother me. How I do miss Fred, who has been twice as gentle to me since his father died, not nearly so cross. It will be five weeks tomorrow that the poor boy has been gone on his fruitless errand. The jury acquitted the murderer, and the Consul wrote me privately that he believes it was due to the blacks being so scared of white Frenchmen having guns. They ignored the murder and ganged up against gun-running. I do find some sympathy with them, I must admit, and wasn't it a shame that Captain J. W. should get involved in such foolishness, but, as the Consul wrote, every skipper visiting Martinique is requested to bring in guns. The situation, he says, is such that the whites, a tiny minority, feel threatened every hour of the day and night and must protect themselves or flee their island.

I got word of Fred's arrival date and telegraphed cousin Roscoe to meet him. Shall try to get shiftless Roy Hupper, he who mismanages the water works, to drive me in the machine to Thomaston when Fred's train arrives.

December 16, 1912

Hurrah! Hurrah! Came a telegram this morning from Fred. He arrived in New York and is coming home at once. I am so glad. He'll get the furnace going and rub my back and play with his little son. Wilfred laughed so coyly at me when I told him his Daddy was coming home. You'd think he almost understood. He is a perfect dear and more fun than a basket of monkeys.

December 17, 1912

Fred came home on the SS *Monhegan* today. I had made fudge and stuffed dates for him. I had also decorated our room with embroidered pillows for his homecoming. I should have known better. All the thanks I got was, "Where in hell have you hidden Nellie's pillow?" Also, I purposely gave up an invitation to meet with my library group because Fred was coming home, and damned if he didn't go out and spend the whole evening with nasty Perce Hupper, his bastard cousin. I do get so everlastingly weary of being the only one to do the square thing. And how my poor back does ache from doing all those things for his arrival. I'd better get him away from his mother soon. Shall we go to sea in the *Hopkins* or in Father J. W.'s *Margaret Thomas?* I don't care, just so long as we go.

Young Kate Shelley Saves the Day

Late in the afternoon of July 6, 1881, a great rainstorm struck the Des Moines River valley in Iowa. Black, fast-rolling clouds had piled up and the farmers of the area had prepared houses, barns and livestock for a bad time. Even so, when the storm struck at twilight it far exceeded their expectations. In a matter of moments the sky became night-black, the wind howled and ripped up trees and fences and the rain poured down. Thunder boomed and seemed to shake the earth. It had been a rainy, stormy spring and summer, but this was the most savage blow of the entire season.

Mrs. Mike Shelley and her five children huddled in their small cottage near the banks of Honey Creek, about a mile and a half from the Des Moines River. They had no thought of bed, even as the night wore on. The downpour was too awesome, the roar of rain and wind too loud for sleep. They stood at the windows of the cottage and watched the creek overflow its banks, carrying with it trees, fence posts and other debris. Their little farmyard became a lake, and the rising creek threatened their stable. Fifteen-year-old Kate, the oldest of the children, went out into the storm to turn loose their horses and cows so they might take care of themselves, and she also rescued a handful of tiny piglets. She returned drenched.

Until his death three years before, Mike Shelley, an Irish immigrant from Tipperary, had been a section foreman on the Chicago and Northwestern Railway. The tracks ran in front of the lonely family cottage. Now, as the younger children dozed, Kate and her mother talked about what the turbulent flood waters might do to the railroad bridge over nearby Honey Creek—and especially what it might do to the long, rickety wooden railroad trestle over the Des

Moines River, which was already weakened by earlier rains. They knew enough about railroads and railroad bridges to be apprehensive.

~

A little after 11 o'clock Kate and her mother heard a familiar sound, the deep panting of a locomotive inching its way through the storm. It was a "pusher," used to help regular trains up the steep grades in that area, and had been sent out from Moingona, a small town on the other side of the Des Moines River, to inspect track and bridge conditions. It was backing cautiously down the track with two of its four-man crew standing on the rear of the tender looking for washouts.

The locomotive chuffed past the Shelley house and rolled on to the bridge over Honey Creek. Suddenly the engine's bell clanged twice, there was a terrible crashing sound, a loud hiss of steam, and locomotive, crew and bridge all fell into the seething water of Honey Creek.

"They've gone down," Kate screamed.

She said later that, despite the violence of the storm, it seemed as still as death, as silent as the grave. A great sense of urgency filled her. What had happened to the men on the locomotive? And, even worse, what would happen to the midnight express which was soon due to roar over the long trestle and then proceed to now-vanished Honey Creek bridge.

~

Kate Shelley was a short, stocky girl, deeply religious and with a sense of responsibility bred in her by having had to help take care of a family without a father. She felt she had to do something. Against her mother's urging, she put on her coat and an absurdly inadequate straw hat, provided herself with a tiny light by mounting a miner's lamp in an old lantern, and set out in the storm. The water was so deep around the house she had to make a long detour to higher ground before she could get near the Honey Creek bridge. When she finally reached it she saw two of the train crew down in the water, clinging to some trees that still stood fast. She shouted down to them and they shouted back, but none could hear the other in the watery tumult. Kate realized she could not rescue the men by herself. Besides, there was the express to think of—and Moingona, the first place where it could be stopped, was a mile and a quarter away.

There was a temporary lull in the storm, and Kate began to run along the tracks toward Moingona. But as she neared the long wooden trestle, the storm redoubled in noise and violence. Kate came to the bridge, and to a desperate decision.

The bridge had only a catwalk beside the tracks, and the railroad had ripped out some of its planks to discourage trespassers. To walk it in full daylight was a perilous enterprise. At night, with a storm raging and the bridge shaken by the swollen river, to try to cross it was suicidal. And there was always the chance that the oncoming express might catch her on the bridge.

The wind rose and, as though timed by a stage director, blew out the tiny lamp Kate carried. She was alone in a howling, black, rain-swept wilderness. Then she thought of the two men clinging to the trees, and of the people on the train. She dropped to her knees and began to crawl across the bridge, feeling for the holes in the planking, seeing where she was going only when the lightning flashed. The bridge was 500 feet long. As she crept from tie to tie, splinters and spikes tore at her clothes and gouged her hands and knees. She felt the bridge shake as the water tore at it and flotsam smashed its piers.

There came a prolonged series of lightning flashes and she saw an enormous tree bearing down on the center of the trestle. The lightning illuminated it so clearly that afterward she could remember seeing the fresh earth that was still clinging to its roots. That great weight must surely carry away the section where she was. She waited in panic. Instead the tree slipped between the piers, its leaves and branches whipping the water and throwing spray over Kate as it passed. She crawled on.

The more she crawled, the more it seemed that she would never reach the end of the bridge. Then suddenly she felt firm ground with her hands and, soaked and bleeding, she stood up and began to run the last quarter mile toward the Moingona station.

~

When she burst into the station—exhausted, tattered, wild-eyed—the first reaction of the men was, "The girl is crazy!" But one of them knew her and understood her warning.

The station agent ran out with a red lamp to halt the express, whose headlight appeared almost instantly. A switch engine's whistle was blown repeatedly to rouse the town. The express came to a halt, its engineer at first indignant at being stopped. When he and the passengers learned what they had been saved from, they crowded together to pass the hat for the young heroine. Meanwhile a rescue train was readied, and Kate guided it across the shaky wooden trestle to the place where the two surviving men of the pusher locomotive still clung to their trees.

Overnight, obscure, cheerful Kate Shelley became the darling of America, and even achieved fame in Europe. For three days she was besieged by reporters, the curious and the important, who thronged the Shelley cottage to congratulate her, ask her questions and beg her to go over the scene again, which she politely did. Then, apparently worn out by her ordeal, she went into a nervous collapse from which she did not recover for three months.

But while she was ill, honors, gifts and tributes of all kinds poured in. Songs and poems were written about her, by amateur and professional artists, one beginning:

> *Have you heard how a girl saved the lightning express,*
> *Of Kate Shelley, whose father was killed on the road?*
> *Were he living today he'd be proud to possess*
> *Such a daughter as Kate. Oh, 'twas grit that she showed*
> *On that terrible evening when Donahue's train*
> *Jumped the bridge and went down, in the darkness and rain!*

Dubuque school children gave her a medal, and so did the state of Iowa, as well as $200. The Chicago *Tribune* launched a fund to pay the Shelley family debts and Kate herself went on a lecture tour to raise money to pay their mortgage. A handsome drinking fountain in a park in Dubuque was named after her. So, some years later, was a new iron railroad bridge over the Des Moines River near Moingona. Kate was given a Simpson College scholarship. The Chicago and Northwestern railroad surpassed itself; not only did it give her a lifetime pass on the railroad, a half barrel of flour and a load of coal, but it issued orders that whenever Kate Shelley traveled by train from nearby Boone, where she occasionally shopped, to her trackside home, the train she took must make a special stop at her front door.

When, in 1903, the station agency at Moingona became vacant Kate applied for the job and had no trouble getting it. She held the post until she died in 1912—of a heart ailment, some said, induced by her heroic efforts that stormy night in 1881. The railroad sent a special train to her home for the funeral.

Adventures in the Klondike (1906)

Luella Day was a practicing physician in Chicago when she decided to take a sabbatical and seek a little adventure. She headed off in 1898 for the Yukon at the peak of the gold rush and learned firsthand of the madness, greed, and grief reaped by miners in search of the great payday. She returned to the United States and self-published her experiences as a message to the government in Washington, D.C., hoping that official action could ease the suffering and poverty she had witnessed. As she put it: "Nature holds her gold in most remote places, and grows her grain in broad fields, but the speculator sharks of the stock exchanges get the profits." Needless to say, no one listened to this remarkable woman's first-hand account of the darker side of the Klondike gold rush:

When I reached Dawson on my return from Bonanza, a period of only two days had elapsed, but in that time those who had followed us arrived at Dawson, and the inhabitants had increased in that brief interval from about 500 to over 12,000 souls. Tents covered the plains between the river and the foot of the mountain, and all was bustle and confusion. Just as soon as the water receded, a period of not more than a few hours, h— broke loose in that camp. Drinking-saloons of the Red Dog variety were opened in profusion, and in them drinking and gambling were rife every hour in the twenty-four. The sun shining all night as well as all day kept the ball rolling, and people would go three days and nights without sleeping.

The miners came down from the creeks every time they had a clean-up, and brought their gold with them, spending most of it in dissipation. I asked Schonburg where they deposited their gold. He started to tell me something, but a man approached and he shut up like a clam. Finally we were alone and he beckoned me into his room. He was embarrassed at having a lady in his room (at least he pretended to be), and quickly lifted the curtain nailed around his bunk and motioned me to look. There, in tin cans and sacks, was a fortune. "Over $300,000 under there," he whispered.

There were no banks and no safes in Dawson at that time, but a man's money anywhere he stowed it was safer than in a bank, as future events proved. The camp was ruled by a vigilance committee and governed by miners' unwritten laws. Any man who stole his neighbor's gold would have been hung higher than Haman on detection. It remained for civilization to bring with it thieves and robbers.

I remained at the primitive hotel for the next ten days. I spent most of my time wandering about looking over the ground and sizing up the situation.

Among the recent arrivals were that class of immoral women who always rush into a new mining-camp, and in a few days dance-halls were opened on the main thoroughfares for the entertainment of the miners who came to Dawson from the mines. The women in these dance-halls were not what you would call raving beauties, but there was a frank exposure of such charms as they imagined they had, for they wore dresses abbreviated at both ends, thus displaying their necks and arms and their legs up to their knees. They were largely Canucks, or Canadian French, and they ranged in ages from children 12 years old to old women of 60, gray-haired but hopeful.

The music was furnished by a cracked fiddle, and the price charged for the privilege of dancing with these sirens was five dollars a head. At one end of the room was a bar where whiskey was retailed at one dollar a drink, and it was customary to buy a drink for the girl you danced with, if you did not, as almost all the men did, treat the whole crowd. One night there was an invasion by a big, rawboned Scotchman with a fine load of what he called "whuskey" in his skin. He volunteered to dance the Highland Fling, and did so, encouraged by the jeers, laughter and applause of the crowd. When he had finished he shouted out, "Now I want some one to donce with, and if you have any one here who can donce, trot her out—any old pig is good enough for me."

There was so much money in the camp that everybody was good-natured, and the rough-house and gun-plays common to mining-camps were conspicuously absent from our lives in Dawson. The life was out of doors and easily seen from the streets. The floors alone were of wood, and they were roofed and walled in with canvas—gambling-dens, boozing-stalls and dance-halls alike.

In about two weeks an illness broke out in the camp, and I was called to prescribe for the wife of a Canuck known as French Curly. I found her in a high fever. It was neither typhoid nor typhus fever. It was a new phase of illness to me, as the bowels were involved seriously. I am of the opinion that the decayed vegetation and the moss and the hot sun pouring down at noonday upon them brought about a deadly miasmatic condition which threatened to decimate the town. The victims were attacked as suddenly as cholera patients are. In a few days about half the population, consisting of 12,000 souls, was stricken, and about one-third of the population died. Many of them left no means of identification and are mourned by their relatives in the East as among the unknown dead. This epidemic lasted from the last of June until the middle of August, when, the weather growing cold, the moss was frozen at night, and the sickness ended as suddenly as it had begun.

I rented a tent, ten by twelve feet, and paid $65 per month for the same. It was of canvas, with a board floor raised two feet from the ground. It was directly adjoining the hotel. Here I opened an office for the practice of my profession. There were two physicians besides myself who had come into the country, but both of them got the gold fever and went up Bonanza Creek prospecting. From one of them I purchased his store of drugs and surgical instruments, and hung out my shingle.

When the epidemic broke out I turned my office into a hospital and filled it with patients. I put my clothing and everything else I could find under their heads for pillows. I had a box in the center of the floor to sit on that was my only furniture.

John Rosine, of Seattle, and now a millionaire steamship-owner and president of the Northwestern Steamship Company, was one of my patients, and lay on that same floor in this rude hospital and was "broke to cases."

For three weeks I never slept day or night, watching over and caring for these unfortunate men. I finally got so worn and weary that I could not eat. I offered a young man a hundred dollars to sit up with the sick just one night so I could get one night's rest and sleep. He declined, saying he would not stay an hour in that tent for a thousand dollars, much less all night. He feared that the fever was contagious, and hastened away.

I walked along the board walk and saw the people dead and dying in nearly every tent, and for the first and only time in my life I became absolutely panic-stricken. I felt that I must get away from that place, and that soon, or I should die myself. But how? I finally decided to get into a small boat, of which there were plenty scattered along the shore, and float down the river. I could not bring myself to leave my dog Napoleon behind, and so took the risk of his upsetting the boat, knowing from experience that if he did so he would land me safe on shore. I packed my dressing-bag and dressed for the journey. Just as I started to leave the tent I turned for a last farewell look around.

It was midnight. At that moment a Mr. Joel, a relative of the late Barney Barnato, opened his eyes and spoke for the first time in three weeks, saying, "Water, water." I had found him unconscious under a fly-tent and got Mr. Franks, the jeweler, to help bring him into my tent. I put down my bag to give him a drink, intending to go on as soon as he had slaked his thirst. But the expression of his large brown eyes and the smile of gratitude that came over his face when I gave him water encouraged me, and I resolved to stay by them. I then noticed that a man named James Smith, of Oregon, who was a friend of Mr. and Mrs. Wilson, was beckoning me to come to him. He was so weak I had to go down on my knees to catch his words. He wanted the pictures of his wife and baby, and I handed them to him. He gazed intently at the portraits, kissed them, reached out and took my hand in his, and in a few minutes he had passed over the "great divide."

Father Judge, of the Roman Catholic Church, came into camp from the Mission of the Holy Cross, in Alaska, about 1,700 miles down the river from Dawson. He came up the river traveling over the ice. He opened a hospital, which he located at the foot of the avalanche where the Indians were lost. Here he pitched several tents, one 40 by 60 feet, and ministered to the sick, shrived the dying, and buried the dead. This good man did not spare himself at any time, and when the epidemic subsided he built a church on the spot where the tent hospital had stood. He was universally beloved, and when death overtook him he was buried in the church he had built, mourned alike by Protestants and Catholics.

The gold was plentiful, and yet many a man died before he got an ounce or a mine. And yet where they were buried the auriferous soil was so rich in gold that their graves are decorated with nuggets. There was no time or opportunity during the epidemic for questions of creed. Catholics and heretics alike lie side by side awaiting the call. At least this must be said for most of these brave men that they laid down their lives not for selfish reasons, but in hope of some day, soon, taking back to their homes the gold which would ensure the future independence of their loved ones.

A Tenderfoot No Longer

Grace Thompson-Seton ends her memoir in triumphant voice. We should all take heart and do likewise:

Now this is the end. It is three years since I first became a woman-who-goes-hunting-with-her-husband. I have lived on jerked deer and alkali water, and bathed in dark-eyed pools, nestling among vast pines where none but the four-footed had been before. I have been sung asleep a hundred times by the coyotes' evening lullaby, have felt the spell of their wild nightly cry, long and mournful, coming just as the darkness has fully come, lasting but a few seconds, and then heard no more till the night gives place to the fresh sheet of dawn. I have pored in the morning over the big round footprints of a mountain lion where he had sneaked in hours of darkness, past my saddle-pillowed head. I have hunted much, and killed a little, the wary, the beautiful, the fleet-footed big game. I have driven a four-in-hand over corduroy roads and ridden horseback over the pathless vasty wilds of the continent's backbone.

I have been nearly frozen eleven thousand feet in air in blinding snow, I have baked on the Dakota plains with the thermometer at 116 degrees, and I have met characters as diverse as the climate. I know what it means to be a miner and a cowboy, and have risked my life when need be, *but,* best of all, I have felt the charm of the glorious freedom, the quick rushing blood, the bounding motion, of the wild life, the joy of the living and of the doing, of the mountain and the plain; I have learned to know and feel some, at least, of the secrets of the Wild Ones. In short, though I am still a woman and may be tender, I am a Woman Tenderfoot no longer.

B R E A K I N G
T H E   B A R R I E R S

Over and over again, those who write of the nation's economic
development celebrate the parade of pioneers and industrialists,
warriors and merchants who rode the bright, awesome machine
of capitalism. And often enough there were women as part of the
story. Some, like Miriam Leslie (who inherited her dead husband's struggling company and built a publishing empire) or
Sarah Todd Astor (the shrewd genius behind the Astor fortune
who charged her husband $500 a day for advice), highlighted the
lives of the privileged. Others were acclaimed journalists who
relentlessly explored the bitter fruits of economic growth, such
as Nellie Bly (one of the first great muckrakers who went around
the world in seventy-two days to international acclaim and died
penniless); Ida Tarbell (who took on John D. Rockefeller with
her investigative reporting and won. "I felt that one had better
die fighting against injustice than to die like a dog or a rat in a
trap," she once said); or Anne Royall (who caught John Adams
swimming naked and said, "Give me an interview and I'll leave").
It is alarming, however, at how hard it was for many of these
audacious women to enter the working life and make their mark.

Some were successful, some were colorful, but all, inevitably, paid a high price for their determination simply to do the thing that every man considered a birthright: work.

It was a male fancy in the nineteenth century to say that if a woman left home for a life of work, she would become a "soiled dove or a painted pigeon." For many women, their options were limited and marriage was the only economic haven, the refuge where the refugee became a hostage. The choice between work and family was deliberately stark, brutal. Without a husband, a woman was considered adrift—or worse—dangerous. In the city, a single woman without means was given the choice of hard labor (factories) or prostitution; in the country, it might be hard labor (fields) or teaching. Either way, self-determination was not an option. Those who spoke out were branded radicals despite their eloquence. Listen to Fanny Fern, one of the first great newspaper columnists in America, who wrote in 1857: "Why shouldn't women work for *pay*? Does anybody object when women *marry for pay*?—without love, without respect, nay with even aversion? . . . How much more to be honored is she who, hewing out her own path, through prejudice and narrowness and even insult, earns honorably and honestly her own independence."

It is only in relatively recent times that adequate attention has been paid to the barriers broken by women, although they have been routinely doing so since America's founding (the determined printer in 1776 who was the first to publish the Declaration of Independence was a woman named Mary Goddard). For too long, the nation's historians and storytellers succumbed to the subtle, irresistible prejudice that reinforced the perception of the great women of America acted merely as supporting players to an American drama made for and by men. Emerson's chilling observation that "woman should not be expected to write or fight or build or compose scores. She does all by inspiring men to do all" played well to many nineteenth century-men and even seemed sensible to a certain kind of woman bred for society and the pleasantries of the parlor. But for other women, Emerson's observation would have had no meaning at all. Belva Lockwood was too busy fighting Congress and the Supreme Court for the right to practice law; Lydia Pinkham, whose cure-all vegetable compound was a bestselling product in the nineteenth century, was already on her way to a fortune; Amelia Earhart had her eyes on the heavens and Susan B. Anthony on the ballot box. Flying planes, voting, publishing, sculpting, legislating, healing, working, building—there was too much to do for American women, and despite the efforts of many men (and with the assistance of still others) they took their places in all aspects of American life.

Thankfully, the ongoing publication of the diaries, letters, and memoirs of women whose principal aim is to recognize their own mental and moral powers is becoming a formidable library. If some still believe that behind this proliferation of books on women and their experiences is the orchestrated pressure of "political correctness," then they are the poorer for the folly. The stories on the following pages are as politically correct as a clenched fist at a Quaker meeting. In the writings of women as different as the 19th-century journalist Fanny Fern or the great 20th-century photographer Margaret Bourke-White, in the speeches of Matilda Gage, Ernestine Rose, and other comrades in the women's movement, there is no apology. If there is sometimes anger it is understandable: when who we are or who we want to be seems to lie just beyond the barriers that loom before us, rage can be a mighty battering ram.

Abigail Adams: "Remember the Ladies . . ."

Braintree March 31, 1776

I long to hear that you have declared an independency—and by the way in the new Code of Laws which I suppose it will be necessary for you to make I desire you would Remember the Ladies, and be more generous and favourable to them than your ancestors. Do not put such unlimited power into the hands of the Husbands. Remember all Men would be tyrants if they could. If perticuliar care and attention is not paid to the Ladies we are determined to foment a Rebelion, and will not hold ourselves bound by any Laws in which we have no voice, or Representation.

That your Sex are Naturally Tyrannical is a Truth so thoroughly established as to admit of no dispute, but such of you as wish to be happy willingly give up the harsh title of Master for the more tender and endearing one of Friend. Why then, not put it out of the power of the vicious and the Lawless to use us with cruelty and indignity with impunity. Men of Sense in all Ages abhor those customs which treat us only as the vassals of your Sex. Regard us then as Beings placed by providence under your protection and in immitation of the Supreem Being make use of that power only for our happiness.

Tough Work (1776)

[*Y*]ou[r] petitioner has been a nurse at the hospital for about a year she has been deligent and carefull in her office, [for] which she your petitioner humbly beg[s] for an augmentation to her pay as she only is allowed two dollars a month she has at this present time sixteen men for to cook and take care off . . . she is oblige[d] to be up day and night with some of the patients and never has been allowed so much as a little Tea, or Coffee which she your Petitioner hopes your honours will take . . . into your consideration and your Petitioner in duty Bound will ever Pray.

—*Alice Redman*

P.S. She your petitioner out of that two dollars pr month is oblig[d] to buy brooms and the soap we wash with. . . .

A Guideline For Female Schoolteachers
(1907)

Do not get married

Do not leave town any time without school board permission

Do not keep company with men

Be home between the hours of 8 P.M. and 6 A.M.

Do not smoke

Do not loiter around in ice cream shops

Do not dress in bright colors

Do not dye your hair

Do not wear any dress more than 2" above the ankle

Do not get into any carriage with any man except your father or brother

Lucy Stone:
"Until she bows down to it no longer." (1876)

The last speaker alluded to this movement [women's rights] as being that of a few disappointed women. From the first years to which my memory stretches, I have been a disappointed woman. When, with my brothers, I reached forth after sources of knowledge, I was reproached with "It isn't fit for you; it doesn't belong to women." Then there was but one college in the world where women were admitted, and that was in Brazil. I would have found my way there, but by the time I was prepared to go, one was opened in the young state of Ohio [Oberlin]—the first in the United States where women and negroes could enjoy opportunities with white men. I was disappointed when I came to seek a profession worthy an immortal being—every employment was closed to me, except those of the teacher, the seamstress, and the housekeeper. In education, in marriage, in religion, in everything, disappointment is the lot of women. It shall be the business of my life to deepen this disappointment in every woman's heart until she bows down to it no longer. I wish that women, instead of being walking show-cases, instead of begging of their fathers and brothers the latest and gayest new bonnet, would ask of them their rights.

"let us have lady doctors . . ." (1849)

*W*e think the men have too long usurped the sole right to practice medicine, and it is time for woman to have some thing to say in the matter. We believe if the system of educating females for physicians be generally adopted, a great amount of suffering and death will be saved. We have too long been subjected to the impositions of Quacks, and quack medicine, and the sooner we learn enough of physiology to take care of ourselves, instead of trusting to them, the better will it be for mankind at large. . . . At any rate, we say let *us* have lady doctors when we need *any,* and the gentlemen may, if they prefer it, employ those of their own sex.

There is always something abhorrent in the thought of having to send for a man if you are a little indisposed, and be subjected to his inquisitiveness. Many a lady we believe had rather suffer much—and in many instances does, to her great injury—rather than undergo the necessary investigation of disease from physicians. But give her one of her own sex, and how much more easily could she unburthen her sorrows, and how much more readily would they be understood.

Fanny Fern Reviews Leaves of Grass (1856)

An astonishing woman full of passion. Humorist, feminist, best-selling novelist, the first great woman columnist in American journalism, Fanny Fern (born in 1811 as Sarah Willis) wasted little time in her adventurous life (her last column being published two days after her death). Nathaniel Hawthorne, who had little patience for women writers, wrote his publishers after reading Fern's novel Ruth Hall: *"Generally women write like emasculated men, and are only distinguished from male authors by greater feebleness and folly; but when they throw off the restraints of decency, and come before the public stark naked, as it were—then their books are sure to possess character and value. Can you tell me anything about this Fanny Fern?" This review of Whitman's* Leaves of Grass *appeared in the newspaper long before anyone gave the bard from Brooklyn a place among the great American poets. It tells us a great deal about this remarkable woman:*

Well baptized: fresh, hardy and grown for the masses. Not more welcome is their natural type to the winter-bound, bed-ridden, and spring-emancipated invalid. "Leaves of Grass" thou art unspeakably delicious, after the forced, stiff, Parnassian exotics for which our admiration has been vainly challenged.

Walt Whitman, the effeminate world needed thee. The timidest soul whose wings ever dropped with discouragement, could not choose but rise on thy strong pinions. . . .

Walt Whitman, the world needed a "Native American" of thorough, out-and-out breed—enamored of *women* not *ladies, men* not *gentlemen;* something beside a mere Catholic-hating Know-Nothing; it needed a man who dared speak out his strong, honest thoughts, in the face of pusillanimous, toadying, republican aristocracy; dictionary-men, hypocrites, cliques and creeds; it needed a large-hearted, untainted, self-reliant, fearless son of the Stars and Stripes, who disdains to sell his birthright for a mess of pottage. . . .

Fresh *Leaves of Grass!* not submitted by the self-reliant author to the fingering of any publisher's critic, to be arranged, rearranged and disarranged to his circumscribed liking, till they hung limp, tame, spiritless, and scentless. No. It were a spectacle worth seeing, this glorious Native American, who, when the daily labor of chisel and plane was over, himself, with toil-hardened fingers, handled the types to print the pages which wise and good men have since delighted to endorse and to honor. Small critics, whose contracted vision could see no beauty, strength, or grace, in these "Leaves," have long ago repented that they so hastily wrote themselves down shallow by such a premature confession. Where an Emerson, and a Howitt have commended, my woman's voice of praise may not avail; but happiness was born a twin, and so I would fain share with others the unmingled delight which these "Leaves" have given me.

I say unmingled; I am not unaware that the charge of coarseness and sensuality has been affixed to them. My moral constitution may be hopelessly tainted—or too sound to be tainted, as the critic wills—but I confess that I extract no poison from these "Leaves"—to me they have brought only healing. Let him who can do so, shroud the eyes of the nursing babe lest it should see its mother's breast. . . .

Sensual? Let him who would affix this stigma upon "Leaves of Grass," write upon his heart, in letters of fire, these noble words of its author:

"In woman I see the bearer of the great fruit, which is immortality. . . . The good thereof is not tasted by *roues,* and never can be. . . ."

I close the extracts from these "Leaves," which it were easy to multiply, for one is more puzzled what to leave unculled, than what to gather, with the following sentiments; for which, and for all the good things included between the covers of his book, Mr. Whitman will please accept the cordial grasp of a woman's hand:

> "*The wife—and she is not one jot less than the husband.*
> *The daughter—and she is just as good as the son,*
> *The mother—and she is every bit as much as the father.*"

The Girl Who Loved Lincoln's Face

While other children played and fished and swung from trees, Vinnie Ream would sit by the riverbank and mold the faces of her family out of mud. She could see spirit and form in a shapeless mound of clay and loved the quick life that would rise up from the work of her fingers. As a little girl, born into an impoverished Wisconsin family in 1847, she was determined to be a sculptor.

During the Civil War, when she lived in Washington, D.C., she apprenticed with a well-known sculptor who recognized her talent and allowed her to use his studio. Would we know of young Vinnie Ream today had she not stood on a streetcorner one afternoon and watched a haggard President Lincoln ride by in a carriage? She knew at once that she wanted to sculpt his face. "He was a man of sorrows," she said years later, "and acquainted with grief." Somehow her request got to him and the president refused to consider the idea ("Why would anyone want to mold my ugly face?"). But Lincoln was moved by Ream's youth—she was barely seventeen—and her modest means, and he relented. He invited her to the White House and sat briefly for her every other day, watching her twist and fold the clay, admiring the deftness of her touch, the subtlety of her craft, while soldiers and statesmen waited impatiently outside his office.

Less than a year after Ream had completed her sculpture, Lincoln was dead. Amidst the national grief, Congress resolved to commission a full-scale statue of the late president for the Capitol rotunda. They solicited proposals from the nation's best sculptors. Ream, the only woman to apply, had never completed a work in marble, but she was the only one to have crafted the great man's face from life, to have seen up close his melancholy eyes and his warm, kindly smile. "When I was summoned before the committee," Ream remembered, "and interrogated about how long I had studied art and if I had ever made a marble statue, my replies must have been incoherent, and later in the privacy of my own home I wept bitter tears that I had ever had the temerity to compete with men in so great an undertaking as the statue of President Lincoln." The Congressional committee astonished everyone by unanimously selecting Ream—the first federal commission awarded to a woman.

Ream began work in a small room in the Capitol. "I approached my sacred task with reverence and with trembling hands." Given Lincoln's bloodstained clothing from the night of his assassination to recreate his truest shape and size, she remembered sitting alone and considering the garments of the man whose face she had come to know and love so well. He had reminisced with her about his youth and his children and had once made her laugh out loud with a story. It would be five years before the final statue was completed. It was unveiled in January of 1871 before President Grant, his cabinet, the members of the Supreme Court, and thousands of dignitaries and diplomats from around the world. The day was bright and clear, the applause deafening. The achievement of the young sculptor was complete.

And what became of the woman who was so talented and passionate at so young an age? While working on a statue of Admiral Farragut to be erected in Farragut Square in Washington in 1875, a young Lieutenant was captivated by her intensity and dedication. He pressed her to marry him and she consented. In the sad tradition of the age, she was prevailed upon to quit sculpting and it would be almost 25 years before she returned again to the art she loved. Before her death in 1914, she completed another statue for the nation's Capitol—of Sequoia, the famous Cherokee chief—but of course it would always be her Lincoln that everyone would remember. You can see the statue today and in the cool marble, in the sad, weary expression, you will see the living soul of America's greatest president. When you stand before it, remember, too, the creator who brought life out of that marble with her small, skillful fingers.

Enid Yandell Poses the Question

The World's Fair in 1893 sponsored the Woman's Building, an exhibit which celebrated the efforts and achievements of women around the world. Among the young artists hired to assist in the project was Enid Yandell, a twenty-two-year-old sculptor. She was introduced to the former First Lady Julia Grant, who had been invited to unveil a statue of her husband, Ulysses S. Grant. Mrs. Bertha Palmer, the Chairwoman of the Board sponsoring the exposition, brought the young artist to meet Mrs. Grant. When the conversation turned to the subject of work, young Enid—

*who must have seemed utterly alien to the grand old woman—*would *have the last word:*

"I want to introduce you to Mrs. Grant," [Mrs. Palmer] said, taking Enid's hand. "Let me present you to Miss Yandell, the young sculptor; she is at work on the Woman's Building and we are very proud of her and think we have conferred on her an honor." Mrs. Grant, a woman of few words, said: "A sculptor! You cut marble?" Miss Yandell replied that she indeed cut marble. "I met one before," Mrs. Grant said, fixing Enid with a steely eye. "She was a great deal about the General, but I don't approve of women sculptors as a rule."

Mrs. Grant was evidently referring to Vinnie Ream Hoxie, who had created a storm of controversy when she was commissioned to execute a statue of Lincoln for the capital; she was only fifteen at the time. Evidently she had spent a lot of time with General Grant.

Mrs. Grant's response cast a damper over the conversation. Mrs. Palmer tactfully introduced another guest. But a little while later, Miss Yandell spotted Mrs. Grant sitting alone. Undaunted, she took up the subject once more. "So you do not approve of me, Mrs. Grant?" Mrs. Grant said that it was nothing personal. "I don't disapprove of *you*, Miss Yandell, but I think every woman is better off at home taking care of husband and children. The battle with the world hardens a woman and makes her unwomanly." "And if one has no husband?" Miss Yandell asked. Mrs. Grant had an answer to that. "Get one," she said. Miss Yandell refused to give up. "But if every woman were to choose a husband the men would not go round; there are more women than men in the world." Mrs. Grant could handle that one too. "Then let them take care of brothers and fathers." She then waxed eloquent. "I don't approve of these women who play on the piano and let the children roll about on the floor, or who paint and write and embroider in a soiled gown and are all cross and tired when the men come home and don't attend to the house or table. Can you make any better housewife for your cutting marble?" "Yes," Miss Yandell said energetically. "I am developing muscle to beat biscuit when I keep house."

This slowed down Mrs. Grant considerably. Miss Yandell was not content to quit when she was ahead. "But, Mrs. Grant," she said, "are there no circumstances under which a woman may go to work?" Mrs. Grant thought it over. "I may be old-fashioned," she said. "I don't like this modern movement. But I don't think so. And yet, there are certain sorts of work a woman may well do:

teaching, being governess, or any taking care of children." Miss Yandell forged ahead. "But suppose a case: a young brother and two strong sisters. The young man makes a good salary but can't get ahead because all his earnings are consumed in taking care of the girls. Hadn't they better go to work and give him a chance to get ahead and have a house of his own, they being as able to work as he? Are they being unwomanly in so doing? Or, the case of a father with a large family of girls and a small income—are they less gentlewomen for helping earn a living, lessening the providing of food for care of so many mouths by adding to the family funds?"

Mrs. Grant stared out the window at the lake. "You may be right. In that case," she said slowly, "they ought to go to work."

Beating Their Wings in Rebellion

"*We women did more than keep house, cook, sew, wash, spin and weave, and garden*," Charlotte Woodward *was to write in her old age*. "*Many of us were under the necessity of earning money besides. We worked secretly, in the seclusion of our bedchambers, because all society was built on the theory that men, not women, earned money, and that men alone supported the family.*" *The excerpt below from Miriam Gurko's* The Ladies of Seneca Falls *offers us a glimpse of Charlotte as she joined the great convention at Seneca Falls, New York, in 1848, the first women's rights gathering in America:*

Early on the morning of July 19, 1848, carriages and wagons began to converge upon Seneca Falls. A young woman, Charlotte Woodward, came with a group of her friends: "At first we traveled quite alone . . . but before we had gone many miles we came on other wagon-loads of women, bound in the same direction. As we reached different cross-roads we saw wagons coming from every part of the county, and long before we reached Seneca Falls we were a procession."

Some had come out of curiosity, but many had been impelled by the same need as Charlotte Woodward. She was one of the large number of women employed by the glove industry of Seneca Falls. Since it was considered unfitting for women to work outside their homes, they did piecework in the seclusion of their own bedrooms. The money they earned was collected—and kept— by their husbands or fathers. "Most women," she wrote, "accepted this condition of society as normal and God-ordained and therefore changeless. But I do not believe that there was any community anywhere in which the souls of some women were not beating their wings in rebellion. . . . Every fiber of my being rebelled, although silently, all the hours that I sat and sewed gloves for a miserable pittance which, after it was earned, could never be mine. I wanted to work, but I wanted to choose my task and I wanted to collect my wages."

When she and her friends reached the Wesleyan Chapel, they formed part of a crowd of three hundred, including about forty men. Men were not supposed to attend the first day's sessions, but since they appeared to be sincerely interested, they were admitted.

At first, however, it looked as though no one would be admitted. The chapel, which was supposed to be opened for the convention, was locked. But Mrs. Stanton's nephew climbed through a window and opened the door from the inside. The waiting crowd entered and took their seats, and the first concerted action to improve the condition of women began.

Although this was to be a convention of and for women, it was unthinkable for a woman to serve as chairman. The most exclusively female organizations had men to chair their meetings. When the Philadelphia Female Anti-Slavery Society held its first meeting some years earlier, a black man had been asked to conduct it. Lucretia Mott commented that "Negroes, idiots and women were in legal documents classed together; so that we were very glad to get one of our own class to come and aid in forming that Society."

In this case, James Mott, Lucretia Mott's husband, served as chairman. If the convention had to be conducted by a man, Mr. Mott was an excellent choice. Impressively handsome and dignified, he gave the proceedings an air of respectability and authority that no woman could have commanded in that era. His wholehearted belief in the equality of women and in the rightness of what the ladies of Seneca Falls were doing added to the sincerity of his manner. The only other participating husband of the five was Thomas McClintock. His wife, Mary Ann McClintock, was appointed secretary.

The first speech, explaining the purpose of the convention, was made by Mrs. Mott, the only one of the organizers who had any experience in public speaking. She was invaluable to the fearful Seneca Falls ladies. She bolstered their failing courage, kept the sessions from wandering off the main issues, and gave the whole proceeding just the right emotional tone. She was followed by Elizabeth Stanton.

During the preceding week, Mrs. Stanton had been filled with increasing terror. It was a combination of stage fright at the prospect of making her first public speech, and consternation at having initiated this unprecedented action by women. A housewife in any period might have quailed at such a formidable undertaking; for a woman in 1848 it was outrageously rash and untraditional, which made it practically earth-shaking.

Nevertheless, she stood up before the audience and, with her confidence growing every minute, read the Declaration of Sentiments. Afterward she delivered a remarkably polished speech, the first of hundreds which were to impress her future listeners. When she had helped write the Declaration and prepared the Resolutions, she had found that she had both competence and pleasure in writing; now she discovered an equal satisfaction in speaking.

On the second day, the convention voted on the Declaration and the Resolutions. Everything was unanimously accepted until the suffrage resolution was proposed. This was too extreme not only for many in the audience but even for the other ladies who, with Mrs. Stanton, had organized the convention. It was argued that so excessive a demand would arouse such antagonism and derision that the movement would be killed before it even got under way.

Mrs. Stanton made an impassioned speech, explaining that through the power of the vote women would be able to win their goals much more quickly. She was warmly supported by Frederick Douglass. Just ten years earlier Douglass, then twenty-one, had escaped from slavery in Baltimore. He made his way first to Massachusetts, where he met William Lloyd Garrison and became an active abolitionist, then moved on to England to avoid being captured and restored to his owner. In 1847, with money raised by British abolitionist sympathizers, he returned to the United States, bought his freedom, and settled in Rochester, New York, where he established the *North Star*, the first newspaper published by a black man in this country.

Elizabeth Stanton had met him when she lived in Boston, and he had long been a friend and frequent visitor of the Motts. Douglass, a firm believer in woman's rights as part of the freedom of all people, had come to lend his assistance to the convention. A highly intelligent and experienced speaker, he made a stirring speech claiming that suffrage was an indispensable basis for winning freedom and equality.

After further debate, some of it acrimonious, a vote was taken. The resolution passed by a small margin. At the end of the final session, one hundred men and women signed the Declaration of Sentiments and Resolutions. Among the signers was young Charlotte Woodward. Of all the women in Seneca Falls that day, she would be the only one alive to cast her first vote seventy-

two years later, when the Federal woman suffrage amendment finally granted
the vote to the female citizens of the United States.

Susan B. Anthony's First Public Speech (1853)

*Some thought her cold, fanatical. She was born a child of reformers—abolitionist,
suffrage-supporting parents. A teacher at first consumed with temperance, Susan Anthony met Amelia Bloomer and Elizabeth Cady Stanton but paid their efforts on
behalf of women little heed. It was the New York State Teachers Association meeting
that gave her a start. Although two-thirds of the attendants were women, men ran the
event, voted the resolutions, laid down the by-laws. The women sat silent until
Anthony stood up to have her say. And when the men tried to shout her down,
she realized that she had to speak for the hundreds of women who sat silently behind her:*

In 1853, the annual convention being held in Rochester, her place of residence, Miss Anthony conscientiously attended all the sessions through three
entire days. After having listened for hours to a discussion as to the reason why
the profession of teacher was not as much respected as that of the lawyer,
minister, or doctor, without once, as she thought, touching the kernel of the
question, she arose to untie for them the Gordian knot, and said, "Mr. President." If all the witches that had been drowned, burned, and hung in the Old
World and the New had suddenly appeared on the platform, threatening vengeance for their wrongs, the officers of that convention could not have been
thrown into greater consternation.

There stood that Quaker girl, calm and self-possessed, while with hasty
consultations, running to and fro, those frightened men could not decide what
to do; how to receive this audacious invader of their sphere of action. At length
President Davies, of West Point, in full dress, buff vest, blue coat, gilt buttons,
stepped to the front, and said, in a tremulous, mocking tone, "What will the
lady have?" "I wish, sir, to speak to the question under discussion," Miss Anthony replied. The Professor, more perplexed than before, said: "What is the
pleasure of the Convention?" A gentleman moved that she should be heard;
another seconded the motion; whereupon a discussion pro and con followed,
lasting full half an hour, when a vote of the men only was taken, and permission granted by a small majority; and lucky for her, too, was it, that the thou-

sand women crowding that hall could not vote on the question, for they would have given a solid "no." The president then announced the vote, and said: "The lady can speak."

We can easily imagine the embarrassment under which Miss Anthony arose after that half hour of suspense, and the bitter hostility she noted on every side. However, with a clear distinct voice, which filled the hall, she said: "It seems to me, gentlemen, that none of you quite comprehend the cause of the disrespect of which you complain. Do you not see that so long as society says a woman is incompetent to be a lawyer, minister, or doctor, but has ample ability to be a teacher, that every man of you who chooses this profession tacitly acknowledges that he has no more brains than a woman? And this, too, is the reason that teaching is a less lucrative profession, as here men must compete with the cheap labor of woman. Would you exalt your profession, exalt those who labor with. Would you make it more lucrative, increase the salaries of the women engaged in the noble work of educating our future Presidents, Senators, and Congressmen."

This said, Miss Anthony took her seat, amid the profoundest silence, broken at last by three gentlemen, Messrs. Cruttenden, Coburn, and Fanning, walking down the broad aisle to congratulate the speaker on her pluck and perseverance, and the pertinency of her remarks. The editor of *The Rochester Democrat* said the next morning, that "whatever the schoolmasters might think of Miss Anthony, it was evident that she hit the nail on the head."

To give the women of to-day some idea of what it cost those who first thrust themselves into these conventions, at the close of the session Miss A. heard women remarking: "Did you ever see anything like this performance?" "I was actually ashamed of my sex." "I felt so mortified I really wished the floor would open and swallow me up." "Who can that creature be?" "She must be a dreadful woman to get up that way and speak in public." "I was so mad at those three men making such a parade to shake hands with her; that will just encourage her to speak again." These ladies had probably all been to theaters, concerts, operas, and gone into ecstasies over Fanny Kemble, Rachel, and Jenny Lind; and Fanny Elsler, balanced on one toe, the other foot in the air, without having their delicacy shocked in the least. But a simple Quaker girl rising in a teachers' convention to make a common-sense remark, modestly dressed, making no display of her neck, or arms, or legs, so tried their delicate sensibilities that they were almost afraid to attend the next session.

At the opening of the next morning's session, after Miss Anthony's début,

Professor Davies, in all his majesty and pomposity, with his thumbs in the armholes of his regulation buff vest, called the Convention to order, and said: "I have been asked by several persons, why no provisions have been made for women to speak, and vote, and act on committees, in these assemblies?" My answer is, "Be pedestal, its shaft, its rich entablature, the crowning glory of the whole. Each and all the parts in their appropriate place contribute to the strength, symmetry, and beauty of the whole. Could I aid in taking down that magnificent entablature from its proud elevation, and placing it in the dust and dirt that surround the pedestal? Neither could I drag down the mother, wife, and daughter, whom we worship as beings of a higher order, on the common plane of life with ourselves."

If all men were pedestals and shafts capable of holding the women of their households above the dirt and dust of common life, in a serene atmosphere of peace and plenty, the good professor's remarks would have had some significance; but as the burdens of existence rest equally on the shoulders of men and women, and we must ever struggle together on a common plane for bread, his metaphor has no foundation. Miss Anthony attended these teachers' conventions from year to year, at Oswego, Utica, Poughkeepsie, Lockport, Syracuse, making the same demands for equal place and pay, until she had the satisfaction to see every right conceded. Women speaking and voting on all questions; appointed on committees, and to prepare reports and addresses, elected officers of the Association, and seated on the platforms.

Anthony and Her Sisters Go to Vote

On November 1, 1872, Susan Anthony asked her sisters to go with her to register in Rochester, New York. The chief registration inspector refused to allow them to do so, saying it was against New York law. Susan Anthony had expected this and come prepared. She had brought along a copy of the Fourteenth Amendment and read aloud the section on which she was basing their right to vote. This, she contended, superseded the New York State constitution.

All the inspectors present listened to the discussion, and two of them agreed to take the responsibility of registering the Anthony sisters. As soon as Susan Anthony left the registration office, she went to ask other women to register. The newspapers carried the story, which persuaded still more women that perhaps they could vote. Altogether, fifty women registered in Rochester.

But when election day came, most of them had second thoughts. It was, after all, illegal for unqualified persons to vote. They could be fined up to $500 and be imprisoned up to three years. Susan Anthony knew this; before she herself tried to vote, she sought legal advice. Several lawyers refused to help her. Finally she found a retired judge, Henry R. Selden, who felt she had valid grounds for her action and agreed to defend her if she ran into trouble. Then she, her sisters, and eleven other women went to vote.

The voting inspectors were reluctant to let the women cast their ballots, since that might make the inspectors guilty of violating the law, but Susan Anthony promised to pay their expenses if they were charged with an illegality. The women then had the incredible experience of exercising the democratic right of all citizens to a voice in their government: They voted.

About two weeks later they were all arrested. Oddly enough, though she knew the law, Susan Anthony had never expected to be actually arrested. She had planned, by proving her own right to suffrage, to bring suit against those inspectors who had refused to register women or accept their vote. This would establish the precedent, once and for all, that inspectors all over the country must accept women as voters.

The pre-trial hearing was held on December 23 before a large audience of newspaper reporters, concerned women, and the curious public. When the militant lawbreakers appeared, they all proved to be, as one newspaper put it, "elderly, matronly-looking women with thoughtful faces, just the sort one would like to see in charge of one's sick-room, considerate, patient, kindly."

Bail was set at $500 each, pending trial. Everyone except Susan Anthony paid. She refused, applying instead for a writ of habeas corpus, planning to challenge the legality of her arrest. The writ was denied, and her bail raised to $1000. Again she refused to pay, saying she would go to jail first. But Judge Selden couldn't bear the thought of Susan Anthony in jail; in spite of her protests, he paid the bond himself. As they were leaving the courtroom, she learned that, by paying bail, she had lost the chance to put the case before the Supreme Court by writ of habeas corpus. She hurried back into the courtroom to get the bond canceled, but it was too late.

The trial took place on June 17, 1873. Before it began, she went through the county delivering a speech—"Is It a Crime for a United States Citizen to Vote?"—in which she discussed the constitutional issues involved. She had not committed any crime, she said, but had only exercised her voting right as a citizen as laid down in the Constitution, which had drawn no distinction between the sexes. In its very preamble, "It was we, the people, not we, the white male citizens, nor yet we, the male citizens, but we, the whole people, who formed this Union."

Some authorities interpreted the use of masculine pronouns—"he," "his," and "him"—as proof that only men were intended to have certain rights under the Constitution. "If you insist on this version of the letter of the law," she said, "we shall insist that you be consistent and . . . exempt women from taxation" and from obeying laws, since "there is no she, or her, or hers, in the tax laws" or in the criminal laws.

The legal papers served on her by the court were all printed forms containing only masculine pronouns. The clerk of the court had altered them to read "she" and "her." If government officials can manipulate pronouns for their purposes, she said, then women can do the same in order to exercise their citizen's right to vote.

The district attorney, fearing that her speech might prejudice a jury in her favor, transferred the trial to another county. She immediately gave her speech in as much of that county as she had time for. The rest of it was covered by another woman's rights leader, Matilda Joslyn Gage, who spoke on "The United States on Trial, not Susan B. Anthony."

The case attracted attention all over the United States. Much of it was sympathetic, especially in Rochester itself, where a local newspaper called her "our Susan B. Anthony" and described her as "a genuine lady—no pretense nor sham—but good Quaker metal . . . cheery, warm-hearted . . . utterly fearless . . . yet having a woman's delicate sensitiveness." The article quoted a woman who, after attending a suffrage convention, had said, "No, I am not converted to what these women advocate, I am too cowardly for that; but I am converted to Susan B. Anthony."

When the trial opened, every seat in the Canandaigua courthouse was filled. There were many lawyers and politicians present, including ex-President Millard Fillmore, all curious to hear how the constitutional question would be handled.

The judge was Ward Hunt, presiding over his first case. Throughout the trial he showed a strong bias against Susan Anthony. He refused to allow her to be called as a witness in her own behalf. Judge Selden, in his defense arguments, stressed the fact that she had acted in good faith, believing, upon his own advice, that she had a right to vote under the provisions of the Fourteenth

Amendment. The only way to prove such a right was by trying to exercise it and then getting a court decision on the legality of such action. Her one motive was to test the constitutional question of woman suffrage.

The district attorney replied that her motives were irrelevant. She had violated the law and was guilty, an argument that he developed in a two-hour speech. Judge Hunt then pulled out of his pocket a written opinion, apparently prepared before the trial, and began reading it to the jury. The privilege of voting, he said, arises from "the Constitution of the State, and not of the United States." In New York the Legislature "has seen fit to say that . . . voting shall be limited to the male sex." Neither the Fourteenth nor the Fifteenth Amendment specifically contained the word "sex" or said that women could vote. Miss Anthony's arguments based on these amendments were therefore not "potent." She knew all this, said the judge, and such knowledge of the facts supplies criminal intent.

He concluded by saying there was nothing for the jury to consider since it was all a question of law "and I have decided as a question of law" that Miss Anthony did not have the right to vote. "I therefore direct that you find a verdict of guilty." He refused to let the jury be polled and, over Judge Selden's protests, cut off all further discussion and discharged the jurors. Several of them said, after they had been dismissed, that they would have voted not guilty.

The next day Judge Selden moved for a new trial, on the grounds that Miss Anthony had been denied her right to a trial by jury. Judge Hunt refused, and pronounced sentence. She was fined $100 and costs. Her response was, "I shall never pay a dollar of your unjust penalty." Ordinarily she would have been imprisoned until she paid, but Judge Hunt carefully refused to order her put in jail, thereby taking away her second chance of bringing the case before the Supreme Court.

After Susan Anthony's trial was over, the election inspectors were tried before Judge Hunt. They were found guilty and fined $25 apiece. Susan Anthony was ready to put up the money, as she had promised, but two of the men decided not to pay as a matter of principle and were jailed. The women who had voted kept them fed with superb meals, and hundreds of Rochester residents came to visit them. At the end of a week, President Grant pardoned them and remitted their fines. The cases against the other women who had voted were dropped. Susan Anthony's fine was never paid, but no further action was taken against her.

Frances Gage Goes to Vote (1872)

She was tough, strong, resourceful. She had been raised as a pioneer farmgirl, the ninth of ten children. After successfully helping her father on the farm one day, he is said to have remarked, "What a pity you are not a boy." "Then and there," she said later, "sprang up my hatred to the limitations of sex. I was outspoken forever afterward." Outspoken indeed. She became a reformer, lecturer and author; she chaired women's conventions with an easy grace and an air of absolute command. While her four sons served in the Civil War, she dedicated herself to the economic and social assistance of freed slaves. Following the war, she joined Stanton, Anthony and the others in pressing again for the rights of women to vote. Her description below of voting attests to her wry humor:

"The fun of the thing was that I had nine women with me in the sitting-room of the hotel. I went down first and offered my vote. They were voting in a bar-room, but the ballot box was on the door into the hall where I stood. I was refused on the ground that I was a *married* woman. So then I took down two *single* women who supported themselves and owned their own home. Their votes were also refused. Then I took down one or more war widows whose husbands' bones had been left to bleach on the battlefield in defense of their country. They, too, were refused, and so on, through the whole nine. With each one offered I made an appropriate argument, and had a big and attentive crowd to hear me. The very worst feature of our case was that it was a corporation tax election; only taxpayers were called on to vote on the raising of money for putting in waterworks, etc. The largest taxpayer in the village was a woman, as was the smallest. The women I offered were all taxpayers, and even I was a taxpayer, in addition to my husband's being one. It created a great stir."

Do You, as a Woman, Want to Vote?

''Some Prominent Women of America Answer the Question''

The following article appeared in the January 1911 edition of *The Ladies' Home Journal:* It is supposed in some quarters that the agitation for woman suffrage which has been so industriously stirred up has won over to its side a majority of the thinking women of this country. The names of well-known women are juggled with in the newspapers until it is not strange that some should ask: How do the women whose works place them in positions of vantage think on this question?

To ascertain the opinions of some of the most prominent women, this page was sent out with the request that each would, in a single sentence, answer the question given at the head:

"Do you, as an American woman, want to vote?"

The answers speak for themselves, and are, to say the least, illuminative.

—*The Editors of the*
Ladies' Home Journal

Where the Real New York Women Stand

The impression is sometimes conveyed that the best part of New York womanhood is in favor of the ballot for woman. But the other side of that impression is reflected by the Committees and Boards governing the two New York organizations that stand as against woman suffrage. Thus there appear as Honorary Vice-Presidents, Directors and members of the Executive Committee of THE NATIONAL LEAGUE FOR THE CIVIC EDUCATION OF WOMEN the following women, representative of the oldest and foremost families of New York:

MRS. GROVER CLEVELAND
 Wife of the Former President of the United States
MRS. ANDREW CARNEGIE
MRS. GEORGE R. SHELDON
MRS. HENRY SELIGMAN
MRS. LIVINGSTON SCHUYLER
MRS. JAMES TERRY GARDINER
MRS. WILLIAM PERRY NORTHRUP
MRS. WILLIAM HAYNES TRUESDALE
MRS. DAVID H. GREER
 Wife of the Bishop of the Diocese of New York
MRS. SCHUYLER VAN RENSSELAER
MRS. CHARLES H. PARKHURST
MRS. ROSSITER JOHNSON
MRS. MABEL DEAN KALBFLEISCH
MRS. WILLIAM PERKINS DRAPER
MRS. DUNLAP HOPKINS
MRS. HIRAM W. SIBLEY

While on the Boards and Committees and member lists of THE NEW YORK STATE ASSOCIATION OPPOSED TO WOMAN SUFFRAGE there appear the names of women equally representative of the foremost New York families:

MRS. ELIHU ROOT

MRS. FRANCIS S. BANGS

MRS. FRANCIS M. SCOTT

MRS. CLEVELAND H. DODGE

MRS. C. GRANT LAFARGE

MRS. HERBERT L. SATTERLEE

MRS. HENRY A. STIMSON

MRS. GEORGE DOUGLAS MILLER

MISS ALICE HILL CHITTENDEN

MRS. JOHN G. MILBURN

MRS. WILLIAM M. POLK

MRS. LOCKWOOD DEFOREST

Those who call themselves suffragettes are making such a noise that I fear there is danger that the public may forget that opposed to these few is the great majority of womankind, proud of being women, and who glory in doing well those things which an All-Wise Creator assigned as woman's part in life.

—Louise Homer

I cannot interest myself in the subject in the slightest degree.

—Mrs. Benjamin Harrison
Wife of the Former President of the United States

No.

—Caroline Hazard
Former President of Wellesley College

No. The active participation of women in politics would be a great and perhaps a hazardous experiment in government. I am opposed to trying it.

—Agnes Irwin
Former Dean of Radcliffe College

The whole suffrage movement seems to me unintelligent, unintelligible and uninteresting. The achievement of universal suffrage would multiply our clubs and divide our homes.

—*Carolyn Wells*

An Authoritative Voice from Colorado

I have voted since 1893: I have been a delegate to the city and State conventions, and a member of the Republican State Committee from my county: I have been a deputy sheriff and a watcher at the polls: for twenty-three years I have been in the midst of the woman-suffrage movement in Colorado. For years I believed in woman suffrage and have worked day in and day out for it—I now see my mistake and would abolish it tomorrow if I could.

No law has been put on the statute book of Colorado for the benefit of women and children that has been put there by the women. The Child Labor Law went through independently of the woman's vote. The hours of working-women have not been shortened; the wages of schoolteachers have not been raised: the type of men that got into office has not improved a bit.

As for the effect of the vote on women personally, I have known scores of women who worked for the Republican party one year and worked for the Democratic party next year, telling me frankly that "the Democrats gave us more money."

Frankly, the experiment is a failure. It has done Colorado no good: it has done woman no good. The best thing for both would be if tomorrow the ballot for women could be abolished.

—*Mrs. Francis W. Goddard*
President of the Colonial Dames of Colorado

Fighting Back (1912)

When Ernestine Hara Kettler picketed the White House for the right to vote she was twenty-one. The adventure of fighting for your faith comes through in this wry account of life as a protester:

But it wasn't just an adventure. As a radical, I believed in justice. It was very just for women to vote and it was highly undemocratic and an outrage that so much opposition had been placed against their getting the ballot. There were, after all, as many women in the country as men. What is this business? Is a woman so far below a man intellectually that she's not fit to vote? When I think of it, it's just incredible! I can't believe it! I condemned it. I was actually outraged that women didn't have the vote! That's why I went down to Washington, D.C.

I don't know how I got there. I didn't have money, so someone must have paid my fare down there, perhaps this Katherine Hodges or the suffrage party. All I remember is that I found myself in Washington, and that I was met at the station and taken to the headquarters of the National Woman's Party. The headquarters was the Little White House; that's where President McKinley died. I was given his room and his bed. I wanted to get out of that room, fast. I didn't want to sleep in anybody's deathbed. Of course, he was only killed, you know, he didn't die of a disease.

What they were doing was picketing in groups of four. Each group had a shift. As soon as one group was arrested, then they sent out another group of four. There was a continuous picket line. That's what drove the policemen crazy—they saw no end to the number of women who were picketing!

I met the other three women in my group at the headquarters. One of them was Peggy Johns from New York. Another, whose name I do not remember, was an organizer in the needle trades in New York. The fourth was a lawyer from one of the Western states, either Wyoming or Arizona. They were all between twenty-five and thirty-five. I was the youngest in the group, twenty-one.

We started picketing the second or third day I was there. We walked back and forth, right in front of the White House gates. We had a banner, but I don't remember whether we each carried one banner or whether the four of us carried one long one with four posts on it. There must have been a saying on it. You can't just have a plain banner without something on it to draw the attention of the people passing by.

A pretty big crowd would gather every day—at least it seemed pretty big to me. There were always men and women standing there harassing us and throwing some pretty bad insults—and pretty obscene ones. The women weren't obscene, but the men were. Our instructions were to pay absolutely no attention to them. I ignored them. I was brave. My goodness, I was fighting for a cause.

We had some support, but they took their lives in their hands. If any of the bystanders supported us, they could be beaten by the rest of the crowd. Towards the end, they started throwing stuff at the women. In fact, during this period somebody fired a shot through the windows of the Little White House, the headquarters. Any woman that happened to be in the right position for it could have been killed. And we couldn't get police protection. We just couldn't get it. The only protection we had was when we were arrested. Then we were protected!

Margaret Sanger: The Early Days

Long heralded for her leadership in the movement to bring birth control to American women, Margaret Sanger (1883–1966) was also a powerful influence on the issue of poverty and population across the world. As one of eleven children raised in Corning, New York, she watched her mother die from disease and remained convinced that constant maternity was a contributing factor. Her subsequent life as a teacher, a nurse, and finally a social activist convinced her that poverty impacted women with a particular fury. She was convinced that women, given their ongoing responsibilities of motherhood, were more vulnerable to the consequences of social upheaval than men, a unique perspective at the time. She argued that birth control, until then associated only with prostitution, was a means by which women could control their lives and escape, should they wish, the confinement of motherhood. She organized birth control clinics (from which the story below comes), launched magazines, and wrote numerous books (What Every Girl Should Know among them). Sanger, herself a liberated woman—she married a second time on the condition that she could have both sexual freedom and access to her wealthy husband's finances!—absorbed immense criticism for her ideas and the way she led her life. She lived to see the first birth control pills, which were put on the market in 1960, a triumphant moment for an extraordinary woman:

The morning of October 16, 1916—crisp but sunny and bright after days of rain—Ethel, Fania, and I opened the doors of the first birth control clinic in America, the first anywhere in the world except the Netherlands. I still believe this was an event of social significance.

Would the women come? Did they come? Nothing, not even the ghost of Anthony Comstock, could have kept them away. We had arrived early, but before we could get the place dusted and ourselves ready for the official reception, Fania called, "Do come outside and look." Halfway to the corner they were standing in line, at least one hundred and fifty, some shawled, some hatless, their red hands clasping the cold, chapped, smaller ones of their children.

Fania began taking names, addresses, object in coming to the clinic, histories—married or single, any miscarriages or abortions, how many children, where born, what ages. Remembering how the Netherlands clinics in recording nothing had made it almost hopeless to measure what they had accomplished from the human point of view, I had resolved that our files should be as complete as it was possible to make them. Fania had a copy of *What Every Girl Should Know* on her desk, and, if she had a free moment, read from it. When asked, she told where it could be bought, and later kept a few copies for the convenience of those who wanted them.

Children were left with her and mothers ushered in to Ethel or me in the rear room, from seven to ten at once. To each group we explained simply what contraception was; that abortion was the wrong way—no matter how early it was performed it was taking life; that contraception was the better way, the safer way—it took a little time, a little trouble, but was well worth while in the long run, because life had not yet begun.

Some women were alone, some were in pairs, some with their neighbors, some with their married daughters. Some did not dare talk this over with their husbands, and some had been urged on by them. At seven in the evening they were still coming, and men also, occasionally bringing their timid, embarrassed wives, or once in a while by themselves to say they would stay home to take care of the children if their wives could come. A hundred women and forty men passed through the doors, but we could not begin to finish the line; the rest were told to return "tomorrow."

In the course of the next few days women appeared clutching minute scraps of paper, seldom more than an inch wide, which had crept into print. The Yiddish and Italian papers had picked up the story from the handbills which bore the clinic address, and the husbands had read them on their way from work and clipped them out for their wives. Women who had seen the brief, inconspicuous newspaper accounts came even from Massachusetts, Pennsylvania, New Jersey, and the far end of Long Island.

Newly married couples with little but love, faith, and hope to save them from charity, told of the tiny flats they had chosen, and of their determination to make a go of it together if only the children were not born too soon. A gaunt skeleton suddenly stood up one morning and made an impassioned speech. "They offer us charity when we have more babies than we can feed, and when we get sick with more babies for trying not to have them they just give us more charity talks!"

Women who were themselves already past childbearing age came just to urge us to preserve others from the sorrows of ruined health, overworked husbands, and broods of defective and wayward children growing up in the streets, filling dispensaries and hospitals, filing through the juvenile courts.

We made records of every applicant and, though the details might vary, the stories were basically identical. All were confused, groping among the ignorant sex-teachings of the poor, fumbling without guidance after truth, misled and bewildered in a tangled jungle of popular superstitions and old wives' remedies. Unconsciously they dramatized the terrible need of intelligent and scientific instruction in these matters of life—and death.

As was inevitable many were kept away by the report that the police were to raid us for performing abortions. "Clinic" was a word which to the uneducated usually signified such a place. We would not have minded particularly being raided on this charge, because we could easily disprove it. But these rumors also brought the most pitiful of all, the reluctantly expectant mothers who hoped to find some means of getting out of their dilemmas. Their desperate threats of suicide haunted you at night.

One Jewish wife, after bringing eight children to birth, had had two abortions and heaven knows how many miscarriages. Worn out, beaten down, not only by toiling in her own kitchen, but by taking in extra work from a sweatshop making hats, she was now at the end of her strength, nervous beyond words, and in a state of morbid excitement. "If you don't help me, I'm going to chop up a glass and swallow it tonight."

A woman wrought to the pitch of killing herself was sick—a community responsibility. She, most of all, required concentrated attention and devotion, and I could not let any such go out of the clinic until her mood had been altered. Building up hope for the future seemed the best deterrent. "Your husband and your children need you. One more won't make so much difference." I had to make each promise to go ahead and have this baby and myself promise in return, "You won't ever have to again. We're going to take care of you."

Day after day the waiting room was crowded with members of every race and creed; Jews and Christians, Protestants and Roman Catholics alike made their confessions to us, whatever they may have professed at home or in church. I asked one bright little Catholic what excuse she could make to the priest when he learned she had been to the clinic. She answered indignantly, "It's none of his business. My husband has a weak heart and works only four days a week. He gets twelve dollars, and we can barely live on it now. We have enough children."

Her friend, sitting by, nodded approval. "When I was married," she broke in, "the priest told us to have lots of children and we listened to him. I had fifteen. Six are living. I'm thirty-seven years old now. Look at me! I might be fifty!"

That evening I made a mental calculation of fifteen baptismal fees, nine baby funerals, masses and candles for the repose of nine baby souls, the physical agonies of the mother and the emotional torment of both parents, and I asked myself, "Is this the price of Christianity?"

But it was not altogether sad; we were often cheered by gayer visitors. The grocer's wife on the corner and the widow with six children who kept the lunch room up the street dropped in to wish us luck, and the fat old German baker whose wife gave out handbills to everybody passing the door sent regular donations of doughnuts. Whenever the pressure became so overwhelming that we could not go out for a meal we were sure to hear Mrs. Rabinowitz call downstairs, "If I bring some hot tea now, will you stop the people coming?" Two jovial policemen paused at the doorway each morning to discuss the weather. Reporters looked in speculating on how long we were going to last. The postman delivering his customary fifty to a hundred letters had his little pleasantry, "Farewell, ladies; hope I find you here tomorrow."

Although the line outside was enough to arouse police attention, nine days went by without interference. Then one afternoon when I, still undiscouraged, was out interviewing a doctor, a woman, large of build and hard of countenance, entered and said to Fania she was the mother of two children and that she had no money to support more. She did not appear overburdened or anxious and, because she was so well fed as to body and prosperous as to clothes, did not seem to belong to the community. She bought a copy of *What Every Girl Should Know* and insisted on paying two dollars instead of the usual tencent fee.

Fania, who had an intuition about such matters, called Ethel aside and said warningly she was certain this must be a policewoman. But Ethel, who was not of the cautious type, replied, "We have nothing to hide. Bring her in anyhow." She talked with the woman in private, gave her our literature and, when asked about our future plans, related them frankly. The sceptical Fania pinned the two-dollar bill on the wall and wrote underneath, "Received from

Mrs. —— of the Police Department, as her contribution." Hourly after that we expected trouble. We had known it must occur sooner or later, but would have preferred it to come about in a different way.

The next day Ethel and Fania were both absent from the clinic. The waiting room was filled almost to suffocation when the door opened and the woman who had been described to me came in.

"Are you Mrs. Sanger?"

"Yes."

"I'm a police officer. You're under arrest."

The doors were locked and this Mrs. Margaret Whitehurst and other plain-clothes members of the vice squad—used to raiding gambling dens and houses of assignation—began to demand names and addresses of the women, seeing them with babies, broken, old, worried, harrowed, yet treating them as though they were inmates of a brothel. Always fearful in the presence of the police, some began to cry aloud and the children on their laps screamed too. For a few moments it was like a panic, until I was able to assure them that only I was under arrest; nothing was going to happen to them, and they could return home if they were quiet. After half an hour I finally persuaded the policemen to let these frightened women go.

All of our four hundred and sixty-four case histories were confiscated, and the table and demonstration supplies were carried off through the patient line outside. The more timid had left, but many had stayed. This was a region where a crowd could be collected by no more urgent gesture than a tilt of the head skyward. Newspaper men with their cameras had joined the throng and the street was packed. Masses of people spilled out over the sidewalk on to the pavement, milling excitedly.

The patrol wagon came rattling up to our door. I had a certain respect for uniformed policemen—you knew what they were about —but none whatsoever for the vice squad. I was white hot with indignation over their unspeakable attitude towards the clinic mothers and stated I preferred to walk the mile to the court rather than sit with them. Their feelings were quite hurt. "Why, we didn't do anything to you, Mrs. Sanger," they protested. Nevertheless I marched ahead, they following behind.

A reporter from the *Brooklyn Eagle* fell into step beside me and before we had gone far suggested, "Now I'll fix it up with the police that you make a getaway, and when we reach that corner you run. I'll stop and talk to them while you skip around the block and get to the station first." It was fantastic for anyone so to misconstrue what I was doing as to imagine I would run around the block for a publicity stunt.

I stayed overnight at the Raymond Street Jail, and I shall never forget it. The mattresses were spotted and smelly, the blankets stiff with dirt and grime. The stench nauseated me. It was not a comforting thought to go without bedclothing when it was so cold, but, having in mind the diseased occupants who might have preceded me, I could not bring myself to creep under the covers. Instead I lay down on top and wrapped my coat around me. The only clean object was my towel, and this I draped over my face and head. For endless hours I struggled with roaches and horrible-looking bugs that came crawling out of the walls and across the floor. When a rat jumped up on the bed I cried out involuntarily and sent it scuttling out.

My cell was at the end of a center row, all opening front and back upon two corridors. The prisoners gathered in one of the aisles the next morning and I joined them. Most had been accused of minor offenses such as shoplifting and petty thievery. Many had weather-beaten faces, were a class by themselves, laughing and unconcerned. But I heard no coarse language. Underneath the chatter I sensed a deep and bitter resentment; some of them had been there for three or four months without having been brought to trial. The more fortunate had a little money to engage lawyers; others had to wait for the court to assign them legal defenders.

While I was talking to the girls, the matron bustled up with, "The ladies are coming!" and shooed us into our cells. The Ladies, a committee from a society for prison reform, peered at us as though we were animals in cages. A gentle voice cooed at me, "Did you come in during the night?"

"Yes," I returned, overlooking the assumption that I was a street walker.

"Can we do anything for you?"

The other inmates were sitting in their corners looking as innocent and sweet as they could, but I startled her by saying, "Yes, you can. Come in and clean up this place. It's filthy and verminous."

The Committee departed hurriedly down the corridor. One more alert member, however, came back to ask, "Is it really very dirty?"

Although I told her in some detail about the blankets, the odors, the roaches, she obviously could not picture the situation. "I'm terribly sorry, but we can't change it."

I was still exasperated over this reply when I was called to the reception room to give an interview to reporters. In addition to answering questions about the raid I said I had a message to the taxpayers of Brooklyn; they were paying money to keep their prisons run in an orderly fashion as in any civilized community and should know it was being wasted, because the conditions at Raymond Street were intolerable.

My bail was arranged by afternoon and when I emerged I saw waiting in front the woman who was going to swallow the glass; she had been there all that time.

I went straight back to the clinic, reopened it, and more mothers came in. I had hoped a court decision might allow us to continue, but now Mr. Rabinowitz came downstairs apologetically. He said he was sorry, and he really was, but the police had made him sign ejection papers, on the ground that I was "maintaining a public nuisance."

In the Netherlands a clinic had been cited as a public benefaction; in the United States it was classed as a public nuisance.

Two uniformed policemen came for me, and with them I was willing to ride in the patrol wagon to the station. As we started I heard a scream from a woman who had just come around the corner on her way to the clinic. She abandoned her baby carriage, rushed through the crowd, and cried, "Come back! Come back and save me!" For a dozen yards she ran after the van before someone caught her and led her to the sidewalk. But the last thing I heard was this poor distracted mother, shrieking and calling, "Come back! Come back!"

Elizabeth Banks: Newspaper Girl (1902)

A journalist at the turn of the century, Elizabeth Banks recounted her experiences in her serialized memoir, The Autobiography of a Newspaper Girl. *Don't be fooled by the quaint title, for though the book is filled with the goggle-eyed excitement of a naive age, there are moments when Banks sharply highlights the infuriating challenges that women faced in the dawning culture of newspaper politics. In our day, where the line between the public and the private sphere is routinely erased by journalists and the readers they serve, the excerpt below seems particularly apt. Though Banks paid a price for protecting a public figure—she would be relegated to writing culture columns for months after the incident—she had honored her own integrity and protected another woman for the right reasons. Her career would bloom as an intrepid reporter willing to catch a breaking story wherever it took her:*

One day a stranger entered the office, and, seeing me in my corner, said, "Ah! I see you've got a lady editor in your office!"

"Well, yes," responded the city editor, "but besides being the lady editor, she's one of the best all-round reporters I've got on my staff."

It could not have been half an hour after that remark was made, when the city editor came over to me, with the air of having an important commission for me.

"I've got a fine thing for you," said he, "if you can pull it through."

Then he explained that a certain well-known actress, who had appeared in a play the night before at one of the theaters, had suddenly forgotten her part, put her hand to her head and gone off the stage, as though in a dream. The play was almost brought to a standstill, but her understudy had managed to take her place till the fall of the curtain. It was thought the actress was intoxicated. In former days she had been an American society leader and had got stage struck. When she had given up her home for the foot-lights a very disagreeable scandal had followed her.

"Now," continued the city editor, "I've sent four different men to see that woman to-day, trying to get an interview and her version of last night's affair on the stage, but she sends down word she's ill and confined to her room and unable to see anyone. But I believe she'd see you, because you're a woman and can go right up to her room. Go and interview her. It'll be a great story, and we'll even scoop the New York papers. Find out if she was drunk last night. Find out everything you can from her. Make a big special of it. You can have all the space you want. If you manage it—well, I'll just say you won't be sorry you tried to please me."

In fifteen minutes I made my way to the hotel where the actress was stopping, sent up my card and was admitted to her bedroom. So beautiful had been the pictures I had seen of this woman, that the wan, thin face, actually ugly from dissipation, that looked up at me from among the pillows, gave me a most disagreeable start.

"I'm glad a woman has come to me at last," she said, as she tossed her head from side to side. "I'm in disgrace, alone, forsaken, even by my own parents. I've made a mess of my life. Listen, and I'll tell you how I did it and about last night at the theater too."

Then, without my having asked her a single question, the woman poured into my astonished ears a story of such pathos and horror as made me start back and cry: "Hush! hush! Don't talk to me any more. You will be sorry to-morrow; but then it will be too late."

"No! I shall not be sorry," she exclaimed, "I must talk or I shall lose my reason. I must tell some one of my troubles. Your face does not look hard and cold. Though you are a stranger, something tells me you are my friend."

"I am a newspaper reporter," I said simply. "You knew it from my card, and I told you I had come from a newspaper as soon as I got to your room."

The woman rose up on her elbows. Her yellow hair lay scattered over the pillows, and with her bloodshot eyes gazing intently into my face and clutching my hands tightly in her own, she exclaimed:

"Yes! Yes! I knew you were a reporter, but you are also a woman and I know you will not write a word of what I have told you. I have told you my story in confidence, and you will keep it."

"No! No! Not that! Not in confidence!" I cried, trying vainly to snatch my hands from her grasp that was now like iron. "You have talked not to me, but to my paper. Oh, you knew it, you knew it. I must print it. I am helpless to keep it out. Why, I'm a woman with a living to earn. I have no one in all the world but myself to depend on. I must do what my editor tells me. He has sent me to get an interview with you, and you have given it to me. I owe a duty to him, to my paper. It would be cheating to hold it back."

The woman's eyes burned into me, her nails dug into the palms of my hands as she tightened her grasp. She had told me, of her own free will, a story for my newspaper, a story for other newspapers, a plot for a novel, and now she said, "I have told you in confidence and you will keep it!" I thought of my city editor, waiting at the office for my return. I could see him smile the "Well done, good and faithful servant" smile upon me when I should walk in and stop at his desk to say: "Yes, I've got a great story from her! She talked and told me everything!" This woman, who clutched my wrists so hard and said to me, "You will keep it!" who was she, that she should cheat me out of what was mine, should block the way to my future success, should hurt me in the beginning of my newspaper career? An outcast! A woman disgraced and spurned and dis-owned!

"Let me go! Let me go! You talked to a reporter, knowing she was a re-porter. Now take the consequences!" I made another effort and got my hands free from her while she sank exhausted on the bed. "I must go now," I contin-ued; "I am sorry I cannot see things the way you seem to see them. I am a working woman, with a hard struggle before me. When my editor tells me to do a thing I have no choice but to obey. The world is very hard on women. I'm sorry for you."

I was turning the handle of the door. "Come back, just one minute," said the woman. "I will not touch you, I won't take your hands again.

"You said just now that the world was hard on women. So it is. And *women* are also very hard on women. I've had more experience than you have had. I know the world. Let me tell you that very seldom has a woman gone to destruction but another woman has had a hand in sending her there. By printing what I have said to you this afternoon, you will ruin me."

"You are ruined already," I said doggedly. "*I cannot hurt you.*"

"You will send me to hell and others with me. You will make my name a by-word in the gutters. By making a public character of me again you will bring renewed shame to my parents. You will make my little sister, who has all her beautiful life before her, hang her head in the presence of all her companions. I say you *will* do this. I mean that you *can* do it. Are you going to do it? Tell me, are you going to do it?"

"I will not do it," I said. My hands fell limply at my side and I stood transfixed. "I will not print a word you have told me, now or ever. I promise." The woman had conquered.

"You have promised! Oh, you have promised!" she exclaimed, a glad look flooding her poor, thin face. "Will you promise me something else?"

"Perhaps," I answered. I was crying now. I was not a journalist. I was only a woman.

"Promise me that in your work, as long as you live, you will never try to get fame or money by writing things that will hurt women like me. Promise that you will never for the sake of your own success tread on another woman and try to crush her."

"I promise!" I answered simply. Then I slipped out and closed the door. Once outside the stifling air of the room and away from the woman's presence, a strange, unaccountable feeling of terror took possession of me. I seemed to have bound myself in chains of iron and when I reached the street I gave myself a shake, under the impression that perhaps the fresh air and the blue sky and the sunlight would make them drop from me; but the chains still seemed to bind me. What had I done? I had entered into a compact which, at that moment it seemed to me, would be a sort of mortgage on my whole future life. I had promised always to refrain from writing anything that would hurt women like the one I had been talking to. I promised never to crush any other woman in my climbing of the ladder to success. Again I shook myself, but the chains still clung, and, thinking that I could really hear them clatter as I walked along the street, I returned to the office.

I passed by the city editor's desk. "Hello! It took a long time!" he exclaimed. "Did she talk?"

"Yes," I answered, "she talked a great deal, but I promised her I would not write a word she said."

He jumped from his chair, an angry light in his eyes. "You promised! What do you mean? Have you a story, the story I sent you after, and do you say you will not write it?"

"That's it, yes," I answered. "She forgot I was a reporter and told me everything, and then I promised I would not write it."

His face grew first red, then white. He was angry and justly so, but he made a tremendous effort to control himself. "If you were a man," he said, quietly, "I would dismiss you from the staff instantly for rank disregard of the interests of your paper. As you are a woman, I will say that you have not the journalistic instinct. You will never be able to do big things in journalism. You can edit your own page, but you'll never be a really successful journalist. The fact is, you're all woman and no journalist."

I remained on the Southern paper for some time after that and attended conscientiously to my woman's page. The city editor grew friendly again, but he gave me no more "special features" to do, for "special features" could only be worked up by "real live journalists," as he frequently explained to me.

Ida Lewis: The Savior of Lime Rock

Off the coast of Newport, Rhode Island, for the years during and after the Civil War, lived one Ida Lewis. Her solitary home belonged first to her father and then, after his death, to her. It was the Lime Rock Lighthouse and she was known up and down New England's rocky coast. Ida was no hermit who simply kept the lamp burning. She took her job seriously, and those who failed to heed her warning light got a second chance should they pile up on the rocks, for she was undaunted by the sea. Hearing calls for help, she would take to her rowboat and head out into the worst storms to rescue those in peril. All in all, Ida saved twenty-two people. Most celebrated was the time she rowed over a half mile in the dead of winter to gather in two sailors who had washed overboard and been given up for dead. The government took her bravery as seriously as the sailors, and she was awarded the Congressional Medal of Honor. But like many in her profession, she sought solitude and independence (she had tried marriage and didn't like it), and these qualities didn't mix well with fame and the curiosity of the public. She thought little of her bravery and assumed it came with the job. They tried to make her a celebrity and she tried to avoid it. In her final years, the cat and mouse game she played with the curious who were determined to see her was as taxing of her strength as any call for help from a tempestuous surf.

Isadora Duncan: On American Dance

She was an artistic revolutionary. In the coil and spring of her dancing, in the robes that floated around her like mist, barefooted, beautiful, uncompromising, she announced to a world certain of itself that nothing was certain. With no regrets, she announced that the classical tradition of ballet was a grave upon which she would dance and weep and sing. No performance artist of her time held the world so breathless. As flamboyant in her personal life as she was on stage, she sought above all to be unconstrained—free from the restrictions of society or the expectations of an adoring public. She bore several children by several men and traveled the world leaving wonder and not a little confusion in her wake. Her death captured the world's attention: While riding in an open convertible, her long, flowing scarf caught in the wheels and snapped her neck. The following excerpt stands as an exuberant manifesto on modern dance:

In a moment of prophetic love for America, Walt Whitman said: "I hear America singing," and I can imagine the mighty song that Walt heard, from the surge of the Pacific, over the plains, the voices rising of the vast Chorale of children, youths, men and women, singing Democracy.

When I read that poem of Whitman's, I, too, had a vision—the Vision of America dancing a dance that would be the worthy expression of the song Walt heard when he heard America singing. This music would have rhythm as great as the exhilaration, the swing of or curves of the Rocky Mountains. It would have nothing to do with the sensual life of the jazz rhythm; it would be like the vibration of the American soul striving upward, through labor, to harmonious life. Nor had this dance that I visioned any vestige of the Fox Trot or the Charleston—rather was it the living leap of the child springing toward the heights, toward its future accomplishment, toward a new great vision of life that would express America.

. . . I often wonder where is the American composer who will hear Walt Whitman's America singing, and who will compose the true music for the American Dance which will contain no Jazz rhythm—no rhythm from the waist down, but from the Solar Plexus, the temporal home of the soul, upwards to the Star-Spangled Banner of the great sky which arches over that stretch of land from the Pacific, over the Plains, over the Sierra Nevadas, over the Rocky Mountains to the Atlantic. I pray you, young American composer, create the music for the dance that shall express the America of Walt Whitman—the America of Abraham Lincoln.

It seems to me monstrous that one should believe that the Jazz rhythm expresses America. Jazz rhythms express the primitive savage. America's music would be something different. It has yet to be written. No composer has yet caught this rhythm of America—it is too mighty for the ears of most. But some day it will gush forth from the great stretches of Earth, rain down from the vast sky spaces, and America will be expressed in some Titanic music that will shape its chaos to harmony, and long-legged shining boys and girls will dance to this music, not the tottering, ape-like convulsions of the Charleston, but a strong, tremendous upward movement, mounting high above the Pyramids of Egypt, beyond the Parthenon of Greece, an expression of beauty and strength such as no civilization has ever known.

I see America dancing, standing with one foot posed on the highest point of the Rockies, her two hands stretched out from the Atlantic to the Pacific, her fine head tossed to the sky, her forehead shining with a Crown of a million stars.

How grotesque that they have encouraged in American schools of so-called bodily culture, Swedish gymnastics, and the ballet. The real American type can never be a ballet dancer. The legs are too long, the body too supple and the spirit too free for this school of affected grace and toe-walking. It is notorious that all great ballet dancers have been short women with small frames. A tall, finely made woman could never dance the ballet. The type that expresses America at its best could never dance the ballet. By the wildest trick of the imagination you could not picture the Goddess of Liberty dancing the ballet. Then why accept this school in America?

Henry Ford has expressed the wish that all the children of Ford's City should dance. He does not approve of the modern dances and says, let them dance the old-fashioned Waltz and Mazurka and Minuet. But the old-fashioned Waltz and Mazurka are an expression of the unctuous servility of courtiers of the time of Louis XVI and hooped skirts. What have these movements to do with the free youth of America? Does not Mr. Ford know that movements are as eloquent as words?

Why should our children bend the knee in that fastidious and servile dance, the Minuet, or twirl in the mazes of the false sentimentality of the Waltz? Rather let them come forth with great strides, leaps and bounds, with lifted forehead and far-spread arms, to dance the language of our Pioneers, the Fortitude of our heroes, the justice, kindness, purity of our statesmen and all the inspired love and tenderness of our Mothers. When the American children dance in this way, it will make them beautiful beings worthy of the name of the Greatest Democracy.

That will be America dancing.

Amelia Earhart's Credo

One of the great pilots of the 20th century, Earhart had little patience for gender debates. Give a girl a chance, she argued, then the girl will do the rest:
For a couple of years I had been pleasantly associated with Purdue University at Lafayette, Indiana, as a periodic and rather peripatetic faculty member. Purdue is a forward-looking institution building an important aviation department. It is one of the few universities in the world that has its own landing field.

Additionally, it is co-educational. Of its 6000 students approximately 1000 are women. The problems and opportunities of these girls were quite as much my concern as aviation matters. Perhaps I have something of a chip on my shoulder when it comes to modern feminine education. Often youngsters are sadly miscast. I have known girls who should be tinkering with mechanical things instead of making dresses, and boys who would do better at cooking than engineering.

One of my favorite phobias is that girls, especially those whose tastes aren't routine, often don't get a fair break. The situation is not new. It has come down through the generations, an inheritance of age-old customs which produced the corollary that women are bred to timidity.

The mechanical-minded boy may have a field-day from the time his legs are long enough to toddle down to the corner garage. For all anyone cares, he may be weaned on piston rings and carburetors, and may remain beautifully

grimy for indefinite periods. But with his sister it is different. With rare excep-
tions, the delights of finding out what makes a motor go, or batting the bumps
out of a bent fender, are joys reserved for masculinity.

The girl who wants to do that sort of thing has such a hard time finding a
place to do it that for long I have harbored a very special pet ambition. Among
my other somewhat suppressed desires it is classified under the letter "T." The
imaginary file card reads, "Tinkering: For Girls Only." The plan is to endow a
catch-as-catch-can machine-shop, where girls may tinker to their hearts content with motors, lathes, jigsaws, gadgets, and diverse hickies of their own
creation. Where they may sprawl on their back, peering up into the innards of
engines, and likely as not get oil in their hair. Where they can make things and
have the fun of finding out how things are made, why engines perk, clocks tick,
radios yowl, and something of the everyday mechanical marvels which—given
the chance—many of them would master quite as well as Brother Bill. And
emerge somewhere in the scale between grease-monkeys and inventors. Or,
negatively, with at least their lack of aptitude revealed.

Amelia Earhart from the Inside

I must say something about the plane which has been my companion aloft for
so many flying hours. It was a craft to delight the eye, its wings and fuselage
painted red with gold stripes down the side. Possibly it may have seemed a trifle
gaudy on the ground but I am sure it looked lovely against one of those white
clouds. It was a closed plane; I drive a closed car and fly a closed plane. I don't
like to be mussed up. Further, the added comfort of a closed plane very definitely lessens fatigue, and fatigue must be considered when one is preparing
for a long flight. The Vega nomally carries six passengers and the pilot, the
passengers in the rear, the pilot in front perched in a cockpit overlooking the
motor with its 500 horses. The six passenger seats had been replaced by large
fuel tanks capable of carrying 520 gallons of gasoline. There are no service
stations between Honolulu and the United States!

My cockpit was a very cozy little cubbyhole. I sat on a cushion just large
enough for me. On the right-hand side of the seat was a large black box, the
radio, with the dials on top so I could reach them easily. On the left was a large
compass and two pump handles, pumps which enabled me to change fuel from
one set of tanks to the other. Some of the fuel was carried in the wing, which is
the normal position in commercial craft, and some in the cabin tanks. In case

my motor-driven pump should fail I could still keep going by using that hand system. I have had to pump as long as six hours on occasion, which is pretty tiring. But it is well worth having that emergency system.

In a little cupboard in the wing, to the right, I carried provisions. I don't drink tea or coffee so I had none with me. On the Atlantic flight I had a thermos bottle of hot soup, but it did not work out very well, so from Honolulu I carried a thermos bottle of hot chocolate. Then I had malted milk tablets, sweet chocolate, tomato juice, and water. One of the Army officer's wives thought I was starting out on a 2400 mile journey with entirely too little to eat so she asked if she couldn't put up a picnic lunch for me. I told her that for some reason or other it was always difficult for me on a long flight to eat much food, but if she packed a lunch I would take it with me. So I had that too.

On the left side there was another little cabinet in which were stored my tools. I don't use hairpins so I have to carry regular tools! Also, there were extra fuses, extra flashlight, pad and pencils, rags, string, odds and ends that might come in handy.

After I asked the men to warm up the motor, I went over to the Weather Bureau for a final check and found that if I did not leave that afternoon, despite local conditions, I would be held indefinitely by storms coming in over the Pacific. So about 4:30 I returned to the plane, which was sitting out on the concrete apron. The motor purred sweetly. I crawled into the cockpit and tested it myself. It sounded perfect. So I told the men to take away the blocks in front of the wheels.

I turned the plane and headed for the take-off pathway, my mechanic running along beside it. I could see him out of the cockpit window and observed that with every step he took the mud squashed up to his shoe tops, so soft was the ground. My mechanic was very gloomy, his cigarette hanging out of the corner of his mouth, his face as white as his coveralls. I wanted to call, "Cheer up, Ernie! It will soon be over." But of course I couldn't make him hear over the sound of the motor.

Glancing to the left, I noticed three fire engines drawn up in front of the hangars, and one ambulance. The Army to a man seemed to have those little squirt fire extinguishers, and the women present had their handkerchiefs out, obviously ready for any emergency.

The take-off with an excessive fuel load is the most hazardous moment, if such could be determined, because of the possibility of fire if anything goes amiss. But please do not compare such a take-off with those of ordinary everyday flying. It is no more fair to compare the two than it is to compare automobile racing and safe automobile driving—if such there be!

When my mechanic had pried loose a great ball of mud and grass that had caked up on the tail skid, I put the plane in take-off position, looked down the long pathway ahead of me, and beyond to the sugar-cane fields stretching to the crest of the mountains which cross the island diagonally. Those mountains usually are sharp in outline but that day they were softened by low-hanging gray clouds.

From the little flags hanging limply on their sticks I saw that what wind I had was with me. That was a disadvantage. You realize a plane takes off against the wind, not with it, just as a small boy flies his kite. He doesn't run with the wind to get his kite into the air, but runs against it. Of course an airplane is simply kite with a motor instead of the small boy.

I pushed the throttle ahead. The Vega started to move and gather speed. I felt the tail come up. The plane got lighter and lighter on the wheels. After rolling about two thousand feet a large bump on the surface of the field threw the plane completely off the ground. I pushed the throttle ahead to the farthest notch, and gave her all the power I had. The plane started to settle, then caught—and we were off.

I have often been asked what I think about at the moment of take-off. Of course no pilot sits and feels his pulse as he flies. He has to be part of the machine. If he thinks of anything but the task in hand then trouble is probably just around the corner.

Amelia and Eleanor Go for a Ride

One night in April, 1933, Amelia Earhart was invited to a formal dinner at the Roosevelt White House. Eleanor Roosevelt in particular much admired Earhart's boldness and sense of adventure. Some time during the dinner, the subject of night flying surfaced. Earhart was eloquent on the matter: the edge of night drawing across the twilight, the sparkle of the lights below, and the stars above that seemed so close you could touch them. It was free up there at night in the cold, dark silence and full of magic. Was it something in Eleanor's eyes as she listened or did she ask outright? In any event, Earhart got on the phone and called someone at Eastern Airlines who confirmed they had a plane (after all, she was Amelia Earhart!). Skipping dessert, Earhart swept the First Lady out—both dressed in satin evening gowns, no less—to the airfield for the first night flight of Eleanor Roosevelt's life. She loved it, and as Earhart swept over the city, the darkened fields of Virginia, and the moonlit coast, the First Lady watched in awe. (Later, Earhart would offer to give Roosevelt private lessons, but the First Lady never took her up on it.) Upon landing, they drove back to the White House only to find, gleaming in the driveway, a new car brought from Cincinnati as a gift for the First Lady. The two women looked at each other. "Let's see how it rides," said Eleanor, and off they went in the middle of the night at high speed, Eleanor at the wheel.

Sylvia Beach and James Joyce

Daughter of Woodrow Wilson's Presbyterian minister, Beach was independent and gloriously bold. She moved to Paris and opened a bookshop which served as the hub to an expatriate literary circle in the years after the First World War when the revolution of the word matched the political madness of the age. She read James Joyce's masterpiece *Ulysses* in manuscript and was determined to see it published. She oversaw the publication through her own bookshop (financed with her own money), and fought to keep the book in print through numerous reprints and revisions. The U.S. Supreme Court's obscenity ruling in 1932 brought the book worldwide attention and in the mad rush to buy the celebrated novel (the American public made Joyce a fortune), his original publisher made not a penny. Though many sought to portray Beach as a wronged business partner, she would have none of it. She had gotten the best of the whole process in her mind—she had seen genius when no one else had; she had been bold enough, brave enough to bring it into the world: "I understood from the first that, working with or for Mr. Joyce, the pleasure was mine—an infinite pleasure—the profits," she added wryly, "were for him."

Caresse Crosby and James Joyce

Some years after Beach's publication of Ulysses, *another bold Paris publisher, Caresse Crosby, would take on the publication of Joyce's work. The vast, thoroughly confusing wordplay which would become* Finnegan's Wake *was originally published by Boston-born Crosby and her husband, the mad poet Harry Crosby. Together the Crosbys had stormed through Paris in the twenties (until Harry's suicide in 1929) where they lived a wild, excessive life, typical of the age. We are lucky that they both loved books and were all too willing to sink their parents' money into The Black Sun*

Press, a marvelous literary press that published Joyce, Lawrence, Proust, Pound, and many others. The Crosbys' design sense was exquisite, their editorial instincts sure, and the books produced magnificent. Caresse was the steadier of the two—she made the press a business and a passion. In this excerpt from her memoirs (The Passionate Years) *she tells a marvelous story of Joyce, her printer, and the unexpected flexibility of genius:*

The first proofs were ready for Joyce early in November and he said he would come to the rue de Lille to correct them one fine afternoon. We waited until dinner time. Just as we were sitting down, a note was handed me, it was from Joyce. He had come as far as our front door, but before Ida could open, he heard Narcisse's watchful bark from within and turned and walked right home again. He said he was very afraid of small animals for his eyes were so bad he might run into them—he had to tap his way with a cane and so could easily be tripped by our dog. He asked me if I would tie Narcisse up, then he would come back next day. I sent the proofs back to him by his messenger so that when he did appear the following afternoon, he had already gone over them, but to my horror they looked like a bookie's score card. Narcisse would never have understood being tied, but I did shut him into my bathroom and locked the door.

The fire was burning in the library. We went up, cautiously, by the bathroom, because Narcisse had yapped (I promised next time to muzzle him as well). Once ensconced in the biggest chair, Joyce changed his glasses and asked for a stronger light (later I ordered a special 150-watt bulb for these sessions). He picked up "The Mookse and the Gripes" and read the opening line, already rewritten beyond recognition.

"Now, Mr. and Mrs. Crosby," Joyce said, "I wonder if you understand why I made that change." All this in a blarney-Irish key.

"No, why?" we chorused, and there ensued one of the most intricate and erudite twenty minutes of explanation that it has ever been my luck to hear, but unfortunately I hardly understood a word, his references were far too esoteric. Harry fared a bit better, but afterward we both regretted that we did not have a dictaphone behind the lamp so that later we could have studied all that had escaped us. Joyce stayed three hours, he didn't want a drink, and by eight he hadn't gotten through with a page and a half. It was illuminating. When he left, Harry guided him down the slippery stairs—Narcisse was happily eating rabbit in the kitchen—and I started to mix some very dry martinis.

A final unexpected incident occurred after Harry's death, for regrettably,

"Tales Told of Shem and Shaun" did not appear until the spring of 1930. (Harry had died in New York in December, 1929.) The pages were on the press and Lescaret in consternation pedaled over to the rue de Lille to show me, to my horror, that on the final "forme," due to a slight error in his calculations, only two lines would fall *en plaine page*—this from the typographer's point of view was a heinous offense to good taste. What could be done at this late date! NOTHING, the other *formes* had all been printed and the type distributed (we only had enough type for four pages at a time). Then Lescaret asked me if I wouldn't beg Mr. Joyce to add another eight lines to help us out. I laughed scornfully at the little man, what a ludicrous idea, when a great writer has composed each line of his prose as carefully as a sonnet you don't ask him to inflate a masterpiece to help out the printer! We will just have to let it go, I groaned, and Lescaret turned and pedaled sadly away—but the next noon when I arrived at 2 rue Cardinale, joy seemed to ooze from the doorway of the Black Sun Press. Lescaret bounced out and handed me that final page. To my consternation eight lines *had* been added.

"Where did you get these?" I accused him.

"Madame, I hope will forgive me," he beamed. "I went to see Mr. Joyce personally to tell him our troubles. He was very nice—he gave me the text right away—he told me he had been wanting to add more, but was too frightened of you, Madame, to do so."

Marian Anderson's Easter Sunday

She was one of America's greatest singers, a contralto who held the nation and the world spellbound with her astonishing voice. Marian Anderson, who began singing in her church choir in Philadelphia in the early twentieth century, was accepted by Yale to study music, but she could not raise the funds for her tuition. As an African-American woman, she had a rich musical heritage, which supplemented her traditional musical education and which she never failed to weave into her repertoire. Her voice evoked no prejudice in her listeners, but her race made life in America very difficult indeed. She traveled to Europe, sang to increasingly larger audiences and was soon an international star. In 1936 she sang to a sold-out Carnegie Hall, but it was 1939 that would forever change her life. The Daughters of the American Revolution refused to allow Anderson to sing at their Constitution Hall, and headlines roared their cowardice, prompting Eleanor Roosevelt to resign from the DAR. A concert was held instead on the steps of the Lincoln Memorial for a crowd of more than seventy-five thousand people. She sang as beautifully there as anyone could remember. Anderson's simple and affecting account of those events follows below:

The division between time spent in Europe and in the United States changed gradually. In my second season under Mr. Hurok's management there was already more to do at home, and less time was devoted to Europe. Soon there were so many concerts to do in the cities of the United States that a trip abroad for concerts had to be squeezed in. There is no doubt that my work was drawing the attention of larger circles of people in wider areas of our country. Fees went up, and I hope that I was making a return in greater service.

Mr. Hurok's aim was to have me accepted as an artist worthy to stand with the finest serious ones, and he sought appearances for me in all the places where the best performers were expected and taken for granted. The nation's capital was such a place. I had sung in Washington years before—in schools and churches. It was time to appear on the city's foremost concert platform—Constitution Hall.

As it turned out, the decision to arrange an appearance in Constitution Hall proved to be momentous. I left bookings entirely to the management. When this one was being made I did not give it much thought. Negotiations for the renting of the hall were begun while I was touring, and I recall that the first intimation I had that there were difficulties came by accident. Even then I did not find out exactly what was going on; all I knew was that something was amiss. It was only a few weeks before the scheduled date for Washington that I discovered the full truth—that the Daughters of the American Revolution, owners of the hall, had decreed that it could not be used by one of my race. I was saddened, but as it is my belief that right will win I assumed that a way would be found. I had no inkling that the thing would become a *cause célèbre.* I was in San Francisco, I recall, when I passed a newsstand, and my eye caught a headline: MRS. ROOSEVELT TAKES STAND. Under this was another line, in bold print just a bit smaller: RESIGNS FROM D. A. R., etc. I was on my way to the concert hall for my performance and could not stop to buy a paper. I did not get one until after the concert, and I honestly could not conceive that things had gone so far.

As we worked our way back East, continuing with our regular schedule, newspaper people made efforts to obtain some comment from me, but I had nothing to say. I really did not know precisely what the Hurok office was doing about the situation and, since I had no useful opinions to offer, did not discuss it. I trusted the management. I knew it must be working on every possible angle, and somehow I felt I would sing in Washington.

Kosti became ill in St. Louis and could not continue on tour. Here was a crisis of immediate concern to me. I was worried about Kosti's well-being and we had to find a substitute in a hurry. Kosti had had symptoms of this illness some time before and had gone to see a physician in Washington, who had recommended special treatment. It was decided now that Kosti should be taken to Washington and hospitalized there.

Franz Rupp, a young man I had never met before, was rushed out to St. Louis by the management to be the accompanist. I had a piano in my hotel room, and as soon as Franz, who is now my accompanist, arrived, we went over the program. I was impressed by the ease with which he handled the situation. He could transpose a song at sight, and he could play many of my numbers entirely from memory. I found out later that he had had a huge backlog of experience playing for instrumentalists and singers. He assured me that I had seen and heard him in Philadelphia when I had attended a concert by Sigrid Onegin years before, as he had been her accompanist.

Mr. Rupp and I gave the St. Louis concert, and then we filled two other engagements as we headed East. Our objective was Washington. We knew by this time that the date in Constitution Hall would not be filled, but we planned to stop in Washington to visit Kosti. I did not realize that my arrival in Washington would in itself be a cause for a commotion, but I was prepared in advance when Gerald Goode, the public-relations man on Mr. Hurok's staff, came down to Annapolis to board our train and ride into the capital with us.

Mr. Goode is another person who made a contribution to my career, the value of which I can scarcely estimate. He was with Mr. Hurok when I joined the roster, and I am sure that he labored devotedly and effectively from the moment of my return from Europe for that first Hurok season in America. His publicity efforts were always constructive, and they took account of my aversion to things flamboyant. Everything he did was tasteful and helpful. And in the Washington affair he was a tower of strength.

Mr. Goode filled me in on developments as we rode into Washington, and he tried to prepare me for what he knew would happen—a barrage of questions from the newspaper people. They were waiting for us in the Washington station. Questions flew at me, and some of them I could not answer because they involved things I did not know about. I tried to get away; I wanted to go straight to the hospital to see Kosti. There was a car waiting for me, and the reporters followed us in another car. I had some difficulty getting into the hospital without several reporters following me. They waited until I had finished my visit, and they questioned me again—about Kosti's progress and his opinion of the Washington situation. Finally we got away and traveled on to New York.

The excitement over the denial of Constitution Hall to me did not die down. It seemed to increase and to follow me wherever I went. I felt about the affair as about an election campaign; whatever the outcome, there is bound to be unpleasantness and embarrassment. I could not escape it, of course. My friends wanted to discuss it, and even strangers went out of their way to express their strong feelings of sympathy and support.

What were my own feelings? I was saddened and ashamed. I was sorry for the people who had precipitated the affair. I felt that their behavior stemmed from a lack of understanding. They were not persecuting me personally or as a representative of my people so much as they were doing something that was neither sensible nor good. Could I have erased the bitterness, I would have done so gladly. I do not mean that I would have been prepared to say that I was not entitled to appear in Constitution Hall as might any other performer. But the unpleasantness disturbed me, and if it had been up to me alone I would have sought a way to wipe it out. I cannot say that such a way out suggested itself to me at the time, or that I thought of one after the event. But I have been in this world long enough to know that there are all kinds of people, all suited by their own natures for different tasks. It would be fooling myself to think that I was meant to be a fearless fighter; I was not, just as I was not meant to be a soprano instead of a contralto.

Then the time came when it was decided that I would sing in Washington on Easter Sunday. The invitation to appear in the open, singing from the Lincoln Memorial before as many people as would care to come, without charge, was made formally by Harold L. Ickes, Secretary of the Interior. It was duly reported, and the weight of the Washington affair bore in on me.

Easter Sunday in 1939 was April 9, and I had other concert dates to fill before it came. Wherever we went I was met by reporters and photographers. The inevitable question was, "What about Washington?" My answer was that I knew too little to tell an intelligent story about it. There were occasions, of course, when I knew more than I said. I did not want to talk, and I particularly did not want to say anything about the D. A. R. As I have made clear, I did not feel that I was designed for hand-to-hand combat, and I did not wish to make statements that I would later regret. The management was taking action. That was enough.

It was comforting to have concrete expressions of support for an essential principle. It was touching to hear from a local manager in a Texas city that a block of two hundred tickets had been purchased by the community's D. A. R. people. It was also heartening; it confirmed my conviction that a whole group should not be condemned because an individual or section of the group does a thing that is not right.

I was informed of the plan for the outdoor concert before the news was published. Indeed, I was asked whether I approved. I said yes, but the yes did not come easily or quickly. I don't like a lot of show, and one could not tell in advance what direction the affair would take. I studied my conscience. In principle the idea was sound, but it could not be comfortable to me as an individual. As I thought further, I could see that my significance as an individual was small in this affair. I had become, whether I liked it or not, a symbol, representing my people. I had to appear.

I discussed the problem with Mother, of course. Her comment was characteristic: "It is an important decision to make. You are in this work. You intend to stay in it. You know what your aspirations are. I think you should make your own decision."

Mother knew what the decision would be. In my heart I also knew. I could not run away from this situation. If I had anything to offer, I would have to do so now. It would be misleading, however, to say that once the decision was made I was without doubts.

We reached Washington early that Easter morning and went to the home of Gifford Pinchot, who had been Governor of Pennsylvania. The Pinchots had been kind enough to offer their hospitality, and it was needed because the hotels would not take us. Then we drove over to the Lincoln Memorial. Kosti was well enough to play, and we tried out the piano and examined the public-address system, which had six microphones, meant not only for the people who were present but also for a radio audience.

When we returned that afternoon I had sensations unlike any I had experienced before. The only comparable emotion I could recall was the feeling I had had when Maestro Toscanini had appeared in the artist's room in Salzburg. My heart leaped wildly, and I could not talk. I even wondered whether I would be able to sing.

The murmur of the vast assemblage quickened my pulse beat. There were policemen waiting at the car, and they led us through a passageway that other officers kept open in the throng. We entered the monument and were taken to a small room. We were introduced to Mr. Ickes, whom we had not met before. He outlined the program. Then came the signal to go out before the public.

If I did not consult contemporary reports I could not recall who was there. My head and heart were in such turmoil that I looked and hardly saw, I listened and hardly heard. I was led to the platform by Representative Caroline O'Day of New York, who had been born in Georgia, and Oscar Chapman, Assistant Secretary of the Interior, who was a Virginian. On the platform behind me sat Secretary Ickes, Secretary of the Treasury Morgenthau, Supreme Court Justice Black, Senators Wagner, Mead, Barkley, Clark, Guffey, and Capper, and many Representatives, including Representative Arthur W. Mitchell of Illinois, a Negro. Mother was there, as were people from Howard University and from churches in Washington and other cities. So was Walter White, then secretary of the National Association for the Advancement of Colored People. It was Mr. White who at one point stepped to the microphone and appealed to the crowd, probably averting serious accidents when my own people tried to reach me.

I report these things now because I have looked them up. All I knew then as I stepped forward was the overwhelming impact of that vast multitude. There seemed to be people as far as the eye could see. The crowd stretched in a great semicircle from the Lincoln Memorial around the reflecting pool on to the shaft of the Washington Monument. I had a feeling that a great wave of good will poured out from these people, almost engulfing me. And when I stood up to sing our National Anthem I felt for a moment as though I were choking. For a desperate second I thought that the words, well as I know them, would not come.

I sang, I don't know how. There must have been the help of professionalism I had accumulated over the years. Without it I could not have gone through the program. I sang—and again I know because I consulted a newspaper clipping—"America," the aria "O mio Fernando," Schubert's "Ave Maria," and three spirituals—"Gospel Train," "Trampin'," and "My Soul Is Anchored in the Lord." I regret that a fixed rule was broken, another thing about which I found out later. Photographs were taken from within the Memorial, where the great statue of Lincoln stands, although there was a tradition that no pictures could be taken from within the sanctum.

It seems also that at the end, when the tumult of the crowd's shouting would not die down, I spoke a few words. I read the clipping now and cannot believe that I could have uttered another sound after I had finished singing. "I am overwhelmed," I said. "I just can't talk. I can't tell you what you have done for me today. I thank you from the bottom of my heart again and again."

It was the simple truth. But did I really say it?

There were many in the gathering who were stirred by their own emotions. Perhaps I did not grasp all that was happening, but at the end great numbers of people bore down on me. They were friendly; all they wished to do was to offer their congratulations and good wishes. The police felt that such a concentration of people was a danger, and they escorted me back into the Memorial. Finally we returned to the Pinchot home.

I cannot forget that demonstration of public emotion or my own strong feelings. In the years that have passed I have had constant reminders of that Easter Sunday. It is not at all uncommon to have people come backstage after a concert even now and remark, "You know, I was at that Easter concert." In my travels abroad I have met countless people who heard and remembered about that Easter Sunday.

In time the policy at Constitution Hall changed. I appeared there first in a concert for the benefit of China Relief. The second appearance in the hall, I believe, was also under charitable auspices. Then, at last, I appeared in the hall as does any other musical performer, presented by a concert manager, and I have been appearing in it regularly. The hall is open to other performers of my group. There is no longer an issue, and that is good.

Margaret Bourke-White: "I knew now what I would not do . . ."

One story which *Fortune* sent me out to cover was in a sphere quite new to me and left a very deep impression on me. This was the great drought of 1934. Word of its severity came so suddenly, and the reports we had were so scanty, that *Fortune* editors didn't know exactly where the chief areas of the drought were. Omaha, Nebraska, seemed as good a starting point as any, since it was in the middle of the corn belt. I left on three hours' notice and on arrival in Omaha found that the drought extended over a vastly greater area than we had known when I was in New York. It ran from the Dakotas in the North to the

Texas panhandle. I was working against a five-day deadline, and it was such an extensive area to cover that I chartered a plane to use for the whole story.

My pilot was a barnstormer of the old school, who earned his livelihood by stunt flying at country fairs. His tiny two-seater was a plane of the old school, too—how old I fortunately did not know until the job was done, when I learned the Curtiss Robin was considered extinct long before the drought reached Nebraska. But luckily, unaware of this, I did not worry on the long hops except about such basic matters as choosing the right place and getting to it in time for the right photographic light, and keeping my film holders freshly loaded and ready for whatever we might meet. The unloading, boxing and reloading was an almost continuous process, which I had to do with my hands and films hidden from the light inside the big black changing bag I carried in my lap. Like woman's work it was never done, and I kept at it whenever we were aloft. The little Robin held up quite well. Crash it finally did, but very gently and only after sundown of my last day. By then I had my pictures and my disturbing memories.

I had never seen landscapes like those through which we flew. Blinding sun beating down on the withered land. Below us the ghostly patchwork of half-buried corn, and the rivers of sand which should have been free-running streams. Sinister spouts of sand wisping up, and then the sudden yellow gloom of curtains of fine-blown soil rising up and trembling in the air. Endless dun-colored acres, which should have been green with crops, carved into dry ripples by the aimless winds.

I had never seen people caught helpless like this in total tragedy. They had no defense. They had no plan. They were numbed like their own dumb animals, and many of these animals were choking and dying in drifting soil. I was deeply moved by the suffering I saw and touched particularly by the bewilderment of the farmers. I think this was the beginning of my awareness of people in a human, sympathetic sense as subjects for the camera and photographed against a wider canvas than I had perceived before. During the rapturous period when I was discovering the beauty of industrial shapes, people were only incidental to me, and in retrospect I believe I had not much feeling for them in my earlier work. But suddenly it was the people who counted. Here in the Dakotas with these farmers, I saw everything in a new light. How could I tell it all in pictures? Here were faces engraved with the very paralysis of despair. These were faces I could not pass by.

It was very hard, after working with the drought and with the people who must weather it through, to return to the advertising world again and glorify that rubber doughnut on which the world rolled. The time was drawing near for another *Satevepost* tire ad, and up in the penthouse the Bourke-White studio must dedicate itself afresh to the making of giant mud pies.

Some readers may remember—and if they do not, they need count it no great loss—the tire ads of the early to middle thirties in which a Gargantuan tire track ran across two center pages, the imprint so big it looked like a road in itself. My assignment in making these was to capture the very soul of the tire, its footprints on the sands of time. But there were no timeless sands up in the penthouse, and ordinary sand would not stand up under the merciless spotlights. By kneading putty with clay and adding various other mysterious oily ingredients, as well as a few handfuls of plebeian mud, the resourceful Oscar made a durable base for our miniature road. It was no reflection on the quality of Oscar's pungent dough that I found I could no longer summon up any enthusiasm over the imprint of an idealized tire on a road of putty. My mind was on another road clogged with fine-blown topsoil and imprinted by the wind. . . .

~

Then I had a dream. I still remember the mood of terror. Great unfriendly shapes were rushing toward me, threatening to crush me down. As they drew closer, I recognized them as the Buick cars I had been photographing. They were moving toward me in a menacing zigzag course, their giant hoods raised in jagged alarming shapes as though determined to swallow me. Run as fast as I could, I could not escape them. As they moved faster, I began to stumble, and as they towered over me, pushing me down, I woke up to find that I had fallen out of bed and was writhing on the floor with my back strained. I decided that if a mere dream could do this to me, the time had come to get out of this type of photography altogether. If I believed in piloting one's own life, then I should go ahead and pilot mine. Since photography was a craft I respected, let me treat it with respect. I made a resolution that from then on, for the rest of my life, I would undertake only those photographic assignments which I felt could be done in a creative and constructive way.

Later that day the phone rang, and appropriately enough it was one of the advertising agencies. A new job had come up—a series of five pictures to be taken in color. Despite my resolve, it was impossible not to feel some curiosity and I inquired about the fee. The fee was to be $1,000 a photograph. I had never received $1,000 for a single picture. I hesitated only a second. It all flooded back, the grotesque unreality, the grief. Why should I go through that again? I found it was not too hard to say, "No, thank you." I recommended another photographer who I thought could do the job well, and I hung up.

Good. I knew now what I would not do, and it was time to figure out what I should do. The drought had been a powerful eye-opener and had shown me that right here in my own country there were worlds about which I knew almost nothing. *Fortune* assignments had given me a magnificent introduction to all sorts of American people. But this time it was not the cross section of industry I wanted. Nor was it the sharp drama of agricultural crisis. It was less the magazine approach and more the book approach I was after. It was based on a great need to understand my fellow Americans better. I felt it should not be an assignment in the ordinary sense but should be as independent of any regular job as my steel mill pictures had been.

What should be the theme, the spine, the unity? I did not consider myself a writer. I felt this book had to be a collaboration between the written word and the image on the celluloid. I needed an author. Yet curiously enough I gave very little thought to what kind of author. I knew it must be someone who was really in earnest about understanding America. But a good writer or a merely competent writer? A novelist or a nonfiction man? A famous author or an obscure one? To all these things I gave no thought. I simply hoped that I would find the right one.

It seemed a miracle that within a week or two I should hear of an author in search of a photographer. He had a book project in mind in which he wanted to collaborate with a photographer. I gathered he had paid little attention to the possibility that there might be mediocre or gifted photographers in the world. He just wanted to find the right one—someone with receptivity and an open mind, someone who would be as interested as he was in American people, everyday people.

He was a writer whose work had extraordinary vitality, an almost savage power. He was the author of an exceedingly controversial book which had been adapted into an equally controversial play. Among the thousands who had seen the play or read the book were many who considered the characters exaggerated, the situations overdrawn. The author wanted to do a book with pictures that would show the authenticity of the people and conditions about which he wrote. He wanted to take the camera to Tobacco Road. His name was Erskine Caldwell.

Mahalia Jackson Sings to the Folklorists

Born into a world of song—gospel, spirituals, the blues—Mahalia Jackson became a true singer. Her life's journey took her from an impoverished childhood in New Orleans to sold-out performances at Carnegie Hall, and through it all, the sound of her own voice kept her alive. Her memoir, Movin' On Up, *is a joyful reminder of the passion and pleasure of doing that thing in life which you were born to do:*

I had begun to make records of my gospel songs, too. One day in 1946 I was in the recording studio practicing. To limber up my voice I sang just to myself an old spiritual song that I had known since I was a little child:

> *One of these mornings I'm going to lay down my cross and get my crown*
> *As soon as my feet strike Zion, I'm going to lay down my heavy burden*
> *I'm gonna put on my robes in glory and move on up a little higher . . .*

A man from Decca Records named Ink Williams was in the studio and happened to hear me.

"What's that you're singing, Mahalia?" he asked.

"Why it's just an old song we used to call 'Movin' On Up,' Ink," I said.

"But who wrote it?" Ink asked.

"Don't anybody know who wrote it, honey," I said. "I've always sung it, since I was a little child down in New Orleans. I like to sing it my own way."

"You sing it just right," Ink said. "Why don't you make a record of it for us?"

I did and a few weeks later "I Will Move On Up a Little Higher" began to move so fast we couldn't keep track of it. Colored folks were buying it in New York, in Chicago, way out West and all over down South. They've kept on buying it until it's sold close to two million copies.

"Movin' On Up" got to be known as my song. It made me famous, but only with Negroes. I still lived far inside the colored world. Then in 1950 the man who always arranged for my appearances in the colored churches in New York telephoned to tell me that he had heard from a white man named Marshall

Stearns who taught music at the New School for Social Research in New York. Stearns spoke to him about a symposium on the origins of jazz music which was going to be held at a place called Music Inn up in the Berkshires in Massachusetts. Music professors from the Juilliard School of Music and a lot of other big places had been invited to come there and discuss and lecture about folk music and jazz.

"What's that got to do with me?" I asked.

"Well, this man Stearns knows all about you and your voice from 'Movin' On Up' and other records and he wanted you to come and sing some gospel songs for them."

"I never expected to be singing for professors," I said. "But if they want me, I'll come, sure enough."

Music Inn, where the symposium was being held, is not far from Tanglewood, where the summer festivals of classical music take place. It's a big old estate that Philip Barber and his wife, Stephanie, bought and fixed up into an inn where people could come to study both jazz and classical music or just to listen to all kinds of music.

When I got up there they were still remodeling the old place. Everybody was running around in all directions carrying ladders and hammers. At night they slept in the cowbarn and the stables and in the ice house. They gave me an old horse stall to sleep in, and I thought to myself, "I finally made it into the white folks' world and look where it landed me!"

After supper Marshall Stearns rounded up music professors and got them into the carriage house, which had been fixed up into a kind of lounge, and asked me to give them a song. I leaned up against the piano and sang "Didn't It Rain, Lord!" and "Jesus, Savior, Pilot Me" and "Movin' On Up."

As soon as I finished, a great big fuss busted loose. Everybody began talking at once. The professors started arguing with each other and asking me all sorts of questions: Where did I learn to sing that way? Who taught me? Where had I learned such tonal shading and rhythm?

After they quieted down a bit, I told them I'd been singing around Baptist churches and gospel tents and at prayer meetings all my life because I loved singing and colored people liked to hear me sing. I told them I'd never had a music lesson. I didn't learn to sing any special way. I just found myself doing it.

Then they began carrying on all over again among themselves and had me sing some more songs and got out tape recorders and played some African bongo music and asked me if it sounded familiar. I told them I didn't know anything about jungle drums, but the beat sounded good; it did something for me.

They argued for a while about that and kept me singing there half the night. When I woke up in my horse stall in the morning, I heard my own voice coming back at me from the carriage house. The professors had already finished breakfast and were playing tape recordings they had made the night before.

"I mean to tell you right now," I said to my accompanist, "we're into something here with these crazy people and I don't know what's going to happen next."

What happened was we stayed on for a whole week while the musicologists and professors and students went around and around with their symposium discussions. They backed me up into a corner and asked me about colored church music and the way some congregations clap their hands and tap their feet. They talked about blues singers, and about the field calls and chants the colored people had made up when they were slaves in the fields of the rice plantations. They kept me singing songs for them and analyzing my style and disputing with me about why I did it just that way until I got all heated up, too.

One young professor kept insisting that I didn't even know my own meter. "You tell us you're singing four-four time," he said, "but I tell you you're not. You're singing twelve-twelve time."

"You're telling me wrong," I shouted. "I stand up here tapping my own foot with a four-four beat and you tell me I'm tapping twelve-twelve. One of us is crazy."

We kept it up all week, but we did a lot of good singing and I moved them with my songs. "Mahalia," Philip Barber told me, "if you'd started out the door and down to the lake while you were singing 'Shall We Gather at the River,' all those experts would have followed you and waded right into the water to be baptized."

Billie Holiday Knows Best

Getting a night's sleep was a continual drag. We were playing big towns and little towns, proms and fairs. A six-hundred-mile jump overnight was standard. When we got to put up at a hotel, it was usually four cats to a room. We might finish at Scranton, Pennsylvania, at two in the morning, grab something to eat, and make Cleveland, Ohio, by noon the next day. The boys in the band had worked out a deal for getting two night's sleep for one night's rent. We'd drive all night, hit a town in the morning, register and turn in early, and sleep until time to go to work. When the job was through, we'd sleep the rest of the night, clear out in the morning, and hit the road. This would work every other day and save loot. On the $125 a week I made, that was still very important.

This would have been fine except that I had to double up with another vocalist. I don't think she liked Negroes much, and especially not me. She didn't want to sleep in the same room with me. She only did because she had to. Artie Shaw had asked me to help her to phrase her lyrics; this made her jealous. Then once I made the mistake of telling somebody we got along fine, and to prove it I mentioned how she let me help her phrase. This made her sore. It was true, there were some places where the management wouldn't let me appear, and I'd have to sit in the bus while she did numbers that were arranged for me. She was always happy when she could sing and I couldn't.

I'll never forget the night we were booked at this fancy boys' school in New England. She was real happy because she was sure I was going to have to sit in the bus all night again because I was too black and sexy for those young boys. But when the time came to open, the head man of the school came out and explained that it wasn't me; they just didn't want any female singers at all. So the two of us had to sit in the bus together all night and listen to the band playing our songs.

Did I razz her! "You see, honey," I said, "you're so fine and grand. You may be white, but you're no better than me. They won't have either of us here because we're both women."

Shirley MacLaine on Power

The biggest surprise brought by success was that suddenly people were interested in what I thought, not because I was older—I was still in my twenties—or because I knew what I was doing, but because I made $800,000 a picture. It was suddenly O.K. for me to call Samuel Goldwyn "Sam," and William Wyler "Willy." They had been people with a Mr. before their names when I was young-and-nobody, but now that stardom was mine I had become *somebody* and we could communicate as equals.

Success in Hollywood forced me to come face to face with certain things: Young or not, ready or not, success forced me to evaluate myself.

Take money for instance. Before Hollywood, I had never had more than fifty dollars I could call "spendable." True, I had never lacked the money for necessities—food and a place to sleep—but luxury money was unknown to me. Now suddenly I had all the luxury money I wanted, but I still acted as though I had only the fifty dollars. I shopped in bargain basements and more often than not bought nothing. Several times I found myself haggling over something that had a fixed price, finally paying the money and leaving the purchase behind on the counter. I felt guilty because I could have what I wanted. I was reluctant to indulge myself, even though I had worked hard for it and economic security had become a reality.

I also found I wanted success and recognition without losing my anonymity. I was haunted by my psychological conditioning as a child to be inconspicuous. It was impossible. I had to adjust to shocking, baseless adulation and an enraging loss of privacy.

Unreasonably, I resented the attention I attracted even though I had fought for it. The most pleasant strangers provoked my fury because they simply looked at me, or watched how I picked up a fork, or stared while I spoke quietly with my daughter, or told me that they had seen the same facial expression on the screen. I felt that it was not their right to stare or to be interested in me. I was wrong, but regardless of how full of admiration their interest might be, I still resented it. I resented my enforced and constant awareness of self; I didn't want to live in a world of only "me."

At first, I reacted with stony hostility, hardly smiling when someone approached me with a compliment. For a while I denied that I was Shirley MacLaine—and I always felt ashamed afterward. After all, how could I call it an invasion of privacy when I had chosen to splash myself across the screen, seeking the applause and approval and attention of strangers?

But I did. I wanted to stand in a supermarket line again with people who were unaware of being observed. I wanted to hear the snatches of personal conversation, notice the way people dressed, the attitudes of their children, and observe the interplay between those who seemed happily married and between those who were miserable. It was all part of what had kept me alive, and it was gone.

I wanted to splash in the waves at Malibu again with Steve and Sachie without being stared at by passersby. Suddenly I felt exposed in a bathing suit, acutely conscious of my white skin that wouldn't tan, embarrassed by my masses of freckles, afraid that my figure might not be what people expected. "Is your mother Shirley MacLaine?" people would ask Sachie. And Sachie would say, "Yes, but she says she's really Shirley Parker." And then she would ask me, "Why are you so special, Mom?" And I would try to explain that I wasn't really special—it was my work that was special. And she would say, "I wish they would leave us alone so we could play again."

But the stardom I had fought for meant that "they" would not leave me alone again. And of course I didn't really want them to. I wanted to be wanted. I needed to be appreciated. I did what I did to win their approval. Behind all my resentment, I was terrified that I would disappoint them.

Instinctively I knew that, if I wanted to maintain an honest level in my work, I would have to remain vulnerable inside myself. If I built a shell and crawled into it, I would fail. People want to see reflections of true human feelings—their own. An actor can only hope to be a mirror of humanity, a mirror to be looked into by audiences. My problem was how to keep myself vulnerable and sensitive while remaining resilient. How to be tough and tender.

~

As my new values emerged I began to realize that I had *power*. Money was one thing, fame and recognition another; both had to be dealt with. But to feel power was devastating.

I found myself with the power to hire and fire people, to impose my opinions on others—to be listened to. What did I think of so-and-so? Did I like his story and the way it was written? Would I accept so-and-so as my director? So-and-so needs a job; would I accept him as co-star or collaborator?

I found myself making decisions because they were part of my new responsibility. Sometimes my decision would wreck the life of someone I'd never met. Although I didn't want to express my opinion—I had never really learned to respect my own opinion because I always believed someone else knew better—I was forced to because I was a *star*. And stars, for some reason, are supposed to know. If they don't, they're supposed to act as though they do.

The power of my position changed the people I had known before. Some who had been direct and honest became wary—wary of offending in my presence, and anxious to be assured of my respect and high evaluation. Others, reacting, became my harshest critics, afraid I might think they were kowtowing to me. I tried to put my old acquaintances at ease, to let them know that nothing basic in me had changed. And I was distressed to discover that often it was they whom I had changed. My success was too much for them. They couldn't handle it. I wondered what they would be like if success had happened to them instead of to me.

B A D G I R L S

Judging from America's astonishing appetite for stories about gunfighters, killers, outlaws, and crooks, it would seem that Americans love bad boys. These malevolent mavericks wander without apology across the borders of law and order we work so hard to patrol, and we seem to offer them a welcome indulgence. Are we less tolerant of our bad girls? There is certainly less written about them. Is there also less ease with stories about women who resolve to do whatever they damn well want, whenever they damn well please? Clichés abound in the anthologies—the only bad girls appear to be madames with hearts of gold or the occasional women outlaws whose only notoriety is their ability to handle a gun and wear a skirt at the same time. American mythologizers appear to have little patience for the wide and interesting array of women who rejected their social roles and, through will or perversity, sought their own solutions. The truth of these women's lives—their anger, their defiance, even the sickness of the choices they sometimes made (or were forced to make)—often seems more interesting than the stick figure desperadoes who dance across American folklore.

Beyond a healthy dose of pure wickedness, for example,

America's bad girls shared a common faith that the law, whether administered by the U.S. government or enforced by state or local authority, was most likely a man's law, and that a free-spirited woman was a man's worst nightmare. They had a right to be "bored crapless," as Bonnie Parker (of Bonnie and Clyde fame) was said to have remarked, but they paid a stiff penalty for their pleasure-seeking. Women out on the edge of appropriate conduct, where many men could live happily, were nearly always tipped out into lawlessness and poverty. In a survey in 1859, for example, 525 women out of 2,000 said destitution drove them to prostitution, but 513 gave as the chief reason "inclination." Women saw the West with the same adventurous hope that men did—the gold was coming up out of the ground, the land was waiting to be claimed, and folks just had to come get it. Hustle was the name of the game, but women had fewer options available to them and their margin for error was small. Unlike Jesse James or the Youngers or Billy the Kid, there seemed little excuse given on behalf of bad women by the American public. We do not hear as much of the pressures of honor or the broken promise that drove them reluctantly to a life of crime. Instead, they are often portrayed as crooks or killers or outlaws without much remorse, as if conscience were a matter of gender.

They are scattered across the national mythology, particularly the American West, like angry wolves in the desert: "Dutch" Jake, who ignored local society and ran her bordello with gusto, often baking cookies for her "girls" and giving them horses to ride; Diamond-tooth Lil, a brash braggart who assured one and all that the diamond stud placed in her front tooth was the least outrageous example of her wild lifestyle (she willed the tooth to a local orphanage to auction, but they buried her before the promise could be kept); Cattle Annie Macdonald, who was lynched for stealing cattle so efficiently that many thought her altogether innocent (she wasn't); Tessie Wall, the murderous madame of California (who said, after killing her lover: "I shot him 'cause I love him goddammit"); Big Nose Kate Fisher, who loved Doc Holliday and saved his skin several times; Fannie Sweet, a New Orleans thief who spied for the Confederate army, practiced a powerful voodoo, and loved poison as a settler of old scores; not to mention a colorful array of women with provocative nicknames like Bertha the Adder, Snake-Hips Lulu, Scarface Liz, Squirrel-tooth Alice and dozens of others. Some have colorful stories that get told in the following pages: women like Mary Read and Anne Bonney, who thieved and murdered with Calico Jack Rackham; Chloroform Kate—widow of Shanghai Johnson— who was buried, after her long life as a hustler, on a garbage scow sent out into San Francisco harbor; Poker Alice Tubbs ("I'd rather play poker than eat"); Miss Piggott and Mother Bronson, two tough San Franciscan saloonkeepers at the turn of the century, who hated and fought one another relentlessly over decades (and to a magnificent conclusion).

At their worst, America's bad girls were very bad indeed, like Cordelia Botkin, who murdered her lover's wife with poisoned candy and languished happily in San Quentin, or Bonnie Parker, who killed with enthusiasm. Some women none of us would want to cross paths with under the best of circumstances. Included in this chapter, however, are some stories of women considered "bad" by a prim and righteous public, but who were, in their own right, gloriously memorable—Tallulah Bankhead, who spoke for bad girls everywhere; Caresse Crosby, who shocked the blue bloods in Boston with her stories of life in Paris in the 1920s; Cassie Chadwick, who duped all of Cleveland into thinking she was the illegitimate daughter of Andrew Carnegie. Whether they were bad to the bone, driven to badness by a hostile society that cornered them, or just inclined to be bad, these women deserve a place distinct from their mean brethren, if only because they demonstrate so colorfully that gender, when it comes to pure wickedness, is not a relevant factor at all.

Mary Read and Anne Bonney

*A*mong the lore of the outlaws on the sea, the only woman to consistently take her place alongside the swaggering blackguards is Mary Read. Her chief distinction appears to be that she dressed like a man and was the outrageous companion of Calico Jack Rackham, a notoriously feared pirate. But Mary Read was much more than a cross-dresser with a taste for adventure. Beneath the standard recitation of her role as a pirate is a strange and poignant story. She was a fatherless daughter, a fraudulent grandson, a servant, a soldier, a lover, a happy wife, a mother, a merciless pirate and a defiant prisoner. One wonders, after trailing her through the tumultuous changes in her life, whether Mary Read had time to learn who she really was, or whether she simply never wanted the rest of us to ever know for certain.

Mary Read's story begins in England. Her mother had married a sailor and become pregnant before being forever widowed by the call of the open seas. She birthed a son, commenced the lonely life of a sailor's widow and, since loneliness often demands an unpayable price from even the most faithful, soon became pregnant again. Mary Read came into the world like her half brother, fatherless. The family was severely impoverished and, while Mary was still small, her half brother died. Though she would not remember her brother, she would forever mourn the loss of him. Unable to make ends meet and fearing starvation, Mary's mother resolved to seek help from her dead son's grandmother, who was a woman of some means. The old woman had not realized that her son had married or fathered a child before going off to sea and was anxious to meet her young grandson. Dressing Mary up in the clothes of her dead half brother, Mary's mother passed Mary off as the precious heir of the departed sailor. The visit went well and the reward for the deception was a crown a week. Mary must have realized for the first time (as she would again and again throughout her life) that identity is in the eye of the beholder.

When Mary was thirteen, the grandmother died. With the weekly stipend gone and Mary's mother unable to help her, Mary was flung out on her own. Once again, her mother recognized the value of a boy's clothing and put Mary to work as a footboy to an elegant French lady. Not one to idle, and ill suited to a life of service and subservience, Mary quit the lady and joined a British man-of-war, working as a powder bearer. She soon grew lithe and strong. But shipboard life was dull and, once again, she fled the known for the new. She went ashore to join the British army where she "bore arms as a cadet" in the Flanders campaign. Cool under fire, she fought with great energy and, it was said, had a particular fondness for the bayonet. She could not purchase a commission, however, as was the custom, so she joined the cavalry. While adventure had been her chief passion, circumstances were to change yet again for young Mary Read—she fell in love with another cavalryman. Her comrades thought her behavior (with all its attendant affection and softness) so unusual that they thought she had gone crazy. The young soldier, daunted at first by Mary's attention, proved altogether thrilled when, one night, she revealed who she really was (she had arranged that they share a tent together!). He immediately proposed to her, she happily accepted, and they both quit the army and opened a tavern together called "The Three Shoes." Business was brisk and they were particularly popular with the soldiers who knew Mary to be one of them. She entered the domestic life and is said to have liked it; we might never have heard from her again had not her young husband soon died. Some said that poor Mary Read was destined to be blown from all the safe havens of her life, but that underestimates the skill and drive of a woman who simply would not wait around when faced with an uncertain future. Once again, it was a man's disguise that allowed her the freedom to avail herself of adventure. She went to sea as a sailor bound for the West Indies. Captured by pirates (who convinced her to join them), she soon learned a different way of life where lawlessness and appetite went unchecked and she liked it. Some accounts say that she abhorred the pirate life, but those who were forced to sail on ships where she was aboard swore that she was as tough, resolute, and as fierce as any pirate they ever saw.

The two great characters of Read's life now make their appearance. Calico Jack Rackham, a forceful, malevolent thief with a reputation for spectacular seamanship and terrible ferocity, welcomed Read aboard as an experienced sailor for his crew. No one would have ever known the truth of her gender (her face was sun-darkened and leathery) had not Rackham's mistress, the bawdy, brassy Anne Bonney, taken quite a shine to the young sailor. Bonney was the illegitimate daughter of an Irish lawyer. She had an outrageous temper (she stabbed her father's maid in a rage) and was disowned by her family when she was old enough to fend for herself. She had fallen for Rackham and sailed with him until she became pregnant. He put her ashore in Cuba to have the baby and when she returned, she noticed the dark and interesting Read among the crew. Unaccustomed to being denied anything she wanted, Bonney pressed her affections until Read was forced to reveal the secret of her gender. Bonney was amazed and delighted and they became great friends—each recognizing in the other the rebellious streak so vital to survival. Soon enough, Rackham grew jealous of the two and one night decided to cut Read's throat for lolling about his mistress. He would have done it had not Bonney told him the truth. Some raconteurs, more comfortable with Read in her appropriate clothing, suggest that following the discovery Rackham loved both women, but this is not true. He kept her secret and she returned to being a pirate. Her true identity was only revealed one night when she wooed another shipmate and her white breasts shone in the candlelight. He too was delighted and they fell happily in love. Mary was not bashful about making her feelings clear. Her lover got into a quarrel with another shipmate, a man much rougher and more bloodthirsty than he was, and they agreed to fight a duel on shore. Mary begged her man to back down but understood that pride would not allow it. She took matters into her own hands. Insulting the same shipmate, she challenged him to a duel two hours *before* his duel with her lover. Needless to say, she killed him quickly and made the later duel unnecessary altogether.

Life for Read and Bonney was fun. They both recognized that notoriety was a living creature in need of constant feeding so they developed a distinctive look with their bell-bottomed trousers, pistols, and cutlasses. The more tenacious and pitiless their pirating, the more awesome their reputation became. Like all legends, however, the end must be the best part of the story: Read and Bonney did not disappoint us. Rackham's ship was cornered by the British authorities, who battered the pirate vessel with cannons and positioned themselves to board it with grappling hooks. Anne and Mary stayed on the deck and fought with bared teeth and curses while Rackham and his crew hid in the hold, hoping to ambush the attackers. The women repeatedly called for help, turning their rage from the enemy to their cowardly shipmates. They fought alone. At one point they were so angry they fired into their own hold killing one of their shipmates and wounding several others. They were soon overwhelmed, Rackham and the crew gave up without a fight, and the entire crew was taken to Jamaica for trial. The women sought mercy on the grounds that both were pregnant. Mary, while awaiting the verdict, caught a fever in the damp jail cell and the life that had begun in poverty ended in the same way. Bonney was freed.

Bonney was allowed to see Calico Jack in prison one last time before he was to hang for his crimes. She stood before her old lover and said evenly, "I'm sorry you are going to die, but if you had fought like a man, you'd need not hang like a dog." Mary Read could not have said it better.

The Sins of the Mothers . . .

Bathsheba Spooner (1746–78) murdered her husband in 1778 with the help of her lover and some accomplices—but the crime that led to her death by hanging (the first capital crime tried in Massachusetts) was more than likely rooted in her background as the daughter of a Tory sympathizer.

Spooner's father fled the country at the outbreak of the Revolution because his loyalties lay firmly with the Crown. Bathsheba married a local man more than thirty years her senior, and his neighbors branded him a Tory by association. Imagine his relief when he came home one evening to find that a young patriot in Washington's army had staggered into his house, wounded and in need of nursing. Who would not now celebrate the Spooner house as a charitable one to the new nation's soldiers? Soon after the invalid recovered, however, the worm turned on old man Spooner. The soldier fell for the mistress of the house (and she for him) and before long, they were plotting Spooner's murder. The soldier hadn't the nerve, blew several opportunities, and taxed Bathsheba's patience. She is said to have convinced two stragglers from the British army to help ambush Spooner on his way home from the tavern. They clubbed him to death and dumped his body in a well. Some poor maid the next morning drew up a bloody bucket. The killers might not have been caught at all had they not flashed Spooner's stolen goods around like the spoils of war. The authorities arrested all of them and the plot was quickly explained. In the eyes of a fervently patriotic public, Bathsheba Spooner's relentless determination to knock off her husband seemed more atrocious than the killing itself (typical, said the locals, of a Tory dame). In any event, the trial was spectacular with some of the country's most notable lawyers for the prosecution and the defense. All four people were found guilty and slated for hanging. According to the patriot newspapers, justice was to be gleefully served.

One last twist held up the proceedings, however, and it gave the story a final grisly ending. Spooner claimed she was pregnant. A special commission was established ("two male midwives and twelve discreet lawful matrons") to determine the truth. Their finding, after careful examination, was that Bathsheba Spooner was not pregnant and, over her passionate objections to wait several months upon an inevitable and indisputable proof, the hangings were scheduled. She put forward the following eloquent request:

> that my body be examined after I am executed by a committee of competent physicians, who will, perforce, belatedly substantiate my claims. I am a woman, familiar with my bodily functions, and am surely able to perceive when my womb is animated. The midwives who have examined me have taken into greater account my father's Royalist leanings than they have the stirrings in my body which should have stirred their consciences. The truth is that they want my father's daughter dead and with her my father's grandchild.

Needless to say, the hangings took place in Worcester, Massachusetts, attended, as expected, by a huge crowd. Incredibly, no one left the scene until the physicians performed the requested autopsy. Their report? To the consternation of all present, the doctors confirmed that the public prosecution was as guilty of murder as Spooner herself—for she was pregnant with a baby boy. Joshua Spooner's grandson became, through no fault of his own, the youngest and most innocent victim of American revolutionary fervor.

Mother Featherlegs

The best thing about her was her name: Although born a Shephard, she was called old Mother Featherlegs by cowboys because she wore long, red pantalettes tied around her ankles. They fluttered in the breeze as she rode through town on the way to the saloon or a secret rendezvous. She was best known as a shrewd go-between for road agents and desperadoes, and it was rumored that she kept vast amounts of stolen jewelry and money in her hideout. She was also known for serving the most foul-smelling rotgut ever to make a cowboy's mouth water. Her kids were outlaws and she was proud to be their mother. Someone thought she got away with too much and ambushed her one day at her well. She was found shot to death and no one ever knew who did it. Perhaps because there was something colorful about this bad woman (her name?), the state of Wyoming put up a monument to her in the town of Goshen in 1964.

Mary Mahaffey's Wedding Night

America loves a con. It must be flawlessly executed and it helps if the victim is someone who actually deserves it. So we go to 1850. Sacramento. One Mary Mahaffey, an elegant young woman of breeding and charm, meets a wealthy rancher in search of a wife. He's used to getting what he wants and the gleam in his eye rivals the one he might have had for a prize steer. He never asks if she is single and she never tells him she isn't. She also never mentions that she has a bawdy collection of friends who love a good time. So lovely Mary accepts his bullish proposal (not to mention his cash) and plans a big wedding. When word gets out that there is going to be a party, especially in Sacramento in 1850, attendance is not an issue. They came from far and wide. One is bound to wonder if the bridegroom noted the hilarity and the general mayhem of Mary's friends—they certainly were not bashful about eating and drinking to the hilt. The bridegroom proved a good fellow, and, undaunted by the calls for more of everything, he footed the whole bill. All noticed the glee with which he watched his new bride, the excitement in his face, and his enthusiasm for her attentions. When the festivities seemed to draw to a close, he looked to his lady love to retire to their wedding chamber. He did not know that the clock was about to strike and that Cinderella's cruel lesson was to be his own: The minister who married them turned into a foul-mouthed gambler for whom the cloth was simply something to wipe his mouth with; the dainty bridesmaids turned surly and demanded payment up front for their dances; most surprising of all, the blushing bride shed the mask and put a gun to his head, robbing him (to the delight of her friends) and kicking him out into the night. He was out a small fortune but intact; she was the belle of the ball that night and ready to marry again!

Calamity Jane

She was a master at spinning her life into legend. She was so American, so perfectly emblematic of a nation that needed to invent itself every day. "I'm the only woman in the west," she would boast, "who worked in a bordello and patronized it at the same time." Without the dime-store writers who fed off any tough with a six-shooter and a mouth to match, she'd have been just another boomtown barfly, a drunk with a flair for camp life and work in the saddle. But the mythmakers loved *her boasts ("I sleep when and where I damn well please!") and believed the stories she told louder and louder as the years passed to anyone who might listen. Her life story traveled well: She was orphaned, took to the outdoor life to survive, was a mule skinner, a scout for Gen. Custer (doubtful), an Indian fighter, a hard-loving, hard-living hustler with fear of no man. She loved Wild Bill Hickock (that's true), claimed to have had his child (that isn't), and bragged how she cornered his killer (that isn't either). When the dust of her life settled, by some swing of chance, she was buried alongside Wild Bill, and her myth was securely fastened to the deathless legend of Boot Hill. The closest thing we have to a real picture of Calamity may well come from this memoir of her last days by a woman who had grown up on the streets of Deadwood, South Dakota:*

Calamity Jane came back to Deadwood after her name had become a tradition. She was a glowing figure in the history of that hectic year of '76 that brought the gold rush into Deadwood Gulch, the crowds of men and scattering of women who followed high adventure wherever it led.

She came back to Deadwood as quietly as she had slipped out, unheralded, dressed in shabby clothes, and leading her little seven-year-old girl by the hand. She was Mrs. Burke then and was considering the schooling of her daughter. Scores of women who looked like her came and went on Deadwood's streets unnoticed every day. But no one like Calamity Jane ever had come into Deadwood Gulch.

She not only was typical of old Deadwood. She was old Deadwood.

Most of her old friends and comrades were gone. Wild Bill, who, according to Calamity herself, was the only man she ever had loved, lay under a life-size pink stone statue of himself in Mount Moriah. The statue was more or less mutilated because the soft rosy sandstone offered a temptation to sightseeing vandals with little knives. A wire screen had been strung around it as a protection but not until after a piece of Bill's nose and a number of chips from his coat and his long hair had been sacrificed to the vandalism that some people call souvenir collecting.

Calamity Jane had been only a name to me as she was to all my generation, but the name had stood for a picturesque bit of adventurous romance that the woman who stood on the corner in front of Pat's Place didn't match at all. But even before I had time to be disappointed I sensed something about her that had assembled this group of the best pioneers to welcome her back to Deadwood. It was the most representative that the town could have assembled.

Many among them were pioneers of '76 who in some way or other had known Calamity Jane in those early days.

I remember noticing at the time how few there were among them of what the papers called "denizens of the badlands." And every one of them was remembering those days in '78 when Calamity Jane alone took care of the smallpox patients in a crude log cabin pesthouse up in Spruce Gulch around behind White Rocks, the tall limestone peak over which the belated morning sun shines down on Deadwood Gulch. Smallpox was the most dreaded scourge of the frontier towns. Usually people died because of dearth of nursing, of facilities for taking care of the sick, and bad sanitary conditions. For the same reasons, it spread with terrifying speed. Those who recovered came from their sickbeds with marred faces. All that a town like Deadwood in '78 knew to do for smallpox patients was to set aside an isolated cabin and notify the doctor.

There were half a dozen patients in the small log pesthouse in Spruce Gulch when Dr. Babcock made his first visit. He said they were all very sick and he was going back after supper. No one offered to go with him, but when he went back he found Calamity Jane there.

"What are you doing here?" he asked.

"Somebody's got to take care of 'em," she replied. "They can't even get 'emselves a drink of water when they want it. You tell me what to do, Doc, and I'll stay right here and do it."

"You will probably get the smallpox," he warned her.

"Yes I know. I'll have to take that chance. I can't leave 'em here to die all alone. Won't they have a better chance if I stay and do what you tell me?"

There was no question but what they would and he told her so. But he looked at her clear olive skin and the firm contours of her face and chin and reminded her that it was not only disease and death she risked. With women of Calamity Jane's sort, beauty was as important almost as life itself. It was their stock in trade. Beauty and bravery were Calamity Jane's best assets. It was doubtful if she ever would lose her courage but, without her beauty, what would she do with her life? He reminded her of this too. But she took nothing into account except that half a dozen very sick men needed her services desperately, and she stayed. The charmed life that had persisted through Indian arrows and guns, through desperate gun fights, various hazards and hardships, held her dark striking beauty for further destruction. She came unscathed through the long smallpox siege and most of her patients lived. Dr. Babcock believed that without her care not one of them could have pulled through.

She never left the pest cabin during those hard weeks except to make hurried trips down to Deadwood for supplies the grocers gave her.

Calamity Jane, I have heard from outsiders, was a woman of many faults. She shattered the commandment that women are supposed to guard against the lightest crack, all the breakage of the third [commandment] was at her tongue's end, and she was given to strong drink. This is the full category of her vices. I never heard about them from the people who had known her. Old Black Hillers seemed never to remember her faults. Certainly they attached no importance to them.

"You should have seen her at her best," my uncle the General said. "She doesn't belong in the kind of clothes she's wearing. She doesn't belong in this day and age. You should have known her when she wore fringed buckskin breeches and carried a gun. She is afraid of nothing, Indians or smallpox, or road agents. That sort of courage hasn't much chance now, with the Indians all herded up in the reservations, and smallpox patients in hospitals, and the road agents either reformed or in the penitentiary. There never was a gunman quicker on the trigger, nor a good Samaritan quicker to help the fellow that needed it. Not much chance nowadays to show those rough rugged virtues that made Calamity beloved."

~

She came into the Black Hills first with General Crook's command in the summer of '75 when he had marched in from Fort Laramie to order the miners out of the Hills until treaties could be made with the Indians. Calamity had been in Cheyenne getting a little bored and restless when she heard of the proposed expedition into a new, wild and dangerous country. The day she heard about it, she hired a team and buggy to "go for a little ride," she told the man at the livery stable. She drove her horses at an easy trot through the streets of Cheyenne, but when she had left the city behind she speeded up and drove as rapidly as her consideration for horses would permit. Arrived at Fort Laramie, she left her rig where its owner could recover it, smuggled herself in among the soldiers, and was too far on the way to the outlaw country to be sent back, before anyone discovered she was a woman.

The General had known her first when she came in with Wild Bill, Colorado Charley, and some others in '76. He was one of those who was entirely blind to her faults and very kind to her virtues. Martha Jane Canary, the General said, rolling the name around behind his blond mustache and beard, was a person of so little consequence that no one knew with any exactness where she was born or from what sort of people she came. By the time she got to be Calamity Jane, notorious from the Missouri River to the heart of the Rockies and from Denver to old Fort Benton, she herself didn't seem to be quite sure.

According to one story, she was born near Burlington, Iowa, about the year 1851, the daughter of a Baptist clergyman, and had run away when she was very young, with an army lieutenant, and gone to Wyoming. At Sidney, Nebraska, she gave birth to a son and the young officer who was its father had sent it back to his parents in "the States," telling them a romantic tale about finding the waif on the plains after its parents had been killed by Indians. A less interesting account gave Calamity's birthplace as Princeton, Missouri, fixing the date definitely as May 1, 1852. It made no mention of her family, but did tell of the seductive young lieutenant, and sent the baby to an orphan asylum.

~

The General was inclined to believe what an old bullwhacker had told him. The bullwhacker had known Jane when she was a little girl in Fort Laramie, and he said she was born at La Bonte's trading post 120 miles northwest of Fort Laramie in 1860, and when she was only two years old her father had been killed and her mother seriously wounded by Sioux Indians. Some one brought her down to Fort Laramie where she was adopted by an army sergeant and his wife. "They were awful kind to her," the bullwhacker had told the General, "but they didn't learn her nothing, and she just run wild around the post."

It was after the affair with the lieutenant that Calamity's mother came into the picture again and Calamity Jane went with her and her stepfather, a man by the name of Hart, to Salt Lake City, where she stayed peaceably for a very brief period. Then she ran away again. This time she went to Rawlins, Wyoming, where she led a wild life according to all reports except those given to her stepfather when he came after her. He was convinced from all he saw and heard that she had developed into a hard-working, well-behaved young woman, and he went back to Utah and let her stay.

Someone from Montana told me once that Jane came honestly by her *penchant* for sinning because her mother was the famous Madame Canary of the Montana mining camps. Her houses were considered "high class" and possibly she would not have wanted her wild, outdoor young daughter with her even if she had cared to come, which probably she would not.

~

Calamity Jane drifted restlessly through the frontier camps and army posts of Wyoming, Nebraska, and Montana learning to tie a diamond hitch with deft fingers, to pack horses, and handle teams with firm, gentle expertness. For a while she held a government position with a pack train. She was willing to do any sort of work that could be done out of doors, or inside when there was sickness and need of nursing, and she cast her lot lightly with any man who lived and worked out of doors and who followed new trails.

Living in a time that kept its women by the hearthstone, in the back seat of a carriage, and in the sidesaddle, she found little legitimate outlet for her tremendous vital energy and her dominant love of excitement. And so she went her way along the frontier, with freighters, soldiers, and placer miners, helping blaze the way and holding out a strong hand to the weaker brothers across the hard places, until her crooked trail led her in the middle Seventies to Deadwood where she seemed to find a home foothold she never had known before. It was the place to which she kept coming back as she got older. It was with Deadwood her name was most closely associated, although all the Black Hills knew her.

Father remembered having seen her once in Rapid City coming out of an old log hotel.

"Say, Judge," she said, "I wonder if I hadn't ought to've done it. Maybe I hadn't. I took that sick kid in there some pickles because he wanted them so bad and the doctor wouldn't let him have 'em. He said he'd die if he ate 'em and the kid thought he'd die if he didn't. He's got mountain fever."

She looked at Father for a moment, not worried but thoughtful. He had nothing to advise. The thing was done and he didn't know much about taking care of mountain fever patients anyway. He would have left it to the doctor but there was no use in saying that now.

"Well," she said finally in a matter-of-fact tone, "I guess it's up to me to see that he don't die." And she did.

The incident had been recalled to Father only the week before in Custer. He had happened to meet "the kid," who told Father then that he owed his life to Calamity Jane's nursing. Perhaps to the pickles, too. You never could tell.

Mrs. McLaughlin, whose husband was the first mayor of Deadwood, said Calamity Jane probably was the only woman in the world who ever ran away from her husband because he gave her too many good clothes and too soft living. That was her second husband. His name was White and he had sold some mining property for quite a lot of money not long after he married Calamity Jane. Mrs. McLaughlin said she used to see Calamity occasionally on the street in Cheyenne and she was a pretty girl then, slim, dark-eyed, and dark-haired, and when White made money the first thing he thought of was to deck her out in fine clothes. He had to buy them because she wasn't enough interested, and she found them uncomfortable and cumbersome. They lived about at the best hotels in Cheyenne and Denver, and she didn't feel at home. She stood the clothes and the hotels as long as she could, and then she ran away. She was with a freighting outfit dressed like a man when he found her and was convinced of the futility of trying to get her back. He never did.

~

The way the benefit for Calamity's daughter worked out showed exactly why she had stumbled so much through life. She didn't have the caliber to carry through her own best plans.

The benefit at the Green Front was a howling success—just that. I don't know how many people went, but I understand there were plenty, and a great many more bought tickets. The money poured in—gold and greenbacks, as lavishly as though it had been gold dust and the time, 1876. There was enough to have kept that child in St. Martin's convent until she was ready for Wellesley or Bryn Mawr. The Green Front turned it over to Calamity and she walked up to the bar to treat the crowd for having been so kind to her child. Her friends tried, after the first drink, to curb her lavishness, but she forgot all about the young daughter, the convent, and higher education for women, and got roaring drunk.

~

It was a long time before Calamity Jane came back to Deadwood again. Her last coming was early in the 20th Century. She was a broken, sick woman, worn out at 50 with the hard careless life she had led. She went through a few more gay carousals and then, on the second of August, the 27th anniversary of the murder of Wild Bill, she died in a miners' boarding house in the gold camp of Terry up in the mountains above Deadwood. It was a high, wild mining camp, perhaps reminding Calamity more of old Deadwood than did Deadwood itself.

She was buried from the Methodist Church in Deadwood. The sermon took no account of the irregularities of her conduct but stressed her high virtues. The church was crowded and a long line of carriages followed Calamity Jane to her grave beside Wild Bill.

The last people leaving the church noticed that a man in the front pew, who had attracted their attention during the service by his grief, was still kneeling and sobbing bitterly. Some one touched him on the shoulder and asked if he had known Calamity Jane.

"Yes," he said between sobs, "I was her first husband. She was the finest woman that ever lived—the kindest."

Until Belle Starr Passes

She's the woman most often cited in the pantheon of desperadoes: an outlaw who stands shoulder to shoulder with Jesse James, the Younger brothers, Billy the Kid, and others. Like them, there is probably less there than meets the eye, but also like them, she caught the popular imagination because she couldn't be bothered abiding by the law. She had four outlaw husbands (including Cole Younger) and outlived them all; she had a daughter who would make her own name as a tough frontier madame. In the end, however, Starr's legend was her own. She rustled cattle, was good with a pistol, loathed authority, rode sidesaddle on a velvet black mare called Venus, and took money from whomever she pleased. Like other outlaw greats, legends about her proliferated in the years after the Civil War and soon enough, any act of innovative thievery or bold gunplay committed by a woman was attributed to Belle Starr. Some stories ring true and are pretty good ones at that.

Her first husband was Bud Shirley, a bushwhacker who was killed by a local militia. Belle is said to have ridden to town to claim his body. She arrived at the same moment that they brought in Shirley in the back of a wagon. The militia (pro-Union men, which must have turned the Confederate sympathizing Starr's stomach) were lolling around waiting for the undertaker. She tied her horse to the wagon and, with all appearances of the grieving widow, climbed aboard to take her dead husband's head in her arms. To everyone's astonishment, she drew his pistols from his belt and stood up firing at his killers. Something of an angry widow's last stand. She did not know that the percussion caps had been removed (standard procedure), and in a fury she hurled the guns at the laughing men and vowed her revenge. She was to take it many times over, though she was more the outlaw than a killer. Her legend grew in her own lifetime, until she was quite a celebrity.

A classic story told by old-timers captures her mystique. It was a hot summer day in a local courthouse. The windows were open and a trial was plodding along when a daydreaming juror happened to gaze out onto the street. Soon the other jurors joined him at the window. The judge was at first indifferent, assuming the jurors were exercising their right to go to the window and spit, but he was soon alarmed by an empty jury box. "What the hell is going on?" he shouted. The foreman turned excitedly and said, "Your honor, Belle Starr is riding into town." Bang went the gavel: "This court will be in recess until Belle Starr passes." With that, the entire courthouse went to the windows to see her ride by.

The Hanging of Cattle Kate: A Newspaper Account (1889)

A DOUBLE LYNCHING . . . the man weakened but the woman cursed to the last.

A man and a woman were lynched near historic Independence Rock on the Sweetwater River in Carbon County [Wyoming] Sunday night. They were postmaster James Averill and a virago who had been living with him as his wife for some months. Their offense was cattle stealing, and they operated on a large scale recruiting quite a bunch of young steers from the range of that section.

News of the double hanging was brought to Rawlins by a special courier and telegraphed to Foreman George D. Henderson of the 76 outfit, who happened to be in the capital. Mr. Henderson's firm has its own ranch in that country and has been systematically robbed by rustlers for years.

Averill and the woman [Cattle Kate] were fearless maverickers. The female was the equal of any man on the range. Of robust physique she was a daredevil in the saddle, handy with a six-shooter and adept with the lariat and branding iron. Where she came from none seems to know, but that she was a holy terror all agreed. She rode straddle, always had a vicious bronco for a mount, and seemed never to tire of dashing across the range.

The thieving pair were ordered to leave the country several times, but paid no attention to the warnings, sending the message that they could take care of themselves, that mavericks were common property, and that they would continue to appropriate unmarked cattle.

Lately it has been rumored that the woman and Averill were engaged in a regular roundup of mavericks and would gather several hundred for shipment this fall. The ugly story was partially verified by the stealthy visit of a cowboy to their place Saturday. He reported that their corral held no less than fifty head of newly branded steers, mostly yearlings, with a few nearly full grown.

The statement of the spy circulated rapidly and thoroughly incensed the ranch men, who resolved to abate the menace to their herds. Word passed along the river, and early in the night from ten to twenty men, made desperate by steady loss, gathered at a designated rendezvous and quietly galloped to the Averill ranch. A few hundred yards from the cabin they dismounted and approached cautiously. This movement was well advised for Averill had murdered two men and would not hesitate to shoot, while the woman was always full of fight.

Within the little habitation sat the thieving pair, before a rude fireplace. The room was clouded with cigarette smoke. A whiskey bottle with two glasses was on the deal table, and firearms were scattered around the interior so as to be within easy reach.

The leader of the regulators stationed a man with a Winchester at each window and led a rush into the door. The sound of "hands up!" sounded above the crash of glass as the rifles were leveled at the strangely assorted pair of thieves. There was a struggle, but the lawless partners were quickly overpowered and their hands bound.

Averill, always feared because he was a murderous coward, showed himself a cur. He begged and whined, and protested innocence, even saying that the woman did all the stealing. The female was made of sterner stuff. She exhausted a blasphemous vocabulary upon the visitors, who essayed to stop the vile flow by gagging her, but found the task too great. After applying every imaginable opprobrious epithet to the lynchers, she cursed everything and everybody, challenging the Deity to cheat her enemies by striking her dead if He dared. When preparations for the short trip to the scaffold were made, she called for her own horse and vaulted to its back from the ground.

Ropes were hung from the limb of a big cottonwood tree on the south bank of the Sweetwater. Nooses were adjusted to the necks of Averill and his wife and their horses led from under them. The woman died with curses on her foul lips. . . .

This is the first hanging of a woman in Wyoming.

Poker Alice Tubbs

She liked her Colt revolver. In her twenties, she was blonde and plump, and some thought her coy. By the time her picture was taken, after years of card playing, hustling, and hard living, she looked like a bulldog. She also liked her cheroot, which stuck in her teeth like a plug. But for all the toughness, the picture tells a tale—her shoulders sag, her eyes have a sadness about them. Born in England, raised in the South—had she expected something different from her life? Did she regret the choices she made or was she just hung over when the photographer got her to sit for the portrait? Who knows. She didn't seem to be one for regrets. Once, in a Pecos Texas saloon, she thought the dealer was cheating, pulled her colt on him, helped herself to $5,000, and went to New York City where she bought fabulous gowns and lingerie before returning penniless to the West. She made a stab at a normal life, became someone's wife, but upon his death, looked once again to make her fortune. She opened a stylish bordello and was known to kill an unruly patron or two when things got out of hand. Poker Alice loved cards above all and would rather have played seven card stud ("with a buy at the end") than eat.

The Worst of the Bad

SALLY SKULL (1813–c.1867) had more than a fearsome name—she had a deadly habit of killing her husbands. Her first husband was killed fighting Indians, she said, though no one knows where or with what tribe he fought. Her second husband left her, complaining she tried to kill him (he was the lucky one!), and then along came husband number three: George Skull. He soon disappeared, as did her next husband (he drowned). Then the next was shot to death by Sally and, incredibly, the court believed her tale of accidental death and wifely grief; she was freed from any wrongdoing. Sally was getting the hang of murder until one day she too disappeared (along with her last husband). Though one day a body believed to be Sally's was found, her husband was never seen again. After killing off her husbands with impunity, many wondered if her last husband had not gotten in his licks first.

~

LYDIA STRUCK (1833–79) used poison to kill just about everyone in her life. She started with her husband, a New York City policeman, who drank too much and battered her. She used arsenic, collected the insurance, and moved to a new state. She had four children, reminders perhaps of her dead husband, so she dispatched each of them with arsenic, too. She married a wealthy widower and he died mysteriously fourteen months later. She married yet again and murdered yet again, including his two children. Where were the police? They only caught on at the end of the trail when too many coincidental deaths were linked to Struck's journey through life. They captured her (preparing to kill yet again), and put her away in prison where she died, unlike her victims, of natural causes.

~

MARY JANE "BRICKTOP" JACKSON (1836–?) was one of the meanest, deadliest criminals that New Orleans had ever seen—which is saying something for a tough town. She killed many men, badly injured many more, and was said never to have lost a fight. She had bright red hair (hence the nickname) and carried a knife, which she handled easily and with guile. She was once in a bar and a patron told her to watch her language. When she ignored him, he made the literally fatal mistake of slapping her and she cut him to shreds. She was freed because the autopsy proved inconclusive as to cause of death! Throughout her life she fought and killed friend and foe with equal abandon. After stabbing her longtime lover to death and being sent to prison, she was pardoned and, to the relief of everyone in New Orleans, she disappeared.

~

BELLE GUNNESS (1859–?) was said to have killed forty-two suitors, two husbands, four children, and a hired maid. Her favorite trick was to place an ad looking for a suitable husband. They had to bring money with them, and when they did she took them in and killed them. She was successful for quite some time and then, with the law closing in, a mysterious fire burned her farm with all her children in it. They found a headless body, presumed to be Belle (not to mention the bodies of scores of victims all around the farm), but those closest to the case thought the conclusion to her deadly gambit was too neat. Though she was never heard of again, rumors of her appearance floated around the country for many decades.

~

FLOSSIE MOORE (1866–?) was a tough African-American woman who operated in Chicago as a mugger and thief. She took after unsuspecting tourists and made sure she got everything of value they owned before beating them up. She was said to have been arrested more than ten times in one day, and she laughed at a judge who fined her $100: "Make it $200," she derided; "I got money to burn." When she was sent away to Joliet Prison she was no better, causing constant trouble and living most of the time in solitary confinement. After her release, she disappeared and was not heard of again.

~

RUTH SNYDER (1895–1928) was known as the "granite woman" because of the shocking murder she committed with her lover. For this crime she would go down in history as the first woman to die in the electric chair. In 1925 Snyder, a married housewife, met Judd Gray, a corset salesman, and they became lovers. It wasn't long before Judd, a weak man with a mother complex, was under Snyder's charismatic spell. He called her "momsie" and soon learned that Snyder had insured her husband's life and had tried numerous times to kill him herself. She had tried to gas him and he hadn't died; she had tried to knock him off a motorboat and he survived; she had even given him poison for the hiccups and he didn't die ("I told her that was one helluva way to cure the hiccups," said Gray later to the police). By the spring of 1927, Snyder was working on Judd to help her kill her resilient husband. At first he refused, but, following Snyder's refusal to sleep with him until he helped her, he agreed. On April 17, they entered her husband's room and smashed a sash weight over his head. He awoke, struggled with Gray, and called for his wife's assistance. She provided it with another smash of the lead weight and picture wire around the neck! At long last, Snyder's husband died. Then Gray tied her up (loosely, as the policemen noted with great suspicion) and fled. When the jewelry that had been "stolen" was found under the bed, and Gray's name turned up in her address book, the police moved on a hunch. They told Snyder that Gray had fingered her (he hadn't) and soon enough, each was singing the other's complete and total guilt. They were both condemned to death. In captivity they each wrote their autobiographies and Snyder received 164 proposals of marriage. At her electrocution, a reporter strapped a camera to his leg and shot a photograph of her death throes (it was spread over the *New York Daily News* the next day), the only known photograph of an execution in American history.

~

MA BARKER (1871–1935) was one of the noted women of the American crime scene in the first part of the twentieth century. She was born in the territory that spawned Jesse James and swore that she had seen him one day riding past her home. Life was never easy for her and got harder following her marriage to an impoverished sharecropper who would father her four sons. She was tough, and believing her sons would need strong guidance in life, she decided to provide it herself. As they grew up and got in more trouble with the law, some speculated that Ma Barker's guidance had more to do with their lives as criminals than as penitent boys in search of the court's forgiveness. Barker often tearfully pleaded at her children's trials and always to great affect. The boys robbed with increasing discipline (Barker was said to be a master of the "getaway"), though few knew for sure how involved Barker really was in either the planning or the execution of the crimes. Following the death of her son Herman at the hands of a policeman, Ma Barker unleashed a continuing series of bank robberies and kidnappings. She was mad as a hornet and made no bones that the FBI was her sworn enemy. In the end, she was killed in a shoot-out along with her youngest son, and though some still say that her bloodthirsty masterminding was all an invention of the FBI who killed her, her long and bloody history suggests otherwise.

~

ANNA HAHN (1906–38) was the first woman electrocuted in Ohio—for mastering the art of marrying rich old men just before they died. The art even extended to their wills, all of which named the young German-born woman as the principal beneficiary. It was only after she got careless with her fifth victim (she refused to pay for his burial despite taking all his money) that police thought to conduct an autopsy. Arsenic abounded, as it did in her other victims (all of whom were dug up and demonstrated similarly lethal levels of the fatal poison). The only man to evade her deadly treachery was one George Heiss, who claimed that he was suspicious of Hahn. Why? Because every time a fly would land on the lip of his beer, it would convulse and die. Observant man; lucky, too.

Lizzie Borden

A mild-mannered schoolteacher in Falls River, Massachusetts, Lizzie Borden is said to have hacked her father and stepmother to death with an axe on an August day in 1892. Everything pointed to her guilt, and the horror of the crime, coupled with the blandness of the accused, transfixed the nation. The thirteen-day trial was avidly followed—Borden's defense attorney kept describing the gruesome murder scene and pointing to the neat Miss Borden, saying: "To find her guilty, you must believe she is a fiend. Gentlemen, does she look it?" As to her guilt or innocence, the public was split (it is said that 1,900 divorces could be directly attributable to the Borden case), but Borden would not confess and the evidence was deemed circumstantial. The deliberations were brief, the jury gone barely an hour. Not guilty, they said. She lived on in Falls River, an outcast, though wealthy with the $500,000 inheritance many thought she had murdered to gain. Why do we remember her more as the murderer gone free than as the faithful daughter wrongly accused? Maybe because of the refrain that the children who lived at the end of her street used to shout at her darkened windows:

> Lizzie Borden took an axe,
> And gave her mother forty whacks;
> When she saw what she had done,
> She gave her father forty-one.

Cordelia Botkin: A Sweet Murder

As bad girls go, she wasn't so bad. But the jury who found her guilty of murder obviously didn't agree. They said she was bad enough to go to San Quentin for life. Cordelia Botkin was sweet-tempered, some said even gracious, and she lived in California at the turn of the century. She loved a newspaper reporter, something of a rogue, whose wife (the daughter of a U.S. Congressman) knew as little about their affair as Cordelia's own husband. They shared a San Francisco flat and lived a wild life on the sly (sometimes with as many as five people dancing and loving the night away). Life was good for Cordelia until the Spanish-American War broke out and her lover smelled an opportunity to make his name as a foreign correspondent. He even suggested before his departure that their illicit passions were on the ebb.

Botkin mourned his departure for a while and then got mad. She figured the war would sharpen his sense of marital devotion, and she obsessed over the wife she had never met. She put in motion a careful plan to eliminate the competition, to ensure that at war's end, there would be no other woman in his life. The fact that he was no longer interested only sharpened her determination.

Why didn't the jury acquit the lovesick Botkin on grounds that she was guilty of a temporary and jealous madness? Why didn't they search their own hearts for the awful feeling of loving someone who no longer loved back?

Because Botkin's murder weapon was so wickedly delicious, so carefully chosen, that every member of the jury was simply appalled. Cordelia Botkin's murder weapon was a box of Haas chocolates lovingly laced with arsenic; her victim's sweet tooth was so keen (and her sister's too) that they ate the candy that came in the mail before reading the card. What appreciation she must have felt for the sender of the surprise sweets, so elegantly wrapped! We will never know to whom she gave loving credit—but considering the amount of arsenic in those chocolates, she had little time for gratitude. She and her sister died immediately, and the guilty finger pointed directly at Cordelia Botkin.

Her trial was swift and the verdict unflinching. It caused quite a sensation, made all the more dramatic when the judge shipped her off to San Quentin, where no woman had ever gone before. They say that she led a good life there; her jailers thought her wonderful and accorded her all sorts of privileges (even a closely monitored shopping spree in San Francisco!), but she died there just the same. Murder, thy name is chocolate.

Miss Piggott and Mother Bronson

Miss Piggott was a ferocious old woman who operated a saloon and boardinghouse on Frisco's Davis Street during the 1860's and 1870's. No one ever knew her first name; she insisted on being addressed, with proper respect, as Miss Piggott. Her only rival of importance as a female crimp [entrapper of sailors] was Mother Bronson, whose establishment was in Steuart Street. Both these ladies were their own bouncers and chief bartenders, but neither enforced her edicts with a bludgeon or a slungshot, as did some other notorious ladies elsewhere along the Barbary Coast. Miss Piggott remained faithful to the bung starter, a sort of wooden mallet used to knock out plugs in barrels, and in the use of this implement as a weapon she developed amazing skill. On the other hand Mother Bronson, who was nearly six feet tall and broad in proportion, scorned to use any other than Mother Nature's weapons. She possessed a fine and strong set of teeth, which she delighted to sink into the anatomy of an obstreperous customer; her enormous feet were encased in No. 12 brogans, and her fist was as hard as a rock and resembled in size a small ham. With the toe of her boot she once hoisted a Chinese from the floor of her saloon to the top of the bar, and she often boasted that she could fell an ox with one blow of her fist.

Sometimes Miss Piggott lacked enough sailors to round out an order,

whereupon Nikko, her runner and right-hand man, prowled through the Barbary Coast until he found a likely-looking prospect and enticed him into the
Davis Street saloon. There he was nudged along the bar until he stood upon a
trapdoor built into the floor. Then Nikko called loudly for drinks, which were
served by Miss Piggott in person. The runner received beer, while for the
stranger Miss Piggott prepared a concoction much used in shanghaiing circles
and called a Miss Piggott Special. It was composed of equal parts of whisky,
brandy, and gin, with a goodly lacing of laudanum or opium.

While the victim was shivering under the terrific impact of this beverage,
Miss Piggott leaned across the bar and tapped him on the head with a bung
starter, while Nikko made matters certain with a blow from a slungshot. As the
prospect began to crumple to the floor, Miss Piggott operated a lever behind
the bar and dumped him into the basement, where he fell upon a mattress that
Miss Piggott had thoughtfully provided, realizing that the man might receive
an injury that would lessen his value. When the object of all these attentions
awoke, he was usually in a ship bound for foreign climes, with no very clear
idea as to how he got there. All of Miss Piggott's regular customers knew the
exact location of the trapdoor and kept away from it, for it was an unwritten
law of the establishment that any man who stood upon the fatal spot was fair
game. The spectacle of Miss Piggott drugging and then slugging a stranger and
dropping him into the basement excited no particular attention. The bystanders might comment judiciously upon the force and accuracy with which the old
lady delivered the knockout blow, but that was about all. What happened to
him was his own affair.

The Burial of Chloroform Kate

Catherine Johnson got her nickname from her habit of sniffing—or even swig-
ging—chloroform as a sort of chaser for the raw whisky she swilled. Kate was
the widow of Shanghai Johnson, who specialized in kidnaping whalers on the
Barbary Coast. She had been a barmaid when he was flourishing and she took
over the business after his demise. Although Kate would drink and carouse
with her customers, and though she mothered some of the regulars like a hen
with a brood, she was likely to answer fresh seamen with a crack on the head.

One day a Royal Navy seaman lurched into her barroom, three sheets to
the wind, and tried to embrace Kate. While Harry the Ape, one of the regulars,
used his fists on the sailor, Kate belabored him with a belaying pin. The Royal

Navy sank by the stern but was soon followed to the floor by Kate. The exertion plus the chloroform-spiked beer she had been tanking up on all day were too much for her heart. The drunken, tearful customers tenderly picked her up and placed her on a table where they splashed water in her face (probably the first time *that* liquid was used in Kate's place). These attempts to arouse her were without effect. She was dead.

The regulars decided to give Chloroform Kate a decent burial at sea, but their booze-fogged brains could not come up with any ideas as to how to get her out to the Golden Gate. God knew, they had neither the money nor the pull to secure a boat to transport the body out to sea. Suddenly Harry the Ape shouted: "I have it! We'll take her aboard the barge at Howard Street Wharf!" A chorus of approving cries and backslaps greeted this suggestion and, after having one for the road, the men bundled the corpse into a tarp and staggered their way under the burden to Howard Street. Sam, as chief mourner, followed Harry and the other pallbearers, carrying an old litho of the clipper *Glory of the Seas* that graced the wall of Kate's bar. They scooped out a shallow grave in the mass of refuse in the scow, and Red Sam gallantly placed the picture with the body. They then sprinkled some brown and wilted gladioli over the tarpaulin and covered her up. When San Francisco's heavily laden garbage scow was towed out the Golden Gate next day, Chloroform Kate made her last voyage and was consigned to the deep.

Cassie Chadwick, "Carnegie's Daughter"

Cassie Chadwick really pulled it off. She played on the snobbery, vanity, greed, and gullibility of every socialite and banker in Cleveland, Ohio, in the mid–1890s. She hit town claiming to be Andrew Carnegie's illegitimate daughter. She deposited promissory notes of more than $5 million signed by Carnegie (they were forgeries) and set herself up with the local bank, which was all too glad to deposit her money. Society follows cash and she was soon seen swanning at all the best functions. On everyone's "A" list, Chadwick, a Canadian grifter, enjoyed herself immensely. She borrowed money, paid it back with borrowed money, and borrowed more. Soon she had millions moving in all directions. She knew that Cleveland society could not, would not, risk the indelicacy of checking with Carnegie himself on the matter and, after all, wasn't she a good citizen? She gave money to all the charities. When it all came apart—some at last began to wonder if they would ever be paid back—the wealthy fools turned out to be a dime a dozen. One of the bank presidents who had supported her borrowing practices was said to have died of a heart attack on getting the news that she was a swindler. They finally caught up to Chadwick and threw her in jail where she died quietly and, no doubt, with a good deal of satisfaction that the social set in Cleveland got what she thought was coming to them.

Bonnie Parker and Clyde Barrow

They were killers. Not Robin Hoods, not misunderstood kids on the run, not well-meaning souls gone wrong—they were raw, sick killers, plain and simple. The scenes that did not make the movie include Bonnie's killing of a traffic cop with a sawed-off shotgun and driving off in wild laughter, and the senseless killing of old men who simply were in the wrong place at the wrong time. Folklore is discomfited by such madness.

Clyde was a small-time thief when he met nineteen-year-old Bonnie. She was waiting tables and impatient to get a life. She had a husband but he was in jail ("Are you married?" he asked her. "Sort of," she said). They began to have fun, and soon after they moved in together, Clyde was arrested for burglary and thrown in jail. Bonnie came to visit him with a gun taped to her thigh, and he broke out and got away. Clyde was arrested yet again and this time did hard time. Pardoned after twenty months following a plea by his mother to the governor of Texas, Clyde, with Bonnie in tow, really got started. They robbed and killed and traveled the open road as self-described desperadoes. They loved the publicity that followed all their exploits.

It was Depression America, and the public's intense interest in the two killers was mixed—horror at the killing and robbery, and admiration for the exuberance of their life of crime. The pair did not disappoint; they posed for pictures with guns and smoked cigars and expressed no regrets ("Tell the public I don't smoke cigars," she said after one such photograph flashed across the nation); they took hostages, told them their story, and let them go to the press. Bonnie even sent poetry to the newspapers. But she knew, as the trail got hotter and the noose tighter (every lawman in the country seemed on the lookout), that life was speeding toward the wall ("When they kill us" she wrote her mother, "please don't let them lay me out in a funeral parlor"). A famous photograph of a picnic lunch with guns and cash spread over a blanket was followed within seconds by an ambush of police and lawmen. Bonnie and

Clyde escaped and left behind the poem quoted below. Less than a year later, the two killers were betrayed by a friend, and the Texas patrolman who had stalked them for months ambushed them on the highway and shot them to death. They got twenty-four bullets out of Clyde and twenty-three out of Bonnie. So ended the life and times of Bonnie and Clyde. So began their legend.

Following are the last stanzas of a poem penned by Bonnie herself and sent to a local newspaper. She understood that she was becoming a folk legend and played it to the hilt:

You have heard the story of Jesse James,
Of how he lived and died,
If you still are in need of something to read,
Here is the story of Bonnie and Clyde.

Now Bonnie and Clyde are the Barrow gang,
I'm sure you all have read
How they rob and steal,
And how those who squeal,
Are usually found dying or dead.

There are lots of untruths to their write-ups,
They are not so merciless as that;
They hate all the laws,
The stool-pigeons, spotters and rats.
If a policeman is killed in Dallas
And they have no clues to guide—
If they can't find a fiend,
They just wipe the slate clean,
And hang it on Bonnie and Clyde.

If they try to act like citizens,
And rent them a nice little flat,
About the third night they are invited to fight
By a submachinegun rat-tat-tat.

A newsboy once said to his buddy:
"I wish old Clyde would get jumped;

"In these awful hard times,
"We'd make a few dimes
"If five or six cops would get bumped."

They class them as cold-blooded killers,
They say they are heartless and mean,
But I say this with pride,
That once I knew Clyde
When he was honest and upright and clean.

But the law fooled around,
Kept tracking him down,
And locking him up in a cell,
Till he said to me,
"I will never be free,
"So I will meet a few of them in hell."

This road was so dimly lighted
There were no highway signs to guide,
But they made up their minds
If the roads were all blind
They wouldn't give up till they died.

The road gets dimmer and dimmer,
Sometimes you can hardly see,
Still it's fight man to man,
And do all you can,
For they know they can never be free.

They don't think they are too tough or desperate,
They know the law always wins,
They have been shot at before
But they do not ignore
That death is the wages of sin.

From heartbreaks some people have suffered,
From weariness some people have died,

But take it all in all,
Our troubles are small,
Till we get like Bonnie and Clyde.

Some day they will go down together,
And they will bury them side by side.
To a few it means grief,
To the law it's relief,
But it's death to Bonnie and Clyde.

Tallulah on Tallulah: A Different Kind of Bad Girl

I have three phobias which, could I mute them, would make my life as slick as a sonnet, but as dull as ditch water: I hate to go to bed, I hate to get up, and I hate to be alone. My inability to cope with these prejudices leads to complications, excesses and heresies frowned upon in stuffier circles, circles I avoid as I would exposure to the black pox. My caprices, born of my fears, frequently find a vent in the romantic pursuits, enthusiasms and experiments at odds with the code affirmed by Elsie Dinsmore.

Over-stimulated, more than once I have breached the peace, curdled the night with monologues, war cries and filibusters. These violations of established order might well land a less artful dodger in the clink, but in these crises my acting skill (isn't it a little early to start bragging?) stands me in good stead. Jug Tallulah, the toast of the Yangtze and the Yukon? What constable would wax so bold?

Testifying for the defense, may I add that I've only been married once, a humdrum record in a profession where husbands come and go like express trains between New York and Philadelphia. By way of compensation my sister Eugenia has been hitched seven times, three times to the same victim. The Bankhead girls strike a high average.

Let's not quibble! I'm the foe of moderation, the champion of excess. If I may lift a line from a die-hard whose identity is lost in the shuffle, "I'd rather be strongly wrong than weakly right." A congenital emotionalist, restive and wired for sound—I operate on either direct or alternating current—I frequently give the impression I'm awash when I haven't had so much as a snifter. On the edge of a crisis I shun the sauce. The climax behind me, I find drink stimulating. It's a worry-extinguisher that up to three in the morning makes for ease and confidence. At three-fifteen the issue may cloud up. I wouldn't think of tippling before an opening night. Once it is behind me and the decision beyond recall, I'm ready for such wassail as is available.

In any drinker's census you'll not find me in the two-cocktails-before-dinner file. After two cocktails I don't want any dinner, or any lunch. The so-called civilized drinkers who follow this tidy pattern are wrestling with desire and remorse at the same time. Food defeats the very thing for which you took the drink. It smothers the glow which the drink lets loose.

I like to drink best when I'm with challenging, exciting people. If I'm in the dumps liquor depresses me further. Circumstance rules my thirst. A thrilling knockout, a ninth-inning finish, a headline that stabs my spine—these can touch me off. I also find drinking pleasant, if not profitable, when I'm in love. It seems to give zest to my emotions, elevate the reading on my romantic thermometer. I'm not fascinated by the taste of liquor. A frozen daiquiri of a scorching afternoon is soothing. It makes living more tolerable. But, given any option, I'll by-pass Martinis and Scotch highballs, stiff-arm those pink or purple concoctions, equal parts of bilge water, anisette and rum, with which hostesses sabotage a party. Asked to name my poison, out of loyalty to the South and my stomach I'll settle for bourbon. If the auspices are favorable, my host under no fiscal strain, I'll go for champagne, the most inspiring of all the juices. Wracked with a hangover I do my muttering over a Black Velvet, a union of champagne and stout. Don't be swindled into believing there's any cure for a hangover. I've tried them all: iced tomatoes, hot clam juice, brandy punches. Like the common cold it defies solution. Time alone can stay it. The hair of the dog? That way lies folly. It's as logical as trying to put out a fire with applications of kerosene.

When overheated I have a tendency to monopolize attention and conversation. I'm not content with boiling. I boil over! Havoc often ensues. I provoke some of my companions into controversy. Others grab their duffel and, to quote J. Caesar, put safety in flight. Edged, my conversation may be spiced with invectives and profanities, condoned in Hemingway, but not in Homer.

Drink reacts on its practitioners in conflicting ways. One brave can knock off a quart of Scotch and look and act as sober as Herbert Hoover. Another, after three Martinis, makes two-cushion caroms off the chaise lounge as he attempts to negotiate the bathroom. One gentleman of my acquaintance bolts upstairs to plough through Proust and James Joyce, after he's latched onto his fourth rum-and-coke. With the same handicap, another sobs his heart out when someone starts to monkey with "Mother Macree" on the piano. As a rule of thumb, liquor sharpens and inflates our natural, if hidden, bent.

Of the mots coined to fit my deportment when on a rampage of good will, the most acid and accurate dropped from the lips of Dorothy Parker. Justly famed for her critiques, her poisonous impeachments of her sex, Dotty Parker is the mistress of the verbal grenade. Miss Parker, after seeing Katharine Hepburn in *The Lake,* wrote of her performance: "She runs the gamut of emotions from A to B." And it was Miss Parker, after swooning through two columns over the imagery and style of James Branch Cabell in *The Silver Stallion,* who concluded by saying: "To save my mother from the electric chair, I couldn't read three pages of it."

A party-tosser of talent, Miss Parker touched off a shindig in tribute to Edie Smith, my secretary and confessor, shortly after my escape from Hollywood in the early thirties. To her hutch in the Algonquin she invited assorted wags, cynics and idlers, among them humorists Frank Sullivan and Corey Ford, screen director George Cukor.

Elated that my friend was to be saluted I made the mistake of taking a few nips before I got to the arena. There I added to my content. I distracted the guests with backbends, cartwheels and monologues. Enough of this shillyshallying! I was noisy, tight and obstreperous!

Miss Parker and Edie were in the kitchen setting up refills, when George Cukor, gentleman and diplomat, decided that in the interests of tranquillity I should go home. Through some ruse he tricked me to the street. Shortly after our departure Miss Parker came out of the kitchen, looked about, then said sweetly: "Oh, has Whistler's mother gone?"

It's true that I once pinwheeled for a block on Piccadilly, but it was three o'clock in the morning. The street was bare and silent. I was only answering a taunt of my companion—Prince Nicholas of Roumania. You know those Roumanian princes! Not all of them are on key.

When I came up from Washington to make my mark on Broadway, I had yet to take a drink other than a sip of eggnog at Christmas. I shuttled about quite a bit in my first two years in Manhattan. I lived for a time with Bijou Martin, a young actress. She was the daughter of Ricardo Martin, the opera star. Her mother was in Europe. I was broke. I welcomed the chance to share her apartment in West Fifty-seventh Street—a five-flight walk-up with two bedrooms, living room and a bath. This shelter was an oddity in that all the doors opened into the corridor. The only way to get from one room to another was to prowl that hall.

One afternoon Biji came home with a bottle of port and suggested we sample it.

"Oh, Biji, I couldn't. I promised Daddy I wouldn't take a drink if he let me go on the stage."

"This isn't a drink," she said. "It's only wine. In Europe children drink wine as we drink water."

My resolve sagged. Eventually I'd get Daddy's permission. I must try everything once. "All right! You're my friend and you'll take care of me. I'll see how it affects me," I said.

We had no wine glasses so we used our toothbrush tumblers. Biji and I filled our mugs to the brim and tossed them off. I had no reaction. Disappointed, I said, "Let's try another." A third beaker, and the roof fell in. Both of us were so tight we couldn't walk. We had to crawl through the hall to our bedrooms on our hands and knees. I don't know which was greater, my horror or my surprise. I felt sick, and I *was* sick. The room was spinning like a top. In my agony I heard Biji moaning. I crawled back down the hall. Biji was trying to get into the bathtub. "I want to take a shower," she pleaded. I saw no flaw in this, though she was fully clothed. I put her hat on her head, she clambered into the vat, and I turned on the water. Then I crawled away to die.

We woke the next morning with devastating hangovers—me in bed, Biji on the bathroom floor. There was a note under the door from Biji's father: "I came to take you and Tallulah to dinner tonight and missed you. You must have gone out." Out indeed! . . .

W O M E N
A N D   W A R

||||||||||||||||||||||||||||||||||||||||||||||||||||||||||||||||||||||||||||||||||||||||||||||||||||||||||||||||

*T*here have always been great women warriors. In older times, powerful women like Boadicea, Eleanor of Aquitaine, Joan of Arc, rose up and led their armies to glory and sometimes grief. In the modern age, women like Golda Meir and Margaret Thatcher did not hesitate to offer the gun as an instrument of political persuasion. In America, however, many men have argued that women should be kept away from the awesome spectacle of the battlefield. Women, so the argument goes, would be a distraction, an impediment. Better for them to remain anxious bystanders, supporting players to the great drama of war enacted by and for men. This is a fool's argument. It is the same nonsense offered by those who think war is principally a matter of generals and military strategies. War is made up of thousands of tiny theaters of action on the field of fire, in the base camps, even in the solemn quiet of home. Since the Revolution of 1776, women have played a variety of parts in all these theaters, and this chapter offers a few stories that highlight the diversity and spirit of their experience.

When we think of war and women we often remember those

who defied military authority in defense of family or country—
women such as Hannah Arnett or Lydia Darrah who embodied
the determination of the warrior spirit on the home front. Readers in the eighteenth and nineteenth centuries loved nothing better than the narrative that touted a lady who would not back
down before an army or its violent intentions. Typical of such
heroines would be Barbara Frietchie, that gray-headed fictional
heroine who stared down Stonewall Jackson. The story ends with
the greater force (full of grudging admiration) backing down before the triumphant, solitary woman. Given that many women
have seen the folly of conflict and not been afraid to mock it,
standing alone is itself a powerful weapon. Consider Jeannette
Rankin, the first woman elected to Congress (at age thirty-seven)
who was not guided by politics but by the conviction that there
should always be someone who casts their vote against war.

When war is inevitable, however, there is also a tradition of
women who went off to fight alongside their husbands, like Molly
Hays or Sally St. Clair; who dressed like men and fought in the
ranks, like Sara Edmonds whose legendary service in the Union
army is well documented. Over the battlefield at Gettysburg
hangs a persistent folktale of women among the Confederate
dead in Pickett's charge. Inevitably, when you scratch beneath
the sentimentality of these stories or peel away the quirkiness,
you find in these women the same turbulent appetite for adventure and experience that drove their husbands, fathers, and boy-
friends into battle. Perhaps some women went to the Revolutionary War to be near their husbands, or others in more modern

wars to be true to a shimmering patriotic ideal, but many went because their blood lusted for adventure. They were bored, stultified in the parlor, and war offered the promise of reality. And since women have had to struggle endlessly for their own reality, why shouldn't the fantasy of war and the battlefield hold the same lure that it does for men?

Of greatest interest, however, may well be the stories of women who participated in America's wars as nurses. Whether in the Civil War or Vietnam, these women took to the battlefields still warm with blood and noisy with pain and suffering. They lived with the carnage, carried the irony and horror of war in their blood like disease. Their voices, though separated by a century and the vast changes in culture, are eerily similar. They share a peculiar invisibility—to the people at home they have become strange; to the military authorities, they barely count. Only with their comrades in war, with whom they "shared the incommunicable horror of war," were they able to find connection, understanding. They provide us with incredible insight into war's true nature.

Warrior Girl (Tewa)

Once there lived a girl of the Cottonwood clan who would not mind her mother or father or uncle. They were always telling her to be a good girl but she got angry very quickly. Finally these people got tired of telling her to be good so they just ignored her. Once when she was grinding corn many enemies began to come close to the village. Her uncle came to her and grabbed her arm and said, "Take your bow and arrows and go and fight with the enemies who are coming. You would not mind us and behaved like a boy. Now it is time for you to go and fight and be brave."

The girl laughed "Ha! Ha!" and said, "I am very anxious to go and fight the enemies. I am not afraid. I will do all I can."

Her uncle handed her a bow and arrows. Then she looked around and there was a rattle hanging on the wall. She stepped up and got it. Then she started to sing. As soon as she stopped singing, she laughed "Ha! Ha!" She sang four times in the room and then she went outside and sang four times. Every time she paused in the singing she laughed "Ha! Ha!" because she was not afraid to fight.

Then she started off toward the enemy. Some of the villagers laughed at her but she just went on, singing and laughing, happy that she was going to fight. Before she met the enemies, she pulled her dress up four times to show the enemies that she was a girl. Then she fought, and she killed all the enemies in one day. When she turned back after the fighting was done, the men saw that she had on a mask—one side was blue and one side was yellow and it had long teeth. The men were afraid of her but they followed her back to the town as she sang and laughed.

That night Pohaha's uncles came to her house and told her that they had been thinking she must be a man and had decided to put her in as war chief. Even if she was a girl, she was a man. As war chief she would have to lead her people against enemies, protect them from sickness, and treat them as her children. After that she became a good woman.

When she died she left her mask and said that it would represent her even if she was dead. "I will be with you all the time," she said; "the mask is me." That is why the Cottonwood people keep the mask.

Brave Woman Counts Coup
(White River Sioux)

To "count coup" is an act of bravery by a warrior to strike the enemy with the first blow or wound:

Over a hundred years ago, when many Sioux were still living in what now is Minnesota, there was a band of Hunkpapa Sioux at Spirit Lake under a chief called Tawa Makoce, meaning His Country. It was his country, too—Indian country, until the white soldiers with their cannon finally drove the Lakota tribes across the Mni Shoshay: The Big Muddy, the Missouri.

In his youth the chief had been one of the greatest warriors. Later, when his fighting days were over, he was known as a wise leader, invaluable in council, and as a great giver of feasts, a provider for the poor. The chief had three sons and one daughter. The sons tried to be warriors as mighty as their father, but that was a hard thing to do. Again and again they battled the Crow Indians with reckless bravery, exposing themselves in the front rank, fighting hand to hand, until one by one they all were killed. Now only his daughter was left to the sad old chief. Some say her name was Makhta. Others call her Winyan Ohitika, Brave Woman.

The girl was beautiful and proud. Many young men sent their fathers to the old chief with gifts of fine horses that were preliminary to marriage proposals. Among those who desired her for a wife was a young warrior named Red Horn, himself the son of a chief, who sent his father again and again to ask for her hand. But Brave Woman would not marry. "I will not take a husband," she said, "until I have counted coup on the Crows to avenge my dead brothers." Another young man who loved Brave Woman was Wanblee Cikala, or Little Eagle. He was too shy to declare his love, because he was a poor boy who had never been able to distinguish himself.

At this time the Kangi Oyate, the Crow nation, made a great effort to establish themselves along the banks of the upper Missouri in country which the Sioux considered their own. The Sioux decided to send out a strong war party to chase them back, and among the young men riding out were Red Horn and Little Eagle. "I shall ride with you," Brave Woman said. She put on her best dress of white buckskin richly decorated with beads and porcupine quills, and around her neck she wore a choker of dentalium shells. She went to the old chief. "Father," she said, "I must go to the place where my brothers died. I must count coup for them. Tell me that I can go."

The old chief wept with pride and sorrow. "You are my last child," he said, "and I fear for you and for a lonely old age without children to comfort me. But your mind has long been made up. I see that you must go; do it quickly. Wear my warbonnet into battle. Go and do not look back."

And so his daughter, taking her brothers' weapons and her father's warbonnet and best war pony, rode out with the warriors. They found an enemy village so huge that it seemed to contain the whole Crow nation—hundreds of men and thousands of horses. There were many more Crows than Sioux, but the Sioux attacked nevertheless. Brave Woman was a sight to stir the warriors to great deeds. To Red Horn she gave her oldest brother's lance and shield. "Count coup for my dead brother," she said. To Little Eagle she gave her second brother's bow and arrows. "Count coup for him who owned these," she told him. To another young warrior she gave her youngest brother's war club. She herself carried only her father's old, curved coupstick wrapped in otter fur.

At first Brave Woman held back from the fight. She supported the Sioux by singing brave heart songs and by making the shrill, trembling war cry with which Indian women encourage their men. But when the Sioux, including her own warriors from the Hunkpapa band, were driven back by overwhelming numbers, she rode into the midst of the battle. She did not try to kill her enemies, but counted coup left and right, touching them with her coupstick. With a woman fighting so bravely among them, what Sioux warrior could think of retreat?

Still, the press of the Crows and their horses drove the Sioux back a second time. Brave Woman's horse was hit by a musket bullet and went down. She was on foot, defenseless, when Red Horn passed her on his speckled pony. She was too proud to call out for help, and he pretended not to see her. Then Little Eagle came riding toward her out of the dust of battle. He dismounted and told her to get on his horse. She did, expecting him to climb up behind her, but he would not. "This horse is wounded and too weak to carry us both," he said.

"I won't leave you to be killed," she told him. He took her brother's bow and struck the horse sharply with it across the rump. The horse bolted, as he intended, and Little Eagle went back into battle on foot. Brave Woman herself rallied the warriors for a final charge, which they made with such fury that the Crows had to give way at last.

This was the battle in which the Crow nation was driven away from the Missouri for good. It was a great victory, but many brave young men died. Among them was Little Eagle, struck down with his face to the enemy. The Sioux warriors broke Red Horn's bow, took his eagle feathers from him, and sent him home. But they placed the body of Little Eagle on a high scaffold on the spot where the enemy camp had been. They killed his horse to serve him in the land of many lodges. "Go willingly," they told the horse. "Your master has need of you in the spirit world."

Brave Woman gashed her arms and legs with a sharp knife. She cut her hair short and tore her white buckskin dress. Thus she mourned for Little Eagle. They had not been man and wife; in fact he had hardly dared speak to her or look at her, but now she asked everybody to treat her as if she were the young warrior's widow. Brave Woman never took a husband, and she never ceased to mourn for Little Eagle. "I am his widow," she told everyone. She died of old age. She had done a great thing, and her fame endures.

> —*Told by Jenny Leading Cloud at White River,*
> *Rosebud Indian Reservation, South Dakota, 1967.*

Abigail's Call to Arms

As a previous dispute with England grew worse, Abigail Adams advised her husband that it was time for the colonies to separate from the mother country:

Braintree, 12 November 1775

The intelligence you will receive before this reaches you, will, I should think, make a plain path, though a dangerous one, for you. I could not join you today, in the petitions of our worthy pastor, for a reconciliation between our no-longer parent state, but tyrant state, and these colonies. Let us separate; they are unworthy to be our brethren. Let us renounce them; and instead of supplications as formerly, for their prosperity and happiness, let us beseech the Almighty to blast their counsels, and bring to nought all their devices.

Hannah Arnett

From the History of Woman Suffrage *comes this marvelous tale of one of America's early Revolutionary War heroines. While she did not take up arms against the British, her words rang as clear as any cannon shot ever fired in defense of the new nation. The scene is Elizabeth, New Jersey, in the dark days when the British army was still considered by all to be the most formidable (and undefeatable) armed force in the world:*

A number of men of Elizabeth assembled one evening in one of the spacious mansions for which this place was rather famous, to discuss the advisability of accepting a proposed amnesty from Cornwallis, who threatened the town with his troops. The question was a momentous one, and the discussion was earnest and protracted. Some were for accepting this proffer at once; others hesitated; they canvassed the subject from various points, but finally decided that submission was all that remained to them. Their hope was gone, and their courage with it; every remnant of patriotic spirit seemed swept away in the darkness of the hour.

But there was a listener of whom they were ignorant; a woman, Hannah Arnett, the wife of the host, sitting at her work in an adjoining room. The discussion had reached her ears, rousing her intense indignation. She listened until she could sit still no longer; springing to her feet she pushed open the parlor door, confronting the amazed men. Can you fancy the scene? A large, low room, with the dark, heavy furniture of the period, dimly lighted by the tall wax candles and the wood fire which blazed on the hearth. Around the table the group of men, pallid, gloomy, dejected, disheartened. In the door-way the figure of the woman in antique costume. Can you not see the proud poise of her head, the indignant light of her blue eyes, the crisp, clear tones of her voice, the majesty, and defiance, and scorn, which clothed her as with a garment?

The men were appalled and startled at the sight. She seemed like some avenging angel about to bring them to judgment for the words they had spoken; and, indeed, such she proved. It was strange to see a woman thus enter the secret councils of men, and her husband hastily approaching her, whispered: "Hannah, Hannah, this is no place for you, we do not want you here just now"; and he tried to take her hand to lead her from the room. But she pushed him gently back, saying to the startled group: "Have you made your decision, gentlemen? Have you chosen the part of men, or traitors?"

They stammered and blundered as they tried to find answer. Things appeared to them in a new light as this woman so pointedly questioned them. Their answers were a mixture of excuses and explanations. They declared the country to be in a hopeless condition; the army starving, half-clothed, undisciplined, the country poor, while England's trained troops were backed by the wealth of a thousand years.

Hannah Arnett listened in silence until the last abject word was spoken, when she rapidly inquired: "But what if we should live after all!" The men looked at each other, but not a word was spoken. "Hannah, Hannah," cried her husband, "do you not see these are no questions for you? We are discussing what is best for us all. Women do not understand these things; go to your spinning-wheel and leave us to discuss these topics. Do you not see that you are making yourself ridiculous?"

But Mrs. Arnett paid no heed. Speaking to the men in a strangely quiet voice, she said: "Can you not tell me? If, after all, God does not let the right perish; if America should win in the conflict, after you have thrown yourselves upon British clemency, where will you be then?" "Then?" spoke a hesitating voice, "why then, if it ever could be so, we should be ruined. We must then leave home and country forever. But the struggle is an entirely hopeless one. We have no men, no money, no arms, no food, and England has everything."

"No," said Hannah Arnett, "you have forgotten one thing which England has not, and which we have—one thing which outweighs all England's treasures—and that is the right. God is on our side; and every volley from our muskets is an echo of His voice. We are poor and weak and few, but God is fighting for us. We counted the cost before we began; we knew the price and were willing to pay; and now, because for the time the day is going against us, you would give up all and sneak back like cravens, to kiss the feet that have trampled upon us! And you call yourselves men; the sons of those who gave up homes and fortune and fatherland to make for themselves and for dear liberty a resting-place in the wilderness! Oh, shame upon you, cowards!"

The words had rushed out in a fiery flood which her husband had vainly striven to check. Turning to the gentlemen present, Mr. Arnett said: "I beg you will excuse this most unseemly interruption to our council. My wife is beside herself, I think. You all know her, and that it is not her custom to meddle with politics. To-morrow she will see her folly; but now I beg your patience."

But her words had roused the slumbering manhood of her hearers. Each began to look upon himself as a craven, and to withdraw from the position he had taken. No one replied to her husband, and Hannah Arnett continued. "Take your protection if you will. Proclaim yourselves traitors and cowards, false to your country and your God, but horrible will be the judgment upon your heads and the heads of those that love you. I tell you that England will never conquer. I know it and feel it in every fiber of my heart. Has God led us thus far to desert us now? Will He who led our fathers across the stormy winter seas forsake their children who have put their trust in Him? For me, I stay with my country, and my hand shall never touch the hand, nor my heart cleave to the heart of him who shames her"; and she turned a glance upon her husband. "Isaac, we have lived together for twenty years, and for all of them I have been a true and loving wife to you. But I am the child of God and of my Country, and if you do this shameful thing, I will never again own you for my husband."

"My dear wife!" he cried, aghast, "you do not know what you are saying. Leave me for such a thing as this?" "For such a thing as this!" she cried, scornfully. "What greater cause could there be? I married a good man and true, a faithful friend, and it needs no divorce to sever me from a traitor and a coward. If you take your amnesty you lose your wife, and I—I lose my husband and my home!" After such a speech, is it any surprise that the men that night swore a solemn oath to stand by the cause they had adopted, and the land of their birth through good or evil, and to spurn as deadliest insult the proffered amnesty of their tyrannical foe?

Lydia Darrah Will Not Tell a Lie

While the American army remained encamped at White Marsh, the British being in possession of Philadelphia, Gen. Howe [the British commander] made some vain attempts to draw Washington into an engagement. The house opposite the headquarters of Gen. Howe, tenanted by William and Lydia Darrah, members of the Society of Friends, was the place selected by the superior officers of the army for private conference, whenever it was necessary to hold consultations.

On the afternoon of the 2d of December, the British Adjutant-General called and informed the mistress that he and some friends were to meet there that evening, and desired that the back room up-stairs might be prepared for their reception. "And be sure, Lydia," he concluded, "that your family are all in bed at an early hour. When our guests are ready to leave the house, I will myself give you notice, that you may let us out and extinguish the candles."

Having delivered this order, the Adjutant-General departed. Lydia betook herself to getting all things in readiness. But she felt curious to know what the business could be that required such secrecy, and resolved on further investigation. Accordingly, in the midst of their conference that night, she quietly approached the door, and listening, heard a plan for the surprise of Washington's forces arranged for the next night. She retreated softly to her room and laid down; soon there was a knocking at her door. She knew well what the signal meant, but took no heed until it was repeated again and again, and then she arose quickly and opened the door. It was the Adjutant-General who came to inform her they were ready to depart. Lydia let them out, fastened the door, extinguished the fire and lights, and returned to her chamber, but she was uneasy, thinking of the threatened danger.

At the dawn of day she arose, telling her family that she must go to Frankfort to procure some flour. She mounted her horse, and taking the bag, started. The snow was deep and the cold intense, but Lydia's heart did not falter. Leaving the grist at the mill, she started on foot for the camp, determined to apprise Gen. Washington of his danger. On the way she met one of his officers, who exclaimed in astonishment at seeing her, but making her errand known, she hastened home.

Preparations were immediately made to give the enemy a fitting reception. None suspected the grave, demure Quakeress of having snatched from the English their anticipated victory; but after the return of the British troops Gen. Howe summoned Lydia to his apartment, locked the door with an air of mystery, and motioned her to a seat. After a moment of silence, he said: "Were any of your family up, Lydia, on the night when I received my company here?" "No," she replied, "they all retired at eight o'clock." "It is very strange," said the officer, and mused a few minutes. "I know you were asleep, for I knocked at your door three times before you heard me; yet it is certain that we were betrayed."

Afterward some one asked Lydia how she could say her family were all in bed while she herself was up; she replied, "Husband and wife are one, and that one is the husband, and my husband was in bed." Thus the wit and wisdom of this Quaker woman saved the American forces at an important crisis, and perhaps turned the fate of the Revolutionary War.

Mrs. Slocum Saves the Man of Her Dreams

"The men all left on Sunday morning. More than eighty went from this house with my husband; I looked at them well, and I could see that every man had mischief in him. I know a coward as soon as I set my eyes upon him. The tories more than once tried to frighten me, but they always showed coward at the bare insinuation that our troops were about.

"Well, they got off in high spirits; every man stepping high and light. And I slept soundly and quietly that night, and worked hard all the next day; but I kept thinking where they had got to—how far; where and how many of the regulars and tories they would meet; and I could not keep myself from the study. I went to bed at the usual time, but still continued to study. As I lay— whether waking or sleeping I know not—I had a dream; yet it was not all a dream. . . . I saw distinctly a body wrapped in my husband's guard-cloak— bloody—dead; and others dead and wounded on the ground about him. I saw them plainly and distinctly. I uttered a cry, and sprang to my feet on the floor; and so strong was the impression on my mind, that I rushed in the direction the vision appeared, and came up against the side of the house. The fire in the room gave little light, and I gazed in every direction to catch another glimpse of the scene. I raised the light; every thing was still and quiet. My child was sleeping, but my woman was awakened by my crying out or jumping on the floor. If ever I felt fear it was at that moment. Seated on the bed, I reflected a few moments—and said aloud: 'I must go to him.' I told the woman I could not sleep and would ride down the road. She appeared in great alarm; but I merely told her to lock the door after me, and look after the child. I went to the stable, saddled my mare—as fleet and easy a nag as ever travelled; and in one minute we were tearing down the road at full speed. The cool night seemed after a mile or two's gallop to bring reflection with it; and I asked myself where I was going, and for what purpose. Again and again I was tempted to turn back; but I was soon ten miles from home, and my mind became stronger every mile I rode. I should find my husband dead or dying—was as firmly my presentiment and conviction as any fact of my life. When day broke I was some thirty miles from home. I knew the general route our little army expected to take, and had followed them without hesitation. About sunrise I came upon a group of women and children, standing and sitting by the road-side, each one of them showing the same anxiety of mind I felt. Stopping a few minutes I inquired if the battle had been fought. They knew nothing, but were assembled on the road to catch intelligence. They thought Caswell had taken the right of the Wilmington road, and gone towards the north-west (Cape Fear). Again was I skimming over the ground through a country thinly settled, and very poor and swampy; but neither my own spirits nor my beautiful nag's failed in the least. We followed the well-marked trail of the troops.

"The sun must have been well up, say eight or nine o'clock, when I heard a sound like thunder, which I knew must be cannon. It was the first time I ever heard a cannon. I stopped still, when presently the cannon thundered again. The battle was then fighting. What a fool! My husband could not be dead last night, and the battle only fighting now! Still, as I am so near, I will go on and see how they come out. So away we went again, faster than ever; and I soon found by the noise of guns that I was near the fight. Again I stopped. I could hear muskets, I could hear rifles, and I could hear shouting. I spoke to my mare and dashed on in the direction of the firing and the shouts, now louder than ever. The blind path I had been following brought me into the Wilmington road leading to Moore's Creek Bridge, a few hundred yards below the bridge. A few yards from the road, under a cluster of trees were lying perhaps twenty men. They were the wounded. I knew the spot; the very trees; and the position of the men I knew as if I had seen it a thousand times. I had seen it all night! I saw all at once; but in an instant my whole soul was centred in one spot; for there, wrapped in his bloody guard-cloak, was my husband's body! How I passed the few yards from my saddle to the place I never knew. I remember uncovering his head and seeing a face clothed with gore from a dreadful wound across the temple. I put my hand on the bloody face; 'twas warm; and an *unknown voice* begged for water. A small camp-kettle was lying near, and a stream of water was close by. I brought it; poured some in his mouth; washed his face; and behold—it was Frank Cogdell. He soon revived and could speak. I was washing the wound in his head. Said he, 'It is not that; it is that hole in my leg that is killing me.' A puddle of blood was standing on the ground about his feet. I took his knife, cut away his trousers and stocking, and found the blood came from a shot-hole through and through the fleshy part of his leg. I looked about and could see nothing that looked as if it would do for dressing wounds but some heart-leaves. I gathered a handful and bound them tight to the holes; and the bleeding stopped. I then went to the others; and—Doctor! I dressed the wounds of many a brave fellow who did good fighting long after that day! I had not inquired for my husband; but while I was busy Caswell came up. He appeared very much surprised to see me; and was with his hat in hand about to pay some compliment: but I interrupted him by asking—'Where is my husband?'

" 'Where he ought to be, madam, in pursuit of the enemy. But pray,' said he, 'how came you here?'

" 'Oh, I thought,' replied I, 'you would need nurses as well as soldiers. See! I have already dressed many of these good fellows; and here is one'—going to Frank and lifting him up with my arm under his head so that he could drink some more water—'would have died before any of you men could have helped him.'

" 'I believe you,' said Frank. Just then I looked up, and my husband, as bloody as a butcher, and as muddy as a ditcher, stood before me.

" 'Why, Mary!' he exclaimed, 'What are you doing there? Hugging Frank Cogdell, the greatest reprobate in the army?'

" 'I don't care,' I cried. 'Frank is a brave fellow, a good soldier, and a true friend to Congress.'

" 'True, true! every word of it!' said Caswell. 'You are right, madam!' with the lowest possible bow.

"I would not tell my husband what brought me there. I was so happy; and so were all! It was a glorious victory; I came just at the height of the enjoyment. I knew my husband was surprised, but I could see he was not displeased with me. It was night again before our excitement had at all subsided. Many prisoners were brought in, and among them some very obnoxious; but the worst of the tories were not taken prisoners. They were, for the most part, left in the woods and swamps wherever they were overtaken. I begged for some of the poor prisoners, and Caswell readily told me none should be hurt but such as had been guilty of murder and house-burning. In the middle of the night I again mounted my mare and started for home. Caswell and my husband wanted me to stay till next morning and they would send a party with me; but no! I wanted to see my child; and I told them they could send no party who could keep up with me. What a happy ride I had back! and with what joy did I embrace my child as he ran to meet me!"

Sara Emma Edmonds: Civil War Soldier

Perhaps the most famous of the hundreds of women who disguised themselves to fight in the Union army, Edmonds took the name Frank and fought well enough to be remembered and admired by the veterans who fought alongside her. None knew her secret but many stepped forward to support her claim after the war that she was entitled to a veteran's pension. Her memoir of the war is a testament to her daring and her formidable skill at weaving a story. The following gives us a taste of both:

I will here relate a little incident illustrative of the peculiarity of my adventures while on this catering business: One morning I started, all alone, for a five-mile ride to an isolated farm-house about three miles back from the Hampton road, and which report said was well supplied with all the articles of which I was in search. I cantered along briskly until I came to a gate which opened into a lane directly to the house. It was a large old-fashioned two-story house, with immense chimneys built outside, Virginia style. The farm appeared to be in good condition, fences all up, a rare thing on the Peninsula, and corn-fields flourishing as if there were no such thing as war in the land.

I rode up to the house and dismounted, hitched my horse to a post at the door, and proceeded to ring the bell. A tall, stately lady made her appearance, and invited me in with much apparent courtesy. She was dressed in deep mourning, which was very becoming to her pale, sad face. She seemed to be about thirty years of age, very prepossessing in appearance, and evidently belonged to one of the "F.F.V's." As soon as I was seated she inquired: "To what fortunate circumstance am I to attribute the pleasure of this unexpected call?" I told her in a few words the nature of my business. The intelligence seemed to cast a deep shadow over her pale features, which all her efforts could not control. She seemed nervous and excited, and something in her appearance aroused my suspicion, notwithstanding her blandness of manner and lady-like deportment.

She invited me into another room, while she prepared the articles which she proposed to let me have, but I declined, giving as an excuse that I preferred to sit where I could see whether my horse remained quiet. I watched all her movements narrowly, not daring to turn my eyes aside for a single moment. She walked round in her stately way for some time, without accomplishing much in the way of facilitating my departure, and she was evidently trying to detain me for some purpose or other. Could it be that she was meditating the best mode of attack, or was she expecting some one to come, and trying to detain me until their arrival? Thoughts like these passed through my mind in quick succession.

At last I rose up abruptly, and asked her if the things were ready. She answered me with an assumed smile of surprise, and said: "Oh, I did not know that you were in a hurry: I was waiting for the boys to come and catch some chickens for you." "And pray, madam, where are the boys?" I asked; "Oh, not far from here," was her reply. "Well, I have decided not to wait; you will please not detain me longer," said I, as I moved toward the door. She began to pack some butter and eggs both together in a small basket which I had brought with me, while another stood beside her without anything in it. I looked at her; she was trembling violently, and was as pale as death. In a moment more she handed me the basket, and I held out a greenback for her acceptance; "Oh, it was no consequence about the pay"; she did not wish anything for it. So I thanked her and went out.

In a few moments she came to the door, but did not offer to assist me, or to hold the basket, or anything, but stood looking at me most maliciously, I thought. I placed the basket on the top of the post to which my horse had been hitched, took my seat in the saddle, and then rode up and took my basket. Turning to her I bade her good morning, and thanking her again for her kindness, I turned to ride away.

I had scarcely gone a rod when she discharged a pistol at me; by some intuitive movement I threw myself forward on my horse's neck and the ball passed over my head. I turned my horse in a twinkling, and grasped my revolver. She was in the act of firing the second time, but was so excited that the bullet went wide of its mark. I held my seven-shooter in my hand, considering where to aim. I did not wish to kill the wretch, but did intend to wound her. When she saw that two could play at this game, she dropped her pistol and threw up her hands imploringly. I took deliberate aim at one of her hands, and sent the ball through the palm of her left hand. She fell to the ground in an instant with a loud shriek. I dismounted, and took the pistol which lay beside her, and placing it in my belt, proceeded to take care of her ladyship after the following manner: I unfastened the end of my halter-strap and tied it painfully tight around her right wrist, and remounting my horse, I started, and brought the lady to consciousness by dragging her by the wrist two or three rods along the ground. I stopped, and she rose to her feet, and with wild entreaties she begged me to release her, but, instead of doing so, I presented a pistol, and told her that if she uttered another word or scream she was a dead woman. In that way I succeeded in keeping her from alarming any one who might be within calling distance, and so made my way toward McClellan's headquarters.

After we had gone in that way about a mile and a half, I told her that she might ride if she wished to do so, for I saw she was becoming weak from loss of blood. She was glad to accept the offer, and I bound up her hand with my handkerchief, gave her my scarf to throw over her head, and assisted her to the saddle. I marched along beside her, holding tight to the bridle rein all the while. When we were about a mile from McClellan's headquarters she fainted, and I caught her as she was falling from the horse. I laid her by the roadside while I went for some water, which I brought in my hat, and after bathing her face for some time she recovered.

For the first time since we started I entered into conversation with her, and found that within the last three weeks she had lost her father, husband, and two brothers in the rebel army. They had all belonged to a company of sharp-shooters, and were the first to fall. She had been almost insane since the intelligence reached her. She said I was the first Yankee that she had seen since the death of her relatives, the evil one seemed to urge her on to the step she had taken, and if I would not deliver her up to the military powers, she would go with me and take care of the wounded. She even proposed to take the oath of allegiance, and seemed deeply penitent. "If thy brother (or sister) sin against thee, and repent, forgive him," are the words of the Saviour. I tried to follow their sacred teachings there and then, and told her that I forgave her fully if she were only truly penitent. Her answer was sobs and tears.

Soon after this conversation we started for camp, she weak and humbled, and I strong and rejoicing. None ever knew from that day to this the secret of that secessionist woman becoming a nurse. Instead of being taken to General McClellan's headquarters, she went direct to the hospital, where Dr. P. dressed her hand, which was causing her extreme pain. The good old surgeon never could solve the mystery connected with her hand, for we both refused to answer any questions relating to the wound, except that she was shot by a "Yankee," which placed the surgeon under obligations to take care of the patient until she recovered—that is to say, as long as it was convenient for him to do so.

The next day she returned to her house in an ambulance, accompanied by a hospital steward, and brought away everything which could be made use of in the hospitals, and so took up her abode with us. Her name was Alice M., but we called her Nellie J. She soon proved the genuineness of her conversion to the Federal faith by her zeal for the cause which she had so recently espoused. As soon as she was well enough to act in the capacity of nurse she commenced in good earnest, and became one of the most faithful and efficient nurses in the army of the Potomac. But that was the first and only instance of a female rebel changing her sentiments, or abating one iota in her cruelty or hatred toward the "Yankees"; and also the only real lady in personal appearance, education, and refinement that I ever met among the females of the Peninsula.

A Nurse's Memory of Lincoln

I was placed in charge of the Confederate wards, and there saw that grandest of men, President Lincoln. . . . Men horribly wounded and sick, from both armies, were rushed into our camp hospital at City Point. I was given especial care of the private Confederates, and my companion . . . took charge of the Confederate officer. I had an orderly to assist me—a boy of sixteen—and what with the cleaning and caring for each sick, torn body, our powers were strained to the utmost limit of endurance. Our patients' cots were so close together that we could just squeeze between, and our ward so long that it required from three to four tents.

One day the orderly rushed in and cried out, "President Lincoln's coming!" I was at the extreme end of the hospital tent, but, girllike, started forward that I might see him. At that instant, oh, such a puny, helpless wail, as of sick and dying infants, issued from every throat: "Oh, don't leave us, Miss! He is a beast! He will kill us!"

I replied: "Oh, no! He is a grand good man!" Again and again came forth that puny wail, "Don't leave us, Miss!" till I finally said, "Well, I'll not leave you, don't fear!" but by that time I had got to the front of the tent and the orderly had pulled back a flap on my request so that I peered out. Within about fifteen or twenty feet were General Grant, with the inevitable cigar, and President Lincoln, so tall, so lank, giving evidence of much sorrow, looming over him. I heard General Grant say distinctly, "These are the Confederate quarters." President Lincoln immediately said, "I wish to go in here alone!"

I drew myself up into the corner as close as possible, and he bent under the open flap and came in. He went at once to a bedside, and reverently leaned over almost double, so low were the cots, and stroked the soldier's head, and with tears streaming down his face he said in a sort of sweet anguish, "Oh, my man, why did you do it?" The boy in gray said, or rather stammered weakly, almost in a whisper, "I went because my State went." On that ground floor, so quiet was the whole ward, a pin could almost have been heard to fall. President Lincoln went from one bedside to another and touched each forehead gently, and with tears streaming asked again the question, and again heard the same reply. When he finally passed out from those boys, some gray and grizzled, but many of them children, there came as from one voice, "Oh, we didn't know he was such a good man! We thought he was a beast!"

"I'm in need of a strong calico dress. . . ."

In the years after the war, Harriet Foote Hawley was mostly referred to as the wife of a Civil War general who became a U.S. senator and governor of Connecticut. During the war, however, this physically frail woman was a dynamic nurse—tireless, outspoken, and extraordinarily effective. Her opinions were fashioned by reality; her experience of war was brutal and direct. The letter below memorably mixes the politics of the age with the hard, practical needs of a woman on the front:

I have not had one minute I could call my own except a very little time when I went and laid down and washed and rested. I find that I must have that rest during the day or be sick. First I worked straight through, from six in the morning till ten at night, but, of course, I couldn't do that long. But you've no idea of the terrible need of it—I thought I knew something about it before but I didn't know anything. I know no words to describe the amount and intensity of this suffering I see around me every moment. . . . I stopped to look at the peaceful face of a poor fellow who had just died eight feet from my chair. One leg had been amputated above the knee ten days ago, and he had suffered terribly and was much wasted. Thank God at least this poor body can suffer no more. . . .

Wednesday morning I came back only to find that another of my poor boys had died just at daylight. I felt hope for him, though I knew he was very low. . . .

Oh, if this baptism of blood does not purify this country and cleanse it of greed and selfish ambitions as well as of slavery, then the nation will deserve to become extinct—for pity's sake, help on this association of the ladies against dress. The pledge to buy no more imported articles is none too strong. The movement ought to have been commenced three years ago. People give and give generously to the soldiers but I do not know of one single family to retrench their expenses since this war broke out. I do not know ten women who have really denied themselves of any comfort for the sake of giving to the soldiers. I don't say it is because they are so selfish—but they don't realize what this war is. I was shocked and pained at the insensibility I saw everywhere when I came from the South in April. I am even more grieved now that I have seen so much more of the unutterable misery that is slowly swelling up to flood all the country by and by. Don't think that I don't appreciate what is done. But I am not so grateful for what is given. Not a day passes that I am not filled with wonder and delight to see how generous people are, but they can't give enough or fear enough, just as it's impossible to keep a hospital supply.

I find I'm in need of a strong calico dress. . . . Now, would you be good enough to buy me a dark calico . . . for I don't want to frighten my boys with any pale thin face, and couldn't some dressmaker there make it up by guess, and so send it on by express? I don't want to be pinched and I don't care what sort of a waist is made. . . . I can't possibly leave my ward to hunt up anything and all the ladies advise me to send East as there's nothing to be bought here and no decent dressmaker. Kate is too sick to send it (she doesn't gain very fast) and mother and Mary have all they can do to live. So here I am, sorry to bother you with all your cares, yet scribbling to do it rather than go ragged and dirty. . . .

Mother Bickerdyke Speaks Out

She was the only woman General Sherman would let come into his camp and, likely as not, it was because he wasn't certain he could stop her anyway. Born in 1817, Bickerdyke was one of the most effective nurses in the Civil War. She served four years and nursed the wounded and the dying through almost twenty battles. Sometimes, in the beginning of the war, before the Sanitary Commission fully organized and staffed the army hospitals, Bickerdyke would work alone. Incredible as it seems to us today, her battlefield duties as a doctor, surgeon, nurse were supplemented by digging graves, washing laundry and even cooking. The soldiers called her "mother" and they loved her. Blunt, strong, she was an organizer, a skillful and courageous woman of action. After the war she lived in near poverty, only receiving a pension from the government more than twenty years after Appomattox. The sum? Twenty-five dollars a month, small change for the sacrifices she had made so relentlessly. On one occasion, following a breakdown of her health (the only one of its kind during the war), Bickerdyke was forced to go North to recuperate. To her dismay, local groups tried to honor her. She refused the attention. In Milwaukee, at a fair for the relief of sick and wounded soldiers, the Milwaukee Chamber of Commerce made an appropriation of twelve hundred dollars a month for hospital relief and asked Bickerdyke to accept the contribution and say a few words. This was her reply:

I am much obliged to you gentlemen for the kind things you have said. I haven't done much, no more than I ought; neither have you. I am glad you are going to give twelve hundred dollars a month for the poor fellows in the hospitals; for it's no more than you ought to do, and it isn't half as much as the soldiers in the hospitals have given for you. Suppose, gentlemen, you had got to give to-night one thousand dollars or your right leg, would it take long to decide which to surrender? Two thousand dollars or your right arm; five thousand dollars or both your eyes; all that you are worth or your life?

But I have got eighteen hundred boys in my hospital . . . who have given one arm, and one leg, and some have given both, and yet they don't seem to think they have done a great deal for their country. And the graveyard behind the hospital, and the battlefield a little farther off, contain the bodies of thousands who have freely given their lives to save you and your homes and your country from ruin. Oh, gentlemen of Milwaukee, don't let us be telling of what we have given, and what we have done! We have done nothing, and given nothing, in comparison with them! And it's our duty to keep on giving and doing just as long as there's soldier down South fighting or suffering for us.

Clara Barton: Snapshots of the Battlefield Angel

Already forty when the Civil War broke out, Clara Barton served with distinction as a nurse and distributor of critical supplies for the wounded. She would live another fifty years after Appomattox, founding the Red Cross and serving as a tireless humanitarian to victims the world over. She directed relief efforts during Florida's yellow fever epidemic in 1887, Johnstown's flood in 1889, the Russian famine in 1891, the

Spanish-American War in 1898, the Armenian genocide in 1896, even the Boer War in 1899. It was, however, her relentless work on the battlefields of the Civil War that earned her her lasting fame:

Clara Barton's Credo

*M*y business is stanching blood and feeding faint men; my post the open field between the bullet and the hospital. I sometimes discuss the application of a compress or a wisp of hay under a broken limb, but not the bearing and merits of a political movement. I make gruel—not speeches; I write *letters home* for wounded soldiers, not political addresses. . . .

The ''Angel''

*W*e may catch a glimpse of her at Chantilly—in the darkness of the rainy midnight bending over a dying boy who took her supporting arm and soothing voice for his sister's—or falling into a brief sleep on the wet ground in her tent, almost under the feet of flying cavalry; or riding in one of her train of army-wagons towards another field, subduing by the way a band of mutinous team-sters into her firm friends and allies; or at the terrible battle of Antietam (where the regular army-supplies did not arrive till three days afterward) furnishing from her wagons cordials [stimulating medicines] and bandages for the wounded, making gruel for the fainting men from the meal in which her medi-cines had been packed, extracting with her own hand a bullet from the cheek of a wounded soldier, tending the fallen all day, with her throat parched and her face blackened by sulphurous smoke, and at night, when the surgeons were dismayed at finding themselves left with only one half-burnt candle amid thou-sands of bleeding, dying men, illumining the field with candles and lanterns her forethought had supplied. No wonder they called her the "Angel of the Battlefield."

We may see her at Fredericksburg, attending to the wounded who were brought to her, whether they wore the blue or the gray. One rebel officer, whose death-agonies she soothed, besought her with his last breath not to cross the river, in his gratitude betraying to her that the movements of the rebels were only a ruse to draw the Union troops on to destruction. It is needless to say that she followed the soldiers across the Rappahannock, un-daunted by the dying man's warning. And we may watch her after the defeat, when the half-starved, half-frozen soldiers were brought to her, having great fires built to lay them around, administering cordials, and causing an old chimney to be pulled down for bricks to warm them with, while she herself had but the shelter of a tattered tent between her and the piercing winds. . . .

A C l o s e C a l l

Clara came closest to losing her life at Antietam as she stooped to give a wounded man a drink. She raised him with her right arm and was holding the cup to his lips with her left hand when she felt a sudden twitch of the sleeve of her dress. In her own words: "The poor fellow sprang from my hands and fell back quivering in the agonies of death. A bullet had passed between my body and the right arm which supported him, cutting through the sleeve and passing through his chest from shoulder to shoulder."

There was no more to be done for him, so Clara left him to his rest. She never mended the hole in her sleeve. "I wonder if a soldier ever does mend a bullet hole in his coat," she speculated. There were to be others in her clothing before her war work was over.

''H e w a s b r o u g h t t o m e — d e a d.''

In twenty minutes we were rocking across the swaying bridge, the water hissing with shot on either side. . . .

An officer stepped to my side to assist me over the debris at the end of the bridge. While our hands were raised in the act of stepping down, a piece of an exploding shell hissed through between us, just below our arms, carrying away a portion of both the skirts of his coat and my dress, rolling along the ground a few rods from us like a harmless pebble into the water.

The next instant a solid shot thundered over our heads, a noble steed bounded in the air, and with his gallant rider, rolled in the dirt, not thirty feet in the rear! Leaving the kind-hearted officer, I passed on alone to the hospital. In less than a half-hour he was brought to me—dead.

"Some of the bravest women I have ever known . . ."

Georgeanna Woolsey was a great nurse—eloquent, direct and sensitive. Her letters home amounted to one of the most vivid records we have of life for a Civil War nurse:

No one knows, who did not watch the thing from the beginning, how much opposition, how much ill-will, how much unfeeling want of thought, these women nurses endured. Hardly a surgeon of whom I can think received or treated them with even common courtesy. Government had decided that women should be employed, and the army surgeons—unable, therefore, to close the hospitals against them—determined to make their lives so unbearable that they should be forced in self-defense to leave. It seemed a matter of cool calculation, just how much ill-mannered opposition would be requisite to break up the system.

Some of the bravest women I have ever known were among this first company of army nurses. They saw at once the position of affairs, the attitude assumed by the surgeons, and the wall against which they were expected to break and scatter; and they set themselves to undermine the whole thing.

None of them were "strong-minded." Some of them were women of the truest refinement and culture; and day after day they quietly and patiently worked, doing, by order of the surgeon, things which not one of those gentlemen would have dared to ask of a woman whose male relative stood able and ready to defend her and report him. I have seen small white hands scrubbing floors, washing windows, and performing all menial offices. I have known women, delicately cared for at home, half fed in hospitals, hard worked day and night, and given, when sleep must be had, a wretched closet just large enough for a camp bed to stand in. I have known surgeons who purposely and ingeniously arranged these inconveniences with the avowed intention of driving away all women from their hospitals.

These annoyances could not have been endured by the nurses but for the knowledge that they were pioneers, who were, if possible, to gain standing ground for others—who must create the position they wished to occupy. This, and the infinite satisfaction of seeing from day to day sick and dying men comforted in their weary and dark hours, comforted as they never would have been but for these brave women, was enough to carry them through all and even more than they endured.

At last, the wall against which they were to break began to totter; the surgeons were most unwilling to see it fall, but the knowledge that the faithful, gentle care of the women nurses had saved the lives of many of their patients, and that a small rate of mortality, or remarkable recoveries in their hospitals, reflected credit immediately upon *themselves,* decided them to give way, here and there, and to make only a show of resistance. They could not do without the women nurses; they knew it, and the women knew it, and so there came to be a tacit understanding about it.

Belle Boyd Saves the Day

She was a celebrated and successful Confederate spy in the Civil War. Her autobiography gives us a glimpse of her boundless enthusiasm and flair for self-dramatization, and though many disputed the events in her book, much of her narrative has held up to the scrutiny of historians. The following excerpt takes place in May, 1862, near Front Royal, Virginia. Boyd has just been warned by her servant that the Union army was getting ready to flee the oncoming Confederate army:

I immediately sprang from my seat and went to the door, and I then found that the servant's report was true. The streets were thronged with Yankee soldiers, hurrying about in every direction in the greatest confusion.

I asked a Federal officer, who just then happened to be passing by, what was the matter. He answered that the Confederates were approaching the town in force, under Generals Jackson and Ewell, that they had surprised and captured the outside pickets, and had actually advanced within a mile of the town without the attack being even suspected.

"Now," he added, "we are endeavoring to get the ordnance and the quartermaster's stores out of their reach."

"But what will you do," I asked, "with the stores in the large dépôt?"

"Burn them, of course!"

"But suppose the rebels come upon you too quickly?"

"Then we will fight as long as we can by any possibility show a front, and in the event of defeat make good our retreat upon Winchester, burning the bridges as soon as we cross them, and finally effect a junction with General Banks's force."

I parted with the Federal officer, and returning to the house, I began to walk quietly up-stairs, when suddenly I heard the report of a rifle, and almost at the same moment I encountered Mr. Clark, who, in his rapid descent from his room, very nearly knocked me down.

"Great heavens! what is the matter?" he ejaculated, as soon as he had regained his breath, which the concussion and fright had deprived him of.

"Nothing to speak of," said I; "only the rebels are coming, and you had best prepare yourself for a visit to Libby Prison."

He answered not a word, but rushed back to his room and commenced compressing into as small a compass as possible all the manuscripts upon which he so much plumed himself, and upon which he relied for fame and credit with the illustrious journal to which he was contributor. It was his intention to collect and secure these inestimable treasures, and then to skedaddle.

I immediately went for my opera-glasses, and, on my way to the balcony in front of the house, from which position I intended to reconnoitre, I was obliged to pass Mr. Clark's door. It was open, but the key was on the outside. The temptation of making a Yankee prisoner was too strong to be resisted, and, yielding to the impulse, I quietly locked in the "Special Correspondent" of the *New York Herald.*

After this feat I hurried to the balcony, and, by the aid of my glasses, descried the advance-guard of the Confederates at the distance of about three-quarters of a mile, marching rapidly upon the town.

To add to my anxiety, my father, who was at that time upon General Garnett's staff, was with them. My heart beat alternately with hope and fear. I was not ignorant of the trap the Yankees had set for my friends. I was in possession of much important information, which, if I could only contrive to convey to General Jackson, I knew our victory would be secure. Without it I had every reason to anticipate defeat and disaster.

The intelligence I was in possession of instructed me that General Banks was at Strasbourg with four thousand men, that the small force at Winchester could be readily re-inforced by General White, who was at Harper's Ferry, and that Generals Shields and Geary were a short distance below Front Royal, while Fremont was beyond the Valley; further, and this was the vital point, that it had been decided all these separate divisions should co-operate against General Jackson.

I again went down to the door, and this time I observed, standing about in groups, several men who had always professed attachment to the cause of the South. I demanded if there was one among them who would venture to carry to General Jackson the information I possessed. They all with one accord said, "No, no. You go."

I did not stop to reflect. My heart, though beating fast, was not appalled. I put on a white sun-bonnet, and started at a run down the street, which was thronged with Federal officers and men. I soon cleared the town and gained the open fields, which I traversed with unabated speed, hoping to escape observation until such time as I could make good my way to the Confederate line, which was still rapidly advancing.

I had on a dark-blue dress, with a little fancy white apron over it; and this contrast of colors, being visible at a great distance, made me far more conspicuous than was just then agreeable. The skirmishing between the outposts was sharp. The main forces of the opposing armies were disposed as follows:

The Federals had placed their artillery on a lofty eminence, which commanded the road by which the Confederates were advancing. Their infantry occupied in force the hospital buildings, which were of great size, and sheltered, by which they kept up an incessant fire.

The Confederates were in line, directly in front of the hospital, into which their artillerymen were throwing shells with deadly precision; for the Yankees had taken this as a shelter, and were firing upon the Confederate troops from the windows.

At this moment, the Federal pickets, who were rapidly falling back, perceived me still running as fast as I was able, and immediately fired upon me.

My escape was most providential; for, although I was not hit, the rifle-balls flew thick and fast about me, and more than one struck the ground so near my feet as to throw the dust in my eyes. Nor was this all: The Federals in the hospital, seeing in what direction the shots of their pickets were aimed, followed the example and also opened fire upon me.

Upon this occasion my life was spared by what seemed to me then, and seems still, little short of a miracle; for, besides the numerous bullets that whistled by my ears, several actually pierced different parts of my clothing, but not one reached my body. Besides all this, I was exposed to a cross-fire from the Federal and Confederate artillery, whose shot and shell flew whistling and hissing over my head.

At length a Federal shell struck the ground within twenty yards of my feet; and the explosion, of course, sent the fragments flying in every direction around me. I had, however, just time to throw myself flat upon the ground before the deadly engine burst; and again Providence spared my life.

Springing up when the danger was passed, I pursued my career, still under a heavy fire. I shall never run again as I ran on that, to me, memorable day. Hope, fear, the love of life, and the determination to serve my country to the last, conspired to fill my heart with more than feminine courage, and to lend preternatural strength and swiftness to my limbs. I often marvel, and even shudder, when I reflect how I cleared the fields, and bounded over the fences with the agility of a deer.

As I neared our line I waved my bonnet to our soldiers, to intimate that they should press forward, upon which one regiment, the First Maryland "rebel" Infantry, and Hay's Louisiana Brigade, gave me a loud cheer, and, without waiting for further orders, dashed upon the town at a rapid pace.

They did not then know who I was, and they were naturally surprised to see a woman on the battle-field, and on a spot, too, where the fire was so hot. Their shouts of approbation and triumph rang in my ears for many a day afterwards, and I still hear them not unfrequently in my dreams.

At this juncture the main body of the Confederates was hidden from my view by a slight elevation which intervened between me and them. My heart almost ceased to beat within me; for the dreadful thought arose in my mind that our force must be too weak to be any match for the Federals, and that the gallant men who had just been applauding me were rushing upon a certain and fruitless death. I accused myself of having urged them to their fate; and now, quite overcome by fatigue, and by the feelings which tormented me, I sank upon my knees and offered a short but earnest prayer to God.

Then I felt as if my supplication was answered, and that I was inspired with fresh spirits and a new life. Not only despair, but fear also forsook me; and I had again no thought but how to fulfill the mission I had already pursued so far.

I arose from my kneeling posture, and had proceeded but a short distance, when, to my unspeakable, indescribable joy, I caught sight of the main body fast approaching; and soon an old friend and connection of mine, Major Harry Douglas, rode up, and, recognizing me, cried out, while he seized my hand—

"Good God, Belle, you here! What is it?"

"Oh, Harry," I gasped out, "give me time to recover my breath."

For some seconds I could say no more; but, as soon as I had sufficiently recovered myself, I produced the "little note," and told him all, urging him to hurry on the cavalry, with orders to them to seize the bridges before the retreating Federals should have time to destroy them.

He instantly galloped off to report to General Jackson, who immediately rode forward, and asked me if I would have an escort and a horse wherewith to return to the village. I thanked him, and said, "No; I would go as I came"; and then, acting upon the information I had been spared to convey, the Confederates gained a most complete victory.

Though the dépôt building had been fired, and was burning, our cavalry reached the bridges barely in time to save them from destruction: The retreating Federals had just crossed, and were actually upon the point of lighting the slow match which, communicating with the bursting charge, would have riven the arches in pieces. So hasty was their retreat that they left all their killed and wounded in our hands.

Although we lost many of our best and bravest—among others the gallant Captain Sheetes, of Ashby's cavalry, who fell leading a brilliant and successful charge upon the Federal infantry—the day was ours; and I had the heartfelt satisfaction to know that it was in consequence of the information I had conveyed at such risk to myself [that] General Jackson made the flank movement which led to such fortunate results. . . .

Buffalo-Calf-Road-Woman at the Battle of the Rosebud

In the summer of 1876, the two greatest battles between soldiers and Indians were fought on the plains of Montana. The first fight was called the Battle of the Rosebud. The second, which was fought a week later, was called the Battle of the Little Bighorn, where General Custer was defeated and killed. The Cheyennes call the Battle of the Rosebud the Fight Where the Girl Saved Her Brother. Let me tell you why.

Well, a hundred years ago, the white men wanted the Indians to go into prisons called "reservations," to give up their freedom to roam and hunt buffalo, to give up being Indians. Some tamely submitted and settled down behind the barbed wire of the agencies, but others did not.

Those who went to the reservations to live like white men were called "friendlies." Those who would not go were called "hostiles." They weren't hostile, really. They didn't want to fight; all they wanted was to be left alone to live the Indian way, which was a good way. But the soldiers would not leave them alone. They decided to have a great roundup and catch all "hostiles," kill those who resisted, and bring the others back to the agencies as prisoners.

Three columns of soldiers entered the last stretch of land left to the red man. They were led by Generals Crook, Terry, and Custer. Crook had the most men with him, about two thousand. He also had cannon and Indian scouts to guide him. At the Rosebud he met the united Sioux and Cheyenne warriors.

The Indians had danced the sacred sun dance. The great Sioux chief and holy man, Sitting Bull, had been granted a vision telling him that the soldiers would be defeated. The warriors were in high spirits. Some men belonging to famous warrior societies had vowed to fight until they were killed, singing their death songs, throwing their lives away, as it was called. They painted their faces for war. They put on their finest outfits so that if they were killed, their enemies would say: "This must have been a great chief. See how nobly he lies there."

The old chiefs instructed the young men how to act. The medicine men prepared protective charms for the fighters, putting gopher dust on their hair or painting their horses with hailstone designs. This was to render them invisible to their foes, or to make them bulletproof. Brave Wolf had the most admired medicine—a mounted hawk that he fastened to the back of his head. He always rode into battle blowing his eagle-bone whistle—and once the fight started, the hawk came alive and whistled too.

Many proud tribes were there besides the Cheyenne—the Hunkpapa, the Minniconjou, the Oglala, the Burned Thighs, the Two Kettles. Many brave chiefs and warriors came, including Two Moons, White Bull, Dirty Moccasins, Little Hawk, Yellow Eagle, and Lame White Man. Among the Sioux was the great Crazy Horse, and Sitting Bull—their holy man, still weak from his flesh offerings made at the sun dance—and the fierce Rain-in-the-Face. Who can count them all! What a fine sight they were!

Those who had earned the right to wear warbonnets were singing, lifting them up. Three times they stopped in their singing, and the fourth time they put the bonnets on their heads, letting the streamers fly and trail behind them. How good it must have been to see this!

Crazy Horse of the Oglala shouted his famous war cry: "A good day to die, and a good day to fight! Cowards to the rear, brave hearts—follow me!"

The fight started. Many brave deeds were done, many coups counted. The battle swayed to and fro. More than anybody else's, this was the Cheyenne's fight. This was their day. Among them was a brave young girl, Buffalo-Calf-Road-Woman, who rode proudly beside her husband, Black Coyote. Her brother, Chief Comes-in-Sight, was in the battle too. She looked for him and at last saw him surrounded, his horse killed from under him. Soldiers were aiming their rifles at him, while their Crow scouts circled around him and waited for an opportunity to count coups. But he fought them off with courage and skill.

Buffalo-Calf-Road-Woman uttered a shrill, high-pitched war cry. She raced her pony into the midst of the battle, into the midst of the enemy. She made the spine-chilling, trilling, trembling sound of the Indian woman encouraging her man during a fight. Chief Comes-in-Sight jumped up on her horse behind her. Buffalo-Calf-Road-Woman laughed with joy and the excitement of battle, and all the while she sang. The soldiers were firing at her, and their Crow scouts were shooting arrows at her horse, but it moved too fast for her and her brother to be hit. Then she turned her horse and raced up the hill from which the old chiefs and the medicine men were watching the battle.

The Sioux and Cheyenne saw what she was doing, and then the white soldiers saw it too. They all stopped fighting and watched the brave girl saving her brother's life. The warriors raised their arms and set up a mighty shout—a long undulating war cry that made one's hair stand up on end. And even some of the soldiers threw their caps in the air and shouted "Hurrah!" in honor of Buffalo-Calf-Road-Woman.

The battle was still young. Not many men had been killed on either side, but the white general was thinking: "If their women fight like this, what will their warriors be like? Even if I win, I will lose half my men." And so General Crook retreated a hundred miles or so. He was to have joined up with Custer, Old Yellow Hair; but when Custer had to fight the same Cheyenne and Sioux a week later, Crook was far away and Custer's regiment was wiped out. So in a way, Buffalo-Calf-Road-Woman contributed to that battle too.

Many who saw what she had done thought that she had counted the biggest coup of all—not taking life, but giving it. That's why the Indians call the Battle of the Rosebud the Fight Where the Girl Saved Her Brother.

The spot where Buffalo-Calf-Road-Woman counted her coup has long since been plowed under. A ranch now covers it. But the memory of her deed will last as long as there are Indians. This is not a fairy tale, but it sure is a legend.

Amelia Earhart: "The memory of the planes remains clearly . . ."

There are two kinds of stones, as everyone knows, one of which rolls. Because I selected a father who was a railroad man it has been my fortune to roll.

Of course, rolling has left its mark on me. What happened to my education is typical. Until the eighth grade I stayed the school year with my grandmother in Atchison, Kansas, and attended a college preparatory school. With the exception of two grades skipped, one spent trying a public school and one conducted at home under a governess-friend, my course was fairly regular—not including time out for travelling. However, it took six high-schools to see me through the customary four-year course. Would it be surprising, considering this record, if I should come out with a right round "ain't" or "he done it" now and then?

Despite such risks there are advantages in a changing environment. Meeting new people and new situations becomes an interesting adventure, and one learns to value fresh experiences as much as old associations.

When the war broke out for the United States I was at Ogontz School, near Philadelphia. My sister was at St. Margaret's College in Toronto and I went to visit her there for the Christmas holidays.

In every life there are places at which the individual, looking back, can see he was forced to choose one of several paths. These turning points may be marked by a trivial circumstance or by one of great joy or sorrow.

In 1918 Canada had been in the war four weary years—years the United States will never appreciate. Four men on crutches, walking together on King Street in Toronto that winter, was a sight which changed the course of existence for me. The realization that war wasn't knitting sweaters and selling Liberty Bonds, nor dancing with handsome uniforms was suddenly evident. Returning to school was impossible, if there was war work that I could do.

I started training under the Canadian Red Cross and as soon as possible completed the first-aid work necessary to qualify as a V.A.D. or nurse's aide. Those four men on crutches!

My first assignment was to Spadina Military Hospital, a rather small institution occupying an old college building converted for war use. Day began at seven and ended at seven, with two hours off in the afternoon. There were many beds to be made and trays and "nurishment" to be carried, and backs to be rubbed—some lovely ones!

Most of the men had been through a physical and emotional crisis. Many were not sick enough to be in bed and not well enough to find real occupation. Even when jobs were offered many lacked the mental stamina to take them— or make good at them, if taken. Spiritually they were tired out. Generally speaking they were a far harder group to care for than the really sick. For with the latter the improvements noted by the patient from day to day are cheerful mile posts, while these poor lads had lost even that means of happiness. . . .

The war was the greatest shock that some lives have had to survive. It so completely changed the direction of my own footsteps that the details of those days remain indelible in my memory, trivial as they appear when recorded.

Days of routine slipped by quickly enough into months of nursing. I hope what we did was helpful. Somebody had to do it. There is so much that must be done in a civilized barbarism like war.

War followed one everywhere. Even entertainments weren't always merely fun. Often they meant having tea with a group of women who were carrying their war work into their homes. I remember, for instance, hours spent with a power sewing machine making pajamas.

The aviation I touched, too, while approached as an entertainment was of course steeped with war. Sometimes I was invited to a flying field, Armour Heights, on the edge of the city. I think there were many planes there; I know there were many young pilots being trained—some very young. (As a matter of fact I wasn't exactly gray with age—twenty, then.)

But the planes were mature. They were full-sized birds that slid on the hard-packed snow and rose into the air with an extra roar that echoed from the evergreens that banked the edge of the field. They were a part of war, just as much as the drives, the bandages, and the soldiers. I remember well that when the snow blown back by the propellers stung my face I felt a first urge to fly. I tried to get permission to go up, but the rules forbade; not even a general's wife could do so—apparently the only thing she couldn't do. I did the next best thing and came to know some of the men fortunate enough to fly. Among them were Canadians, Scotch, Irish, and even Americans who could not pass our rigorous tests but were accepted in Canada at that time.

They were terribly young, those air men—young and eager. Aviation was the romantic branch of the service and inevitably attracted the romanticists. The dark side did not impress the enlisted men or me. To us there was humor in the big padded helmets, despite their purpose, which was to prevent scalp wounds in the crashes that were frequent in those days. The boys smeared their faces with grease, to prevent freezing, and that seemed funny, too. The training planes were often under-powered, but no matter how well that was understood, the pilots joked about possible unpleasantness.

I have even forgotten the names of the men I knew then. But the memory of the planes remains clearly, and the sense of the inevitability of flying. It always seemed to me one of the few worth-while things that emerged from the misery of war.

"I want to go to Vietnam."

She had heard John F. Kennedy speak of the sacrifice required to keep the torch of democracy alight in the world; she thought that "if our boys were being blown apart, then somebody better be over there putting them back together again." Lynda Van Devanter's idealism and will and sense of adventure took her halfway across the world to the battlefield hospitals of Vietnam. We shall learn more about what she found there and what she came home to; for the moment, though, let's listen to the simple sound of youth lunging toward the action of life and war in the early pages of her memoir, Home Before Morning:

Although our three nursing school years were spent totally immersed in the medical world, by the time I reached my senior year, I began to realize again that there was a different kind of world outside the walls of Mercy Hospital, a world where all was not clean sheets and morning roll calls. The images from the seven o'clock news in the dorm's first-floor lounge began my return to consciousness. One night Walter Cronkite talked about body counts while sweating soldiers ran across the screen firing rifles. Another night, Huntley and Brinkley talked about American victories while wounded soldiers were being carried into a helicopter. I started to pay closer attention to the stories and found the images intruding into my life more and more frequently. Every evening, at seven and eleven, human destruction was brought into the homes of millions by television.

"Those guys look so young," I said one night.

Barbara nodded. "Most of them are no more than eighteen or nineteen," she replied. "My father said half of them learn about death before they even learn to shave."

"Was your father over there?"

"In '62, as an advisor," she said. "He was there before the troop buildup. He says if he were healthier, he'd be back there right now."

Although I had hardly paid any attention to the news of Vietnam before, I now began to search out information. From my naïve perspective, I saw the United States pursuing a course that President Kennedy had talked about in his inaugural address: We were saving a country from communism. There were brave boys fighting and dying for democracy, I thought. And if our boys were being blown apart, then somebody better be over there putting them back together again. I started to think that maybe that somebody should be me.

By January of 1968, when an Army sergeant arrived at Mercy to talk to us about opportunities in the military, it didn't take much convincing for me to sign up. Shortly after that, Barbara joined, too.

"Are you crazy?" Gina said. "You go in the Army, they'll send you to Vietnam. It's dangerous over there."

"I want to go to Vietnam," I told her.

"But what if you get killed?"

Barbara provided the answer to that one. "The sergeant told us that nurses don't get killed," she said. "They're all in rear areas. The hospitals are perfectly safe."

Gina was unconvinced. "I think you're both nuts. If you had any brains, you'd do exactly what I'm going to do: find a decent job, get married, and have a house full of kids. Leave the wars to the men."

When I told my parents of my decision, my mother had a similar response, although she wasn't as outspoken as Gina. My father said very little. He mostly listened as I gave him the same talk the recruiter had given me. I mentioned the benefits, the pay, the extra training, the free travel, the excitement, and the challenge.

"It's a job that somebody has to do," I said.

"I understand," he replied. "But I'm worried about my little girl." In spite of those words, I thought I saw a gleam in his eyes. He was proud of me.

Flight Nurse's Creed

I will summon every resource to prevent the triumph of death over life. I will stand guard over the medicines and equipment entrusted to my care and insure their proper use. I will be untiring in the performances of my duties and I will remember that, upon my disposition and spirit, will in large measure depend the morale of my patients. I will be faithful to my training and to the wisdom handed down to me by those who have gone before us. I have taken a nurse's oath, reverent in man's mind because of the spirit and work of its creator, Florence Nightingale. She, I remember, was called the "lady with the lamp." It is now my privilege to lift this lamp of hope and faith and courage in my profession to heights not known by her in her time. Together with the help of flight surgeons and surgical technicians, I can set the very skies ablaze with life and promise for the sick, injured, and wounded who are my sacred charges. This I will do; I will not falter in war or in peace.

"I didn't want this money."

I was stationed at Fort Bragg before Vietnam. I was close to a guy from the eighty-second Airborne Division. We weren't close like boy friend and girl friend. He was like a younger brother, probably the same age as my brother back home. He took out a fifty-thousand dollar life insurance policy on himself before he left and I get this check for fifty-thousand dollars when I'm in 'Nam because he dies over there and I was his beneficiary. I had to get his parents' address. I didn't want this money. It was a big laugh when we were in North Carolina but it wasn't a laugh now that this nineteen-year-old guy is dead. I didn't care what they did with the money but I wasn't taking any of it.

"It's not going to get your leg back."

Over and over and over. I used to see these people—they'd come in and give them Purple Hearts on the ward. And I'd look at them as they'd get their Purple Heart. At that point, it looked like it might be meaningful to them, so I didn't say anything. I never said anything, never said anything about what a waste it was. I would never dream of doing that, because they knew it and it would hurt like hell if they heard it anyway. But I would watch this ridiculous little ceremony, and they'd get a Purple Heart for what was left of them, and I'd think, "You're getting this? What are you getting this for? It's not going to get your leg back. It's not going to get your looks back. It's not going to make you avoid all the pain you're going to have to face when you go home and see your family and get back into society. It's all sitting in front of you and you're going to have to deal with it . . . and nothing will make up for that."

I remember one young man, he had lost his leg and he was walking around on crutches. He had adjusted pretty well. This was probably the first few weeks after he lost his leg. We didn't keep them more than sixty days. Our standard was: If you couldn't cure them or kill them in sixty days, you had to lose them somehow. And he went down and called his mother and told her he had lost his leg. He had been doing pretty well up to this point. I said, "What did your mother say?" He said, "Well, she cried." And I could see he was going to get a little teary-eyed, but he didn't want to because it was a twenty-two bed ward. All the guys are looking at each other and they don't like to cry in front of each other. So I just gave him a hug, in front of all the guys, and that made him feel good.

"*I hate them dying alone.*"

The excerpt below is from Winnie Smith's memoir, American Daughter Gone to War. *No longer the idealistic young woman fearful that the action will take place without her, she finds that the horror, as it always does, has patiently waited for her. Her grisly initiation—she works around the clock in the combat wards in Saigon—leaves her no time for medals or speeches or etiquette; there is only the endless struggle and sadness as she and her comrades try to keep the fatally wounded (the ones she calls "expectants") from slipping away:*

~

Sliding behind the yellow curtain screens, I see one expectant gazing calmly at the face of another expectant on a gurney next to his. Has there been some dreadful mistake? I take the man's blood pressure: eighty systolic. What's he doing behind the screen? I speed up his IV, pull back the sheet to check out his wounds.

At first I see only one arm missing at the shoulder. Then I see why he's here. Where there should be chest wall are only dressings saturated with coagulated blood.

The soldier watches with a look of vague curiosity. I replace the sheet.

"Water," he whispers.

"Sure. Anything else?"

"Hurts. Hurts like hell."

"I'll get you something for it."

I'm so tired. I wish I could take a break, but as I come out from behind the curtains, I notice an IV that's almost empty. And I remember that one routine [patient] has poor urine output and see another's leg dressing is saturated with blood.

I find Hooper in the medication room. I ask for fifty milligrams of morphine.

Hooper raises an eyebrow to ask if I'm sure.

I'm sure. I slip back behind the yellow curtain, hold the expectant's head so he can sip the water. He runs his tongue over his parched lips, nodding gratefully.

"Sorry, no ice," I joke.

"No sweat, Lieutenant. Thanks." He smiles weakly.

"This is pain medicine," I tell him, sticking the needle into his IV tubing. He smiles again. "You're an angel, Lieutenant. Maybe now I can get some rest."

My hands tremble slightly, but I do not hesitate.

When I look into his face to say a last good-bye, his eyes are already closed.

Oh, what I wouldn't give to sit in the shade of a tree with a tall glass of iced tea!

As busy as we are, there's a command performance in ICU. A general is here to pin Purple Hearts on the patients, something none of us has seen done before. The journalists love it. So does the general, smiling benevolently upon wounded soldiers as he angles Purple Hearts to be conspicuous in photographs.

He starts at bed one, ceremoniously reads off name, rank, and serial number as if he were playing a part in some cornball flick. Only there's a glitch. The general can't pin the medal on because the recipient wears no pajamas. Seeing the general's fluster, the wounded man holds out one hand, nonchalantly salutes, and smiles.

As the general approaches the next patient, the general's aide hisses, "Straighten up, soldier!"

"Yes, sir!" barks the soldier, whipping out a brisk salute.

We grin, give him the thumbs-up. But the moment is lost when the general passes up his buddy, wounded a few days later in another skirmish.

"Hey, you forgot the Dude," he calls.

No, someone says, they haven't forgotten. The Dude was hit by our side. There are no Purple Hearts for those wounded by friendly fire.

The next recipient has not been in-country for long, easily seen by his lack of a tan. Racked by high fevers, horrified by the green pus oozing from his belly, and terrified of dying, he believes the general is a priest come to say last rites. Eyes wild, teeth bared, he swipes erratically at the IV bottle hanging between them.

The general is obviously ill at ease. He hands over the medal and backs away, glances with irritation at the bedside fan blowing over them to reduce the soldier's fever. He runs his hands down his chest to his waist to straighten his uniform, then squares his shoulders.

On to a head injury, trached and on a respirator, who gurgles while the general is making his spiel.

Enough of this bullshit. Breaking ranks, I roll a suction machine to the bedside and turn it on. The soldier's secretions slurp through the catheter into the tubing. I rinse the tubing with water, turn off the machine, and replace the catheter in a bottle of Wescodyne.

"Is he all right?" the general asks anxiously.

The soldier's right frontal lobe has been blown away. If he lives to get back to the States, he may never get out of the hospital. But I say nothing of these things. I focus on the patient rather than face the general. Answer: "Yes, sir."

We're way behind in our work when I return to the recovery room. I admit a routine rolling through the doors, check his IV, grab a bottle for his Foley, suction his trach, hook his chest tubes up to suction, note his dressings are dry and intact, insert a stomach tube, change the oxygen tank.

The corpsman says something about a falling blood pressure on the middle third bed, and I can see from here that the shoulder dressing is soaked. I grab some silver nitrate sticks and take down the dressing to cauterize the bleeder. They're rolling in another patient from the operating room.

It's too much for us; see if the ICU can take one of the overflows.

They don't have an empty bed. To make space, they roll one of their patients behind the expectant screens.

Did I blow the whistle too soon? Could one of the other nurses have done better? It doesn't matter. I'm the only nurse here.

I step behind the curtains to see whom I have banished to certain death. Another soldier with fixed and dilated pupils.

I jump and whirl at a touch on my shoulder. "Has he slipped away yet?" Sheila asks matter-of-factly.

"No." I'm ashamed to be caught just standing here after having asked for help.

"I come here, too," she says quietly. "I hate them dying alone."

Coming Home

We heard young Lynda Van Devanter rushing off to war; now listen to her coming home. Beyond the strange dislocation sensed by all Vietnam vets coming back to America was an even deeper angst felt by the combat nurses, whose ex-

perience was often discounted even by the soldiers she had once sought to save. Though Van Devanter suffered mightily in the years after the war, she went on to become the National Women's Director of the Vietnam Veterans of America, in which position she has assisted thousands of her comrades—men and women—to recover a sense of life and purpose in the aftermath of the nation's traumatic war in Vietnam:

There were hundreds of GIs at the San Francisco Airport, waiting to get home. Some had waited for more than twenty-four hours. They had spent the night on benches and on the floor, using old field jackets for blankets and duffel bags for pillows. Some who had tried to save money by flying "Space Available" found themselves bumped. A few walked around in a daze, as if they couldn't believe that they were finally out of Vietnam.

I quickly went to a ladies' room and stripped off my fatigues and jungle boots, for the last time, I realized. I donned my green summer cord uniform, fixed the brass and ribbons, and ran a brush through my hair. I looked down at the pile of dirty fatigues and boots for a second. It almost seemed that they *were* Vietnam. I stuffed them into the duffel bag, yanked it closed, and went out to find the nearest airline with the next flight to D.C.

"Can you hear it?" a corporal asked me while we waited in line to book our flights. On his uniform he had the crossed rifles of the infantry and three rows of ribbons. In his eyes, I could see a lifetime's worth of sadness.

" 'Nam still sucks," I answered. "But I can't hear it anymore."

"Sure you can," he said. "Everybody does. It never stops."

I was one of the lucky ones in San Francisco. I got a seat on a direct flight to Washington that was leaving within an hour. The corporal, who was trying to get to some backwater town in Louisiana, found out he would have to wait until midnight before a seat would be open on something going his way. And with layovers, he wouldn't get home until the next night.

When I called my parents' house to give them my arrival time, I could barely contain my excitement. My mother answered the phone. Her voice cracked when I told her I was coming home.

"I'll make a pan of lasagna," she said.

"I'd like that."

"Lynda, I want you to know . . ." She was fighting tears. I closed my eyes. I could almost see the quiver of her jaw as my mother, who had always been so proper, struggled with her emotions while she tried to get out the words. ". . . I want you to know that . . . that your father and I missed you. We missed you very much."

"I missed you too, Mom."

I had a quick drink in the airport and another on the plane to make me sleep. I was exhausted; hadn't slept in more than twenty-four hours. As we were passing over the Midwest, I began to doze. But before I was able to reach a deep sleep, I saw an image that startled me awake. It was the bloody, blown away face of the young bleeder into whom I had pumped blood six months earlier. *Gene and Katie, May 1968.* He was wearing his tux and dancing with Katie, but his face was all exposed meat and bone. Blood was running like tears down the area that was once his cheeks, and it was drip-drip-dripping onto Katie's exposed shoulder and inching down her back, staining her gown. I tried to warn her that she was ruining her dress, but the words wouldn't come out. Then finally, I made a sound, a low moaning that took every bit of strength I had. Katie turned to look at me. Her face, too, was blown away.

She laughed.

I screamed.

The elderly businessman next to me touched my shoulder. When I opened my eyes, I was drenched with cold sweat and shaking. He asked the stewardess to bring me a blanket, which I clutched tightly to my chest. It was a few minutes before I realized where I was. By that time, I'm sure they all thought I was crazy.

"It was only a bad dream," I said, still shivering.

Although the nightmares had started early in my tour in Vietnam, they had gotten progressively worse during the last few months, especially after that long fruitless operation on Gene. On the way back from 'Nam, I had spent a few days in Hawaii, partly because I though this might be my only chance to visit the islands and partly because I wanted to decompress before facing my family. Although the days in Hawaii were enjoyable—as soon as I arrived, I had a McDonald's hamburger, french fries, and a Coke—the nights were pure hell, with the dreams coming one after another, until I was afraid to go to sleep.

I tried drinking myself into oblivion; that was only effective about half the time.

When I had asked Carl about the bad dreams, he had shrugged my questions off. "Of course you'll have nightmares," he said. "Everybody in this hole does. It's part of the price we pay."

"But when will they stop?"

"I don't know. Maybe when you get back to the world."

That was one of the few things about which he was wrong.

I ordered another drink from the stewardess and tried reading a magazine. I couldn't concentrate. My mind kept bouncing back and forth between my life in Vietnam and the world I would face when I got home. I wondered about the soldiers I had worked on: What about the guy who had fallen into the pungi pit (a North Vietnamese trap) last week? Had he survived? And the guy I had saved from the expectant room a few weeks earlier? Did he make it? Or the chest cases? How many of them lived? Were they in Japan now, or already in graves back in the world?

I worried a lot about Jack. How was he doing at the DMZ? Had the casualties let up yet? Did he miss me? Would he get through the rest of his tour safely? Or would I get a letter telling me that something had happened? Or if something happened, would anybody in his unit even know to send me a letter? Would they find my parents' address in his wallet?

My biggest worries came not from the life I had left behind, but from the life that was ahead of me. I knew that this year had changed me drastically, probably more than I realized. My parents would be meeting an entirely different Lynda than they had said good-bye to only twelve months ago. They told me they loved me and missed me, but would they love me when they got to know me again? Would they even like me? What would I do if they didn't like me? How would I ever fit in?

I tried a couple more drinks to help me forget all the worries, but again the alcohol did no good. I stayed sober and anxious. By the time the pilot announced that we were approaching National Airport in D.C., my hands were shaking, my heart pounding, my palms sweating, and my throat dry. I had a headache that wouldn't quit and a lump in my throat that I thought would choke me to death. I had trouble breathing. It felt as though someone were sitting on my chest.

My parents are waiting. They're on the ground.

The plane began its descent. I gripped the arms of my seat. Sweat beaded up on my forehead and rolled down the side of my face. I grabbed a Kleenex from my purse and wiped it off, my hands shaking the whole time.

As I looked out the window trying to find some familiar landmarks, the pilot's voice came back over the speaker system. "We're in a bit of a traffic jam," he said. "The tower hasn't given us clearance to land yet, so we're going to circle. We'll be in the air another twenty minutes. Relax and enjoy the scenery."

Relax? My stomach was tied in knots. I felt like I would throw up. I wanted to go to the bathroom, but the overhead sign told us to keep our seat belts fastened. I opened a barf bag in case I needed it.

The plane descended lower. A few clouds floated past. They were soft, white, and fluffy, kind of like I had always pictured the floor of heaven. I wiped more sweat from my forehead and squeezed the armrests tighter. My heart was pounding so loudly I thought I might explode. I felt like I was going to pass out.

We came lower and went into a sharp turn. "We're on the final leg of our approach to Washington National," the stewardess said. "Please make sure your seat belts are buckled, seat backs are up, all tray tables in the full upright position, and any carry-on luggage securely stowed under the seat in front of you."

When we broke through a thin layer of clouds, I could see all the land-marks that I had come to know as a child. There was the Washington Monu-ment, where my friends and I had climbed to the top singing folk songs while one of the boys played a guitar; the Capitol, where we had gone with our civics class to listen to the senators and congressmen debate the Civil Rights Act in 1964; the White House, where an embattled and untrustworthy president now resided; and the Pentagon, that enormous sandstone building where generals made decisions that would affect my life and the lives of more than a million others in uniform.

I took a deep breath and felt the tears welling up as the plane's wheels screeched against the runway. The pilot reversed the engines to bring us to a stop. My ears popped from the pressure. *I can't cry,* I told myself out of habit. *I have to be strong.*

Then it hit me that I didn't have to be strong all the time anymore, that maybe now I would be able to start relaxing, that now people's lives were no longer dependent on me holding things together. There would be no more calls in the middle of the night. No more helicopters bearing wounded young boys. No more rocket attacks. No more monsoons. No more Viet Cong. No more seventy-two-hour stretches at the operating table. No more trying to turn pieces of meat and bone back into human beings. In a few more minutes, when the plane stopped at the terminal and I walked down the ramp, I would be home.

We taxied off the runway and slowly made our way toward the building.

There was another slight delay while we waited for a departing plane to leave our gate. The stewardesses, in their bright, cheery way, welcomed us to Washington, gave us the local time and temperature, and suggested that on our next trip, we fly their airline. I was a tightly wound spring about to snap, and as each moment passed, I got tighter and tighter. It seemed like we'd never get there. By now my heart was racing faster than the speed of sound and my body was shaking uncontrollably. As soon as we came to a stop, I grabbed my carry-on bags and jumped over my seatmate. People in front were moving into the aisle. I pushed past them all.

I wanted to scream with frustration as I waited an interminable length of time for the man outside to hook up the ramp so the stewardess could open the door. I stared at that door, and silently cursed it for being there. It was the last obstacle between me and home. I wanted it moved.

Now!

Suddenly, it was open.

And at the other end of the ramp, I saw two anxious faces.

I broke into a broad smile.

They both smiled at the same time.

Then I laughed.

I heard my mother call first. "Lynda," she said in a special way, pronouncing each syllable slowly and crisply as only she could. Unencumbered happiness was in every tone of her voice.

I burst through the door and ran down the ramp.

Then I heard my father's voice. "My little girl's home," he said.

I couldn't run fast enough. In a moment I was in his arms, laughing and crying as I hugged and kissed my father and mother. I felt the strength from those protective arms and I wanted to melt into them. I wanted somebody to pick me up and hold me like a baby. I didn't ever want to be strong again. I wanted to be somebody's child. My father's child. And my mother's child.

The three of us squeezed each other so tightly it's a wonder we didn't all turn blue. I couldn't stop the tears and neither could my parents. For that moment, I felt loved more than I ever had in my entire life. Finally, I stepped back and looked at them. "You don't know how great you both look," I said.

They laughed. "You look great, too," they said.

After a few more moments, my mother hugged me again. I noticed something about her face. She had been worried. Now, she seemed relieved. "At least they fed you over there," she said. "You've put on a little weight, haven't you, dear?"

Lest We Forget

*I*st Lt. Sharon Ann Lane, 2nd Lt. Carol Drazba, 2nd Lt. Elizabeth Jones, Lt. Col. Annie Graham, 2nd Lt. Pamela Donovan, Capt. Mary Klinker, 1st Lt. Hedwig Orlowski, and Capt. Eleanor Alexander—the eight women on the wall of the Vietnam memorial in Washington, D.C.

Jeannette Rankin: "But I cannot vote for war."

"*I* want to stand by my country," declared Jeannette Rankin, the first woman ever elected to the U.S. Congress, "but I cannot vote for war." The year was 1917, the Lusitania had been sunk, Europe was spilling its youth's blood into the muddy trenches of Ypres and Arras, and America was furiously debating whether or not to join the fight. Rankin's vote against U.S. involvement, along with a handful of congressmen and six senators, was but a whisper in the storm for war that swept over the country. She had come a long way to cast her vote and could not have imagined how far she had yet to go.

Rankin was born into a wealthy family in the territory of Montana in 1880 (Montana became a state in 1889) and raised on the western traditions of feminine independence. She was drawn to the suffrage movement at a young age and worked tirelessly for women's right to vote. To her surprise, she found herself on a suffrage ticket that won, placing her in the odd position of being a congresswoman with the right to vote in the House of Representatives before she herself could vote in a general election.

Almost immediately after her election, Rankin joined those adamantly opposed to the war in Europe. She argued that America's obligation to the world was as a peacemaker, and she should use her authority and moral guidance to contribute toward the construction of a lasting peace. As she said later, "America has the war habit. It is one we must break before we are broken by it." Over her eloquent objections, America joined the struggle abroad.

In 1920 she lost her district to gerrymandering (inspired, in part, by those who held her principles against her); she ran for the U.S. Senate and lost.

America's contribution to victory in World War I had been held out as proof of her lack of judgment. To the contrary, insisted Rankin, no one is victorious in war, and she crisscrossed the country speaking on behalf of world peace and disarmament. Her political spirit had caught on with other women—consider the slogan of Alice Mary Robertson's successful congressional campaign (the second woman elected): "I cannot be bought, I cannot be sold, I cannot be intimidated."

As the tempests of World War II gathered, Rankin again sought elective office and, in 1940, won. (This time, of course, she was able to cast a vote on her own behalf!) She had little time to savor her victory, for when Pearl Harbor awakened the wrath of the nation, Rankin became the only member of either house to vote "nay" on the declaration of war against Japan: She again stood alone for the same principles that had led to her vote in 1917. The members of Congress and the public were outraged and shunned her in public and private. She was vilified and cursed at and treated with contempt. Her political future was over before it had begun, just as had happened nearly twenty-five years before. As with all people who follow the dictates of conscience, Rankin neither shrank from nor changed her passionate view that war is a sin and wrong, whatever the cause. In fact, though few had listened to her, the "habit" of war was taken up again, and before it was all over, the face of the world was once again scarred by it.

Rankin continued to argue for disarmament. Her last hurrah came in January of 1968 when, at the age of eighty-eight, she joined a march of five thousand women in front of the Jeannette Rankin Brigade banner in Washington, D.C. The cause? A protest against the war in Vietnam.

WOMEN OF FAITH, WOMEN OF FIRE

The road that conscience follows is long and exacting. In our youth it is a lovely path, flat, certain, and we are all on it together. Our shared faith—that we shall do what is right, that we shall be true to our truest nature—is carried along like a bright banner. But soon enough, the way begins to buckle and twist and steepen. The crossroads keep coming and companions break off onto different paths with brave good-byes and promises to meet again. Who among us claims to know the way? The walking gives way to climbing and the journey seems more a matter of stamina, of will. What we once held aloft as banners we now need as torches, and we see them burning in the mountains around us, marking the progress of solitary, faithful travelers in a mighty darkness. In the end, though many began, few make it above the treeline. We come to love those few—they offer us hope, inspiration, and a reminder of the journey we began so long ago when our faith was simple, clear, and indestructible.

There are so many astonishing American women who did not drop off the path, who did not quit in the name of conformity or accede to the temptations of fatigue, depression, or despair. However much they may have wanted to belong to a merry band of fellow pilgrims, they endured the isolation that their faith demanded. They were not afraid to risk their reputations, their happiness, even their lives for the convictions they held. There were the women who fought slavery with their whole selves, such as Harriet Tubman, who built her Underground Railroad without rest, and Sojourner Truth, Harriet Jacobs, and Fanny Kemble, who all testified against slavery with a soaring eloquence. The women's rights movement in the mid-nineteenth century produced fiery souls like those of the Grimké sisters, Lucretia Mott, Elizabeth Cady Stanton ("Radical reform must start in our homes, in our nurseries, in ourselves . . ."), Abigail Duniway, and many others. Their challenges to an institutionalized and formidable sexism laid the foundation for the heroism of the twentieth-century civil-rights activists and feminists. We are all stronger as citizens, as human beings, because of the righteous resolve these women possessed and their determination to follow the rigorous, unyielding dictates of conscience.

The First Trial for Witchcraft in America
(1648)

At this court one Margaret Jones of Charlestown was indicted and found guilty of witchcraft, and hanged for it. The evidence against her was, 1. that she was found to have such a malignant touch, as many persons, (men, women, and children) whom she stroked or touched with any affection or displeasure, or, etc., were taken with deafness, or vomiting, or other violent pains or sickness, 2. she practising physic, and her medicines being such things as (by her own confession) were harmless, as aniseed, liquors, etc., yet had extraordinary violent effects, 3. she would use to tell such as would not make use of her physic, that they would never be healed, and accordingly their diseases and hurts continued, with relapse against the ordinary course, and beyond the apprehension of all physicians and surgeons, 4. some things which she foretold came to pass accordingly; other things she could tell of (as secret speeches, etc.) which she had no ordinary means to come to the knowledge of, . . . 6. in the prison, in the clear daylight, there was seen in her arms, she sitting on the floor, and her clothes up, etc., a little child, which ran from her into another room, and the officer following it, it was vanished. The like child was seen in two other places, to which she had relation; and one maid that saw it, fell sick upon it, and was cured by the said Margaret, who used means to be employed to that end. Her behavior at her trial was very intemperate, lying notoriously, and railing upon the jury and witnesses, etc., and in the like distemper she died. The same day and hour she was executed, there was a very great tempest at Connecticut, which blew down many trees, etc.

Anne Hutchinson

Her biographers describe her in many ways: Some say she was misunderstood, others that she was unafraid, still others that she was a saint, a bold sinner, or even the first great feminist in America. She was all of these things and because she was brave and brilliant and a woman, she would suffer colonial America's supreme damnation.

She emigrated from England to Massachusetts Bay in 1634 at the age of forty-three. She had birthed twelve children (and seen three of them die) and bore her last child upon her arrival in America. Something of a midwife and nurse, Hutchinson soon developed quite a following among the women in the fledgling colony for her deeply spiritual nature. She had come to the New World with new ideas; she had little patience with the political emphasis on outward piety. The grace of God, she argued before larger and larger groups, was not to be awarded by ministers or exclusively owned by Massachusetts Bay religious leaders, but was rather a gift from God to those whose hearts were receptive. Intermediaries, while helpful, were not essential. Many people found her thinking sensible and compelling. She offered hope to those who had no established place within the strict theological hierarchy of the community. She suggested that she herself had heard the words of God directly, a clear voice to her deepest conscience.

Needless to say, such thoughts (particularly from a woman) were considered heretical, and Hutchinson was branded a renegade by the church fathers. They particularly objected to the gatherings that Hutchinson conducted at her own home and accused her of activities that bordered on witchcraft. Soon enough, the political winds were strong enough that Anne Hutchinson was brought to trial. She faced a tribunal of church elders, led by the Rev. John Winthrop, who saw himself as the willful shepherd to his New World flock. The transcripts of the several trials she endured are astonishing: One woman faced her unjust accusers all at once, answering questions, jousting, debating, admonishing her accusers on matters of religious training, moral instruction, and social behavior. Worn down but unbeaten, Hutchinson gave as good as she got. Toward the end, she sought something of a compromise and relied on friends like Cotton Mather to argue on her behalf, but she had made too many enemies, had left too many critics calling for her total submission. Winthrop recognized that she was becoming more and more of a political problem the longer she stood her ground and finally threatened her one last time. Would she recant her ideas? She would not. She knew that capitulation to the charges against her would grossly undermine her own spiritual convictions and those who believed in her. Knowing full well the consequences, she refused to recant. The tribunal summoned all its fury:

> "Forasmuch as you, Mrs. Hutchinson, have highly transgressed and offended . . . and troubled the Church with your Errors and have drawn away many a poor soule, and have upheld your Revelations; and foras-

much as you have made a Lye . . . Therefor in the name of our Lord
Jesus Christ . . . I doe cast you out and . . . deliver you up to Sathan
. . . and account you from this time forth to be a Hethen and a Publi-
can. . . . I command you in the name of Christ Jesus and of this church
as a Leper to withdraw your selfe out of the Congregation."

Hutchinson faced her accusers in silence. She had argued her points,
conceded on matter of her own arrogance and smaller points of theology, but
she must have known that there could be no further compromise with these
elders. Total submission had been required and only God had the right to ask
that of her. These were stubborn, political, frightened men, not messengers of
a divine will. She would not submit. She turned toward a fearful, awestruck
congregation and walked slowly, elegantly down the aisle towards the church
door. To much astonishment from the congregation, Mary Dyer, a younger
woman who loved Hutchinson as her mentor and friend, stepped from the
crowd. Dyer smiled at Hutchinson and quietly took her arm and together they
walked out of the church. At the door a man sniped, "The Lord sanctifie this
unto you." Hutchinson answered calmly as she stepped with her comrade into
the sunlight, "The Lord judgeth not as man judgeth. Better to be cast out of
the Church than to deny Christ."

Dyer would later be hung on the Boston Common by these same church
elders for professing the Quaker faith, while brave Anne Hutchinson would be
slain by Indians in the forests of Long Island where she had gone to be free of
religious persecution. Both would be the greater for their faith than any of the
men who tried and convicted them; both would live on as inspirations to spiritual seekers for generations to come.

Jemima Wilkinson

Born a Quaker in Rhode Island in 1752, Jemima Wilkinson was largely self-taught.
She had memorized much of the Bible and knew her Quaker teachings, in many
cases, verbatim. During a severe illness in her mid-twenties she had a vision and saw
herself as a new soul resurrected. She recovered and announced to her astonished
family and community that she was no longer the Jemima they had known but had
been reborn as "the Publick Universal Friend." For nearly fifty years she pursued her
mission to minister to the sick and the sinful alike. A wonderful story about her

suggests that, like some of our modern TV evangelists, Wilkinson understood the deli-
cate line between faith and credulity:

One time Wilkinson was said to have finally caved in to local pressure to demonstrate her divine authority: She would walk on water. At the appointed day and hour a mighty crowd gathered at the water's edge to see this astonishing event. Wilkinson arrived and delivered a powerful sermon, which periodically roused the crowd with the passionate question, "Do ye have faith?" With each query the crowd's answer became more ebullient and enthusiastic. Finally she cried, "Do ye have faith that I can do this thing?" The crowd cheered and gave its overwhelming assent—"We believe!" Wilkinson stopped and held the crowd breathless for a moment and then said, "It is good that ye have such faith for with it, ye need no other evidence." She departed amidst a bewildered and admiring crowd, her legend intact.

Sacajawea

Thomas Jefferson gave Meriwether Lewis and William Clark clear and decisive instructions: "The object of your mission is single," he wrote them in 1803, "the direct water communication from sea to sea formed by the bed of the Missouri & perhaps the Oregon." It is the storyteller's pleasure to connect random events into one seamless narrative; the more accurate and comprehensive the telling, the closer the storyteller comes to the historian. So, let the historians recount that revelatory journey across the new nation's newly acquired territory that was the Lewis and Clark expedition; leave it to the storytellers to linger over the wonderful, willful woman who led the expedition west.

We pick up her trail in life following a sharp, violent fight between the Shoshones of the Rocky Mountains and the Hidatsas. The Hidatsas won the day and seized captives, among them a young Shoshone girl named Sacajawea (the Birdwoman). Dark and watchful, she was alert to the ways of the woods and the animals. She survived among the Hidatsas because she was resourceful and tough, and for that survival Lewis and Clark would come to be very grateful indeed. Living among the Hidatsas was a French Canadian named Toussaint Charbonneau, a wandering, opportunistic trapper who recognized the value of the self-possessed Sacajawea. He won her in a bet from the braves who had captured her, and he recognized the assistance she could bring him both as a worker and as a wife (he had several others). It was business and he knew he had traded well.

One day a party of white men worked their way up the river toward Charbonneau's camp. They came to see him because they needed a guide to take them up the Missouri River. While he knew some of the ground, he did not want to go; he was lazy, cautious, noncommittal. Sacajawea, now pregnant, stood listening carefully to the explorers; she must have recognized that they could be her first real opportunity to get home. She had longed for the mountains, the sheer ravines, the daunting rocks, and the fast water of her childhood and she remembered all the trails, narrow passes, and pastures. While her husband hesitated, she did not: "I will take you," she said with authority. "I speak the language. I am a Shoshone." We don't know what transpired at that moment but can speculate: Charbonneau must have smelled an opportunity; Lewis and Clark were short of options and must have hesitated, seeing her condition; Sacajawea is likely to have been impatient and sure of herself. We do know that she made it simple: "Wait a few days," she said. "The child will come very soon and I will take it along with us." They did and Baptiste Charbonneau was born as expected. Six weeks later, strapped to his mother's back, the papoose became the youngest member of America's most celebrated expedition. Sacajawea would carry her son every step of the nearly five-thousand-mile journey.

Lewis and Clark's journals make little reference to their guide, but from the entries that are made, her importance seems unmistakable. At one point, Charbonneau mistakenly overturned a canoe carrying all the expeditions' journals (he seemed of very little use to the group), but Sacajawea dove into the white water and rescued every page. At another point, she became quite ill; she told the party to go on without her. And though Lewis and Clark may well have appeared gallant by staying behind until she recovered, the truth was that they knew better. They needed her and could not press on until she could help them find the way.

When they reached the country of the Snake people, the land of Sacajawea's birth, they were met by Shoshone warriors, and the chief who came forward to meet the expedition and determine its intent looked immediately familiar to the Birdwoman. How long was it before Sacajawea recognized the chief as her own brother? How long before the brother saw the face of the little sister he had lost so many years ago? It was surely a joyful occasion (Sacajawea, who Lewis had thought never showed emotion, wept through most of the first day) and one that brought Lewis and Clark great relief, food, fresh horses, and protection. The site of the reunion became known as Camp Fortunate. Sacajawea was to guide the expedition through the bewildering lands that today are Montana and Wyoming. On the verge of returning to Washington, William Clark thanked her, paid her nothing (her husband was paid $500), and returned to an impatient, young nation anxious to hear of the promise that lay beyond the Mississippi.

As for Sacajawea, though some say she died young, most agree that she lived a very long time, dying in 1884 at the Wind River Reservation in Wyoming—the year that Mark Twain published *Huckleberry Finn* and Harry Truman was born! The Reverend John Roberts, a noted western missionary, performed the service. She "sleeps with her face towards the dawn on the sunny side of the Rocky Mountains," he wrote. Over 1,000 people attended her funeral. Her son, who had ridden his mother's shoulders into history would die only a year later, like his mother, a respected guide and lover of nature. Legends sprang up about the Birdwoman—some fantastic and, because the written record was so sparse, most entirely speculative, but of this we can be sure: With resourcefulness she survived, with courage she guided the most celebrated explorers in American history, and with determination she made her way home.

Hannah Fox's Harrowing Tale

Miss Hannah Fox tells the following story of an adventure she had while engaged in felling trees in her mother's woods in Rhode Island, in the early colonial days:

We were making fine progress with our clearing and getting ready to build a house in the spring. My brother and I worked early and late, often going without our dinner, when the bread and meat which we brought with us was frozen so hard that our teeth could make no impression upon it, without taking too much of our time. My brother plied his axe on the largest trees, while I worked at the smaller ones or trimmed the boughs from the trunks of such as had been felled.

The last day of our chopping was colder than ever. The ground was covered by a deep snow which had crusted over hard enough to bear our weight, which was a great convenience in moving from spot to spot in the forest, as well as in walking to and from our cabin, which was a mile away. My brother had gone to the nearest settlement that day, leaving me to do my work alone.

As a storm was threatening, I toiled as long as I could see, and after twilight felled a sizeable tree which in its descent lodged against another. Not liking to leave the job half finished, I mounted the almost prostrate trunk to cut away a limb and let it down. The bole of the tree was forked about twenty feet from the ground, and one of the divisions of the fork would have to be cut asunder. A few blows of my axe and the tree began to settle, but as I was about to descend, the fork split and the first joints of my left-hand fingers slid into the crack so that for the moment I could not extricate them. The pressure was not severe, and as I believed I could soon relieve myself by cutting away the remaining portion, I felt no alarm. But at the first blow of the axe which I held in my right hand, the trunk changed its position, rolling over and closing the split, with the whole force of its tough oaken fibers crushing my fingers like pipe-stems; at the same time my body was dislodged from the trunk and I slid slowly down till I hung suspended with the points of my feet just brushing the snow. The air was freezing and every moment growing colder; no prospect of any relief that night; the nearest house a mile away; no friends to feel alarmed at my absence, for my mother would suppose that I was safe with my brother, while the latter would suppose I was by this time at home.

The first thought was of my mother. "It will kill her to know that I died in this death-trap so near home, almost within hearing of her voice! There must be some escape! but how?" My axe had fallen below me and my feet could almost touch it. It was impossible to imagine how I could cut myself loose unless I could reach it. My only hope of life rested on that keen blade which lay glittering on the snow.

Within reach of my hand was a dead bush which towered some eight feet above me, and by a great exertion of strength I managed to break it. Holding it between my teeth I stripped it of its twigs, leaving two projecting a few inches at the lower end to form a hook. With this I managed to draw towards me the head of the axe until my fingers touched it, when it slipped from the hook and fell again upon the snow, breaking through the crust and burying itself so that only the upper end of the helve could be seen.

Up to that moment the recollection of my mother and the first excitement engendered by hope had almost made me unconscious of the excruciating pain in my crushed fingers, and the sharp thrills that shot through my nerves, as my body swung and twisted in my efforts to reach the axe. But now, as the axe fell beyond my reach, the reaction came, hope fled, and I shuddered with the thought that I must die there alone like some wild thing caught in a snare. I thought of my widowed mother, my brother, the home which we had toiled to make comfortable and happy. I prayed earnestly to God for forgiveness of my sins, and then calmly resigned myself to death, which I now believed to be inevitable. For a time, which I afterwards found to be only five minutes, but which then seemed to me like hours, I hung motionless. The pain had ceased, for the intense cold blunted my sense of feeling. A numbness stole over me, and I seemed to be falling into a trance, from which I was roused by a sound of bells borne to me as if from a great distance. Hope again awoke, and I screamed loud and long; the woods echoed my cries, but no voice replied. The bells grew fainter and fainter, and at last died away. But the sound of my voice had broken the spell which cold and despair were fast throwing over me. A hundred devices ran swiftly through my mind, and each device was dismissed as impracticable. The helve of the axe caught my eye, and in an instant by an association of ideas it flashed across me that in the pocket of my dress there was a small knife—another sharp instrument by which I could extricate myself. With some difficulty I contrived to open the blade, and then withdrawing the knife from my pocket and gripping it as one who clings to the last hope of life, I strove to cut away the wood that held my fingers in its terrible vise. In vain! the wood was like iron. The motion of my arm and body brought back the pain which the cold had lulled, and I feared that I should faint.

After a moment's pause I adopted a last expedient. Nerving myself to the dreadful necessity, I disjointed my fingers and fell exhausted to the ground. My life was saved, but my left hand was a bleeding stump. The intensity of the cold stopped the flow of blood. I tore off a piece of my dress, bound up my fingers, and started for home. My complete exhaustion and the bitter cold made that the longest mile I had ever traveled. By nine o'clock that evening I had managed to drag myself, more dead than alive, to my mother's door, but it was more than a week before I could again leave the house.

Frances Anne Kemble: Life on a Plantation

Frances Anne Kemble was an English actress who came to the United States in 1832. She married a wealthy Philadelphian who, two years after their wedding, inherited a significant rice and cotton plantation in Georgia. Long opposed to the idea of slavery, Fanny Kemble was suddenly the owner of more than seven hundred slaves. Over the winter of 1838–39, she lived with her husband on the plantation, visiting the slave villages, talking with the men, women, and children *who worked the fields. Her husband did not share her horrors of slave life (it would subsequently lead to their divorce), and she was forced to confide in her diary— an extraordinary documentation of the inhumanity and indifference that slavery inspired. The publication in England in 1863 of* Journal of a Residence on a Georgia Plantation *was said to have influenced the British people in their decision not to come to the aid of the Confederacy in the Civil War. Though the modern reader will note her patronizing tone about her slaves, Kemble's voice is direct and without apology. This excerpt captures the essence of her observations during those two long months:*

I was summoned into the wooden porch, or piazza, of the house to see a poor woman who desired to speak to me. This was none other than the tall, emaciated-looking Negress who, on the day of our arrival, had embraced me and my nurse with such irresistible zeal. She appeared very ill today, and presently unfolded to me a most distressing history of bodily afflictions. She was the mother of a very large family, and complained to me that, what with childbearing and hard field labor, her back was almost broken in two.

With an almost savage vehemence of gesticulation, she suddenly tore up her scanty clothing and exhibited a spectacle with which I was inconceivably shocked and sickened. The facts, without any of her corroborating statements, bore tolerable witness to the hardships of her existence. I promised to attend to her ailments and give her proper remedies; but these are natural results, inevitable and irremediable ones, of improper treatment of the female frame; and, though there may be alleviation, there cannot be any cure when once the beautiful and wonderful structure has been thus made the victim of ignorance, folly, and wickedness.

After the departure of this poor woman, I walked down the settlement toward the infirmary, or hospital, calling in at one or two of the houses along the row. These cabins consist of one room, about twelve feet by fifteen, with a couple of closets, smaller and closer than the staterooms of a ship, divided off from the main room and each other by rough wooden partitions, in which the inhabitants sleep. They have almost all of them a rude bedstead, with the gray moss of the forests for mattress, and filthy, pestilential-looking blankets for covering.

Two families (sometimes eight and ten in number) reside in one of these huts, which are mere wooden frames pinned, as it were, to the earth by a brick chimney outside, whose enormous aperture within pours down a flood of air, but little counteracted by the miserable spark of fire which hardly sends an attenuated thread of lingering smoke up its huge throat. A wide ditch runs immediately at the back of these dwellings, which is filled and emptied daily by the tide. Attached to each hovel is a small scrap of ground for a garden, which, however, is for the most part untended and uncultivated.

Such of these dwellings as I visited today were filthy and wretched in the extreme, and exhibited that most deplorable consequence of ignorance and an abject condition, the inability of the inhabitants to secure and improve even such pitiful comfort as might yet be achieved by them. Instead of the order, neatness, and ingenuity which might convert even these miserable hovels into tolerable residences, there was the careless, reckless, filthy indolence which even the brutes do not exhibit in their lairs and nests, and which seemed incapable of applying to the uses of existence the few miserable means of comfort yet within their reach. . . .

In the midst of the floor, or squatting round the cold hearth, would be four or five little children from four to ten years old, the latter all with babies in their arms, the care of the infants being taken from the mothers (who are driven afield as soon as they recover from child labor) and devolved upon these poor little nurses, as they are called, whose business it is to watch the infant, and carry it to its mother whenever it may require nourishment. To these hardly human little beings I addressed my remonstrances about the filth, cold, and unnecessary wretchedness of their room, bidding the older boys and girls kindle up the fire, sweep the floor, and expel the poultry.

For a long time my very words seemed unintelligible to them, till, when I began to sweep and make up the fire, etc., they first fell to laughing and then imitating me. The incrustations of dirt on their hands, feet, and faces were my next object of attack, and the stupid Negro practice (by-the-by, but a short time since nearly universal in enlightened Europe) of keeping the babies with their feet bare, and their heads, already well capped by nature with their wooly hair, wrapped in half a dozen hot, filthy coverings.

Thus I traveled down the "street," in every dwelling endeavoring to awaken a new perception, that of cleanliness, sighing, as I went, over the futility of my own exertions, for how can slaves be improved? Nevertheless, thought I, let what can be done; for it may be that, the two being incompatible, improvement may yet expel slavery; and so it might, and surely would, if, instead of beginning at the end, I could but begin at the beginning of my task. If the mind and soul were awakened instead of mere physical good attempted, the physical good would result and the great curse vanish away; but my hands are tied fast, and this corner of the work is all that I may do. Yet it cannot be but, from my words and actions, some revelations should reach these poor people; and going in and out among them perpetually, I shall teach and they learn involuntarily a thousand things of deepest import. They must learn, and who can tell the fruit of that knowledge alone, that there are beings in the world, even with skins of a different color from their own, who have sympathy for their misfortunes, love for their virtues, and respect for their common nature—but oh! my heart is full almost to bursting as I walk among these most poor creatures.

The infirmary is a large two-story building, terminating the broad orange-planted space between the two rows of houses which form the first settlement; it is built of whitewashed wood, and contains four large-sized rooms. But how shall I describe to you the spectacle which was presented to me on entering the first of these? But half the casements, of which there were six, were glazed, and these were obscured with dirt, almost as much as the other windowless ones were darkened by the dingy shutters, which the shivering inmates had fastened to in order to protect themselves from the cold.

In the enormous chimney glimmered the powerless embers of a few sticks of wood, round which, however, as many of the sick women as could approach were cowering, some on wooden settles, most of them on the ground, excluding those who were too ill to rise; and these last poor wretches lay prostrate on the floor, without bed, mattress, or pillow, buried in tattered and filthy blankets, which, huddled round them as they lay strewn about, left hardly space to move upon the floor. And here, in their hour of sickness and suffering, lay those whose health and strength are spent in unrequited labor for us; those who, perhaps even yesterday, were being urged on to their unpaid task; those whose husbands, fathers, brothers, and sons were even at that hour sweating over the earth; whose produce was to buy for us all the luxuries which health can revel in, all the comforts which can alleviate sickness.

I stood in the midst of them, perfectly unable to speak, the tears pouring from my eyes at this sad spectacle of their misery, myself and my emotion alike strange and incomprehensible to them. Here lay women expecting every hour the terrors and agonies of childbirth; others who had just brought their doomed offspring into the world; others who were groaning over the anguish and bitter disappointment of miscarriages. Here lay some burning with fever;

others chilled with cold and aching with rheumatism, upon the hard cold ground, the drafts and dampness of the atmosphere increasing their sufferings, and dirt, noise, and stench, and every aggravation of which sickness is capable, combined in their condition. Here they lay like brute beasts, absorbed in physical suffering; unvisited by any of those Divine influences which may ennoble the dispensations of pain and illness, forsaken, as it seemed to me, of all good; and yet, O God, Thou surely hadst not forsaken them! Now pray take notice that this is the hospital of an estate where the owners are supposed to be humane, the overseer efficient and kind, and the Negroes remarkably well-cared for and comfortable.

As soon as I recovered from my dismay, I addressed old Rose, the midwife, who had charge of this room, bidding her open the shutters of such windows as were glazed and let in the light. I next proceeded to make up the fire; but, upon my lifting a log for that purpose, there was one universal outcry of horror, and old Rose, attempting to snatch it from me, exclaimed: "Let alone, missis—let be; what for you lift wood? You have nigger enough, missis, to do it!" I hereupon had to explain to them my view of the purposes for which hands and arms were appended to our bodies, and forthwith began making Rose tidy up the miserable apartment, removing all the filth and rubbish from the floor that could be removed, folding up in piles the blankets of the patients who were not using them, and placing, in rather more sheltered and comfortable positions, those who were unable to rise. It was all that I could do, and having enforced upon them all my earnest desire that they should keep their room swept and as tidy as possible, I passed on to the other room on the ground floor, and to the two above, one of which is appropriated to the use of the men who are ill.

They were all in the same deplorable condition, the upper rooms being rather the more miserable inasmuch as none of the windows were glazed at all, and they had, therefore, only the alternative of utter darkness, or killing drafts of air from the unsheltered casements. In all, filth, disorder, and misery abounded; the floor was the only bed, and scanty begrimed rags of blankets the only covering. I left this refuge for Mr. ——'s sick dependents with my clothes covered with dust and full of vermin, and with a heart heavy enough, as you will well believe.

Harriet Ann Jacobs:
My Story Ends with Freedom

"*I* was born a slave," wrote Harriet Ann Jacobs (1813–97) in her remarkable memoir Incidents in the Life a Slave Girl, "*but I never knew it till six years of happy childhood had passed away.*" *Pass away it did. She was sent first to the home of her mistress and then bequeathed, at the age of twelve, to her mistress's five-year-old niece. The memoir is painfully vivid, documenting the unwanted advances of her owner's father, the cruelty and callousness she was subjected to while coming of age. In 1835, at the age of twenty-two and now the mother of two children by a white man, Jacobs fled the closing noose of slavery. She spent seven years hiding, planning all the while for a way to help secure the safety of the two children (their father had promised his children freedom and reneged). In 1842 she made her way to New York and a decade later won her freedom. She published her astonishing memoir under a pseudonym and, as it had been edited by the abolitionist writer Lydia Child, many refused to believe that a self-educated black woman could have accomplished such an achievement on her own. History is filled with those who cannot recognize the authenticity of passion and outrage. Jacobs was the author; the life she lived was true. The following excerpt talks of the years in hiding while the world rolled on by her cramped attic space:*

They told me a place of concealment had been provided for me at my grandmother's. I could not imagine how it was possible to hide me in her house, every nook and corner of which was known to the Flint family. They told me to wait and see. We were rowed ashore, and went boldly through the streets, to my grandmother's. I wore my sailor's clothes, and had blackened my face with charcoal. I passed several people whom I knew. The father of my children came so near that I brushed against his arm; but he had no idea who it was.

"You must make the most of this walk," said my friend Peter, "for you may not have another very soon."

I thought his voice sounded sad. It was kind of him to conceal from me what a dismal hole was to be my home for a long, long time. . . .

A small shed had been added to my grandmother's house years ago. Some boards were laid across the joists at the top, and between these boards and the roof was a very small garret, never occupied by any thing but rats and mice. It was a pent roof, covered with nothing but shingles, according to the southern custom for such buildings. The garret was only nine feet long and seven wide. The highest part was three feet high, and sloped down abruptly to the loose board floor. There was no admission for either light or air. My uncle Phillip, who was a carpenter, had very skillfully made a concealed trap-door, which communicated with the storeroom. He had been doing this while I was waiting in the swamp. The storeroom opened upon a piazza. To this hole I was conveyed as soon as I entered the house. The air was stifling; the darkness total. A bed had been spread on the floor. I could sleep quite comfortably on one side; but the slope was so sudden that I could not turn on the other without hitting the roof. The rats and mice ran over my bed; but I was weary, and I slept such sleep as the wretched may, when a tempest has passed over them. Morning came. I knew it only by the noises I heard; for in my small den day and night were all the same. I suffered for air even more than for light. But I was not comfortless. I heard the voices of my children. There was joy and there was sadness in the sound. It made my tears flow. How I longed to speak to them! I was eager to look on their faces; but there was no hole, no crack, through which I could peep. This continued darkness was oppressive. It seemed horrible to sit or lie in a cramped position day after day, without one gleam of light. Yet I would have chosen this, rather than my lot as a slave, though white people considered it an easy one; and it was so compared with the fate of others. . . .

My food was passed up to me through the trap-door my uncle had contrived; and my grandmother, my uncle Phillip, and aunt Nancy would seize such opportunities as they could, to mount up there and chat with me at the opening. But of course this was not safe in the daytime. It must all be done in darkness. It was impossible for me to move in an erect position, but I crawled about my den for exercise. One day I hit my head against something, and found it was a gimlet. My uncle had left it sticking there when he made the trap-door. I was as rejoiced as Robinson Crusoe could have been at finding such a treasure. It put a lucky thought into my head. I said to myself, "Now I will have some light. Now I will see my children." I did not dare to begin my work during the daytime, for fear of attracting attention. But I groped round; and having found the side next the street, where I could frequently see my children, I stuck the gimlet in and waited for evening. I bored three rows of holes, one above another; then I bored out the interstices between. I thus succeeded in making one hole about an inch long and an inch broad. I sat by it till late into the night, to enjoy the little whiff of air that floated in. In the morning I watched for my children. The first person I saw in the street was Dr. Flint. I had a shuddering, superstitious feeling that it was a bad omen. Several familiar faces passed by. At last I heard the merry laugh of children, and presently two sweet little faces were looking up at me, as though they knew I was there, and were conscious of the joy they imparted. How I longed to *tell* them I was there! . . .

Autumn came, with a pleasant abatement of heat. My eyes had become accustomed to the dim light, and by holding my book or work in a certain position near the aperture I contrived to read and sew. That was a great relief to the tedious monotony of my life. But when winter came, the cold penetrated through the thin shingle roof, and I was dreadfully chilled. The winters there are not so long, or so severe, as in northern latitudes; but the houses are not built to shelter from cold, and my little den was peculiarly comfortless. The kind grandmother brought me bed-clothes and warm drinks. Often I was obliged to lie in bed all day to keep comfortable; but with all my precautions, my shoulders and feet were frostbitten. . . .

Dr. Flint and his family repeatedly tried to coax and bribe my children to tell something they had heard said about me. One day the doctor took them into a shop, and offered them some bright little silver pieces and gay handker-chiefs if they would tell where their mother was. Ellen shrank away from him, and would not speak; but Benny spoke up, and said, "Dr. Flint, I don't know where my mother is. I guess she's in New York; and when you go there again, I wish you'd ask her to come home, for I want to see her; but if you put her in jail, or tell her you'll cut her head off, I'll tell her to go right back."

~

Mr. Sands was elected [to Congress], an event which occasioned me some anxious thoughts. He had not emancipated my children, and if he should die they would be at the mercy of his heirs. Two little voices, that frequently met my ear, seemed to plead with me not to let their father depart without striving to make their freedom secure. Years had passed since I had spoken to him. I had not even seen him since the night I passed him, unrecognized, in my disguise of a sailor. I supposed he would call before he left, to say something to my grandmother concerning the children, and I resolved what course to take.

The day before his departure for Washington I made arrangements, to-wards evening, to get from my hiding-place into the storeroom below. I found myself so stiff and clumsy that it was with great difficulty I could hitch from one resting place to another. When I reached the storeroom my ankles gave way under me, and I sank exhausted on the floor. It seemed as if I could never use my limbs again. But the purpose I had in view roused all the strength I had. I crawled on my hands and knees to the window, and, screened behind a barrel, I waited for his coming. The clock struck nine, and I knew the steam-boat would leave between ten and eleven. My hopes were failing, but presently I heard his voice, saying to some one, "Wait for me a moment. I wish to see Aunt Martha." When he came out, as he passed the window, I said, "Stop one moment, and let me speak for my children." He started, hesitated, and then passed on, and went out of the gate. I closed the shutter I had partially opened, and sank down behind the barrel. I had suffered much; but seldom had I experienced a keener pang than I then felt. Had my children, then, become of so little consequence to him? And had he so little feeling for their wretched mother that he would not listen a moment while she pleaded for them? Painful memories were so busy within me, that I forgot I had not hooked the shutter, till I heard some one opening it. I looked up. He had come back. "Who called me?" said he, in a low tone. "I did," I replied. "Oh, Linda," said he, "I knew your voice; but I was afraid to answer, lest my friend should hear me. Why do you come here? Is it possible you risk yourself in this house? They are mad to allow it. I shall expect to hear that you are all ruined." I did not wish to implicate him, by letting him know my place of concealment; so I merely said, "I thought you would come to bid grandmother good-by, and so I came here to speak a few words to you about emancipating my children. Many changes may take place during the six months you are gone to Washington, and it does not seem right for you to expose them to the risk of such changes. I want nothing for myself; all I ask is, that you will free my children, or authorize some friend to do it, before you go."

He promised he would do it, and also expressed a readiness to make any arrangements whereby I could be purchased.

~

I hardly expect that the reader will credit me, when I affirm that I lived in that little dismal hole, almost deprived of light and air, and with no space to move my limbs, for nearly seven years. But it is a fact; and to me a sad one, even now; for my body still suffers from the effects of that long imprisonment, to say nothing of my soul. . . .

Harriet Tubman

Every year, during Black History Month, she rises from her legend and comes alive. We remember her as the woman who walked north from slavery and who, once free, knew she had to return to get others out. On the anvil of her will and spirit, she forged a mighty chain that pulled her black brothers and sisters up and out of bondage; the architect of the Underground Railroad, she hammered one safe house after another into a link of freedom.

They called her the Moses of her people and, like her namesake, her life's work was centered on getting her people out of bondage. She had faced the bleak and empty dawn when she herself had reached the promised land, the shining North, only to find that no arms waited to embrace her, no welcoming words or encouragement. She never forgot her shock at being a lone black woman with no money, no friends, no home. It was an empty, scary feeling because when you are no one, you are likely to have to find out who you are. But Tubman recognized that the grim prospect of a life to be made from scratch was better than no opportunity to start a life at all. She understood that all across the South were men and women who must have the right to face their own self-creation, however hard, however daunting.

There are many stories of Harriet Tubman, though one is particularly haunting. It was a summer night. The heat had not left the fields and the air was thick, oppressive. Tubman, still a slave, was called by her vexed mistress to the main house. It didn't matter that Tubman had worked all day in the fields, was tired and sore and anxious to sleep. The mistress had a baby who was sick and would not stop crying. The mother had no patience for the child who was only quiet when its cradle was rocked. Tubman was instructed to rock the cradle all night and the mistress returned to her bed where, coiled on the pillow beside her, lay a horsewhip. When Tubman fell asleep, a sickening and immediate chain reaction commenced: The cradle was stilled, the baby woke and cried, the mother arose and savagely whipped Tubman across her neck and back (she would carry scars from that night the rest of her life). It was the mark of Tubman's awesome spirit that she took from the horror of that night a valuable admonition, which she would use to greater purpose than her mistress. Be alert. Stay awake. Do not rest. "I had reasoned it out in my mind," she said later, "there was one of two things I had a *right* to, liberty or death; if I could not have one, I would have the other." In the long night marches, as she brought hundreds of slaves to freedom, she kept herself and them moving through woods and thickets, crossing rivers, climbing mountains. Be alert. Stay awake. Do not rest. Traveling along moonlit roads to darkened houses, she did not hesitate, when her comrades tired, faltered or wanted to go back, to offer them the same choice she had reasoned out so clearly. First she used the softer lashes of persuasion; then she cajoled them, spoke to them of the life ahead, pushed them through the fear and fatigue. When, at last, one or another finally gave up and turned south to return to the horrific home that was, at least, familiar, she would draw her pistol and level it without remorse: "Dead niggers tell no tales—go on or die" she would say. She knew what they could not—that the only way home was out. Freedom had no acceptable alternative.

Harriet Tubman did more than escape slavery, though that feat required courage enough; she returned to hell to bring others out, and such is the true heroic journey.

Sojourner Truth: "Ain't I a woman?"

Most beautiful soul. Brave woman who walked out of slavery to freedom. Talker whose tongue could bring pause to haters and fear mongers. Brilliant archer of metaphor. Sojourner Truth carried with her a Book of Life, and she took the signature of interesting people she met along the way as she traveled the North speaking out against slavery. Lincoln signed her book. People who brought a grandeur to their character regardless of station signed as well. She reasoned with a fresh and honest care; she spoke with passion and calm all at once. She delivered the speech below to a packed crowd at the Ohio Women's Rights Convention, who feared being addressed by a black woman. Abolitionism and women's rights were uneasy allies at first, but Truth recognized their natural and abiding connection. She works the connection with great subtlety, shifting the emphasis so that her listeners are touched by her gender and her race at the same time. As she took to the podium, many in the crowd hissed and booed. Truth pressed on and soon enough brought everyone to their feet with her ringing address. "I have never in my life," wrote an eyewitness, "seen anything have the magical influence that subdued the snobbish spirit of the day":

Well, children, where there is so much racket there must be something out of kilter. I think that 'twixt the Negroes of the South and the women at the North, all talking about rights, the white man will be in a fix pretty soon. But what's all this here talking about? That man over there [the previous speaker] says that women need to be helped into carriages and lifted over ditches, and to have the best place everywhere? Nobody ever helps me into carrriages, or over mud puddles, or gives me any best place. And ain't I a woman? Look at me! Look at my arm. I have plowed and planted and gathered into barns, and no man could head me. And ain't I a woman? I could work as much and eat as much as a man—when I could get it—and bear the lash as well. And ain't I a woman? I have borne thirteen children, and seen them most all sold off into slavery, and when I cried out with a mother's grief, none but Jesus heard me! And ain't I a woman?

They talk about this thing in the head, what's this they call it? [Someone near her whispers "intellect."] That's it, honey. What's that got to do with women's rights or Negroes' rights? If my cup won't hold but a pint and yours holds a quart, wouldn't you be mean not to let me have my little half-measure full?

Then that little man in black there [a minister], he says women can't have as much rights as men, 'cause Christ wasn't a woman. Where did your Christ come from? Where did your Christ come from? *Where did your Christ come from?* From God and a woman! Man had nothing to do with Him. If the first woman God ever made was strong enough to turn the world upside down all alone, these together ought to be able to turn it back and get it right side up again. And now they is asking to do it, the men better let them.

Obliged to you for hearing on me, and now old Sojourner hasn't got nuthing more to say.

"It is not my shame, but yours . . ."

From her new home in Battle Creek, Michigan, Sojourner Truth traveled into Indiana on a speaking tour with her old friend from New England, Parker Pillsbury. Indiana was a rough place for abolitionists. The rolling hills and rich black earth had attracted many settlers from the South. More than once hecklers made it impossible for the tall, old woman and the stocky black-bearded minister to hold their meetings.

In Kosciusko County, a rumor was circulated that Sojourner Truth was an imposter, a man disguised in women's clothing. A large number of pro-slavery people turned up at one of the meetings. Their leader, a local doctor, had bet forty dollars that Sojourner was a man. Just as she started to speak, he stepped forward, hands raised above his head.

"Hold on," he shouted. "There is strong doubt in the minds of many persons here regarding the sex of the next speaker. A majority of us, in fact, are convinced that the speaker is not a woman but a man disguised as a woman. For the speaker's own sake, we demand, if it be a she, that she expose her breast to the gaze of some of the ladies present so that they may report back and dispel the audience's doubts."

Sojourner noticed many of the women flushing with embarrassment and anger at the man's suggestion. Pillsbury, who was hearing the rumor for the first time, strode quickly toward the doctor. His hand was raised and his face was crimson. Sojourner feared he would hurl the doctor to the ground. She rose hastily.

"Why do you suppose me to be a man?"

"Your voice is not the voice of a woman," replied the doctor. "It is the voice of a man and we believe that you are a man." He turned to face the audience and called out, "Let's put the matter to a vote. Is this person a man?"

The crowd roared "Aye."

Quietly, her fingers steady, Sojourner began to untie the white kerchief across her breast. Slowly her hands moved to undo the buttons at the top of her dress.

"I will show my breast," she announced as the last button came undone, "but to the entire congregation." And as she opened her blouse, she added with slow emphasis, "It is not my shame, but yours that I do this."

Julia Ward Howe Writes "Mine Eyes Have Seen the Glory"

It would be impossible for me to say how many times I have been called upon to rehearse the circumstances under which I wrote the "Battle Hymn of the Republic." I have also had occasion more than once to state the simple story in writing. As this oft-told tale has no unimportant part in the story of my life, I will briefly add it to these records. I distinctly remember that a feeling of discouragement came over me as I drew near the city of Washington at the time already mentioned. I thought of the women of my acquaintance whose sons or husbands were fighting our great battle; the women themselves serving in the hospitals, or busying themselves with the work of the Sanitary Commission. My husband, as already said, was beyond the age of military service, my eldest son but a stripling; my youngest was a child of not more than two years. I could not leave my nursery to follow the march of our armies, neither had I the practical deftness which the preparing and packing of sanitary stores demanded. Something seemed to say to me, "You would be glad to serve, but you cannot help any one; you have nothing to give, and there is nothing for you to do." Yet, because of my sincere desire, a word was given me to say, which did strengthen the hearts of those who fought in the field and of those who languished in the prison.

We were invited, one day, to attend a review of troops at some distance from the town. While we were engaged in watching the manoeuvres, a sudden movement of the enemy necessitated immediate action. The review was discontinued, and we saw a detachment of soldiers gallop to the assistance of a small body of our men who were in imminent danger of being surrounded and cut off from retreat. The regiments remaining on the field were ordered to march to their cantonments. We returned to the city very slowly, of necessity, for the troops nearly filled the road. My dear minister was in the carriage with me, as were several other friends. To beguile the rather tedious drive, we sang from time to time snatches of the army songs so popular at that time, concluding, I think, with

> *"John Brown's body lies a-mouldering in the ground;*
> *His soul is marching on."*

The soldiers seemed to like this, and answered back, "Good for you!" Mr. Clarke said, "Mrs. Howe, why do you not write some good words for that stirring tune?" I replied that I had often wished to do this, but had not as yet found in my mind any leading toward it.

I went to bed that night as usual, and slept, according to my wont, quite soundly. I awoke in the gray of the morning twilight; and as I lay waiting for the dawn, the long lines of the desired poem began to twine themselves in my mind. Having thought out all the stanzas, I said to myself, "I must get up and write these verses down, lest I fall asleep again and forget them." So, with a sudden effort, I sprang out of bed, and found in the dimness an old stump of a pen which I remembered to have used the day before. I scrawled the verses almost without looking at the paper. I had learned to do this when, on previous occasions, attacks of versification had visited me in the night, and I feared to have recourse to a light lest I should wake the baby, who slept near me. I was always obliged to decipher my scrawl before another night should intervene, as it was only legible while the matter was fresh in my mind. At this time, having completed my writing, I returned to bed and fell asleep, saying to myself, "I like this better than most things that I have written."

The poem, which was soon after published in the "Atlantic Monthly," was somewhat praised on its appearance, but the vicissitudes of the war so engrossed public attention that small heed was taken of literary matters. I knew, and was content to know, that the poem soon found its way to the camps, as I heard from time to time of its being sung in chorus by the soldiers.

As the war went on, it came to pass that Chaplain McCabe, newly released from Libby Prison, gave a public lecture in Washington, and recounted some of his recent experiences. Among them was the following: He and the other Union prisoners occupied one large, comfortless room, in which the floor was their only bed. An official in charge of them told them, one evening, that the Union arms had just sustained a terrible defeat. While they sat together in great sorrow, the negro who waited upon them whispered to one man that the officer had given them false information, and that the Union soldiers had, on the contrary, achieved an important victory. At this good news they all rejoiced, and presently made the walls ring with my Battle Hymn, which they sang in chorus, Chaplain McCabe leading. The lecturer recited the poem with such effect that those present began to inquire, "Who wrote this Battle Hymn?" It now became one of the leading lyrics of the war. In view of its success, one of my good friends said, "Mrs. Howe ought to die now, for she has done the best that she will ever do." I was not of this opinion, feeling myself still "full of days' works," although I did not guess at the new experiences which then lay before me.

"But Life is not all Love."

The following reminiscence of Emily Dickinson by her cousin Clara Newman Turner speaks for itself, a touching yet vivid portrait of one of America's great poets:

My own personal acquaintance with Emily Dickinson began when I was a young school girl, and many were the interests I took to her at our trysting-place, on the top stair of the flight leading down to a side hall. It was almost dark but opened into many retreats for my fawn-like friend. On a few never-to-be-forgotten occasions she read to me there a verse or two before enclosing in some friendly letter asking me to tell her what it meant to me and calling me her little *World*. I think I can never feel more proud than when she honored me by thinking I understood her. . . .

In the first years of my knowing her, she would sometimes come across the grounds to her brother's home and spend an hour in chatting with us all. Gradually these "angel visits became few and far between" indeed, and more and more quaint like herself. For instance—I remember, as I confided my hopes and fears to her ever-sympathetic listening ear before the severe examinations (taken alone) for entrance to the High School—then equal to the College examination—she would only repeat "I am sure of success, I see nothing else," until I met it brave in her courage. The morning of the dreaded ordeal came a little note on this wise,—"A little flower is sitting beside me waiting to be a Crown."

Released from my hard day only just before supper, I had no time to take her word that her kind prophecy was true, but I had no need, for, being summoned from the table, I found Emily in the dark just outside the door holding out the fair flower, and her sweet voice said, "Nobody came to tell us, and the little flower was so impatient to be a crown, it insisted upon bringing me over."

As this retirement grew upon her she rarely saw anyone outside her immediate home circle, although one and another of the Literati of the country have come—at times far—to see her. A glass of wine and a flower, accompanied with a note or line (as in one instance with a Cape Jessamine, the quotation "I, Jesus, send mine angel") and the visitor must be sufficed, if the Spirit within that strange little self did not move her to be seen.

I have been asked repeatedly what led to this withdrawing of herself from the world—was it some disappointment? If, by this, disappointment in love is meant, implying love unrequited, I answer almost an indignant *No*. If disappointment in *Life* is meant, consider her intensely sensitive nature, and exceeding individual mind and its longings, and you will readily accept my reply that I am sure there were *many*—but Life is not all Love, you know, although Love may be the sweetest part of all life. It began by simply not joining in some things which were not congenial and a gradual withdrawing from many things which we none of us hardly realized so subtly did it come, until *others* spoke of her as a Recluse. You know how imperceptibly such changes *can* approach.

One or two more little home incidents. Her little nephew, boy-like, had a way of leaving anything superfluous to his immediate needs at Grandma's. After one of these little "Sins of Omission," over came his high-top rubber boots, standing erect and spotless on a silver tray, their tops running over with

Emily's flowers. At another time the little overcoat was returned with each velvet pocket pinned down, and a card with "Come in" on one, and "Knock" on the other. The "Come in" proved to be raisins;—the "Knock," cracked nuts. Do you blame the little fellow for leaving his things round over there? The boy was my care, but I never could be generous enough to discourage the failing.

She was very fond of music, and at one time played not a little on the piano. When I knew her, her Repertoire was quite limited—consisting of but three tunes. One of these she called "The Devil," and it was weird and quaint enough to warrant the title. She had learned it on an old-fashioned piano, two octaves shorter than the modern "Chickering" which then stood in her home parlor, and always before seating herself to play, she covered these superfluous octaves, that the keyboard might accord with her education. After she became more reclusive, and gave up the piano entirely I had the pleasure of playing for her and quite often would come to me just some little word as, "Emily is tired, and the sweet voice in the parlor cannot speak to her alone," or "There's a voice in the down-stairs; I call, but it does not answer." I answered the summons when I could, and never without some acknowledgement. Sometimes a flower on the piano stool, again a little plate of fresh cookies, or, best of all, a word written out for me. How I regret we had not known the Angel-Genius we were entertaining, and so had preserved these little missives! Is it always "Unawares"? What hourly caution lies in the answer!

Returning each year after my marriage, for short stays to her own home, so long as my Uncle lived, my visits with Emily were always in her own room after the evening was done below stairs, and by appointment her door was left ajar. "I don't speak things like the rest" was her apology and her "speaking things" like herself would delight my very soul often far into the night, or even early morning. I was not present at Mr. Dickinson's funeral. The following Christmas when I enclosed a Christmas wreath for his grave with the little remembrances for the living, Emily wrote thus in acknowledgement, "I am sure you must have remembered that Father had become 'as little children' or you would never have dared send him a Christmas gift, for you know how he frowned upon Santa Claus, and all such prowling gentlemen."

The next time I saw her was at the burial of her Mother. Arriving only in time for the service, I saw nothing of Emily, save a line asking for a word as I went away. On our way to the train, we stopped at the door just a moment and Emily, calling me *behind* the door, looking pale and worn with her anxious watching and grief, said she just wanted to thank Mr. Turner and myself for coming so far "to speak to Mother. She cannot thank you herself today, you know, but some other day," and this was the last time I ever saw her sweet face.

She *died* (as we say) quite suddenly May 15th, '86, of a disease which owing to her extreme reticence and retirement of disposition, and reluctance to confer with a physician, was hastened, no doubt, when it might possibly have been retarded, though not cured. Two years before—breaking through all reserve, and at night—she had had a chill while ministering to death in her brother's house, and was taken home unconscious. Three times during those two years she had similar attacks, and from little casual remarks doubtless she knew within herself that her note of warning had been sounded and she had heard. On Thursday, May 13th, '86, the message came very tenderly, for she became unconscious almost at once and so remained until Saturday afternoon, when Death gave her Life "the other side." I think it must have been during these two years, (although there is no date) that she wrote these poems.

Greatly to my regret, I was unable to attend Emily's funeral, being called to sickness by a telegram received the same hour with that which called me to her. They folded her in a little white wrap I had sewed for her myself the last Christmas, little dreaming I was weaving her shroud, and she lay in her white casket in the hall of her father's house, while the bees and the butterflies she had immortalized, buzzed a Requiem without the open door. A knot of field blue violets lay at her throat, and a wreath of the same modest flower was the only decoration on her casket. The service was very simple. The Pastor of the Congregational Church of Amherst read from the Scriptures. Rev. Mr. Jenkins of Portland led in prayer, and Col. Higginson followed with the reading of Emily Brontë's last Poem, prefacing the reading by this introduction, "I will read a poem, our friend who has just now put on Immortality, and who seemed scarce ever to have taken it off, used to read to her sister."

The brief service concluded, six stalwart men, with whose faces she had been familiar, and who had rendered glad service as she toiled among her outdoor friends—the flowers—lifted her on their shoulders and bore her—into the street? Ah no! That would have been a way almost as strange and unknown for her, to pass, as is to us today that upon which she has entered, while we stand without, as yet unbidden to follow.

The Cemetery lay three fields away, and the bars being lowered between— the light little burden led the way through meadows *filled* with buttercups and daisies, and they stood sentinels of her path, or bowed their heads as the funeral train brushed them by.

Angelina Grimké Speaks to the Mob (1838)

*T*wo sisters, Angelina and Sarah Grimké. Two daughters born into South Carolina society at the turn of the nineteenth century, prepared for a life of ease and
privilege. What a strange course their lives were to follow! True women of conscience, they would spend their lives in vivid opposition to the society in which
they came of age. The price they paid for speaking out against slavery (to packed
crowds in the North) and on behalf of women's rights was social isolation and
bitter, venomous criticism from Southerners and angry Northern men alike. Writers
of books, articles, and political tracts on a range of subjects, they never rested
against injustice. By their old age, they were testing the 15th Amendment in Massachusetts by trying to vote. Angelina, the younger, was bolder, more outspoken. Her
speech below in Philadelphia in 1838 was delivered despite a furious crowd outside
the building where she spoke. Sarah's speech (see page 392), under less dramatic
circumstances, nevertheless reminds us in words as true and direct as if spoken last
week:

Pennsylvania Hall was one of the most commodious and splendid buildings in
the city, scientifically ventilated and brilliantly lighted with gas. It cost upward
of $40,000. Over the forum, in large gold letters, was the motto, "Virtue,
Liberty, Independence." On the platform were superb chairs, sofas, and desk
covered with blue silk damask; everything throughout the hall was artistic and
complete. Abolitionists from all parts of the country hastened to be present at
the dedication; and among the rest came representatives of the Woman's National Convention, held in New York one year before.

Notices had been posted about the city threatening the speedy destruction
of this temple of liberty. During this three days' Convention, the enemy was
slowly organizing the destructive mob that finally burned that grand edifice to
the ground. There were a large number of strangers in the city from the South,
and many Southern students attending the medical college, who were all active
in the riot. The crowds of women and colored people who had attended the
Convention intensified the exasperation of the mob. Black men and white
women, walking side by side in and out of the hall, was too much for the
foreign plebeian and the Southern patrician.

As it was announced that on the evening of the third day some ladies were
to speak, a howling mob surrounded the building. In the midst of the tumult
Mr. Garrison introduced Maria Chapman, [she was the positive power of so

much anti-slavery work, that James Russell Lowell spoke of her as "the coiled-up mainspring of the movement"] of Boston, who rose, and waving her hand to the audience to become quiet, tried in a few eloquent and appropriate remarks to bespeak a hearing for Angelina E. Grimké, the gifted orator from South Carolina, who, having lived in the midst of slavery all her life, could faithfully describe its cruelties and abominations. But the indescribable uproar outside, cries of fire, and yells of defiance, were a constant interruption, and stones thrown against the windows a warning of coming danger. But through it all this brave Southern woman stood unmoved, except by the intense earnestness of her own great theme . . . :

Do you ask, then, "What has the North to do?" I answer, cast out first the spirit of slavery from your own hearts, and then lend your aid to convert the South. Each one present has a work to do, be his or her situation what it may, however limited their means or insignificant their supposed influence. The great men of this country will not do this work; the Church will never do it. A desire to please the world, to keep the favor of all parties and of all conditions, makes them dumb on this and every other unpopular subject.

As a Southerner, I feel that it is my duty to stand up here to-night and bear testimony against slavery. I have seen it! I have seen it! I know it has horrors that can never be described. I was brought up under its wing. I witnessed for many years its demoralizing influences and its destructiveness to human happiness. I have never seen a happy slave. I have seen him dance in his chains, it is true, but he was not happy. There is a wide difference between happiness and mirth. Man can not enjoy happiness while his manhood is destroyed. Slaves, however, may be, and sometimes are mirthful. When hope is extinguished, they say, "Let us eat and drink, for to-morrow we die." [Here stones were thrown at the windows—a great noise without and commotion within.]

What is a mob? What would the breaking of every window be? What would the levelling of this hall be? Any evidence that we are wrong, or that slavery is a good and wholesome Institution? What if the mob should now burst in upon us, break up our meeting, and commit violence upon our persons, would that be anything compared with what the slaves endure? No, no; and we do not remember them, "as bound with them," if we shrink in the time of peril, or are unwilling to sacrifice ourselves, if need be, for their sake. [Great noise.] I thank the Lord that there is yet life enough left to feel the truth, even though it rages at it; that conscience is not so completely seared as to be unmoved by the truth of the living God. [Another outbreak of the mob and confusion in the house.]

How wonderfully constituted is the human mind! How it resists, as long as it can, all efforts to reclaim it from error! I feel that all this disturbance is but an evidence that our efforts are the best that could have been adopted, or else the friends of slavery would not care for what we say and do. The South know what we do. I am thankful that they are reached by our efforts. Many times have I wept in the land of my birth over the system of slavery. I knew of none who sympathized in my feelings; I was unaware that any efforts were made to deliver the oppressed; no voice in the wilderness was heard calling on the people to repent and do works meet for repentance, and my heart sickened within me. Oh, how should I have rejoiced to know that such efforts as these were being made. I only wonder that I had such feelings. But in the midst of temptation I was preserved, and my sympathy grew warmer, and my hatred of slavery more inveterate, until at last I have exiled myself from my native land, because I could no longer endure to hear the wailing of the slave.

I fled to the land of Penn; for here, thought I, sympathy for the slave will surely be found. But I found it not. The people were kind and hospitable, but the slave had no place in their thoughts. I therefore shut up my grief in my own heart. I remembered that I was a Carolinian, from a State which framed this iniquity by law. Every Southern breeze wafted to me the discordant tones of weeping and wailing, shrieks and groans, mingled with prayers and blasphemous curses. My heart sank within me at the abominations in the midst of which I had been born and educated. What will it avail, cried I, in bitterness of spirit, to expose to the gaze of strangers the horrors and pollutions of slavery, when there is no ear to hear nor heart to feel and pray for the slave? But how different do I feel now! Animated with hope, nay, with an assurance of the triumph of liberty and good-will to man, I will lift up my voice like a trumpet, and show this people what they can do to influence the Southern mind and overthrow slavery. [Shouting, and stones against the windows.]

We often hear the question asked, "What shall we do?" Here is an opportunity. Every man and every woman present may do something by showing that we fear not a mob, and in the midst of revilings and threatenings, pleading the cause of those who are ready to perish. Let me urge every one to buy the books written on this subject; read them, and lend them to your neighbors. Give your money no longer for things which pander to pride and lust, but aid in scattering "the living coals of truth upon the naked heart of the nation"; in circulating appeals to the sympathies of Christians in behalf of the outraged slave.

But it is said by some, our "books and papers do not speak the truth"; why, then, do they not contradict what we say? They can not. Moreover, the South has entreated, nay, commanded us, to be silent; and what greater evidence of the truth of our publications could be desired?

Women of Philadelphia! allow me as a Southern woman, with much attachment to the land of my birth, to entreat you to come up to this work. Especially, let me urge you to petition. Men may settle this and other questions at the ballot-box, but you have no such right. It is only through petitions that you can reach the Legislature. It is, therefore, peculiarly your duty to petition. Do you say, "It does no good!" The South already turns pale at the number sent. They have read the reports of the proceedings of Congress, and they have seen that among other petitions were very many from the women of the North on the subject of slavery. Men who hold the rod over slaves rule in the councils of the nations; and they deny our right to petition and remonstrate against abuses of our sex and our kind. We have these rights, however, from our God. Only let us exercise them, and, though often turned away unanswered, let us remember the influence of importunity upon the unjust judge, and act accordingly. The fact that the South looks jealously upon our measures shows that they are effectual. There is, therefore, no cause for doubting or despair.

It was remarked in England that women did much to abolish slavery in her colonies. Nor are they now idle. Numerous petitions from them have recently been presented to the Queen to abolish apprenticeship, with its cruelties, nearly equal to those of the system whose place it supplies. One petition, two miles and a quarter long, has been presented. And do you think these labors will be in vain? Let the history of the past answer. When the women of these States send up to Congress such a petition our legislators will arise, as did those of England, and say: "When all the maids and matrons of the land are knocking at our doors we must legislate." Let the zeal and love, the faith and works of our English sisters quicken ours; that while the slaves continue to suffer, and when they shout for deliverance, we may feel the satisfaction of "having done what we could."

The mob burned the building down but the words of brave Grimké remain.

Sarah Grimké: "Woman must be willing to see herself as she is . . ."

When an insect emerges with struggles from its chrysalis state, how feeble are all its movements, how its wings hang powerless until the genial air has dried and strengthened them, how patiently the insect tries again and again to spread them, and visit the flowers which bloom around, till at last it enjoys the recompense of its labors in the nectar and the fragrance of the garden.

This illustrates the present condition of Woman. She is just emerging from the darkness and ignorance by which she has been shrouded. She looks forth from her chrysalis and sees the natural and intellectual world lying around her clothed in radiant beauty, and inviting her to enter and possess this magnificent inheritance. How came I, she asks, to be excluded from all these precious privileges? I will arise and go to my Father and say, "Father, permit me to share the labors of my brethren and partake of the fruits which they enjoy." "Go, my daughter," is the paternal response. "Be unto man, in an infinitely higher sense than heretofore, a help-meet." How is woman fulfilling her divine mission? Is she looking on the benefits she is commissioned to bestow on the human race, or is she keeping her eye on her own interests and seeking her own elevation, with little of that expansive benevolence, that philosophical foresight which seeks the development of all?

Woman is now in the transition state, a glorious mission is before her, a glorious destiny awaits her. To fulfill that mission, to be worthy of that destiny, she must patiently wait and quietly hope, blessing those who scorn and deride her feeble and often unsuccessful efforts, to free herself from her entanglements. She must expect many failures in her attempts to emancipate herself from the thralldom of public opinion. Those who have long held the reins of power and the rank of superiority, naturally look with distrust on a movement which threatens to overturn long established customs and transform the baby and the toy into an intellectual being, desiring equal rights with themselves and asserting her claim to all the immunities they enjoy. Woman must be willing to see herself as she is, the slave of fashion, assuming all the Proteus forms she invents, without reference to health or convenience. She must remember how few of us give evidence of sufficient development to warrant our claims; and whilst we feel a divine impulse to proceed in achieving the enlargement of woman, whilst we hear a voice saying, "Ye have compassed this mountain long enough; speak to the people that they go forward," let us not be dismayed at the hindrances we shall encounter from those whom we are laboring to release from the swaddling bands of infancy, or the grave-clothes of superstition, time-honored opinion and crushing circumstances. We are now in a perilous and difficult position. We feel all the inconveniences of our past condition, all the disadvantages and uneasiness of the one we are constrained to occupy, and see in bold relief all the advantages which a change will yield us. But let us remember that our transition state, although replete with temptations and suffering, is necessary to our improvement; we need it to strengthen us and enable us to bear hardships as good soldiers of truth.

To regard any state of society as fixed, is to regard it as the ultimate good, as the best condition to which we can attain. But when man has progressed, when his morality and his religion have assumed a higher tone, it is impossible to perpetuate his childhood, or to give permanence to institutions and opinions whose days are numbered. When reform has truth for its basis and is instinct with the life of progression, no power can dress it in the habiliments of the grave, and bury it out of sight, either in the Potter's-field or under the magnificent mausoleum. There is nothing so precious to man as progress; he has defended it with his heart's best blood, and according to his development has aided it, although sometimes in his blindness he has scattered fire and sword, destruction and misery around, in endeavoring to force mankind to adopt the truths he thought essential to progress. "Woman has come on the stage," says Horace Mann, "6,000 years after man, to profit by his misdeeds and correct his errors." Until now, the world was not prepared to receive, in full measure, the hallowed influence which woman is designed to shed. Her holy mission is to bring peace on earth and goodwill to man. She does not ask for irresponsible power; she has seen that from the earliest records of the human race the possession of such power is fraught with danger, that it has always made tyrants. She feels Divinity stirring within her, and its irrepressible aspirings can not, should not, be controlled. Mankind have always rejected the means appointed by Infinite Wisdom to assist their upward flight. Let us then go calmly forward, alike regardless of the scorn and ridicule of the shallow, the grave denunciations of the bigot, or the weighty counsel of the narrow-minded and selfish, who would point out the exact position fitted for us to occupy, and with seeming condescension invite us to fill some posts of honor and profit, while they undertake to confine us within their bounds, leaving nothing to our good sense, intelligence, intuitive desires, and aspiring hopes. The truth is, "It is not in man that walketh to direct his steps." God alone is competent to do this, and in the present movement His power, wisdom, and will, are so conspicuous, that it will be well to set no bounds to His work, but let it have free course, expecting that contradictions and inconsistencies will mar it, but believing that those contradictions will cease, those inconsistencies disappear, and the perfected human being be developed.

If we adopt as our watchword the language of Margaret Fuller, we can not but overcome all obstacles, outlive all opposition: "Give me Truth. Cheat me by no illusion. Oh, the granting of this prayer is sometimes terrible; I walk over the burning plowshares and they sear my feet—yet nothing but Truth will do."

Lucretia Mott Remembered

Lucretia Mott was a Quaker, a teacher, a mother of six children, a wife of fifty-seven years, an abolitionist, an effective public speaker and, arguably, one of the greatest of the nineteenth-century women activists. Anti-slavery was her first cause. She spoke out in black churches, led a formal boycott of Southern goods, and founded the American Anti-Slavery Society. Following the passage of the Anti-Fugitive Act of 1850, Mott openly welcomed runaway slaves in direct and public violation of a law she found abhorrent. The Civil War sorely tested her pacifist principles and she pressed for peace with vigor. Following the war, however, she resumed an aggressive new course with her advocacy of women's rights. She considered herself an independent voice: Surprisingly, the right to vote was not a passion and she resisted the divorce laws deemed so important by her sisters in the cause (her critics argued that her happy marriage to a man who supported her life's work made her blind to the issue). Her essential goal was to gain and secure the civil rights for women and blacks. The excerpt below from the monumental History of Woman Suffrage *offers us some touching details on the life and character of this remarkable woman:*

There are often periods in the lives of earnest, imaginative beings, when some new book or acquaintance comes to them like an added sun in the heavens, lighting the darkest recesses and chasing every shadow away. Thus came Lucretia Mott to me, at a period in my young days when all life's problems seemed inextricably tangled; when, like Noah's dove on the waters, my soul found no solid resting-place in the whole world of thought. The misery of the multitude was too boundless for comprehension, too hopeless for tender feeling; despair supplanted all other emotions, and the appalling views of the future threw their dark shadows over the sweetest and most innocent pleasures of life. Before meeting Mrs. Mott, I had heard a few men of liberal opinions discuss various political, religious, and social theories, but with my first doubt of my father's absolute wisdom came a distrust of all men's opinions on the character and sphere of woman; and I naturally inferred that if their judgments were unsound on a question I was sure I did understand, they were quite likely to be so on those I did not. Hence, I often longed to meet some woman who had sufficient confidence in herself to frame and hold an opinion in the face of opposition, a woman who understood the deep significance of life to whom I could talk freely; my longings were answered at last.

In June, 1840, I met Mrs. Mott for the first time, in London. Crossing the Atlantic in company with James G. Birney, then the Liberty Party candidate for President, soon after the bitter schism in the anti-slavery ranks, he described to me as we walked the deck day after day, the women who had fanned the flames of dissension, and had completely demoralized the anti-slavery ranks. As my first view of Mrs. Mott was through his prejudices, no prepossessions in her favor biased my judgment. When first introduced to her at our hotel in Great Queen Street, with the other ladies from Boston and Philadelphia who were delegates to the World's Convention, I felt somewhat embarrassed, as I was the only lady present who represented the "Birney faction," though I really knew nothing of the merits of the division, having been outside the world of reforms. Still, as my husband and my cousin, Gerrit Smith, were on that side, I supposed they would all have a feeling of hostility toward me. However, Mrs. Mott, in her sweet, gentle way, received me with great cordiality and courtesy, and I was seated by her side at dinner.

No sooner were the viands fairly dispensed, than several Baptist ministers began to rally the ladies on having set the Abolitionists all by the ears in America, and now proposing to do the same thing in England. I soon found that the pending battle was on woman's rights, and that unwittingly I was by marriage on the wrong side. As I had thought much on this question in regard

to the laws, Church action, and social usages, I found myself in full accord
with the other ladies, combating most of the gentlemen at the table; our only
champion, George Bradburn, was too deaf to hear a word that was said. In
spite of constant gentle nudgings by my husband under the table, and frowns
from Mr. Birney opposite, the tantalizing tone of the conversation was too
much for me to maintain silence. Calmly and skillfully Mrs. Mott parried all
their attacks, now by her quiet humor turning the laugh on them, and then by
her earnestness and dignity silencing their ridicule and sneers. I shall never
forget the look of recognition she gave me when she saw by my remarks that I
fully comprehended the problem of woman's rights and wrongs. How beautiful
she looked to me that day.

I had always regarded a Quaker woman, as one does a Sister of Charity, a
being above ordinary mortals, ready to be translated at any moment. I had
never spoken to one before, nor been near enough to touch the hem of a
garment. Mrs. Mott was to me an entire new revelation of womanhood. I
sought every opportunity to be at her side, and continually plied her with
questions, and I shall never cease to be grateful for the patience and seeming
pleasure with which she fed my hungering soul. Seeing the lions in London
together, on one occasion with a large party we visited the British Museum,
where it is supposed all people go to see the wonders of the world. On entering,
Mrs. Mott and myself sat down near the door to rest a few moments, telling the
party to go on, that we would follow. They accordingly explored all the departments of curiosities, supposing we were slowly following at a distance; but
when they returned, after an absence of three hours, there we sat in the same
spot, having seen nothing but each other, wholly absorbed in questions of
theology and social life. She had told me of the doctrines and divisions among
"Friends," of the inward light, of Elias Hicks, of Channing, of a religion of
practical life, of Mary Wollstonecroft, her social theories, and her demands of
equality for women. I had been reading Combe's "Constitution of Man" and
"Moral Philosophy," Channing's works, and Mary Wollstonecroft, though all
tabooed by orthodox teachers, but I had never heard a woman talk what, as a
Scotch Presbyterian, I had scarcely dared to think.

On the following Sunday I went to hear Mrs. Mott preach in a Unitarian
church. Though I had never heard a woman speak, yet I had long believed she
had the right to do so, and had often expressed the idea in private circles; but
when at last I saw a woman rise up in the pulpit and preach as earnestly and

impressively as Mrs. Mott always did, it seemed to me like the realization of an oft-repeated happy dream. The day we visited the Zoological Gardens, as we were admiring the gorgeous plumage of some beautiful birds, one of the gentlemen opponents remarked, "You see, Mrs. Mott, our Heavenly Father believes in bright colors. How much it would take from our pleasure if all the birds were dressed in drab." "Yes," said she, "but immortal beings do not depend on their feathers for their attractions. With the infinite variety of the human face and form, of thought, feeling, and affection, we do not need gorgeous apparel to distinguish us. Moreover, if it is fitting that woman should dress in every color of the rainbow, why not man also? Clergymen, with their black clothes and white cravats, are quite as monotonous as the Quakers." . . .

~

An amusing incident occurred the first year, 1869, we held a Convention in Washington. Chaplain Cray, of the Senate, was invited to open the Convention with prayer. Mrs. Mott and I were sitting close together, with our heads bowed and eyes closed, listening to the invocation. As the chaplain proceeded, he touched the garden scene in Paradise, and spoke of woman as a secondary creation, called into being for the especial benefit of man, an afterthought with the Creator. Straightening up, Mrs. Mott whispered to me, "I can not bow my head to such absurdities." Edward M. Davis, in the audience, noticed his mother's movements, and knowing that what had struck his mind had no doubt disturbed hers also, he immediately left the hall, returning shortly after Bible in hand, that he might confound the chaplain with the very book he had quoted. He ascended the platform just as Mr. Gray said "amen," and read from the opening chapter of Genesis, the account of the simultaneous creation of man and woman, in which dominion was given to both alike over every living thing. After Mr. Davis made a few pertinent remarks on the allegorical character of the second chapter of Genesis, Mrs. Mott followed with a critical analysis of the prayer, and the portion of the Scripture read by her son, showing the eternal oneness and equality of man and woman, the union of the masculine and feminine elements, like the positive and negative magnetism, the centripetal and centrifugal forces in nature, pervading the animal, vegetable, and mineral kingdoms, the whole world of thought and action, as there could have been no perpetuation of creation without these elements equal and eternal in the Godhead. The press commented on the novelty of reviewing an address to the throne of grace, particularly when uttered by the chaplain of Congress.

Mrs. Mott remarked on these criticisms, "If we can teach clergymen to be as careful what they say to God as to man, our Conventions at the capital will be of great service to our representatives."

As a writer Mrs. Mott was clear and concise; her few published sermons, her charming private letters and diary, with what those who knew her best can remember, are all of her thoughts bequeathed to posterity. As a speaker she was calm, clear, and unimpassioned; indulged but little in wit, humor, or pathos, but by her good common sense and liberality on all questions, by her earnestness and simplicity, she held the most respectful attention of her audiences. Hence an occasional touch of humor or sarcasm, or an outburst of eloquent indignation came from her with great power. She had what the Friends call unction; that made the most radical utterances from her lips acceptable. In her conversation she was original and brilliant, earnest and playful. Such was her persuasiveness of voice and manner that opinions received with hisses from another speaker, were applauded when uttered by Mrs. Mott.

Josiah Allen's Wife Meets Victoria Woodhull

What a pair: Josiah Allen's wife, the comical creation of Marietta Holley, and Victoria Woodhull, the larger-than-life figure who distinguished herself first as a Wall Street stockbroker (she helped build Commodore Vanderbilt's fortune) and then as a political figure (she ran for President on a free love platform)! Woodhull was charismatic, outspoken, and a thorny ally of the women's rights advocates who admired and feared her social, moral, and political independence. In this marvelous (and fictitious) scene rendered by Holley, we confront head on the clash of the old world and the new in America's nineteenth-century struggle for equity between the sexes:

The other lady was smart and sensible lookin', but she was some like me, she wont never be hung for her beauty. This was Susan B. Anthony. Betsey Bobbet sot down on a chair pretty nigh the door, but I had considerable talk with Susan. The other two was awful long discussin' some question with Miss Woodhull.

Susan said in the course of her remarks that "she had made the 'Cause of Wimmen's Rights,' her husband, and was going to cleave to it till she died."

I told her I was deeply interested in it, but I couldn't marry myself to it, because before gettin' acquainted with it, I had united myself to Josiah."

We had considerable reasonable and agreeable talk, such as would be expected from two such minds as mine and hern, and then the three ladies departed. And Miss Woodhull came up to me agin kinder friendly, and says she,

"I am glad to meet you Josiah Allen's wife," and then she invited me to set down. As I turned round to get a chair I see through a door into another room where sot several other wimmen—some up to a table, and all dreadful busy readin' papers and writin' letters. They looked so business-like and earnest at their work, that I knew they could not have time to backbite their neighbors, and I was glad to see it. . . .

"She is a Strong Wimen's Righter, she is one of us."

"No, Victory [Victoria]; I haint one of you, I am Josiah Allen's wife." Then I sithed. And says I, "Victory you are in the right on it, and you are in the wrong on it," and says I, "I come clear from Jonesville to try to set you right where you are wrong." Says I, almost overcome with emotion. "You are younger than I Victory, and I want to talk with you jest as friendly as if I was your mother in law."

Says she, "Where do you think I am in the right, and where do you think I am in the wrong?"

Says I, "You are right in thinkin' what a solemn thing it is to bring up children as they ought to be. What an awful thing it is to bring the little creeters into the world without their votin' on the subject at all, and then neglect 'em, and abuse 'em, and make their poor little days awful long in the world, and then expect them to honor you for it. You are right in your views of health, and wimmin's votin' and etcetery—but you are wrong Victory, and I don't want you to get mad at me, for I say it with as friendly feelin's as if I was your mother in law,—you are wrong in this free love business, you are wrong in keepin' house with two husbands at the same time."

"Two husbands! it is false; I was divorced from him, and my husband and I found him perishing in the streets, and we took him home and took care of him 'till he died. Which would the Lord have done Josiah Allen's wife, passed by on the other side, or took pity on him?

"I don't know what the Lord would have done Victory, but I believe I should have sent him to a good horsepittle or tarven, and hired him took care of. I never could stand it to have another husband in the same house with me and Josiah. It would seem so kind o' curious, somethin' in the circus way. I never could stand it never."

"There have been a good many things Josiah Allen's wife that you have not been required to stand, God and man united you to a good husband whom you love. But in your happiness you shouldn't forget that some other woman has been less fortunate. In your perfect happiness, and harmony—"

"Oh!" says I candidly, "I don't say but what Josiah and me have had our little spats Victory. Josiah will go in his stockin' feet considerable and—"

But she interrupted of me with her eyes a flashin',

"What would you say to livin' with a man that forgot every day of his life that he was a man, and sunk himself into a brute. Leaving his young wife of a week for the society of the abandoned? What would you say to abuse, that resulted in the birth of a idiot child? Would you endure such a life? Would you live with the animal that he had made himself? I married a man. I never promised God nor man that I would love, honor and obey the wild beast he changed into. I was free from him in the sight of a pure God, long enough before the law freed me."

I let her have her say out, for Josiah Allen's wife is one to let every man or mouse tell thier principles if they have got any. And if I was conversin' with the overseer of the bottomless pit (I don't want to speak his name right out, bein' a Methodist), I would give him a chance to get up and relate his experience. But as she stopped with her voice kinder choked up, I laid my brown cotton glove gently onto her shoulder, and says I,

"Hush up Victory," says I "wimmen must submit to some things, they can pray, and they can try to let their sorrows lift 'em nearer to heaven, makin' angels of 'em." . . . Says I, "men as a general thing think that wimmen have got to do up all the angel business there is done. Men seem to get the idee that they can do as they are a mind to and the Lord will wink at 'em. And there are lots of things that the world thinks would be awful coarse in a woman, but is all right in a man. But I don't believe a man's cigar smoke smells any sweeter to the Lord than a woman's would. And I don't believe a coarse low song sounds any sweeter and purer in the ears of angels, because it is sung in a base voice instead of a sulfereno. I never could see why men couldn't do somethin' in the angel line themselves, as well as to put it all on to the wimmen, when they have got everything else under the sun to do. Not but what" says I, "I am willen' to do my part. I never was a shirk, and Josiah Allen will tell you so, I am willin' to do my share of the angel business." And says I, in a generous way, "I would do it all, if I only had time. But I love to see justice and reason. Nature feathers out geese and gander's equally, or if there is any difference the gander's wings are the most foamin' lookin'. Men's shoulders are made jest the same way that wimmen's are; feathers would look jest as well on 'em as on a woman, they can cultivate wings with jest as little trouble. What is the purest and whitest unseen feathers on a livin' angel's hidden wing, . . . Victory? They are purity, goodness, and patience, and men can grow these unbeknown feathers jest as easy as a woman can if they only set out."

Ernestine Rose: "A heroism which woman possesses."

Another word from the brilliant Polish expatriate who came to mean so much to the woman's movement in the nineteenth century:

Mothers, women of America! when you hear the subject of Woman's Rights broached, laugh at it and us, ridicule it as much as you please; but never forget, that by the laws of your country, you have no right to your children—the law gives the father as uncontrolled power over the child as it gives the husband over the wife; only the child, when it comes to maturity, the father's control ceases, while the wife never comes to maturity. The father may bequeath, bestow, or sell the child without the consent of the mother. But methinks I hear you say that no man deserving the name of man, or the title of husband and father, could commit such an outrage against the dearest principles of humanity; well, if there are no such men, then the law ought to be annulled, a law against which nature, justice, and humanity revolt, ought to be wiped off from the statute book as a disgrace; and if there are such—which unhappily we all know there are—then there is still greater reason why the laws ought to be changed, for bad laws encourage bad men and make them worse; good men can not be benefited by the existence of bad laws; bad men ought not to be; laws are not made for him who is a law unto himself, but for the lawless. The legitimate object of law is to protect the innocent and inexperienced against the designing and the guilty; we therefore ask every one present to demand of the Legislatures of every State to alter these unjust laws; give the wife an equal right with the husband in the property acquired after marriage; give the mother an equal right with the father in the control of the children; let the wife at the death of the husband remain his heir to the same extent that he would be hers, at her death; let the laws be alike for both, and they are sure to be right; but to have them so, woman must help make them.

We hear a great deal about the heroism of the battle-field. What is it? Compare it with the heroism of the woman who stands up for the right, and it sinks into utter insignificance. To stand before the cannon's mouth, with death before him and disgrace behind, excited to frenzy by physical fear, encouraged by his leader, stimulated by sound of the trumpet, and sustained by the *still emptier sound of glory*, requires no great heroism; the merest coward could be a hero in such a position; but to face the fire of an unjust and prejudiced public opinion, to attack the adamantine walls of long-usurped power, to brave not only the enemy abroad, but often that severest of all enemies, your own friends at home, requires a heroism that the world has never yet recognized, that the battle-field can not supply, but which woman possesses.

Frances Gage:
"Let woman speak for herself . . ."

Gage was chosen to act as President of the Akron Convention (for the enfranchisement of women) in May, 1851. On taking the chair she sought to lay out the rights of women using the cornerstone principles of the new republic. Her stirring analogy succeeded quite well:

I am at a loss, kind friends, to know whether to return your thanks, or not, for the honor conferred upon me. And when I tell you that I have never in my life attended a regular business meeting, and am entirely inexperienced in the forms and ceremonies of a deliberative body, you will not be surprised that I do not feel remarkably grateful for the position. For though you have conferred an honor upon me, I very much fear I shall not be able to reflect it back. I will try.

When our forefathers left the old and beaten paths of New England, and struck out for themselves in a new and unexplored country, they went forth with a slow and cautious step, but with firm and resolute hearts. The land of their fathers had become too small for their children. Its soil answered not their wants. The parents shook their heads and said, with doubtful and foreboding faces: "Stand still, stay at home. This has sufficed for us; we have lived and enjoyed ourselves here. True, our mountains are high and our soil is rugged and cold; but you won't find a better; change, and trial, and toil will meet you at every step. Stay, tarry with us, and go not forth to the wilderness."

But the children answered: "Let us go; this land has sufficed for you, but the one beyond the mountains is better. We know there is trial, toil, and danger; but for the sake of our children, and our children's children, we are willing to meet all." They went forth, and pitched their tents in the wilderness. An herculean task was before them; the rich and fertile soil was shadowed by a mighty forest, and giant trees were to be felled. The Indians roamed the wild, wide hunting-grounds, and claimed them as their own. They must be met and subdued. The savage beasts howled defiance from every hill-top, and in every glen. They must be destroyed. Did the hearts of our fathers fail? No; they entered upon their new life, their new world, with a strong faith and a mighty will. For they saw in the prospection a great and incalculable good. It was not the work of an hour, nor of a day; not of weeks or months, but of long struggling, toiling, painful years. If they failed at one point, they took hold at another. If their paths through the wilderness were at first crooked, rough, and dangerous, by little and little they improved them. The forest faded away, the savage disappeared, the wild beasts were destroyed, and the hopes and prophetic visions of their far-seeing powers in the new and untried country, were more than realized.

Permit me to draw a comparison between the situation of our forefathers in the wilderness, without even so much as a bridle-path through its dark depths, and our present position. The old land of moral, social, and political privilege seems too narrow for our wants; its soil answers not to our growing, and we feel that we see clearly a better country that we might inhabit. But there are mountains of established law and custom to overcome; a wilderness of prejudice to be subdued; a powerful foe of selfishness and self-interest to overthrow; wild beasts of pride, envy, malice, and hate to destroy. But for the sake of our children and our children's children, we have entered upon the work, hoping and praying that we may be guided by wisdom, sustained by love, and led and cheered by the earnest hope of doing good.

I shall enter into no labored argument to prove that woman does not occupy the position in society to which her capacity justly entitles her. The rights of mankind emanate from their natural wants and emotions. Are not the natural wants and emotions of humanity common to, and shared equally by, both sexes? Does man hunger and thirst, suffer cold and heat more than woman? Does he love and hate, hope and fear, joy and sorrow more than woman? Does his heart thrill with a deeper pleasure in doing good? Can his soul writhe in more bitter agony under the consciousness of evil or wrong? Is the sunshine more glorious, the air more quiet, the sounds of harmony more soothing, the perfume of flowers more exquisite, or forms of beauty more soul-satisfying to his senses, than to hers? To all these interrogatories every one will answer, No!

Where then did man get the authority that he now claims over one-half of humanity? From what power the vested right to place woman—his partner, his companion, his helpmeet in life—in an inferior position? Came it from nature? Nature made woman his superior when she made her his mother; his equal when she fitted her to hold the sacred position of wife. Does he draw his authority from God, from the language of holy writ? No! For it says that "Male and female created he *them,* and gave *them* dominion." Does he claim it under law of the land? Did woman meet with him in council and voluntarily give up all her claim to be her own law-maker? Or did the majesty of might place this power in his hands?—The power of the strong over the weak makes man the master! Yes, there, and there only, does he gain his authority.

In the dark ages of the past, when ignorance, superstition, and bigotry held rule in the world, might made the law. But the undertone, the still small voice of Justice, Love, and Mercy, have ever been heard, pleading the cause of humanity, pleading for truth and right; and their low, soft tones of harmony have softened the lion heart of might, and, little by little, he has yielded as the centuries rolled on; and man, as well as woman, has been the gainer by every concession. We will ask him to yield still; to allow the voice of woman to be heard; to let her take the position which her wants and emotions seem to require; to let her enjoy her natural rights. Do not answer that woman's position is now all her natural wants and emotions require. Our meeting here together this day proves the contrary; proves that we have aspirations that are not met. Will it be answered that we are factious, discontented spirits, striving to disturb the public order, and tear up the old fastnesses of society? So it was said of Jesus Christ and His followers, when they taught peace on earth and good-will to men. So it was said of our forefathers in the great struggle for freedom. So it has been said of every reformer that has ever started out the car of progress on a new and untried track.

We fear not man as an enemy. He is our friend, our brother. Let woman speak for herself, and she will be heard. Let her claim with a calm and determined, yet loving spirit, her place, and it will be given her. I pour out no harsh invectives against the present order of things—against our fathers, husbands, and brothers; they do as they have been taught; they feel as society bids them; they act as the law requires. Woman must act for herself.

Oh, if all women could be impressed with the importance of their own action, and with one united voice, speak out in their own behalf, in behalf of humanity, they could create a revolution without armies, without bloodshed, that would do more to ameliorate the condition of mankind, to purify, elevate, ennoble humanity, than all that has been done by reformers in the last century.

Carry Nation Gets Her Start

The image of Carry Nation bursting through the saloon door with her hatchet in hand is one that Americans have written into the folkloric history of women. "The old battle-axe" was an apt expression used more often by men than women. To many people Nation stood for something like a vengeful and uncompromising mother intent on chasing her drunken children home. And while it is true that she did smash saloons and even carried a hatchet (selling little miniature ones to raise money for the cause of temperance), she was a formidable social activist who understood the very real impact alcohol was having on American family life. As she often argued, she was only enforcing laws that were already in place (saloons were to be closed on Sunday), and drunken husbands could be abusive and dangerous to women who did not have the protection or the sympathy of the courts. Much of her reputation was eroded by the unhappy circumstances in her private life and the fact that she claimed to hear voices, but she stood up for what she believed at an age (mid fifties) when society was telling women to take their seat and be quiet. She smashed her first saloon in 1899 and her last in 1910 (where she was badly beaten up by the owner of the saloon—a woman). This excerpt from her autobiography (The Use and Need of Carry Nation) *recounts the early events that led to the creation of the legendary Carry Nation:*

God has given me a mean fight, a dirty and dangerous fight; for it is a war on the hidden things of darkness. I am, in this book throwing all the light I can on the dangerous foe to liberty, free speech and Christianity, the Masonic Lodge, which is the father of all the other secret orders. Through this Mystic Order of Brotherhood managing the primaries and elections, they got into office from constable up to the governor, the tools of the liquor power. The great question that was then discussed was "re-submission." Every representative to congress at Topeka was in favor of the re-submission without an exception. Money was sent into Kansas by the thousands from brewers and distillers to be used by politicians for the purpose of bringing about re-submission. Kansas was the storm center. If the liquor men could bring back saloons into Kansas then a great blow would be struck against prohibition in all the states. This would discourage the people all over. Their great word was, "you can't," "prohibition will not prohibit." I do not belong to the "can't" family. When I was born my father wrote my name Carry A. Moore, then later it was Nation, which is more still. C. A. N. are the initials of my name, then C. (see) A. Nation! And all together Carry A. Nation! This is no accident but Providence. This does not mean that I will carry a nation, but that the roused heart and conscience will, as I am the roused heart and conscience of the people. There are just two crowds, God's crowd and the Devil's crowd. One gains the battle by can, and the other loses it by can't.

My Christian experience will give you the secret of my life, it is God indwelling. When I found I could effect nothing through the officials, I was sad, indeed. I saw that Kansas homes, hearts and souls were to be sacrificed. I had lost all the hopes of my young life through drink, I saw the terrible butchery that would follow. I felt that I had rather die than to see the saloons come back into Kansas. I felt desperate. I took this to God daily, feeling that he only could rescue. On the 5th of June, 1899 before retiring, I threw myself face downward at the foot of my bed at my home in Medicine Lodge. I poured out my grief and agony to God, in about this strain: "Oh Lord you see the treason in Kansas, they are going to break the mothers' hearts, they are going to send the boys to drunkards' graves and a drunkard's hell. I have exhausted all my means, Oh Lord, you have plenty of ways. You have used the base things and the weak things, use me to save Kansas. I have but one life to give you. If I had a thousand, I would give them all, please show me something to do." The next morning I was awakened by a voice which seemed to be speaking in my heart, these words, "Go to Kiowa," and my hands were lifted and thrown down and the words, "I'll stand by you." The words, "Go to Kiowa," were spoken in a murmuring, musical tone, low and soft, but, "I'll stand by you," was very clear, positive and emphatic. I was impressed with a great inspiration, the interpretation was very plain, it was this: "Take something in your hands, and throw at these places in Kiowa and smash them." I was very much relieved and overjoyed and was determined to be, "obedient to the heavenly vision." (Acts 26:19.) I told no one what I heard or what I intended to do.

I was a busy home keeper, did all my house work, was superintendent of two Sunday schools, one in the country, was jail evangelist, and president of the W. C. T. U. and kept open house for all of God's people, where all the Christian workers were welcome to abide at my house.

When no one was looking I would walk out in the yard and pick up brick bats and rocks, would hide them under my kitchen apron, would take them in my room, would wrap them up in newspapers one by one. I did this until I got quite a pile. A very sneaking degenerate druggist in Medicine Lodge named Southworth, had for years been selling intoxicating liquors on the sly. I had gotten in his drug store four bottles of Schlitz Malt. I was going to use them as evidence to convict this wiley dive keeper.

One of the bottles I took to a W. C. T. U. meeting and in the presence of the ladies I opened it and drank the contents. Then I had two of them to take me down to a Doctor's office. I fell limp on the sofa and said: "Doctor, what is the matter with me?"

He looked at my eyes, felt my heart and pulse, shook his head and looked grave.

I said: "Am I poisoned?" "Yes," said the Doctor.

I said: "What poisoned me is that beer you recommended Bro. —— to take as a tonic." I resorted to this stratagem, to show the effect that beer has upon the system. This Doctor was a kind man and meant well, but it must have been ignorance that made him say beer could ever be used as a medicine.

There was another, Dr. Kocile, in Medicine Lodge who used to sell all the whiskey he could. He made a drunkard of a very prominent woman of the town, who took the Keeley cure. She told the W. C. T. U. of the villainy of this doctor and she could not have hated any one more. Oh! the drunkards the doctors are making! No physician, who is worthy of the name will prescribe it as a medicine, for there is not one medical quality in alcohol. It kills the living and preserves the dead. Never preserves anything but death. It is made by a rotting process and it rots the brain, body and soul; it paralyzes the vascular circulation and increases the action of the heart. This is friction and friction in any machinery is dangerous, and the cure is not hastened but delayed.

Any physician that will prescribe whiskey or alcohol as a medicine is either a fool or a knave. A fool because he does not understand his business, for even saying that alcohol does arouse the action of the heart, there are medicines that will do that and will not produce the fatal results of alcoholism, which is the worst of all diseases. He is a knave because his practice is a matter of getting a case, and a fee at the same time, like a machine agent who breaks the machine to get the job of mending it. Alcohol destroys the normal condition of all the functions of the body. The stomach is thrown out of fix, and the patient goes to the doctor for a stomach pill; the heart, liver, kidneys, and in fact, the whole body is in a deranged condition, and the doctor has a perpetual patient. I sincerely believe this to be the reason why many physicians prescribe it. . . .

I got to Kiowa at half past eight, stayed all night. Next morning I had my horse hitched and drove to the first dive kept by a Mr. Dobson, whose brother was then sheriff of the county. I stacked up these smashers on my left arm, all I could hold. They looked like packages wrapped in paper. I stood before the counter and said: "Mr. Dobson, I told you last spring to close this place, you did not do it, now I have come down with another remonstrance, get out of the way. I do not want to strike you, but I am going to break this place up." I threw as hard, and as fast as I could, smashing mirrors and bottles and glasses and it was astonishing how quickly this was done. These men seemed terrified, threw up their hands and backed up in the corner. My strength was that of a giant. I felt invincible. God was certainly standing by me.

I will tell you of a very strange thing. As the stones were flying against this "wonderful and horrible" thing, I saw Mr. McKinley, the President, sitting in an old fashion arm chair and as the stones would strike I saw them hit the chair and the chair fell to pieces, and I saw Mr. McKinley fall over. I did not understand this until very recently; now I know that the smashing in Kansas was intended to strike the head of this nation the hardest blow, for every saloon I smashed in Kansas had a license from the head of this government which made the head of the government more responsible than the dive-keeper. I broke up three of these dives that day, broke the windows on the outside to prove that the man who rents his house is a partner also with the man who sells. The party who licenses and the paper that advertises, all have a hand in this and are *particeps criminis*. I smashed five saloons with rocks, before I ever took a hatchet.

In the last place, kept by Lewis, there was quite a young man behind the bar. I said to him: "Young man, come from behind that bar, your mother did not raise you for such a place." I threw a brick at the mirror, which was a very heavy one, and it did not break, but the brick fell and broke everything in its way. I began to look around for something that would break it. I was standing by a billiard table on which there was one ball. I said: "Thank God," and picked it up, threw it, and it made a hole in the mirror.

By this time, the streets were crowded with people: most of them seemed to look puzzled. There was one boy about fifteen years old who seemed perfectly wild with joy, and he jumped, skipped and yelled with delight. I have since thought of that as being a significant sign. For to smash saloons will save the boy.

I stood in the middle of the street and spoke in this way: "I have destroyed three of your places of business, and if I have broken a statute of Kansas, put me in jail; if I am not a law-breaker your mayor and councilmen are. You must arrest one of us, for if I am not a criminal, they are."

One of the councilmen, who was a butcher, said: "Don't you think we can attend to our business."

"Yes," I said. "You can, but you won't. As Jail Evangelist of Medicine Lodge, I know you have manufactured many criminals and this county is burdened down with taxes to prosecute the results of these dives. Two murders have been committed in the last five years in this county, one in a dive I have just destroyed. You are a butcher of hogs and cattle, but they are butchering men, women and children, positively contrary to the laws of God and man, and the mayor and councilmen are more to blame than the jointist, and now if I have done wrong in any particular arrest me." When I was through with my speech I got into my buggy and said: "I'll go home."

The Wit of Abigail Scott Duniway

While Carry Nation was smashing saloons, other women were busy trying to separate suffrage issues from issues of prohibition. Abigail Duniway, a major leader in the women's rights movement, traveled extensively throughout the far West arguing that women should not let anti-prohibition sentiments cloud the issue of women's right to vote. Duniway was politically very astute and understood that the political initiative to win the right for women to vote had enough adversaries of its own, She did not want to exacerbate the male voter who, if his right to drink were not threatened, would vote on behalf of women. She was right, and though her efforts were vilified by many women who objected to the morality of alcohol, her work was part of the long, tricky road to 1920. This excerpt from her memoir Path Breaking *offers some amusing anecdotes from her life on the stump:*

On one occasion, while I was campaigning in Idaho in 1889, I stopped over in a railroad town to deliver two lectures. Churches were no longer closed against me anywhere; but I had learned that only a small fraction of the men, and but few women, would attend a lecture in a small town in any other church but their own; so I went to the chairman of the committee having charge of the one public hall in the place, who agreed to let me have it at a reasonable price, if I were not a member of the Woman's Christian Temperance Union, against which he seemed to have a grievance. I had a good audience, before which I read a note from the Circuit Judge, tendering me the Court House for the next evening's meeting, at which there was an augmented crowd. In reply to a question from some one in the audience, I was forced to state my views on the temperance problem. As prohibition had recently become a live political issue, and I was trying to steer clear of it, at least till women would get the right to vote, I complied with reluctance; but I never was successful as a dodger, so I said, in substance: "With all due deference to everybody's opinion, whether coinciding with my own or not, I will say, frankly, that I am opposed to two kinds of prohibition. One of these would prohibit woman from the use of her right to vote, and the other would prohibit a man's right to sell a sober man a drink of liquor if he should want to buy. If one of you were to call a physician to prescribe for an abscess in the side, and the doctor should order the abscess to be overspread with a rigid prohibition plaster big enough to cover both the diameter and the circumference of the entire ulcer, a ten-year-old boy who was having the benefit of the common schools, and understood something about the circulation of the blood, could tell you that your doctor was a quack. He would know, if you didn't, that the virus thus confined would burrow deeper and yet deeper into the body of the man, and would ultimately rot him to death. The abscess in the Nation's side is drunkenness. It is a disease of the Nation's blood; you cannot cure it by sumptuary laws. You must treat it openly, with the sanitary usages of common sense. The large majority of men who use intoxicants are not drunkards; yet there are men who fall victims to the disease of drunkenness, just as there are men who are victims of gluttony. We should have laws to quarantine and cure the drunkard; and we should fine or imprison any man, or set of men, who would supply a drunkard with intoxicants. But you would not think of compelling every man to walk with crutches because now and then some man walks lame; nor would you think of prohibiting the existence of all women because a man is sometimes guilty of coveting his neighbor's wife."

The necessary little exercise of taking the collection was then in order, and I was keeping up a running fire of little jokes during the performance, when a man who had been sitting in a corner at my left, arose and said: "I was formerly opposed to women's rights; but I had begun to believe in 'em, because I thought women would be sure to vote for prohibition. But," and his voice reached a high key as he exclaimed, "I don't want any woman to vote unless they'll all vote for prohibition!" To this I replied: "The gentleman reminds me of Brigham Young, who at one time advocated Equal Rights for the women of Utah, in the firm belief that all women would vote for polygamy. In like manner the gentleman who has just spoken has been led to advocate Equal Rights for women, but only because he has thought that all women would vote his ticket. And, like Brigham Young, my friend will in due time discover his mistake. He'll find that there is but one thing in the world a little stronger than a woman's will, and that is—her won't. Of what good would the ballot be to women, if my friend here could have control of barbed hooks fastened in their jaws, with strings attached and himself clothed with arbitrary power to yank every string?" The house laughed and applauded, and I added: "Would you compel every man to go into quarantine because some man gets the smallpox? I know the argument my friend will use in reply to this. He'll say, 'We prohibit the spread of smallpox. Wouldn't *you?*' " My reply was easy. I said: "Everybody wants to avoid smallpox. Can't my hearers see the point? If the Snake River flowed intoxicants, and pure water was prohibited to flow at all, unless held in licensed leash, like liquor, the secret demand for the water would increase to the law-breaking point. Then, children would learn to shun intoxicants and hunt for water, just as calves and colts, and lambs and pigs hunt for it, just as they instinctively shun the alkali puddles of the desert." The gentleman looked the chagrin and disappointment he felt, and I got a little sorry for him, so I added, "I know, good friends, that my opponent here isn't half as narrow as he thinks he is. There is only one streak of tyranny in him, and, of course, there is a cause for that, somewhere. A man is what his mother makes him; and somebody must have sinned against this man's mother, or he wouldn't have that one streak of tyranny in his mental makeup."

The house roared, and a comely little woman came laughingly forward, as the discomfited speaker escaped through a side door. Laying a half dollar on the desk, the lady said, "The collection missed me, and this discussion is worth half a dollar." The general laughter continued until after the close of the meeting; and on my way back to the hotel, I said to the landlady at my side, "I can't see what everybody is laughing about. I surely didn't say anything cute enough to arouse so much merriment." "That man," said the lady in reply, "is the alleged illegitimate son of a Southern governor. We all knew you didn't know about it, so nobody blamed you; and that pleasant little woman, who laid that half dollar on the desk, is his wife." I was afterwards informed that my opponent was in reality a good husband, whose streak of tyranny—though only a streak—was excusable under the circumstances.

Mother Jones

Mother Jones was tough. She hated rich folks and couldn't stand anyone whose ease came at the expense of another. Capitalism's darker side was her obsession. As a middle-aged woman, she became enamored of the single greatest value of a union—its ability to strike. While her speech was blunt, colorful, fiery—marked by a gorgeous capacity for swearing—she was wise and shrewd in the ways of power. In the industrial boom of the late nineteenth century, when fortunes were being made in steel, coal, alcohol, and minerals, Jones was ubiquitous. This is the fighting age, she told a striking crowd; "Put on your fighting clothes." Indeed. Strikers admired her, but striking wives adored her. She looked to the wives for the strength in every strike. It is you, she would tell the women, who will bring the muscle and grit to the strike. Stand fast and your man will follow you and do the same. She lived to be a hundred and to see much of the work she had fought for accomplished. Summarize her? She did it best herself: "Pray for the dead and fight like hell for the living." The following selections from her autobiography capture her zeal and the furious determination of her will:

I was born in the city of Cork, Ireland, in 1830. My people were poor. For generations they had fought for Ireland's freedom. Many of my folks have died in that struggle. My father, Richard Harris, came to America in 1835, and as soon as he had become an American citizen he sent for his family. His work as a laborer with railway construction crews took him to Toronto, Canada. Here I was brought up but always as the child of an American citizen. Of that citizenship I have ever been proud.

After finishing the common schools, I attended the Normal school with the intention of becoming a teacher. Dress-making too, I learned proficiently. My first position was teaching in a convent in Monroe, Michigan. Later, I came to Chicago and opened a dress-making establishment. I preferred sewing to bossing little children.

However, I went back to teaching again, this time in Memphis, Tennessee. Here I was married in 1861. My husband was an iron moulder and a staunch member of the Iron Moulders' Union.

In 1867, a yellow fever epidemic swept Memphis. Its victims were mainly among the poor and the workers. The rich and the well-to-do fled the city. Schools and churches were closed. People were not permitted to enter the house of a yellow fever victim without permits. The poor could not afford nurses. Across the street from me, ten persons lay dead from the plague. The dead surrounded us. They were buried at night quickly and without ceremony. All about my house I could hear weeping and the cries of delirium. One by one, my four little children sickened and died. I washed their little bodies and got them ready for burial. My husband caught the fever and died. I sat alone through nights of grief. No one came to me. No one could. Other homes were as stricken as was mine. All day long, all night long, I heard the grating of the wheels of the death cart.

After the union had buried my husband, I got a permit to nurse the sufferers. This I did until the plague was stamped out.

I returned to Chicago and went again into the dress-making business with a partner. We were located on Washington Street near the lake. We worked for the aristocrats of Chicago, and I had ample opportunity to observe the luxury and extravagance of their lives. Often while sewing for the lords and barons who lived in magnificent houses on the Lake Shore Drive, I would look out of the plate glass windows and see the poor, shivering wretches, jobless and hungry, walking along the frozen lake front. The contrast of their condition with that of the tropical comfort of the people for whom I sewed was painful to me. My employers seemed neither to notice nor to care.

Summers, too, from the windows of the rich, I used to watch the mothers come from the west side slums, lugging babies and little children, hoping for a breath of cool, fresh air from the lake. At night, when the tenements were stifling hot, men, women and little children slept in the parks. But the rich, having donated to the charity ice fund, had, by the time it was hot in the city, gone to seaside and mountains.

In October, 1871, the great Chicago fire burned up our establishment and everything that we had. The fire made thousands homeless. We stayed all night and the next day without food on the lake front, often going into the lake to keep cool. Old St. Mary's church at Wabash Avenue and Peck Court was thrown open to the refugees and there I camped until I could find a place to go.

Near by in an old, tumbled down, fire scorched building the Knights of Labor held meetings. The Knights of Labor was the labor organization of those days. I used to spend my evenings at their meetings, listening to splendid speakers. Sundays we went out into the woods and held meetings.

Those were the days of sacrifice for the cause of labor. Those were the days when we had no halls, when there were no high salaried officers, no feasting with the enemies of labor. Those were the days of the martyrs and the saints. . . .

In Arnot, Pennsylvania, a strike had been going on four or five months. The men were becoming discouraged. The coal company sent the doctors, the school teachers, the preachers and their wives to the homes of the miners to get them to sign a document that they would go back to work.

The president of the district, Mr. Wilson, and an organizer, Tom Haggerty, got despondent. The signatures were overwhelmingly in favor of returning on Monday.

Haggerty suggested that they send for me. Saturday morning they telephoned to Barnesboro, where I was organizing, for me to come at once or they would lose the strike.

"Oh Mother," Haggerty said, "Come over quick and help us! The boys are that despondent! They are going back Monday."

I told him that I was holding a meeting that night but that I would leave early Sunday morning.

I started at daybreak. At Roaring Branch, the nearest train connection with Arnot, the secretary of the Arnot Union, a young boy, William Bouncer, met me with a horse and buggy. We drove sixteen miles over rough mountain roads. It was biting cold. We got into Arnot Sunday noon and I was placed in the coal company's hotel, the only hotel in town. I made some objections but Bouncer said, "Mother, we have engaged this room for you and if it is not occupied, they will never rent us another."

Sunday afternoon I held a meeting. It was not as large a gathering as those we had later but I stirred up the poor wretches that did come.

"You've got to take the pledge," I said. "Rise and pledge to stick to your brothers and the union till the strike's won!"

The men shuffled their feet but the women rose, their babies in their arms, and pledged themselves to see that no one went to work in the morning.

"The meeting stands adjourned till ten o'clock tomorrow morning," I said. "Everyone come and see that the slaves that think to go back to their masters come along with you."

I returned to my room at the hotel. I wasn't called down to supper but after the general manager of the mines and all of the other guests had gone to church, the housekeeper stole up to my room and asked me to come down and get a cup of tea.

At eleven o'clock that night the housekeeper again knocked at my door and told me that I had to give up my room; that she was told it belonged to a teacher. "It's a shame, mother," she whispered, as she helped me into my coat.

I found little Bouncer sitting on guard down in the lobby. He took me up the mountain to a miner's house. A cold wind almost blew the bonnet from my head. At the miner's shack I knocked.

A man's voice shouted, "Who is there?"

"Mother Jones," said I.

A light came in the tiny window. The door opened.

"And did they put you out, Mother?"

"They did that."

"I told Mary they might do that," said the miner. He held the oil lamp with the thumb and his little finger and I could see that the others were off. His face was young but his body was bent over.

He insisted on my sleeping in the only bed, with his wife. He slept with his head on his arms on the kitchen table. Early in the morning his wife rose to keep the children quiet, so that I might sleep a little later as I was very tired.

At eight o'clock she came into my room, crying.

"Mother, are you awake?"

"Yes, I am awake."

"Well, you must get up. The sheriff is here to put us out for keeping you. This house belongs to the Company."

The family gathered up all their earthly belongings, which weren't much, took down all the holy pictures, and put them in a wagon, and they with all their neighbors went to the meeting. The sight of that wagon with the sticks of furniture and the holy pictures and the children, with the father and mother and myself walking along through the streets turned the tide. It made the men so angry that they decided not to go back that morning to the mines. Instead they came to the meeting where they determined not to give up the strike until they had won the victory.

Then the company tried to bring in scabs. I told the men to stay home with the children for a change and let the women attend to the scabs. I organized an army of women housekeepers. On a given day they were to bring their mops and brooms and "the army" would charge the scabs up at the mines. The general manager, the sheriff and the corporation hirelings heard of our plans and were on hand. The day came and the women came with the mops and brooms and pails of water.

I decided not to go up to the Drip Mouth myself, for I knew they would arrest me and that might rout the army. I selected as leader an Irish woman who had a most picturesque appearance. She had slept late and her husband had told her to hurry up and get into the army. She had grabbed a red petticoat and slipped it over a thick cotton night gown. She wore a black stocking and a white one. She had tied a little red fringed shawl over her wild red hair. Her face was red and her eyes were mad. I looked at her and felt that she could raise a rumpus.

I said, "You lead the army up to the Drip Mouth. Take that tin dishpan you have with you and your hammer, and when the scabs and the mules come up, begin to hammer and howl. Then all of you hammer and howl and be ready to chase the scabs with your mops and brooms. Don't be afraid of anyone."

Up the mountain side, yelling and hollering, she led the women, and when the mules came up with the scabs and the coal, she began beating on the dishpan and hollering and all the army joined in with her. The sheriff tapped her on the shoulder.

"My dear lady," said he, "remember the mules. Don't frighten them."

She took the old tin pan and she hit him with it and she hollered, "To hell with you and the mules!"

He fell over and dropped into the creek. Then the mules began to rebel against scabbing. They bucked and kicked the scab drivers and started off for the barn. The scabs started running down hill, followed by the army of women with their mops and pails and brooms.

A poll parrot in a near by shack screamed at the superintendent, "Got hell, did you? Got hell?"

There was a great big doctor in the crowd, a company lap dog. He had a little satchel in his hand and he said to me, impudent like, "Mrs. Jones, I have a warrant for you."

"All right," said I. "Keep it in your pill bag until I come for it. I am going to hold a meeting now."

From that day on the women kept continual watch of the mines to see that the company did not bring in scabs. Every day women with brooms or mops in one hand and babies in the other arm wrapped in little blankets, went to the mines and watched that no one went in. And all night long they kept watch. They were heroic women. In the long years to come the nation will pay them high tribute for they were fighting for the advancement of a great country.

I held meetings throughout the surrounding country. The company was spending money among the farmers, urging them not to do anything for the miners. I went out with an old wagon and a union mule that had gone on strike, and a miner's little boy for a driver. I held meetings among the farmers and won them to the side of the strikers.

Sometimes it was twelve or one o'clock in the morning when I would get home, the little boy asleep on my arm and I driving the mule. Sometimes it was several degrees below zero. The winds whistled down the mountains and drove the snow and sleet in our faces. My hands and feet were often numb. We were all living on dry bread and black coffee. I slept in a room that never had a fire in it, and I often woke up in the morning to find snow covering the outside covers of the bed. . . .

Other strikes come to my mind, strikes of less fire and flame and hence attracting less national notice. The papers proclaimed to stockholders and investors that there was peace, and there was no peace. The garment workers struck and won. In Roosevelt, New Jersey, the workingmen in the fertilizing plant of Williams and Clark struck.

Two strikers were shot dead—shot in the back by the hired gunmen. The guards were arraigned, let out on bail, and reported back on the job. The strikers were assembled in a vacant lot. Guards shot into their midst, firing low and filling the legs of the workers with bullets.

"Mother," the strikers wrote to me, "come help us with our women!"

I went. "Women," said I, "see that your husbands use no fire arms or violence no matter what the provocation. Don't let your husbands scab. Help them stand firm and above all keep them from the saloons. No strike was ever won that did not have the support of the womenfolk." . . .

Emma Goldman Goes to the Mines

Born in Lithuania, Emma Goldman emigrated to the United States in 1885. She came to New York City where she looked for work amidst appalling conditions and soon developed a deep hatred for capitalism and its attendant abuses. She joined a fledgling anarchist movement and worked the streets, giving speeches to small crowds, handing leaflets to passing strangers. She was arrested in 1893 for incitement to riot, but the real riot was taking place within her own conscience. She was testing the boundaries of her own morality, her own sexual identity, even the nature of love and family life. She determined that she would be no one's wife or mother. She announced that she was neither owned by any man, nor an owner of one. Events continually challenged her positions but she never backed down. Revolution in-

trigued her; strikes inspired her; wars drove her to a maddened rage against national-ism. She was a pacifist in World War I and, in 1917, was tried and convicted for her protests against the draft. Following her release from jail, she earned her next badge of honor with her deportation by a jittery U.S. government to Russia, a nation to which she at first seemed sympathetic. Goldman was to be a shill for no nation, however, and soon enough, after she had spoken out against the Russian regime, she was expelled. Next stop England. She lived for a time in Wales, agi-tated on behalf of the miners (and married one) before heading to Spain for the Spanish Civil War. She died in Toronto after a hard but uncompromising life. Her autobiography, Living My Life, *includes a memory from her days as a strike-breaker:*

In Pennsylvania I found the condition of the miners since the "settlement" of the strike worse than in 1897 when I had gone through the region. The men were more subdued and helpless. Only our own comrades were alert, and even more determined since the shameful defeat of the strike, brought about by the treachery of the union leaders. They were working part time, barely earning enough to live on, yet somehow they managed to contribute to the propaganda. It was inspiring to see such consecration to our cause.

Two experiences stood out on my trip. One happened down in a mine, the other in the home of a worker. As on my previous visits, I was taken to the pit to talk to the men in one of the shafts during lunch-hour. The foreman was away, and the miners eager to hear me. I sat surrounded by a group of black faces. During my talk I caught sight of two figures huddled together—a man withered with age and a child. I inquired who they were. "That's Grandpa Jones," I was told; "he's ninety and he has worked in the mines for seventy years. The kid is his great-grandchild. He says he's fourteen, but we know he's only eight." My comrade spoke in a matter-of-fact manner. A man of ninety and a child of eight working ten hours a day in a black pit!

After the first meeting I was invited by a miner to his home for the night. The small room assigned me had already three occupants: two children on a narrow cot, and a young girl in a folding bed. I was to share the bed with her. The parents and their infant girl slept in the next room. My throat felt parched; the stifling air in the room made me cough. The woman offered me a glass of hot milk. I was tired and sleepy: the night was heavy with the breathing of the man, the pitiful wailing of the infant, and the monotonous tramp of the mother trying to quiet her baby.

In the morning I asked about the child. Was it ill or hungry that it cried so much? Her milk was too poor and not enough, the mother said; the baby was bottle-fed. A horrible suspicion assailed me. "You gave me the baby's milk!" I cried. The woman attempted to deny it, but I could see in her eyes that I had guessed correctly. "How could you do such a thing?" I upbraided her. "Baby had one bottle in the evening, and you looked tired and you coughed; what else could I do?" she said. I was hot with shame and overcome with wonder at the great heart beneath that poverty and those rags.

Helen Keller Remembers

When she was only nineteen months old, Helen Keller took ill and, as a result, became deaf, blind, and severely speech-impaired. The story of her struggle toward language is a part of every American's folklore—we see in her will and drive the qualities we wish for ourselves. Keller has become a kind of American metaphor—an emblem of the certainty that none of us has to stay forever blind to the light and wisdom of life. Her account of the breakthrough she and her beloved teacher Anne Sullivan achieved, called The Story of My Life, *was initially serialized to wide acclaim in 1903 while Keller was still at Radcliffe College. Below, the excerpt of the key moment when the haze and mystery of meaning sharpened into the radiant glory of language:*

Dr. Bell advised my father to write to Mr. Anagnos, director of the Perkins Institution in Boston, the scene of Dr. Howe's great labours for the blind, and ask him if he had a teacher competent to begin my education. This my father did at once, and in a few weeks there came a kind letter from Mr. Anagnos with the comforting assurance that a teacher had been found. This was in the summer of 1886. But Miss Sullivan did not arrive until the following March.

Thus I came up out of Egypt and stood before Sinai, and a power divine touched my spirit and gave it sight, so that I beheld many wonders. And from the sacred mountain I heard a voice which said, "Knowledge is love and light and vision."

~

The most important day I remember in all my life is the one on which my teacher, Anne Mansfield Sullivan, came to me. I am filled with wonder when I consider the immeasurable contrasts between the two lives which it connects. It was the third of March, 1887, three months before I was seven years old.

On the afternoon of that eventful day, I stood on the porch, dumb, expectant. I guessed vaguely from my mother's signs and from the hurrying to and fro in the house that something unusual was about to happen, so I went to the door and waited on the steps. The afternoon sun penetrated the mass of honey-suckle that covered the porch, and fell on my upturned face. My fingers lingered almost unconsciously on the familiar leaves and blossoms which had just come forth to greet the sweet southern spring. I did not know what the future held of marvel or surprise for me. Anger and bitterness had preyed upon me continually for weeks and a deep languor had succeeded this passionate struggle.

Have you ever been at sea in a dense fog, when it seemed as if a tangible white darkness shut you in, and the great ship, tense and anxious, groped her way toward the shore with plummet and sounding-line, and you waited with beating heart for something to happen? I was like that ship before my educa-tion began, only I was without compass or sounding-line, and had no way of knowing how near the harbour was. "Light! give me light!" was the wordless cry of my soul, and the light of love shone on me in that very hour.

I felt approaching footsteps. I stretched out my hand as I supposed to my mother. Some one took it, and I was caught up and held close in the arms of her who had come to reveal all things to me, and, more than all things else, to love me.

The morning after my teacher came she led me into her room and gave me a doll. The little blind children at the Perkins Institution had sent it and Laura Bridgman had dressed it; but I did not know this until afterward. When I had played with it a little while, Miss Sullivan slowly spelled into my hand the word "d-o-l-l." I was at once interested in this finger play and tried to imitate it. When I finally succeeded in making the letters correctly I was flushed with childish pleasure and pride. Running downstairs to my mother I held up my hand and made the letters for doll. I did not know that I was spelling a word or even that words existed; I was simply making my fingers go in monkey-like imitation. In the days that followed I learned to spell in this uncomprehending way a great many words, among them *pin, hat, cup* and a few verbs like *sit, stand* and *walk*. But my teacher had been with me several weeks before I understood that everything has a name.

One day, while I was playing with my new doll, Miss Sullivan put my big rag doll into my lap also, spelled "d-o-l-l" and tried to make me understand that "d-o-l-l" applied to both. Earlier in the day we had had a tussle over the words "m-u-g" and "w-a-t-e-r." Miss Sullivan had tried to impress it upon me that "m-u-g" is mug and that "w-a-t-e-r" is water, but I persisted in confounding the two. In despair she had dropped the subject for the time, only to renew it at the first opportunity. I became impatient at her repeated attempts and, seizing the new doll, I dashed it upon the floor. I was keenly delighted when I felt the fragments of the broken doll at my feet. Neither sorrow nor regret followed my passionate outburst. I had not loved the doll. In the still, dark world in which I lived there was no strong sentiment or tenderness. I felt my teacher sweep the fragments to one side of the hearth, and I had a sense of satisfaction that the cause of my discomfort was removed. She brought me my hat, and I knew I was going out into the warm sunshine. This thought, if a wordless sensation may be called a thought, made me hop and skip with pleasure.

We walked down the path to the well-house, attracted by the fragrance of the honeysuckle with which it was covered. Some one was drawing water and my teacher placed my hand under the spout. As the cool stream gushed over one hand she spelled into the other the word water, first slowly, then rapidly. I stood still, my whole attention fixed upon the motions of her fingers. Suddenly I felt a misty consciousness as of something forgotten—a thrill of returning thought; and somehow the mystery of language was revealed to me. I knew then that "w-a-t-e-r" meant the wonderful cool something that was flowing over my hand. That living word awakened my soul, gave it light, hope, joy, set it free! There were barriers still, it is true, but barriers that could in time be swept away.

I left the well-house eager to learn. Everything had a name, and each name gave birth to a new thought. As we returned to the house every object which I touched seemed to quiver with life. That was because I saw everything with the strange, new sight that had come to me. On entering the door I remembered the doll I had broken. I felt my way to the hearth and picked up the pieces. I tried vainly to put them together. Then my eyes filled with tears; for I realized what I had done, and for the first time I felt repentance and sorrow.

I learned a great many new words that day, I do not remember what they all were; but I do know that *mother, father, sister, teacher* were among them—words that were to make the world blossom for me, "like Aaron's rod, with flowers." It would have been difficult to find a happier child than I was as I lay in my crib at the close of that eventful day and lived over the joys it had brought me, and for the first time longed for a new day to come. . . .

~

I had now the key to all language, and I was eager to learn to use it. Children who hear acquire language without any particular effort; the words that fall from others' lips they catch on the wing, as it were, delightedly, while the little deaf child must trap them by a slow and often painful process. But whatever the process, the result is wonderful. Gradually from naming an object we advance step by step until we have traversed the vast distance between our first stammered syllable and the sweep of thought in a line of Shakespeare.

At first, when my teacher told me about a new thing I asked very few questions. My ideas were vague, and my vocabulary was inadequate; but as my knowledge of things grew, and I learned more and more words, my field of inquiry broadened, and I would return again and again to the same subject, eager for further information. Sometimes a new word revived an image that some earlier experience had engraved on my brain.

I remember the morning that I first asked the meaning of the word, "love." This was before I knew many words. I had found a few early violets in the garden and brought them to my teacher. She tried to kiss me; but at that time I did not like to have any one kiss me except my mother. Miss Sullivan put her arm gently round me and spelled into my hand, "I love Helen."

"What is love?" I asked.

She drew me closer to her and said, "It is here," pointing to my heart, whose beats I was conscious of for the first time. Her words puzzled me very much because I did not then understand anything unless I touched it.

I smelt the violets in her hand and asked, half in words, half in signs, a question which meant, "Is love the sweetness of flowers?"

"No," said my teacher.

Again I thought. The warm sun was shining on us.

"Is this not love?" I asked, pointing in the direction from which the heat came. "Is this not love?"

It seemed to me that there could be nothing more beautiful than the sun, whose warmth makes all things grow. But Miss Sullivan shook her head, and I was greatly puzzled and disappointed. I thought it strange that my teacher could not show me love.

A day or two afterward I was stringing beads of different sizes in symmetrical groups—two large beads, three small ones, and so on. I had made many mistakes, and Miss Sullivan had pointed them out again and again with gentle patience. Finally I noticed a very obvious error in the sequence and for an instant I concentrated my attention on the lesson and tried to think how I should have arranged the beads. Miss Sullivan touched my forehead and spelled with decided emphasis, "Think."

In a flash I knew that the word was the name of the process that was going on in my head. This was my first conscious perception of an abstract idea.

For a long time I was still—I was not thinking of the beads in my lap, but trying to find a meaning for "love" in the light of this new idea. The sun had been under a cloud all day, and there had been brief showers; but suddenly the sun broke forth in all its southern splendour.

Again I asked my teacher, "Is this not love?"

"Love is something like the clouds that were in the sky before the sun came out," she replied. Then in simpler words than these, which at that time I could not have understood, she explained: "You cannot touch the clouds, you know, but you feel the rain and know how glad the flowers and the thirsty earth are to have it after a hot day. You cannot touch love either; but you feel the sweetness that it pours into everything. Without love you would not be happy or want to play."

The beautiful truth burst upon my mind—I felt that there were invisible lines stretched between my spirit and the spirits of others.

"I want to ride!"

A century before Rosa Parks refused to move to the back of the bus, Sojourner Truth challenged the public transportation authorities in Washington, D.C.:

While Sojourner was engaged in the hospital, she often had occasion to procure articles from various parts of the city for the sick soldiers, and would sometimes be obliged to walk a long distance, carrying her burdens upon her arm. She would gladly have availed herself of the street cars; but, although there was on each track one car called the Jim Crow car, nominally for the accommodation of colored people, yet should they succeed in getting on at all they would seldom have more than the privilege of standing, as the seats were usually filled with white folks. Unwilling to submit to this state of things, she complained to the president of the street railroad, who ordered the Jim Crow car to be taken off. A law was now passed giving the colored people equal car privileges with the white.

Not long after this, Sojourner, having occasion to ride, signaled the car, but neither conductor nor driver noticed her. Soon another followed, and she raised her hand again, but they also turned away. She then gave three tremendous yelps, "I want to ride! *I want to ride!!* I WANT TO RIDE!!! Consternation seized the passing crowd—people, carriages, go-carts of every description stood still. The car was effectually blocked up, and before it could move on, Sojourner had jumped aboard. Then there arose a great shout from the crowd, "Ha! ha! ha!! She has beaten him," &c. The angry conductor told her to go forward where the horses were, or he would put her out. Quietly seating herself, she informed him that she was a passenger. "Go forward where the horses are, or I will throw you out," said he in a menacing voice. She told him that she was neither a Marylander nor a Virginian to fear his threats; but was from the Empire State of New York, and knew the laws as well as he did.

Several soldiers were in the car, and when other passengers came in, they related the circumstance and said, "You ought to have heard that old woman talk to the conductor." Sojourner rode farther than she needed to go; for a ride was so rare a privilege that she determined to make the most of it. She left the car feeling very happy, and said, "Bless God! I have had a ride."

Returning one day from the Orphan's Home at Georgetown, she hastened to reach a car; but they paid no attention to her signal, and kept ringing a bell that they might not hear her. She ran after it, and when it stopped to take other passengers, she succeeded in overtaking it and, getting in, said to the conductor, "It is a shame to make a lady run so." He told her if she said another word, he would put her off the car, and came forward as if to execute his threat. She replied, "If you attempt that, it will cost you more than your car and horses are worth." A gentleman of dignified and commanding manner, wearing a general's uniform, interfered in her behalf, and the conductor gave her no further trouble.

At another time, she was sent to Georgetown to obtain a nurse for the hospital, which being accomplished, they went to the station and took seats in an empty car, but had not proceeded far before two ladies came in, and seating themselves opposite the colored woman began a whispered conversation, frequently casting scornful glances at the latter. The nurse, for the first time in her life finding herself in one sense on a level with white folks and being much abashed, hung her poor old head nearly down to her lap; but Sojourner, nothing daunted, looked fearlessly about. At length one of the ladies called out, in a weak, faint voice, "Conductor, conductor, does niggers ride in these cars?" He hesitatingly answered, "Ye-yea-yes," to which she responded, " 'T is a shame and a disgrace. They ought to have a nigger car on the track." Sojourner remarked, "Of course colored people ride in the cars. Street cars are designed for poor white, and colored, folks. Carriages are for ladies and gentlemen. There are carriages [pointing out of the window], standing ready to take you three or four miles for sixpence, and then you talk of a nigger car!!!" Promptly acting upon this hint, they arose to leave. "Ah!" said Sojourner, "now they are going to take a carriage. Good-by, ladies."

Mrs. Laura Haviland, a widely known philanthropist, spent several months in the same hospital and sometimes went about the city with Sojourner to procure necessaries for the invalids. Returning one day, being much fatigued, Mrs. Haviland proposed to take a car although she was well aware that a white person was seldom allowed to ride if accompanied by a black one. "As Mrs. Haviland signaled the car," says Sojourner, "I stepped one side as if to continue my walk and when it stopped I ran and jumped aboard. The conductor pushed me back, saying, 'Get out of the way and let this lady come in.' Whoop! said I, I am a lady too. We met with no further opposition till we were obliged to change cars. A man coming out as we were going into the next car, asked the conductor if 'niggers were allowed to ride.' The conductor grabbed me by the shoulder and jerking me around, ordered me to get out. I told him I would not. Mrs. Haviland took hold of my other arm and said, 'Don't put her out.' The conductor asked if I belonged to her. 'No,' replied Mrs. Haviland, 'She belongs to humanity.' 'Then take her and go,' said he, and giving me another push slammed me against the door. I told him I would let him know whether he could shove me about like a dog, and said to Mrs. Haviland, Take the number of this car.

"At this, the man looked alarmed, and gave us no more trouble. When we arrived at the hospital, the surgeons were called in to examine my shoulder and found that a bone was misplaced. I complained to the president of the road, who advised me to arrest the man for assault and battery. The Bureau furnished me a lawyer, and the fellow lost his situation. It created a great sensation, and before the trial was ended, the inside of the cars looked like pepper and salt; and I felt, like Poll Parrot, 'Jack, I am riding.' A little circumstance will show how great a change a few weeks had produced: A lady saw some colored women looking wistfully toward a car, when the conductor, halting, said, 'Walk in, ladies.' Now they who had so lately cursed me for wanting to ride, could stop for black as well as white, and could even condescend to say, 'Walk in, ladies.' "

Rosa L. Parks

Hers was a simple refusal, but it started one of the great social protests of our nation's history—I will not sit at the back of the bus. Simple testimony in service of the profound and enduring pride possessed by every human being:

I had had problems with bus drivers over the years, because I didn't see fit to pay my money into the front and then go around to the back. Sometimes bus drivers wouldn't permit me to get on the bus, and I had been evicted from the bus. But as I say, there had been incidents over the years. One of the things that made this get so much publicity was the fact the police were called in and I was placed under arrest. See, if I had just been evicted from the bus and he hadn't placed me under arrest or had any charges brought against me, it probably could have been just another incident.

I had left my work at the men's alteration shop, a tailor shop in the Montgomery Fair department store, and as I left work, I crossed the street to a drugstore to pick up a few items instead of trying to go directly to the bus stop. And when I had finished this, I came across the street and looked for a Cleveland Avenue bus that apparently had some seats on it. At that time it was a little hard to get a seat on the bus. But when I did get to the entrance to the bus, I got in line with a number of other people who were getting on the same bus.

As I got up on the bus and walked to the seat I saw there was only one vacancy that was just back of where it was considered the white section. So this was the seat that I took, next to the aisle, and a man was sitting next to me. Across the aisle there were two women, and there were a few seats at this point in the very front of the bus that was called the white section. I went on to one stop and I didn't particularly notice who was getting on the bus, didn't particularly notice the other people getting on. And on the third stop there were some people getting on, and at this point all of the front seats were taken. Now in the beginning, at the very first stop I had got on the bus, the back of the bus was filled up with people standing in the aisle and I don't know why this one vacancy that I took was left, because there were quite a few people already standing toward the back of the bus. The third stop is when all the front seats were taken, and this one man was standing and when the driver looked around and saw he was standing, he asked the four of us, the man in the seat with me and the two women across the aisle, to let him have those front seats.

At his first request, didn't any of us move. Then he spoke again and said, "You'd better make it light on yourselves and let me have those seats." At this point, of course, the passenger who would have taken the seat hadn't said anything. In fact, he never did speak to my knowledge. When the three people, the man who was in the seat with me and the two women, stood up and moved into the aisle, I remained where I was. When the driver saw that I was still sitting there, he asked if I was going to stand up. I told him, no, I wasn't. He said, "Well, if you don't stand up, I'm going to have you arrested." I told him to go on and have me arrested.

He got off the bus and came back shortly. A few minutes later, two police-men got on the bus, and they approached me and asked if the driver had asked me to stand up, and I said yes, and they wanted to know why I didn't. I told them I didn't think I should have to stand up. After I had paid my fare and occupied a seat, I didn't think I should have to give it up. They placed me under arrest then and had me to get in the police car, and I was taken to jail and booked on suspicion, I believe. The questions were asked, the usual ques-tions they ask a prisoner or somebody that's under arrest. They had to deter-mine whether or not the driver wanted to press charges or swear out a warrant, which he did. Then they took me to jail and I was placed in a cell. In a little while I was taken from the cell, and my picture was made and fingerprints taken. I went back to the cell then, and a few minutes later I was called back again, and when this happened I found out that Mr. E.D. Nixon and Attorney and Mrs. Clifford Durr had come to make bond for me.

In the meantime before this, of course . . . I was given permission to make a telephone call after my picture was taken and fingerprints taken. I called my home and spoke to my mother on the telephone and told her what had happened, that I was in jail. She was quite upset and asked me had the police beaten me. I told her, no, I hadn't been physically injured, but I was being held in jail, and I wanted my husband to come and get me out. . . . He didn't have a car at that time, so he had to get someone to bring him down. At the time when he got down, Mr. Nixon and the Durrs had just made bond for me, so we all met at the jail and we went home. . . .

Where Did You Go, Virginia Dare?

Strangely appropriate, her disappearance. What became of Virginia Dare, the first European child born in the New World, is America's earliest mystery. She was named triumphantly in honor of the rich, refulgent paradise by Governor John White, her grandfather. He was the determined leader of the hundred men, women, and children who landed on Roanoke Island in the summer of 1587. What rising faith for all of them after the long, hard journey across the Atlantic! What soaring promise to live differently, to become something altogether new! But great ideals have their dark side. Beautiful as the land was, it was not hospitable. The local natives, increasingly agitated by the white visitors who appeared determined to stay, disturbed the night with cries and weird calls. The birds swung south at the turning of the leaves; the wind and sea were uneven. The fledgling colony staked out their homes on the edge of the forest and grew anxious as winter came. Virginia's birth brought pleasure, celebration, but little solace.

Governor White worried more as a leader than as a grandfather. He thought the solution lay in more bodies, more food, more guns. Strength was needed. This is our land, he argued, and if we leave it because we are faint of heart, we do not deserve to be its owners. He would return to England and come back to save them all. "Leave a mark," he told them with a strange omniscience, "so I know where you went." What did he know? What did he see in the anxious faces of his family and friends or sense in the wilderness that led him to imagine they might go anywhere at all? No matter. His decision was firm, resolute. More is needed and I will go get it. So he left them and sailed for home. He left his granddaughter, the newborn, the sweet new shoot that he had barely set into the fresh and promising ground.

He was gone a long time, longer than he had planned. By the time he returned (ironically, unable to bring much of anything with him), more than two years had passed. As they neared the coastline the winds rose, the clouds gathered. Thunder broke over a high surf and lightning ripped bright veins in the sky. Don't come back, said the sea. Stay away. They took to the boats to row ashore but could not. One capsized and seven sailors drowned. Frantic to see his family, to save them all as he had planned, he waited offshore, helpless, useless. At dusk the winds fell. "We espied the light of a great fire through the woods. We rowed toward it, and when we were opposite the place we let fall our grappling anchor near the shore, sounded a trumpet call, and then played the tunes of many familiar English songs. We hailed the shore with friendly greetings but got no answer. At daybreak we landed, and when we approached the fire we found the grass and some rotten trees burning." White was learning a hard immigrant lesson: that the music from the Old World would find no answering call in this land. Old tunes will not soothe a wild country.

No one was there. On a post (or a tree) was a simple carved word: "Croatan." The word would ever after stand for the ambiguous message that the lost leave behind them. Across the bay was Croatan Island where the native inhabitants were friendlier, more accommodating. Quick, he told his sailors, sail the bay and we will find them safe. At Croatan, no one was there either. No signs. No marks. Only when White understood that his people were forever gone did the winds return. The sea roiled again and dragged the anchors of the ships. The sailors were alarmed; they wanted to get out to the open water. White called out again and again. Not tunes now, but his own real, raw voice. He was no longer the Governor; he was an aging grandfather who had not stayed. He had gone for help and left those behind, helpless. Did he blame himself as he stood at the ship's rails, calling for those he had left on an alien shore? The sailors shook their heads and turned the ships for home, their home. England. As the land fell away, and the sails swelled with a returning wind, he must have thought: *Where is my home now?* An enduring question for men who forsake their families for the greater good.

When questions have no answers, we ask the storytellers. Their tales about the lost colony abound: Gray-eyed Indians on Hatteras swore their great-grandparents were light skinned and spoke in a foreign tongue; others whispered of a ghost ship sailing the coast with the forlorn faces, still searching, still passing away. But many of the stories that were told around the campfires at night were about that first immigrant girl, little Virginia Dare. Virginia, you who were neither European, nor British, nor Native American. You who marked a fresh beginning and whom no one ever saw again. They say you became a white doe and ran the beaches and forests and could not be caught. Your wildness was your magic, your meaning. They say too that a young, handsome man, who was given a silver arrow from the Queen of England, joined the hunt for you. He stalked you to the sea and his arrow brought you down. At the instant of your death, you looked into his eyes and whispered "Virginia Dare."

Is it true? Some would say it was so. They would point to the man who left you here and to the man who sought to slay you for the magic you had found, both as conclusive proof that a woman's unfettered life could not be tolerated. But I don't think so. Like us all, you were born into an alien world and abandoned in it. The storytellers transformed you, took your uncreated youth, and gave it a wild and lively form. They were wise. You cannot be slain because you are bold and quick and resolute. You cannot die because you have mastered the power of becoming. Your power has passed like a torch to other women who, like you, were left to discover their own lives in America. They learned, as you did, that they possessed a greater power, a cresting passion to follow their own lives at whatever the cost. You have touched their hearts with fire and they, in turn, have touched ours.

P E R M I S S I O N S

I N D E X